A House for All Nations

A CENTENNIAL HISTORY OF THE BAPTIST SPANISH PUBLISHING HOUSE

A House for All Nations

A CENTENNIAL HISTORY OF THE BAPTIST SPANISH PUBLISHING HOUSE

by

Joe T. Poe

Published in partnership by
Baptist Spanish Publishing House Foundation
and
Baptist Spanish Publishing House
7000 Alabama Street, El Paso, Texas 79904

BAPTIST SPANISH PUBLISHING HOUSE

A HOUSE FOR ALL NATIONS

Copyright© 2004 Casa Bautista de Publicaciones.

Unless otherwise noted, Scripture quotations are from the Holy Bible:
New International Version, Copyright© 1973, 1978, 1984 by the International
Bible Society. Used by permission of Zondervan Bible Publishers.

Cover design by Carlos Santiesteban
Typography by José Amézaga

The cover design by Carlos Santiesteban utilizes a projected mural created by CBP
Trustee Leandro González, who is both a pastor and a talented artist from the Dominican Republic. The many-faceted mural represents multiple elements of Casa's publication ministry across its hundred years of service.

First Edition: 2004
Dewey Decimal System: 266.01
Subject: History, Baptist Spanish Publishing House/
Editorial Mundo Hispano

ISBN Number 0-311-15046-2
CBP Number 15046

Printed in U.S.A.

Dedicated in

loving memory to

Frank W. Patterson

and

Pauline Gilliland Patterson

Contents

Introduction

A hundred years for God is barely the blink of an eye. But for us humans, it is a long time: 36,525 days. 876,600 hours. 52,596,000 minutes. Even measured in weeks and months, the totals stay quite impressive: Almost 5,218 weeks. Or: 1,200 months.

Despite scientific advances which have prolonged the average life span for human beings, achieving a hundred birthdays is still unusual. (And the quality of life for those that do get to a hundred often leaves much to be desired.)

But Casa Bautista de Publicaciones (Baptist Spanish Publishing House, a.k.a., Editorial Mundo Hispano or Hispanic World Publishers) is celebrating, in 2005, its centennial! The hundredth anniversary of its founding!

Such calls for celebration! Even though institutions often outlive their founders, it is still the exception for an institution to survive and thrive to a hundred or more years. A high percentage of "new businesses" fail in their first five years, and a consultant for Christian Social Ministries told me that most Christian ministries don't last longer than that either. This book purposes to acquaint you with CBP's life and work–for a full hundred years! My hope is that with this story you will want to be a part of that celebration, with actions and with attitude.

When Bruce McIver wrote his history of the Youth Revival Movement in Texas and elsewhere, of the 1940s and 50s, he called it "a personal history." Thus the wording is frequently in first person, which allows Bruce to include personal perceptions and judgments where pertinent. After all, he was not only a recorder of that history; he had been a major participant!

In contemplating this record covering CBP's history of service for a hundred years, I have seriously considered the methodology, or literary approach, that McIver used. I have been related to this ministry, both as an observer of and as an active participant in it, for almost all the second half of its century of service. I, like McIver of the Youth Revival Movement, have impressions, appreciations, perceptions, and opinions about the things that have happened over these years. (I am reminded of the dictum that history is event plus interpretation.) However, after considering this "personal method," I have decided against it. Except for this introduction, I will write in third person syntax, even when referring to myself. I feel there are convincing reasons to adopt this method:

I want the story to be the Casa's story—not mine. I have asked for—and received—input from all the living (present and former) General Directors and from many employees and missionaries who have served, or are still serving, with this ministry. Without pretending absolute objectivity (a goal that perpetually eludes us), I want to be fair with their input.

Still another reason is my desire that you, the reader, be free to make your own judgments and form your own opinions relative to this ministry, its impact, and its effectiveness. My commitment to it should be obvious, for I have essentially planted my entire adult life here. But in these pages, I will sincerely try to report—factually and historically–, leaving value judgments largely to the reader.

Yet another reason has to do with what might be called "denominational politics." While it can be argued that organizational life, in any circle and at any level, implies "politics" (one dictionary definition of the word is: "the total complex of relations between men in society"), frequently if not always there is the element of competition between individuals or groups that represent differing interests or opinions. It is not the purpose of this book or its author to further the "political agenda" of any particular individual or group within our denominational structure. Rather, the book proposes to celebrate Casa's century of service to the Baptist denomination in particular and to evangelical Christianity in general.

Welcome to the celebration!

As a part of the festivities, thanks are in order: Thanks to colleagues (who have encouraged the author in his task and been helpful with input as indicated above). Thanks to librarians, researchers, and archivists— in El Paso, Dallas, Nashville, Richmond, Kansas City, Valley Forge, and elsewhere. (Publications like this one would be virtually impossible without such libraries, their investigative resources and professional staffs.) Thanks to the Baptist Spanish Publishing House Foundation, and specifically to Dr. and Mrs. Burton Patterson, and to their Foundation for the Advancement of Christianity, for funding to make the publication possible. Their generosity has been expressed in honor of Dr. and Mrs. Frank W. Patterson, Burton's father and mother, whose years of service with the Publishing House will be narrated in the book (see chapters 3 and 4). The volume is thus dedicated to Dr. Frank W. Patterson and to his beloved wife, Pauline. They labored long with CBP, and their commitment to this ministry of Christian publications in Spanish has shown itself in a thousand different ways—even in the years after their retirement from active duty. Our memories—and joyful thanks—overflow! Thanks—first, last, and always—to God Himself. For His Providence, His Provisions, His Patience—with erring children who, however faultingly, desire to serve Him and see His kingdom grow. Before the story begins, let it be noted that the flow of data has been organized around the nine persons who have to date served as "General Directors," the title used for at least the last forty-five years to designate the principal administrative leader of this ministry. The author acknowledges his indebtedness to William R. Estep for a model along these lines. Estep's book *WHOLE GOSPEL WHOLE WORLD,* a sesquicentennial history of the Foreign Mission Board, SBC, was organized around the ten men who have served as leaders of this Board's work since its inception in 1845. I am sure that such was not intended to imply that these leaders were the only players or even that they were the most important elements in the ministry at all times. It does imply that the leaders play key roles which ought not to be ignored in a survey of work done across a span of years. Recognizing that the size of operations is vastly different, I nevertheless contend that a similar principle holds true for the Casa Bautista de Publicaciones. Each General Director has left his stamp on the work accomplished. Thus each will be highlighted in some detail, but in full knowledge that a general without troops is a lost cause, even before the battle begins. Because of the length of time served and consequent impact on the work accomplished, two chapters each are given to the years of Dr. Davis' leadership and to those of Dr. Patterson. Together their time at the helm measures nearly two thirds of the century being celebrated!

For practical reasons, endnotes are used instead of footnotes; they are placed at the close of each chapter. In addition to documentation, these notes often contain additional information beyond the text. The careful reader is hereby forewarned of their importance and encouraged to give attention to them. They are a vital part of the full Casa story.

Enough preamble. "Pull the curtain!" "Let the story begin!" And, "...to God be the glory!"

Joe T. Poe
El Paso, Texas

100 AÑOS

1905　　2005

CBP

Chapter 1

The J. Edgar Davis Years—Part I

Jones Edgar Davis and Mary Gamble Davis were the missionary founders of Casa Bautista de Publicaciones. The starting place was the kitchen of their home in Toluca, Mexico. It happened in the year 1905.

Early Life and Ministry

Some eleven years earlier, J. E. and Mary had linked their lives in a simple wedding ceremony in Harper, Kansas. They became an indomitable team of Christian workers whose lives and ministries yielded abundant fruit for the cause of Christ during the rest of their lives.

That either Edgar or Mary should have been in Harper, Kansas, in 1894 was, in itself, little short of a miracle—and could easily give rise to a romantic novel or some healthy western fiction were this work not determined to be "pure history." Neither was a native of Kansas, and in fact neither had been in Harper very long.

Harper is a small town, with an elevation of about 1400 feet, on the plains of Kansas about 75 miles southwest of Wichita at the intersection of what is known today as US Highway 160 (which runs east and west) and State Highway 14 (which runs north and south). It bears the same name as the county, but has never been the county seat. In 1894 its population would have been nearing 2,000, and its connecting line to the outside world was the Hutchinson & Southern Railway (which later became a part of the Atchison, Topeka and the Santa Fe). Exactly how Edgar and Mary came to Harper has yet to surface; but what they were doing there in 1894 is well known. He was pastor of the Baptist church; she was a teacher in the town's school.

Edgar had been born on a farm near Lone Jack, Missouri, on March 2, 1873. His parents, John and Sarah Davis, were active Baptist Christians. John, a native of North Carolina, was a teacher by profession, but he also farmed a tract of land that he had likely homesteaded, as a part of the country's great push westward, during the 19th Century. Both Missouri and Kansas had been a part of the Louisiana Purchase, successfully negotiated by President Thomas Jefferson, in 1803. Missouri was admitted to the Union as the 24th state, in 1821; Kansas achieved the same status in 1861, becoming the 34th state. John Davis served as a deacon in the local Baptist church where he and Sarah were raising their family of four boys and one girl. Sarah Powell Davis, a redhead whose maternal grandparents bore the name Adams, ran a well-disciplined household and was remembered especially as "a praying Christian." A distant cousin of Sarah was a missionary and evangelist named Thomas L. Powell. It was during one of "Cousin Tom's" series of meetings in the old Greenton Baptist Church, of Lafayette County, that Edgar made his public profession of faith in Christ. The date was July 4, 1886. Baptized by the evangelist himself about a week later in a small Missouri stream not far from the Davis' home place, Edgar's age was thirteen years and four months.[1]

In place of "teenage rebellion," Edgar determined to stay close to Christ and grow in his Christian walk. Even the word "circumspect" seems inadequate to describe the cleanliness of life this young believer endeavored to practice. He himself recalled an incident that happened on the day of his baptism when "in an unguarded moment," he "almost cursed" some stubborn horses his father had sent him to herd into the barn. But with the words forming on his tongue, he restrained himself and later felt "mortified" to the point of barely forgiving himself. It was a lesson, he said, that cured him from foul language. "From that day I have never been tempted to swear."[2]

Another glimpse of Edgar's circumspect behavior was recounted by his brother V.A. "At one time our father promised us boys that he would give a sum of money –quite a respectable sum, too, at that time– if we would neither swear, drink, nor use tobacco before we reached the age of 21. Edgar was the only one of us who received the reward." This brother also reported that whereas the other siblings developed ways of avoiding the "unpleasant consequences" of dis-obeying the rules in this rather puritanical home, Edgar "would not lie" or deceive; he would always just "take his medicine."[3]

Responding to the felt call of God, Edgar was licensed to preach by the Greenton church in August 1890. He was seventeen. The action of the church gave him the opportunity to preach his first sermon and made him aware of both the joys of ministry and the heavy responsibilities that fall on a pastor. The following month (September 1890) he entered William Jewell College, at Lib-erty, Missouri, to prepare himself for a career in ministry. Apparently his first year there was spent in the pre-baccalaureate program. The College's history goes back to 1843 when Dr. William Jewell, a prominent physician of Columbia, Missouri, offered $10,000 toward the establishment of a Baptist college in the state. Initial difficulties were surmounted, and the state legislature issued a charter in early 1849. Instruction finally began in January of 1850. Financial and war difficulties forced closing of the college during the periods 1855-1857 and 1861-1868, but by 1890, when Edgar Davis entered, the college had made a good comeback. W. R. Rothwell, who had begun as a professor in 1871, became the chairman of the faculty two years later and served a decade in this position. When Edgar began his first year, Professor James G. Clark was chairman. The course for the Bachelor of Arts degree had been arranged into four classes (freshman, sophomore, junior, and senior) since 1885. While Edgar was studying at William Jewell, the trustees, in 1892, elected John Priest Greene as president. He left the pastorate of Third Baptist Church of St. Louis to assume this post, and it was during his long tenure of some thirty years that William Jewell really became one of the outstanding colleges of the Middle West. Principal faculty members during Greene's administration are said to have included James G. Clark, J. R. Eaton, R. I. Fulton, J. R. Gibbs, Harry G. Parker, Richard P. Rider, W. R. Rothwell, Robert B. Semple, J. H. Simmons, Charles Lee Smith, and John O. Turnbaugh,[4] Undoubtedly Jones Edgar Davis absorbed much from his classes with several of these outstanding teachers. Books in "The Davis Collection" of the Library at the Casa Bautista de Publicaciones specifically reflect Davis' studies in English, Greek, and Biblical subjects.

Beginning in 1890, Edgar studied continuously for three years. As Ross reports, "... by hard work he was able to pay most of his expenses. It became necessary, however, for him to secure a student loan from the college in order to meet some of his financial obligations. Burdened by a loan he was unable to repay and without sufficient income to meet the expenses of a new school term, Davis in 1893 dropped out of school for a year and took a full-time job with the intention of saving enough to return to college and finish his course. Three years were to pass, however, before he was able to re-enter."[5] During this time, he sought opportunities to serve full time in a pastorate. Harper, Kansas, gave him his first opportunity. Just before receiving the invitation to go to Harper, Davis experienced a disappointing parenthesis in his life that probably served to reconfirm his call to be a preacher. It had to do with an attempt to stake a claim in the Cherokee Strip of the Oklahoma Territory. On September 16, 1893, this Strip was opened by a "run." Some would-be settlers raced by horse (with or without carriage), others went on foot, and some traveled by train. Edgar Davis tried his luck by train, getting off quickly at what would later be the town of Alva, to stake his claim and wait for the land recorder to fully legalize his ownership. Sadly Edgar learned that he had driven his stake in an area laid off for an alley. Dejectedly he returned home, probably concluding that the Lord who had so definitely closed the land rush door would surely open another. That's when the invitation from Harper came.

The Baptist church in Harper was not very old when, through providential circumstances, it made contact with the 20-year-old preacher from Missouri (with three years of study at William Jewell to his credit) and invited Edgar Davis as supply preacher in early fall of 1893. "Shepherd" and "flock" apparently meshed quickly and well, for barely a month later the Harper church called him as its regular pastor and convoked a council to ordain him officially. The ordination took place on November 2, 1893. Technically, it was the beginning of a ministerial career that would last more than 50 years.

Mary Gamble was also in Harper, Kansas, by providential circumstances. She had, as a western ballad extols, "come a long way to live in the West." Her parents were Virginians, and Mary had been born and raised in the forested Appalachians of Virginia, not far from the state line with West Virginia. The nearest town was Tazeville. Her parents were Nancy Peyton and G. F. Gamble. G. F. ran a lumber mill, and always sought to live near well timbered areas. Mary, born on November 18, 1873, was the first of nine children. Siblings came to include two sets of male twins, one other brother, and three sisters. Since Mary was the oldest, she shared heavy responsibilities with her mother as the family grew. The parents were fervent Methodists, and early in Mary's life she received infant baptism, according to longstanding Methodist practice. It represented the serious Christian faith that permeated this home in the mountains of western Virginia, about 50 miles northeast of Bristol and some 90 miles west of Roanoke.

Mary thoroughly enjoyed growing up in the mountains, with their multicolored butterflies in season and gorgeous hues when the leaves changed colors in the fall. The commodious house in which the family lived was somewhat isolated both from any neighbors and from their church, but it was filled with the sounds of a loving family and blessed with the bounty of nature. Flowers and fruit trees grew in abundance. Family devotions were regularly practiced, and Sundays brought special times of family worship that included singing, prayers, and Bible reading—if it proved impossible to make the trip to the church itself, some miles away. Methodist pastors traveling through the area were frequent visitors to the Gamble home. Christmas celebrations were remembered with special joy, both for what the season brought in extra activities at church and what it brought at home as well.

Schools were "few and far between" in the isolation of the mountains, but fortunately the economy of the family permitted the employment of tutors, or private instructors, for the children. Of course the parents always chose Christian teachers, and the children learned to love them dearly. One of the tutors took a special interest in Mary and her spiritual life. Understanding Mary's sensibilities, the teacher sought to approach her in the tenderest way possible to help her see the need of having Christ as personal Savior. The teacher, Mary later remembered, presented very clearly to her the need every sinner has for a Savior and emphasized that one's only assurance of heaven is to accept Jesus as personal Lord. Mary was disposed to do exactly what the teacher suggested. And she did! Her age was fourteen, but sixty-eight years later, when she shared data with Olivia Lerín for her book,[6] Mary's memory of the decision to become a Christian was crystal clear and her gratitude to that

Christian tutor who had led her to Christ was deep and abiding. Two years after her private decision, she formally united with the Methodist church her family was attending.

When Mary had finished the equivalent of secondary education, received from the tutors and private instructors, her parents were able to send her for additional studies to what was then called Centenary College, in Cleveland, Tennessee. This was one of several Methodist schools that have worn the Centenary name, and apparently connects with what today is known as Lee University, in Cleveland. Going to college was definitely Mary's first experience in living away from her parental home, and likely represented her first separation from the family. Olivia Lerín reports that Mary was a model student, both in personal conduct and in her dedication to the program of studies. Mary recalled wanting to learn all she possibly could while God allowed her the privilege of being in those educational surroundings.[7] Ross says that Mary was able to study in Centenary College for two years (evidently the years 1890-91 and 91-92), and that she then started teaching in the Kansas public schools in 1892.[8] We are left to wonder what specific link God used to connect her from Cleveland, in east Tennessee, to the teacher needs of new Kansas towns like Harper, a thousand miles distant in the mid-west. However it was, it happened. And when the Baptist church in Harper called Jones Edgar Davis as its pastor in the fall of 1893, Mary Gamble, from Virginia and Tennessee, was there as a teacher—and probably in her second year.

In places like Harper, weddings very easily became social events for nearly everybody in town. And so it was in January 1894 that both J. E. Davis and Mary Gamble attended a wedding and its subsequent reception for another couple, there in Harper. According to Olivia Lerín, Mary was one of the bridesmaids.[9] Details are lacking, but some mutual friend introduced them. J. E. was almost twenty-one (his birthday was coming up in early March) and Mary was a few months behind him (her birthday fell in November). Their attraction must have been close to "love at first sight." Mary's conversation (content and style) evidently impressed Edgar; and Mary is said to have liked Davis' combination of seriousness and joviality as well as his refined manners and ample knowledge.[10] The result was that it did not take long for them to realize how God in His providence had brought them together. The courtship was short; and their marriage took place in Harper, on September 12, of the same year they met (1894). Both had already established a pattern of "following Jesus wherever He led." Before long it led Mary to become a Baptist Christian, like her husband. In fact he himself baptized her. Olivia Lerín makes a point of clarifying that this denominational change came not from J. E.'s pressure but from serious study on Mary's part,[11] perhaps several months after the wedding. In fact it must have already been late fall or winter, for the stream where the baptism was to occur already had a cap of ice which had to be broken before Edgar would have the joy of immersing his beloved Mary in the symbolic waters of New Testament baptism.[12]

Lasher's *Baptist Ministerial Directory*, published at the close of the 19th Century, lists a variety of sites for the pastoral ministry of this young dedicated team in the waning years of that century. The length and variety of the list is probably to be explained by the practice of "an annual call" for pastors plus the likelihood that some of the pastorates were not "full time," essentially overlapped, and were thus conducted simultaneously. The *Directory* shows Davis to have served as pastor in the following churches and places: "Harper, '93-94; Chicaskia, '93-95; Norwich, Kan., '94-95; Kingsville, Centropolis Ch., Kansas City, Mo., '98."[13] Ross adds a mention of the church in Star Center (as well as Norwich) following his service in Harper.[14] William Jewell College has confirmed that Davis was able to renew his studies there in the fall of 1896. Thus during his last years in college, he was "a part time student and a full time pastor." Graduation from William Jewell finally came on June 7, 1899, and with honors.[15]

Soon after graduation, Edgar was called as pastor of the Baptist church in Richmond, Missouri. Richmond is about 40 miles east of Kansas City, in Ray county, just north of the Missouri River (which forms the county's southern boundary). Just south of the river is Lafayette county where Edgar Davis had been raised. The Richmond Public Library conserves archives of the *Richmond Conservator* newspaper which reported in its May 18, 1899, weekly edition that "Rev. J. E. Davis, of Liberty, Mo." would "preach at the Baptist church in this city next Sunday morning and evening at the usual hours." It added that "at the evening service the rites of baptism" would "be administered to those who applied for membership to the church during the Methodist revival."[16] Somewhat curiously, the paper reported two months later (on July 20) that the Baptist church was canvassing its membership and soliciting donations "for a pastor's salary." But eventually, Davis was called and moved to Richmond; there he no doubt felt much nearer his home territory.

In J.E.'s second year in Richmond (1900), the preacher for the summer Revival was his brother W. E., seven years his junior and likely a student at William Jewell at the time. W. E. later served as pastor of the church in Richmond, from 1930 through 1944, subsequently making his retirement home there till his death in 1964.[17]

An anecdote from Davis' pastorate there is preserved on the Internet in the form of a newspaper report of his opposition to the building of a theater on a site adjacent to the Baptist church building.[18] And the *Richmond Conservator* announced in its edition of April 18, 1901, that "Rev. J. E. Davis will preach at the Baptist church next Sunday morning and evening as usual. The theme of his sermon for the evening is 'Richmond's Greatest Sin: A Monster Dragged to Light.' " "City officials" and "all who are interested in this question" were "cordially invited to attend."[19] Ross reports that it was in Richmond that Davis first conceived the idea of a small church periodical. The idea matured and pastor Davis did, in fact, begin what would be his long career in Christian publications. In his Autobiographical Notes, Davis later recalled concerning the paper: "It can not be said that it was a great success, yet after experimenting some, I decided to purchase a small printing press, which I did, and took my first lessons in printing."[20] In a sense, one can say that the Casa Bautista de Publicaciones had its beginning in Richmond, Missouri!

The *Richmond Conservator* carried the following announcement in its edition of December 26, 1901: "Rev. J. E. Davis, who has been the pastor of the Richmond Baptist church for the past two years, and who recently tendered his resignation to the congregation, has accepted the call recently tendered him to the pastorate of the Baptist church in Moberly and will leave for that city with his family the first of the new year. Although young in ministry, Rev. Davis is a most excellent preacher, and during his residence in Richmond his every act has been that of a Christian gentleman and has won him the esteem of this entire community. During his services as pastor of the Baptist church here 152 new members have been added to the church roll, almost as many as the entire enrollment when he came to Richmond, and during the same time he has also baptized 119 persons."[21]

Moberly was a fairly important town, in central Missouri, about 70 miles north of the state capital of Jefferson City. The Davises moved from Richmond to Moberly in the closing days of 1901, for J. E. to be pastor of the Baptist Church there. If the idea of a church paper had been born in Richmond, it came to full maturity in Moberly. A deacon in the church, named. J. E. McQuitty, was a printer by profession. He gave pastor Davis helpful advice (and probably some practical assistance) for *The Baptist Messenger*, which Davis published weekly as long as he was pastor in Moberly. (A collection of these papers still exists in the library of the Baptist Spanish Publishing House, in El Paso.) In fact, Edgar purchased a larger press than the one he had used in Richmond and some additional equipment. The basement of the Davis home was essentially converted into a miniature print shop. This too presaged what would happen in the kitchen of their home later in Toluca, Mexico.[22]

Call and Appointment to Missionary Service in Mexico

The Davises were in their third year of service in Moberly when circumstances came together that occasioned their appointment as missionaries to Mexico. Viewed from the standpoint of present procedures, their designation for work in Mexico was accomplished in a very brief amount of time. But factors behind their request for appointment dated back a number of years.

Precisely during the last decade and a half of the 19th Century, and with early encouragement from evangelist D. L. Moody and interested leaders from universities like Princeton and Oberlin, the Student Volunteer Movement for Foreign Missions had been born and was impacting numerous college campuses, including William Jewell. J. E. Davis felt this influence. Fellow students like John W. Lowe (later a Baptist missionary to China for forty-two years) and John S. Cheavens (one of the early Baptist missionaries in Mexico) helped awaken his missionary interest. Davis participated in a mission study class, sponsored by the Volunteer Band, during his years at William Jewell. The book *Dawn on the Hills of T'ang*, by Harlan Beach, particularly impacted Edgar. He later commented, "It awakened in me a profound longing for the salvation of the heathen as well as deeper convictions of my own duty. I felt God's hand upon me drawing me toward the great mission work."[23] Olivia Lerín records Mary's memory that during their first year in Moberly (1902), the church there sent Edgar to the Southern Baptist Convention which convened in Asheville, North Carolina, and that Edgar returned commenting on his feeling that the Lord would eventually lead them into foreign mission service.[24] But it was the moving appeal of R. J. Willingham, at the 1904 session of the Southern Baptist Convention, held in Nashville, Tennessee, that brought the matter to a head. Willingham had served the Foreign Mission Board as its executive leader (then called Corresponding Secretary) since 1893 and had come to the position from the pastorate of First Baptist Church, Memphis, Tennessee. Jones Edgar Davis, as one of the 1,095 messengers registered at the 1904 Convention (having been sent by his church in Moberly), heard Willingham's message at the session set aside for emphasis on foreign missions. Davis later said he considered it "the most stirring missionary appeal I ever heard. I shall never forget how he, out of his great love for the kingdom of our Lord,... pled with tear-dimmed eyes for men and women to go into all the world to proclaim the Gospel message to the lost multitudes."[25] Davis and over forty others responded to Willingham's appeal, offering themselves for missionary service.

In what now seems like an unbelievably short time for the application process, J. E. and Mary Davis were appointed as missionaries to Mexico on July 5, 1904. And by early December, they were there!

The determination of their place of service is another story of God's providential workings. Davis apparently conferred with Willingham on the possibilities of missionary service before leaving the Convention in Nashville. While China would have been his first choice, Willingham indicated that field was temporarily closed, and the subject was left pending for Davis to return to Missouri and discuss it with Mary.

During the Convention, Davis had learned that his friend and former classmate, missionary John S. Cheavens, was in attendance. Return travel plans coincided, and Davis was able to discuss his missionary interest with

Cheavens on the train as the two made their way back to Missouri. Davis later acknowledged that as Cheavens presented the challenge of missions in Mexico, "his appeal gripped my heart." And when Davis mentioned to Cheavens that he had a small printing operation (for his weekly church paper), Cheavens told him that there was a great need for a publishing plant in Mexico.[26]

Back home in Moberly, J. E. discussed the matter with Mary. Her dedication to the cause of Christ dated back to her teen-age years. The idea of missionary service was not new, but its time had come. A dramatic monologue reports Mary as replying to Edgar's question, "Will you go with me?" "Yes, of course," was Mary's answer. "I, too, have been listening to God's voice and am ready to go with you."[27] Ross reports that on Davis' formal application to the Foreign Mission Board, he wrote: "China is my choice, but my wife does not feel as I do about that field, and calling to mind that some of our ablest missionaries went to fields other than their personal choices, I decided on the possibility of Mexico which is more satisfactory to my wife. She is willing to go to Mexico."[28] Davis' availability to become a "printer for God—in Mexico"[29] may well have accelerated the appointment process. At the Board's request, the Davises traveled by train to Richmond, Virginia, barely over a month later and were appointed as missionaries to Mexico on July 5, 1904.

The rest of the summer was spent winding up things in Moberly and preparing to go to Mexico. Edgar sold his small press for $45, and the church gave him a little over $100 toward a press to be bought in Mexico. There were three children that had been born to J. E. and Mary; the eldest was named Inez (nicknamed "Lula"); the second, Irene; and the third, Frank. Getting them ready for an international move required special attention from the just appointed missionary parents. However, by September, the family was ready to leave Moberly.

Where the Davises would locate in Mexico was still very much undecided. When the North Mexican Mission met in Saltillo, Mexico on August 17, it recommended that the new appointees go to Torreón "for the present" where Davis could "be of real service in the English work while learning the language and until his field be definitely determined."[30] Davis' friend Cheavens was apparently a resident missionary in Torreón and was agreeable to this plan. (He was back in Mexico for the August mission meeting, according to the minutes.) Davis himself liked this idea.[31] Hermosillo (in the state of Sonora) and Morelia (in the state of Michoacán) also came under consideration. However, after further contact between Davis and Willingham, and also between Willingham and the two Missions in Mexico (the North Mexican Mission, and the South Mexican Mission), it was decided the Davises would go to Toluca, in south central Mexico.

The month of October was spent in Arkansas, where Davis had accepted invitations to preach some evangelistic campaigns prior to their departure for

Mexico. Mary later called these Arkansas experiences times when "we learned patience and ultimate dependence on God's grace and strength."[32]   While there, Mary came down with typhoid fever and required intense attention from her faithful husband. At times, her life seemed to hang in the balance. Edgar, nevertheless, was able to fulfill his preaching commitments for revivals and associational meetings, during Mary's recuperation. In fact, there were over a hundred professions of faith in his meetings![33] And the church in Waldron, Arkansas, where Davis' parents were then members, made a good contribution to "the press fund," so that a total of $455 was in Davis' hand before departure by train for Mexico. (Edgar had Dr. Willingham's permission to make these solicitations for the press fund.)

In early December, the five Davises boarded iron horses that moved steel wheels against steel rails, and the trains carried them from Arkansas, all the way across Texas. Passing through Dallas and San Antonio, entering Mexico probably at Laredo and continuing ever southward, they finally arrived in Toluca on December 4, 1904. Moberly must have seemed like two thousand miles—and two thousand light years—to the north. Though there were no bands nor "hallelujah choruses" to welcome them, Mexico was their "Macedonia" and the Davises were delighted to arrive. It would be their home for the next dozen years, and a major part of "their field" till the end of the journey.

Mexico, a Mission Field for Baptists—in 1904

Though it is entirely legitimate to think of J. E. and Mary Davis as pioneer Baptist missionaries to Mexico, they were not the first. Evangelical work there already had a history of at least four decades, and Baptist work dated back thirty years or more. Estep and Patterson (in English) and Treviño and Anderson (in Spanish) turn out to be our best sources for understanding the status of Baptist mission work in Mexico when the Davises arrived in Toluca on that December day of 1904.[34] Anderson's summary of Baptist history in Mexico uses about fifty pages. It begins with the "pre-history" work of a Scotch Bible colporteur and teacher named James Thompson who traveled through various Latin American countries in the years immediately following their independence from Spain. Thompson's work in Mexico as early as 1829 is seen to later connect with work of the American Bible Society and the American Baptist Home Mission Society. A Bible Society agent named W. H. Norris is said to have accompanied the American army to Mexico during the War of 1846-47 and distributed some Bibles in Spanish, both to troops and the Mexican populace.

A third "precursor" was an Irishman named James Hickey who is credited with founding the first organized Baptist work in Mexico. His international pilgrimage and varied circumstances took him from Ireland to Canada to the United States and finally to Mexico. (Davis would have been interested in the fact that Hickey sojourned a time in Missouri and that there he became inter-ested in the Mexican people and in the Spanish language.) In the early 1860s, he served as an agent for both the American Tract Society and the American Bible Society. Evidences exist to signal Hickey's presence in various parts of Mexico (such as León, Durango, Monterrey, and Matamoros). Anderson under-stands that he made long trips by horseback, visiting ranches, towns, and cities. More a colporteur and explorer than a pastor, Hickey is nonetheless recognized as the founding pioneer of Baptist work in Mexico. Hickey's contact with the Westrup family in Monterrey provided the circumstances for the first organized Baptist church in the country. Hickey was the catalyst, but Tomás Westrup be-came the pastor. The date was January 30, 1864. Primera Iglesia Bautista (First Baptist Church) of Monterrey still traces its origin to this event.

Though a series of difficulties and controversies prevented the quick growth that Hickey's and Westrup's work had seemed to promise early on, the Baptist work did not die; and Westrup himself became the first Baptist mission-ary in Mexico, supported by the American Baptist Home Mission Society of New York. His appointment by that society occurred in 1870, and this is considered to be the beginning date of "a Baptist denomination" in Mexico. The decade of the 1870s brought numerous ups and downs to the nascent Baptist denomina-tion in Mexico, and it was not until September 1880 that the Foreign Mission Board of the Southern Baptist Convention, with specific financial and moral support from Baptists in Texas, adopted the work being conducted by John Westrup (younger brother of Thomas). Barely two months after his appoint-ment, John (known in Mexico as Juan) and his riding companion Basilio Flores were brutally murdered, by unidentified assailants. (Anderson asserts that at this point in Mexican history, the authorities didn't even bother to investigate the deaths of Protestants!)[35] Treviño reports that many attributed the deaths to Catholic fanatics.[36] Thomas Westrup temporarily took up his brother's work but was re-appointed by the American Baptist Home Mission Society the following year.

A bit of time elapsed before William Flournoy and William (W. D.) Powell were named missionaries to Mexico by the Foreign Mission Board, SBC. The Flournoys were named in 1881 and had a relatively short ministry—and a short life—, mainly in the area near Laredo and Nuevo Laredo. The Powells were appointed in 1882 and had a long and fruitful—though not uncontrover-sial—ministry in Mexico.[37] They were no longer in Mexico when the Davises arrived. In fact, Powell had been at the center of an internal controversy in the mid 1890s that had led to the resignation of several Southern Baptist mission-aries,[38] eventually including Powell himself. It was sometimes called an "exo-dus."[39] All this had happened in the years prior to 1904. By that time, the Missions in Mexico had been reorganized and reinforced, largely overcoming the negative effects of the earlier decade. Anderson concludes that by 1903, Baptist work related to the Foreign Mission Board, SBC, had recovered from "the exodus" and was in a state of "plena marcha" (frank advance).[40] By then, there were more than eighty Baptist churches in the country, three associations, several schools, some early Baptist publications, and more than 2,000 baptized members in the churches. It was time to unify the work by organizing a National Convention. Such was done in September, 1903. J. G. Chastain, W. H. Sloan, and Alejandro Treviño were prime movers. Treviño was the first president. Anderson detects "un desarrollo vertiginoso" (astounding—literally "dizzying"—development) in the Baptist life of Mexico till the end of the decade. This is the context for the arrival of the Davises in the country, and the immediate setting for the birth of the Casa Bautista de Publicaciones.

Barely three weeks after arrival in Toluca, J. E. Davis journeyed to Mexico City and bought a small press, a paper cutter, and a small quantity of type. He used the $455 he had brought in "the press fund." In the early days of 1905, the equipment was installed in the kitchen of the house the Davis family occupied in Toluca. Very shortly, tracts and some other small publications came from the press. During the spring months, Davis received a request to print *El Expositor Bíblico* and *Nuestros Niños*, both being edited by missionary J. G. Chastain, in Guadalajara. Though the name was yet to appear, in effect Casa Bautista de Publicaciones had been born.[41]

Forerunner Publications

Reference to *El Expositor Bíblico* and *Nuestros Niños* gives opportunity to explore the antecedents that Ross calls "forerunner publications" for what was to become Casa Bautista de Publicaciones. Just as a baby is not born as a full grown person, a Christian institution such as the Publishing House did not come into existence "full-grown." Rather, it developed upon the foundation laid by pioneer Baptist editors in Mexico. And "the first Baptist periodical in Mexico was started a little more than twenty years before the Publishing House was founded"[42] During these twenty years, some publications were started; some suffered discontinuance, and some were officially merged with others. During this initial period, all the Baptist publications enjoyed either the patronage of the American Baptist Home Mission Society or the Foreign Mission Board, SBC.

Publications related to the American Baptist Home Mission Society included *El Mexicano Bautista* (1884-1887); *La Luz* (1885-1905), and *El Cristiano Bautista* (1904-1910).

It is interesting that Anderson credits Thomas Westrup with making two requests of the American Baptist Home Mission Society, after being named its first missionary to Mexico in 1870: (1) "a printing press" to produce materials in Spanish and (2) "financial support" for various national pastors in the country. Anderson says the Society granted the second request immediately but waited some four years before granting the first.[43] Ross does not mention the delay and cites the ABHMS Annual Report for 1870 as indicating the press was to be used for publishing tracts, hymns, a newspaper, and other religious literature.[44] When the Home Mission Society suspended its operations in Mexico, in 1876, "the press was placed in the custody of the Mexican Baptist Mission Society, but was returned to Westrup in 1883 for the publication in Spanish of a small monthly paper."[45] The paper was launched in December of 1883, changed names in March 1884, and again in September (1884) to become *El Mexicano Bautista*. Westrup continued publishing it until 1887.

La Luz was begun by William H. Sloan, another missionary of the ABHMS. It dates from January 1885, and its place of publication was Mexico City. Sloan had earlier served for a time as superintendent of the mission press in Madras, India. Then, after a period back in the United States because of his wife's health, he was given a missionary appointment to go to Mexico (he had spoken Spanish as a child). And when he went, he carried some printing equipment, thanks to the generosity of the church he had been pastoring in New York state and the generosity of a Christian lady in New York City. He named his paper, *La Luz*. In April 1887, it was consolidated with Westrup's *El Mexicano Bautista* and with *El Heraldo Mexicano* (see below). Either under Sloan's editorship or that of someone else, and with the respect and cooperation of Baptist leaders from all over Mexico, and even from outside the country, *La Luz* continued uninterrupted service for some twenty-one years. Its last issue appeared in December of 1905.[46]

El Cristiano Bautista existed from 1904 until 1910. It was launched by the Nuevo León Baptist Association. Jonás García, Alejandro Treviño and Tobías Treviño were its leaders. Ernesto Barocio was also linked to this paper beginning in 1907. The discontinuance of *La Luz* (at the end of 1905) increased the need for *El Cristiano Bautista*. In 1910, it was merged with *El Atalaya Bautista*, then being edited by J. E. Davis (see below).

Publications related to the Foreign Mission Board, SBC, included *El Heraldo Mexicano* (1883-1887), *El Expositor Bíblico* (1890-present), and *Nuestros Niños* (1905-1984).

El Heraldo Mexicano was published by W. D. Powell, from his base in Saltillo, with José M. Cárdenas as co-editor. At first it was published in both English and Spanish, and circulated mainly in Saltillo and nearby areas. Its early circulation of about 500 copies was greater than the combined membership of Baptist churches in Mexico at the time. It was consolidated with *El Mexicano Bautista* of Monterrey and *La Luz* of Mexico City in April of 1887.

El Expositor Bíblico was created as a Sunday school periodical for young people and adults. It was founded by David A. Wilson, a Southern Baptist missionary, in Guadalajara, in 1890.[47] Though started as a twelve page monthly, it became a quarterly by the turn of the century. Besides Wilson, Southern Baptist missionaries Sarah Hale, John S. Cheavens, and J. G. Chastain served as editors during the first fifteen years, before Davis arrived in Mexico. Though it has evolved into an annual, it still merits Ross' comment as having "the longest life of any Baptist publication established in Mexico."[48]

Nuestros Niños was a children's Sunday school paper, which according to Ross, Chastain added in 1905, almost simultaneously with the arrival of the Davises in Mexico.[49]

Thus there were at least four Baptist publications being done in Mexico when J. E. and Mary Davis arrived in Toluca in 1904. These were: *La Luz, El Cristiano Bautista, El Expositor Bíblico* and *Nuestros Niños*.

Six Good Years

In hindsight, it would seem appropriate for J. E. Davis, upon arrival in Toluca, to have dreamed a dream like the one reported in Genesis 41. Pharaoh's dream, as interpreted by Joseph, foretold the coming of seven good years (in the dream, symbolized by seven well fattened cattle), followed by seven lean years (symbolized by seven lean cattle—"ugly and gaunt"— that devoured the seven "sleek and fat" ones). The significant differences would have had to do with the numbers (six and six, rather than seven and seven) and the point of reference (the newly founded ministry of Christian publications in Spanish rather than grain production to feed a nation). It is nonetheless impressive that the first six years (1905 through 1910) were years of exuberant growth, but they were followed by six years (1911 through 1916) that brought exasperating difficulties, in a kind of swelling uncontrollable tide, that all but devoured the young Casa de Publicaciones. And did provoke its relocation from Mexican soil.

What follows are excerpts from Davis' own reports to the South Mexican Mission, plus some quotes from key correspondence between J. E. and Foreign Mission Board executives, and a few special stories or anecdotes that give insight into what these years must have meant in the lives and ministries of J. E. and Mary Davis—and the Christian publishing house they founded.

1905—The meeting was held in Toluca, where the Davises had located. J. E. was elected president of the Mission. Davis reported: "The Printing establishment has been started, a good printing outfit purchased, and quite a number of tracts, etc., printed. With a small appropriation from the Board this year," he hopes to make the work self-sustaining thereafter.[50] J.E. is named also to serve as Mission treasurer during Bro. Mahon's forthcoming absence. The Davises are given approval to move "to some other field, our preference being León, Guanajuato."[51]

1906—Available Minutes reflect Davis' move to León and his decision "to remain" there, despite implied discussions with the North Mexican Mission that might have taken the publishing ministry to Torreón.

1907—Davis reports: "...We finished the printing of 500 copies of Immersion,[52] and have about one-third of the History of the Baptists[53] printed. We have printed... a good many tracts." The value of the printing plant is calculated at $2,875. Chastain gives the report for *El Expositor Bíblico*, noting that the subscription list is up to 1700 a quarter. "The influence of this periodical is growing... [this means] that the Baptist Sunday Schools in this and other Spanish-speaking countries are taking greater interest in the study of the Sunday School lessons."[54] Circulation of *Nuestros Niños* is considerably less, but there is a base to build on. Davis is elected editor of all the Sunday School literature and of a proposed Baptist weekly newspaper. He is also to continue as the South Mexican Mission's representative on a joint committee to plan "a complete Commentary on the New Testament." Growth of the publication work provokes the question of purchasing property for it in León. J. E. Davis is "requested to take up the matter with the Board."[55] The promise of continued growth leads the Mission to request appropriations "for the enlargement of the plant." These requests come to slightly less than $2,000, but the Board does not find it possible to grant them just now.

1908—Davis' report is optimistic and positive:[56]

"This has been a good year in this department of our work. We have been employing from one to four men all the year.

"The Expositor Bíblico has grown very satisfactorily. We are now issuing 2,000 copies and they are none too many. We increased the number of pages at the beginning of the year to 60.

"Nuestros Niños was made a weekly at the beginning of the year, and we are printing 600 copies each week.

"El Atalaya Bautista was established January 1, as an 8 page weekly, but was made a 12 page paper about July 1. Much interest is taken in the weekly and much material is being sent in constantly. We print 600 each week. We have almost 500 subscribers at present.

"The 'Short History of the Baptists,'[57] with an appendix on Baptist history in Mexico, has been finished and 250 copies [have been] bound and [are] for sale.

"During the first half of the year, we printed about one million pages of literature. We are doing more since.

"...Teófilo Barocio [has been] translating Dr. Frost's book on The Memorial Supper.[58] We have about 100 pages now printed. The issue [will be] 500 copies... Other works [are] in process... which we hope to print soon... We plan to take in job work of a certain kind this year and hope to earn a part of the expenses of the plant."

Progress on the Commentary project is reported as "very slow."[59] But the Board has appropriated some $1,500 dollars for equipment, and a new press has been purchased and installed. Thus plant capacity has been considerably enlarged. Receipts for the year have totaled almost $3,000 and expenses, about $100 less. Preaching services are held nightly during the Mission Meeting, and Davis preached on Thursday night. Continuing in the tradition of "the annual call," the Mission unanimously elected "Mr. Davis" as "editor of all the periodicals, business manager and director of the printing plant."[60] Davis reports baptisms as increasing in León. He also comments on the conversion of two printers and how this might be the signal of "what good might result from an industrial school."[61]   The Neals are reported to be actively cooperating in the publishing work in León (apart from other responsibilities), even helping to set type.[62]

1909—The Meeting was held in Guadalajara, on July 7, 8, and 9. Mary is present for the meeting, but apparently circumstances prevented J. E. from being in Guadalajara. The Minutes say that "Mrs. Davis made a short report on the work of the printery. The work is growing and now it is easy to employ printers, whereas last year it was almost impossible. Five or six men are employed regularly."[63] The C. L. Neals are expected "to leave León and the [field] work [will be left] in the hands of Mr. and Mrs. Davis."[64] At this meeting Neal reports: "I have compiled a little hand-book for Christian workers, taking up almost every dogma of the Catholic church and refuting it with the Scripture. There are also chapters on the divinity of Christ with many of the prophecies and fulfillments."[65] Other details about the book are given, along with the explanation: "It is now being printed, at my expense of course, in the Baptist printery at León."[66] This book, with the title *Manual para los Obreros Cristianos,* has been in continuous circulation for more than ninety years, and is still listed in the CBP general catalog.

An "extra meeting" of the South Mexican Mission was held on October 19, "just after the close of the Convention." The agenda consisted of two items: "the examinations of the missionaries in the Spanish language, and the consolidation of the two Baptist religious periodicals of Mexico." The references are to *El Cristiano Bautista* and *El Atalaya Bautista*. A consolidation plan is approved, and though the "editorial staff" is to represent the traditions and backgrounds of both papers, "Mr. Davis [is] to have entire control of business of the paper and it is to remain entirely under the control of the South Mexican Mission."[67] It is interesting to note that a "publishing committee" was created "to select the books and tracts" to be translated and/or published.[68]

1910—Thirteen members were "enrolled" as present for the "Tenth Annual Meeting of the South Mexican Mission," held August 10, 11, and 12, in León, among them both Mary and J. E. Davis. The Minutes extend to twenty-three typed pages. They report, generally in glowing terms, progress on all "fields" and in all ministries. An early reference to "the books printed by our publishing house" may constitute the first use in Mission minutes of this term to describe the publications work.[69] Davis alludes to the conversion of a former Catholic priest "who promises to be a very valuable addition" to the work. This would have been Félix Buldain who indeed worked fruitfully with Davis for several years. J. E. also reported "that opening the printing plant to public work" had given the Baptist presence more influence in the town of León. He says, "We have the work of nearly all the business concerns in the town and all speak well of us... The business men are openly our friends; they will stop and speak to us on the streets openly, and while it is not evangelizing, it is liberalizing the people."[70]

Davis' written report begins with characteristic optimism: "It is a great pleasure to submit the following report which is by far the best we have been able to make in the history of the Casa Bautista de Publicaciones. We give all praise and glory to God, who has helped us from year to year to build up this plant from a very small beginning five years ago until it has assumed very respectable proportions."[71] Plant inventory at the beginning of 1910 is reported to value slightly over $8,000. Work for the public has been conducted under the name of La Imprenta Americana (opened on August 14, of 1909), after "necessary steps" were taken "under the law for this purpose."[72]

"This has been a year of advance for our papers."[73] Circulation of *El Expositor Bíblico* is up to 2,600 copies a quarter, with a tenth of that going to "Western Cuba."[74] The print run for *Nuestros Niños* has grown to 1700 copies a week. "*El Bautista* is the result of the consolidation of *El Atalaya Bautista* and *El Cristiano Bautista*." The agreement, authorized last year and finally concluded in April of this year, was put into effect in May. The Mission is given more detail concerning the agreement. The print run of the new paper is 1500 copies a week. It has met with "the general satisfaction" of both missionaries and nationals.[75] Several new books have been published or are in process, including a new edition of Pendleton's Theology, originally translated into Spanish by Sloan.[76]

With excitement veiled in understatement, Davis writes of "our new quarters," saying, "Of course it is not necessary to mention the purchase of the property here for the church and printing plant."[77] He announces: "We are now located permanently. Our machinery once installed will not have to be moved at the heavy expense and great danger of breakage. The public will know we are permanently established."[78] The Foreign Mission Board had appropriated $10,000 for this first "permanent" location of the Casa. Davis relishes the growth being experienced, gives a financial report showing about $10,000 in total receipts (about half of which were operational funds from the Board), and proposes still greater capacity if the Board can provide an additional $2,500 for equipment and materials. "We can, if properly outfitted now, make this plant self-supporting in a few years."[79]

When the definitely "up-beat" meeting concluded, it would likely have been impossible for Davis to believe that he—and Casa Bautista de Publicaciones—were within a few months of the beginning of the lean years. But such was the case.

****

Before recapping the circumstances in Mexico that triggered "the lean years," it is appropriate to recall that even during the good years, there were serious moments of crises. Mary and J. E. are almost heard to shout from heaven, "Oh yes! Many!" Two of the most serious crisis moments had to do with appendicitis. In one case with "Lula," the Davises' older daughter. In the other case, with J. E. himself.

Lula's illness began scarcely two months after the Davis family arrived in Toluca (December, 1904). Stomach aches turned into serious abdominal pain, and concerned parents took Lula to the doctor. He prescribed medication, but there was no improvement. In the absence of adequate diagnostic procedures, appendicitis went undetected. The illness continued till the appendix ruptured. And Lula–age: nine and a half—died. She was buried in Toluca. These were days of heavy sorrow for the entire family, but especially for the young missionary parents, still essentially strangers in a foreign land. But when Mary gave Olivia Lerín her recollections of this bitter trial, her comment was that neither she nor J. E. "vacillated for a moment in their determination to continue serving the Lord," with faithfulness to his purpose.[80] In fact, it appears that their response was to give themselves yet more completely to the publications work. Olivia reports that both J. E. and Mary put in twelve hour shifts in "the printery"—from 6:00 a.m. till 6:00 p.m. Mary learned to set type and help in other ways. Both were close to being "workaholics."[81]

The second case came to J. E. himself. He suffered an attack of acute appendicitis in October of 1908. Lula's death from this illness was still too painful in their minds for unnecessary risks to be taken. While Christian brethren prayed, in León and elsewhere, Mary determined that her husband should go to the United States for the surgery he apparently needed.[82] "Davis was kept in ice packs until the pain eased, and ... he went [by train] all the way to St. Louis, Missouri, for the operation."[83] Mary accompanied him. By the time Dr. W. H. Mayfield, the surgeon in St. Louis, examined Edgar, it seemed probable that the appendix had burst; an operation would be very risky. Davis might not live. "Dr. Mayfield," J. E. is reported to have said to the doctor, "I did not come here to die; I came to get well." While brethren in Mexico concentrated on prayer to the Great Physician, Dr. Mayfield did the surgery. Davis not only survived, but within a few days was "sitting in bed writing articles for his Spanish Baptist paper" in Mexico.[84] Mary stayed at his side for two weeks. By then the physicians felt he was out of serious danger. Alone, this mother and publications missionary returned to León where she had left her children and where she went to keep things moving at Baptist Printery/Publications House. J. G. Chastain, who had temporarily substituted for Davis during the time for surgery in St. Louis, could not remain longer, and Mary found herself essentially managing the Casa de Publicaciones. She gave herself so completely to the demands of the work that she came near to a nervous collapse herself. Extended rest eventually became necessary for Mary, and the episode affected her health for the rest of her days.[85] In St. Louis, Davis himself was hospitalized for several weeks, but by Christmas was able to return to Mexico and reassume his duties there. He received a happy welcome from family, friends, and colleagues!

Another moment during the good years that represented crisis mixed with great joy was the birth of a second son. The Davises had decided for Mary to give birth in a Presbyterian-sponsored mission hospital named for the Good Samaritan, which was located in the city of Guanajuato, not far from León. Circumstances—and dedication to the publication work—required that Mary make the journey to the hospital alone. J. E. followed slightly later. And the baby was born on February 1, 1907.[86]

By the summer of 1910, these crises had been weathered, and the Davises–and their colleagues—seemed poised for a Decade of Advance. But the Mexican Revolution broke out on November 20, 1910—and everything changed.

Six Lean Years

As in Pharaoh's dream, the good years were followed by lean ones. And the "ugly and gaunt" cattle began to eat the "sleek and fat" ones.[87] Glimpses of these years are available from Mission Minutes, correspondence, and other sources.

1911—The annual meeting of the South Mexican Mission was held in Morelia, August 9-11. A certain afterglow of the good years is still perceivable, as Davis reports that "the Printery has had the best year's work that it has ever had, notwithstanding the Revolution." Literature circulation has increased, and good quantities are going to Cuba and several South American countries. Admittedly, "the Revolution caused a falling off in subscriptions to the weekly paper, *El Bautista.*"[88] So far, the Revolution was apparently having mixed effects on Baptist work. Missionary R. P. Mahon reported that "until the Revolution began, the work was in a very hopeful condition." He comments also that while the Revolution did not reach the city of Morelia, it reached the rest of his field, and sometimes with surprising results. "Some of the pastors were leaders in the Revolution," he says, and "now they have large crowds of men to attend their services."[89] The written report of "Casa Bautista de Publicaciones, León,

Guanajuato" begins with a disclaimer: "Despite the political troubles in the Republic and calamities of different kinds in other parts of the field where our publications circulate,..." The content of the report is positive: growth in literature circulation; several new books published or in process, including Harvey's book on the Church;[90] finances in balance at approximately the $10,000 mark. (Income, including almost $4,000 in operational funds received from the Foreign Mission Board, exceeded expenditures, though by only $47.87.) And the report ends hopefully, though with caution: "If there is no further trouble, we expect to do more work and make better progress the coming year... We need better equipment, but we do not think it advisable under the present circumstances to ask for any increase over last year."[91]

1912—Though the 1911 sessions ended with an agreement for the 1912 meeting to begin on Wednesday of the second week in August, and in Toluca, the meeting was actually held partly in Aguascalientes and partly in León, on October 14 and 15. Transportation problems were playing havoc with meeting plans—and with shipments of materials. Davis' verbal report "about the success of the Publishing House" and "its good influence on the City of León" almost seems hollow, but then so do the recommendations of the Mission to the Foreign Mission Board concerning the "Judson Memorial Fund" (that three year effort by Southern Baptists to raise $1,250,000 "to be used by the Foreign Mission Board for educational missions," an effort done to appropriately commemorate "the 100th anniversary of the sailing of Adoniram Judson, first American foreign missionary").[92] The Mission recommended: "$25,000 for the Publishing House; $25,000 for a Hospital; $50,000 for Schools; and $25,000 to build meeting houses at Toluca, Guadalajara, Colima, León, Uruapan, and Tacámbaro."[93] In March, 1912, Davis had written the Board: "Our work is almost completely paralyzed. Worse than last year. Our papers are being published regularly however, and we hope there will be no cause for suspending any of them... things are going from bad to worse..."[94] The violence that had erupted beginning in November of 1910, when Francisco I. Madero called for a general insurrection to end the long and repressive regime of Porfirio Díaz, could not be stopped even by Madero himself (who had been elected president in the fall of 1911). Regional leaders like Emiliano Zapata, Venustiano Carranza, Álvaro Obregón, and Francisco ('Pancho') Villa, had put together regional armies which at times seized cities or controlled areas in such a way as to impact seriously the life of the entire nation. Several small revolts were staged in 1912, and "the propertied classes were dismayed by the government's inability to restore and maintain order."[95] Though in some ways 1912 was an acceptable year, the dark shadows of the Revolution still hung over the country. The future of the Publishing House still hung in the balance.

1913—Ross reports that somewhat curiously Davis felt enough ease of mind in early 1913 to leave his wife and family in Mexico and journey to the

United States for several months to visit his aging parents and attend the Southern Baptist Convention, held that year in St. Louis, Missouri.[96] Mary Davis, assisted by missionary James Benson, kept Casa Bautista de Publicaciones "going strong!" During these months, there was another chapter in the ongoing saga of the Mexican Revolution. President Francisco I. Madero was overturned by a triumvirate of Félix Díaz, Bernardo Reyes, and Victoriano Huerta, with Huerta assuming the presidency. Madero and his vice-president Pino Suárez were murdered "by the officials who held them in custody."[97] When Davis returned to León in June, "the revolution appeared to be over;" the situation was "static if not calm." In July "Davis sent his wife and children to Mexico City...so the children could attend the American School there."[98] The South Mexican Mission finally had its "annual meeting" in Toluca, on September 12, with only three members present: J. E. Davis, C. L. Neal and his wife Dr. Hallie Garrett Neal. Some of the other missionaries had already left the country. Ross reports that by the fall of this year, "there was nearly a complete stagnation of business." Davis reduced the plant staff by 50%. Prospects for the future were dimming rapidly. Davis was apprehensive about the presidential election scheduled for October. He concluded that American (political and/or military) intervention would eventually become necessary and wrote the Board: "If worse comes to worst, we would move to Veracruz and there we'll be safe while matters are at their worst. If we think then we should go home, we will go..."[99] In fact, things did get to the point in November that Davis went to Mexico City, got his family, and took them to Veracruz for a couple of weeks. Then it appeared conditions were safe enough for the family to return to Mexico City. Davis accompanied them there, then proceeded north to León. In sizing up the situation he found it necessary to suspend publication of *El Bautista* at the end of the year. He gave three reasons for this action: (1) the revolution and its effects upon churches, transportation, etc., (2) the increase in prices for paper, ink, etc., making it impossible "to make ends meet," and (3) the American Baptist Home Mission Society was withdrawing its financial support for the paper. Thus ended year three of the lean ones. The remaining three only went from bad to worse.

1914—Apparently there are no Minutes from a meeting of the South Mexican Mission for 1914. It may be assumed that there was no meeting. Ross reports that "early in 1914 Davis concluded that it would be more practical for him to leave a man in charge of the shop in León so that he could join his family in Mexico City. He continued to write the Sunday School lessons for *El Expositor Bíblico* and made occasional trips to León to check on the work at the plant." [100] He was in León when American troops landed at Veracruz on April 21, 1914. (The immediate background for the American incursion was the alleged inappropriate treatment to the crew of the American warship *U.S.S. Dolphin*, which had landed without Mexican permission at Tampico; the larger background was the context of Revolution since late 1910.) Not knowing what had taken place in Veracruz, Davis planned to take the night train from León to Mexico City. But anti-Americanism, already on the rise, found expression in León (by some who had probably learned of the American invasion). Davis and other Americans on the train were ordered off. After being searched, "they spent the night with the manager of the electric light plant." Warned the next morning by the very mayor of León to stay in hiding, because of an anti-American demonstration that was being planned, the Americans (including Davis) waited until the mayor could assure their safety. A Mexico City newspaper actually reported that Davis had been killed in León and his body dragged through the streets. With diplomatic assistance from several South American countries, the United States and Mexico (and their presidents Wilson and Huerta) agreed to arbitration. Davis was finally able to get back to Mexico City.[101]

In the late fall Davis seriously considered leaving the country. Revolution had so destroyed the necessary infrastructure for normal life and ministry that it seemed futile to try to continue. Anti-Americanism was still running high, and, in fact, most Americans—including missionaries—had already left. Edgar wrote the Board concerning his uneasiness and seeking counsel. (To complicate matters, apparently the church in Moberly had offered him a call to return to the pastorate he had left to come to Mexico.) Even without air mail (which didn't exist yet), mail by train had earlier been regular and relatively rapid. Now, however, the mail service was suffering so many interruptions that it was mid-December before Davis received the Board's counsel. By that time he had determined that it was God's leading that he—and his family—stay in Mexico. He wrote: "The Lord has made me to see again, and perhaps more clearly than ever before, that he has been able to take care of me and mine, that he has work for me to do here in Mexico..." The question of what to do with his family still bothered him. "If I did not love my family, it would not make so much difference, but it is a real cross to be separated from them... Missionary life... is real hardship now, but the will of the Lord be done." And separations of weeks or even months did occur. Railways were cut, bridges were blown up, telegraph wires were down. Life was hard; but the Davises stayed—another year and a half.[102]

1915—As strange as it now seems, Davis began this year by starting a new publication (*El Foro Cristiano*) and by receiving from the Foreign Mission Board a $1,000 grant (from the Judson Centennial Fund) for a new press. The first issue of *El Foro* (designed in part to substitute *El Bautista*, which had been suspended) came out on January 7, 1915. "Its four-month existence was filled with interruptions and setbacks."[103] Revolutionary conditions finally forced Davis to suspend *El Foro Cristiano* indefinitely as of May 6, 1915. As Davis himself would likely have said it, "By the hardest and sometimes slightly delayed," he managed to publish *El Expositor Bíblico* without interruption as long as he was in Mexico. Regarding the issue for the second quarter of 1915, Davis explained: "We are publishing this issue with great difficulty and much fear, for the time is almost at hand to mail it and there are no trains."[104]

Again there are no Mission Minutes for the South Mexican Mission for this year. From the other sources available, one detects the Revolution was becoming a way of life. Patterson has commented that "the designs of the revolution were at first political, but soon became social in purpose and socialistic in method. The Díaz regime had left the masses as poverty-stricken and neglected as they had been a century before. The battle cry of the people became: ¡Tierra y Libertad!— (Land and liberty)." Then Patterson reflects agreement with a Chilean historian who perceived "that the revolutionists gradually adopted a four-plank program: just distribution of land to the people, just labor laws, cessation of favoritism toward foreigners, and further curbing of the Church's powers."[105] Today it would seem hard to oppose these seemingly legitimate goals, but the road to their achievement was violent, tortuous, disruptive, and seemingly unending. This year brought more conflict between the regional warlords, especially between Carranza and Villa.

Davis was even forced (and sometimes paid) to do printing for whichever warlord controlled León. Villa paid for one of his printing jobs with new fifty cent bills, of his own issue. Davis wisely spent all the money immediately for supplies, knowing that as soon as Villa left town the money would be worthless.[106]

In early September J. E. found an opportunity to leave León and join his family in Mexico City. The train "was made up of a number of antiquated boxcars, most of them in need of repairs. Davis joined in with the crowd trying to get to Mexico City. The only space he could find on the train was on top of one of the cars, and toward nightfall the train stopped at Irapuato and was placed on a siding, leaving Davis stranded. In looking around the yard, he discovered a locomotive that had just arrived from Zacatecas, and he was told that it would be leaving for the Mexico City in about two hours. Davis was able to find space atop one of the oil tanks and, after a miserable night, the train got as far as the little village of Tula. From there he was able to hide in a boxcar on a military train, and arrived in Mexico City the following day, September 10, 1915. Rather than return to León, he decided to "set up shop" in the Mexico City and print *El Expositor Bíblico* there. After all, the new press he had bought the year before (with the grant from the Judson Centennial Fund) was still in Mexico City (he had been unable to ship it to León), and paper was more available in the capital city than in León.[107] But the new arrangement did not last long.

1916—One can only wonder if deep down Mary and J. E. Davis began this year knowing that this would be when the last "ugly and gaunt" cow would eat the last "sleek and fat" one. Their sojourn in Mexico was coming to an end, but God would intervene and give them strength for new beginnings.

"In January 1916 some of the Villistas stopped a train at Santa Isabel, Chihuahua [in northern Mexico], and shot sixteen American engineers who were aboard. Two months later Villa personally led a raid on Columbus, New Mexico, killing sixteen Americans and burning a part of the town."[108] With additional disturbances along the border, the American president, Woodrow Wilson, was forced to act. With permission of the Mexican president Venustiano Carranza, Wilson sent General Pershing and his troops into Mexico to capture Villa. The mission was not really successful, and perhaps only served to heighten the anti-American sentiment in all of Mexico. Davis and his family were in real danger. Upon investigating his options, Davis found that he could have *El Expositor Bíblico* printed in El Paso, Texas, at a reasonable cost and that missionary G. H. Lacy, living there, could and would help with the editorial work. In May 1916, he wrote the Board: "We are right now in a panic here. Everything has gone up and there is nothing in sight to live on. Do not know how it will be settled. I only wish we were out, but we can't go now. Hope to get out before matters get very much worse."[109] During the same month, the American State Department urged all remaining North Americans to leave Mexico as soon as possible. Davis was determined to stay until he could finish the fourth quarter issue of *El Expositor Bíblico* for 1916. He hoped to be in El Paso in time to get out the issue for the first quarter of 1917.

Because conditions steadily worsened, Davis was unable to finish the *Expositor* for the fourth quarter before he and his family found it necessary to board the train for Veracruz on June 26, 1916. Though the train was fired-on numerous times by revolutionaries, no serious damage was done and they reached Veracruz before nightfall. The next day they were taken aboard the U.S. battleship *Nebraska*, where they remained four days. (J. E.'s first correspondence with the Board after arrival was written on notepad paper from the *U.S.S. Nebraska*.) Then they were transferred to an army transport ship named *Sumner*, which had been dispatched precisely to bring the refugees to a U.S. port. Finally they sailed for Tampa. Mary's memories of the journey fill several pages in Olivia Lerín's book.[110] The boat was crowded with 655 refugees. During the ten-day trip to Tampa, the ship passed through a tropical storm that left most of the passengers ill and occasioned some equipment and baggage to be thrown overboard to be sure the boat and its human cargo survived. Mary remembered the considerable embarrassment all experienced upon arrival in Tampa, because their clothes were filthy and their personal hygiene deplorable. But they were "home"—at least inside their home country.

By mid-July they were back in Missouri, where J. E.'s parents now lived in Mt. Washington. Davis' July 15 letter to Dr. T. B. Ray reflects his relief to be out of Mexico, his assumption that unsettled times there would continue, and his proposal of a meeting in St. Louis or New Orleans to discuss the future of the publications ministry. Already El Paso was under consideration. He writes:

"If it seems best to go to El Paso temporarily, I hope to get there by October 1st. In short, [I] would want to go before to make my arrangements." Their plan, after some time in Missouri, was to visit "Mrs. Davis' folks" in Colorado. Though the family might spend the winter there (in Lamar, Colorado), J. E. says he would soon "be ready for the *Expositor* work." The letter includes his expense report from Mexico to Missouri, noting that the Government had given the refugees train tickets from Tampa to their destination. Apologizing for the lengthy letter (which "seemed necessary"), J. E. Davis, signs the letter as "Yours for the work of His Kingdom."[111]

Ross states: "Thus ended a brave struggle to keep the Publishing House operating in Mexico. Davis' persistence in the face of such odds is to be greatly commended. Anyone with lesser courage and determination would have abandoned the work in the early days of the Revolution."[112]

After some much-needed rest, the Davises—founders of Casa Bautista de Publicaciones—would indeed go to El Paso and make a new start in the publication work that meant so much to them—and to the whole of evangelical work in Spanish.

Endnotes

1. See J. Wilson Ross, Sowing the Seed in Spanish, El Paso: Baptist Spanish Publishing House, 1962, p. 12.

2. Ibid., p. 13.

3. Ibid.

4. See Encyclopedia of Southern Baptists, vol. 2, pp. 1498-1500

5. Ross, Sowing the Seed, p. 14.

6. See Olivia S. D. de Lerín, María Gamble Davis: Heroína de la Fe, El Paso: Casa Bautista de Publicaciones, Segunda Edición, 1959, pp. 18-20.

7. Ibid., p. 20.

8. Ross, Sowing the Seed, p. 15.

9. Lerín, María, p. 22.

10. Ibid., p. 23.

11. Ibid., pp. 25-26.

12. Ibid.

13. See Lasher's Baptist Ministerial Directory, p. 199.

14. Ross, Sowing the Seed, p. 16.

15. See excerpted pages from Catalogue for 1898-'99, supplied by William Jewell College.

16. Richmond Conservator, May 18, 1899, p. 2.

17. See data (historical booklets, newspaper clippings, etc.) supplied by pastor Dallas Bundy and longtime member Milford Wyss, First Baptist Church, Richmond, Missouri.

18. Report published in the Richmond Missourian.

19. Richmond Conservator, April 18, 1901, p. 1.

20. See Ross, Sowing the Seed, p. 16.

21. Richmond Conservator, December 26, 1901, p. 1.

22. See Ross, Sowing the Seed, p. 16

23. Quoted by Ross, Sowing the Seed, p. 17.

24. Lerín, María, p. 33.

25. Ross, Sowing the Seed, p. 17.

26. Ibid., p. 18.

27. Dramatic Monologue, n.d., Part I, p. 3.

28. Ross, Sowing the Seed, p. 18.

29. See J. Edgar Davis of Mexico: Printer for God, by Frank W. Patterson, Broadman Press, 1953; Spanish edition: Impresor al Servicio de Dios, F. W. Patterson, Trad., Roberta Ryan, CBP, 1966.

30. See Minutes, IMB Archives, date Aug. 23, 1904, signed by J. W. Newbrough, secretary of the mission.

31. See Ross, Sowing the Seed, p. 19.

32. Dramatic Monologue, Part I, p. 3.

33. Ibid.

34. See William R. Estep, Whole Gospel Whole World: The Foreign Mission Board of the Southern Baptist Convention, 1845-1995, Nashville: Broadman and Holman Publishers, 1994; Frank W. Patterson, A Century of Baptist Work in Mexico, El Paso: Baptist Spanish Publishing House, 1979; Alejandro Treviño, Historia de los Trabajos Bautistas en México, El Paso: Casa Bautista de Publica - ciones, 1939; and Justo Anderson, Historia de los Bautistas, Tomo III, El Paso: Casa Bautista de Publicaciones, 1990.

35. Anderson, Historia de, p. 28.

36. Treviño, Historia de los, p. 32.

37. Estep credits the Powells with eighteen years of service in Mexico. See Estep, Whole Gospel, p. 234.

38. See Joe T. Poe, Missions for a New Century, El Paso: Baptist Spanish Publishing House Foundation, 2002, pp. 29-30, 59-61, 66-67.

39. See Patterson, A Century of, pp. 56-58.

40. Anderson, Historia de, p. 39.

41. See Ross, Sowing the Seed, pp. 21, 22.

42. See John Wilson Ross, "A History of the Baptist Spanish Publishing House in El Paso, Texas," an unpublished thesis submitted to the Graduate Faculty of Texas Technological College, for the Master of Arts degree, June, 1958, p. 1; and J. Wilson Ross and José Tomás Poe, Noventa Años de Historia y Ministerio, El Paso: Casa Bautista de Publicaciones, 1995, p. 3.

43. Anderson, Historia de, p. 24.

44. Ross, "A History of," p. 3.

45. Ibid.

46. Ibid., pp. 4-6.

47. See Poe, Missions for a New Century, pp. 25, 73, 82-89, 127-128.

48. Ross, "A History of," p. 9.

49. Ibid., p. 13.

50. Minutes, pp. 3-4.

51. Ibid., p. 8

52. CBP's first book; Spanish title: La Inmersión: El Acto del Bautismo Cristiano, by J. T. Christian.

53. By Vedder; CBP's second book; Spanish title: Breve Historia de los Bautistas, by H. C. Vedder. Was maintained in print until about 1990.

54. Minutes, p. 10.

55. Ibid., p. 12.

56. See several pages, following p. 8 of the Minutes.

57. By Vedder; see footnote 53.

58. According to Ross, eventually published without date and reprinted in 1935; the Spanish title is La Cena Conmemorativa de Nuestro Señor, trad. Teófilo Barocio.

59. Minutes, p. 9.

60. Ibid., p. 10.

61. Ibid., p. 12.

62. Ibid.

63. Minutes, p. 2.

64. Ibid., p. 3.

65. Ibid., pp. 4-5.

66. Ibid., p. 3.

67. Minutes, special meeting, p. 1; see also paragraph "Forerunner publications," on El Cristiano Bautista.

68. Minutes, special meeting, p. 4.

69. Minutes, p. 1; see also p. 7 where the "Report of Printery" is also titled in parenthesis "Casa Bautista de Publicaciones."

70. Minutes, p. 3.

71. Ibid., p. 7.

72. Ibid, p. 8.

73. Ibid.

74. Ibid.

75. Minutes, p. 10.

76. See Poe, Missions for a New Century, p. 129; Spanish title of the Pendleton book, Compendio de Teología.

77. Minutes, p. 10.

78. Ibid.

79. Ibid., p. 11.

80. See Lerín, María, p. 43.

81. Ibid.

82. Ibid., p. 50.

83. Patterson, Printer for, p. 14.

84. Ibid.

85. See Lerín, María, pp. 50-52.

86. Ibid., p. 49.

87. See Genesis 41:2-4, NIV.

88. Minutes, p. 2.

89. Ibid.

90. Spanish title, La Iglesia: su Forma de

Gobierno y Sus Ordenanzas; it enjoyed a very lengthy circulation; noteworthy also is its translator: Sarah Hale.

91. CBP Report to 1911 Mission meeting, p. 2.

92. See Encyclopedia of Southern Baptists, vol. 1, pp. 715-716.

93. Minutes p. 3.

94. Cited by Ross, Sowing the Seed, p. 40.

95. Ross, Sowing the Seed, p. 40.

96. Ibid., p. 42.

97. Ibid., p. 43.

98. Ibid.

99. See letter, Davis to R. J. Willingham, October 25, 1913; also cited by Ross, Sowing the Seed, p. 44.

100. Ross, Sowing the Seed, p. 45.

101. Ibid., pp. 47-48.

102. See letter, Davis to R. J. Willingham, December 20, 1914; also cited by Ross, Sowing the Seed, p. 50.

103. Ross, Sowing the Seed, p. 52.

104. Ibid., p. 53.

105. Patterson, A Century of, p. 106.

106. See Ross, Sowing the Seed, p. 55.

107. Ibid., p. 58

108. Ibid.

109. Ibid., p. 59

110. See Lerín, María, pp. 83-86.

111. Letter, Davis to T. B. Ray, July 15, 1916; IMB Archives.

112. Ross, Sowing the Seed, p. 60.

Chapter 2

The J. Edgar Davis Years—Part II

Relocation and New Answers to Old Questions

The chronological parameters for this chapter are from June 1916 until March 31, 1943: From the arrival of J. E. and Mary Davis (and their family) from Mexico, essentially as refugees from the never-ending Mexican revolution, until Davis' obligatory retirement, according to policies of the time, at the end of the month in which he reached age 70. These parameters make for a period of almost 27 years.

Consciously the reader should avoid any tendency to consider CBP's move from León to El Paso as comparable to a minutely planned and carefully executed corporate relocation, like when the J. C. Penney Company moved its corporate headquarters from New York City to Plano (a suburb north of Dallas, Texas), or when Boeing moved its central offices from Seattle to Chicago, or when El Paso Natural Gas Company left its name-sake city to relocate in Houston. Apart from differences in size (Casa Bautista evidently never had over twenty employees in León), there were radical differences in kind: This was a move forced by unexpected and undesired circumstances. Everything that had been "nailed down" came loose and was suddenly "up for grabs." Basic determinations on Who, Where, What, When, Why, and How again had to be addressed. Even tentative answers required time.

Who? Though J. E. and Mary Davis had weathered the storm of "six lean years" in Mexico, and though they apparently arrived back in the States with the firm intention to keep the publications ministry going, a perusal of their correspondence with leaders of the Foreign Mission Board indicates that their continuation was open to question. It was at least dependent on recovering from the extreme fatigue that apparently both felt, fatigue such as to put them at the point of exhaustion if not nervous collapse. In a letter from Davis to Dr. J. F. Love, the Board's "Corresponding Secretary" [i.e., chief executive leader], dated July 25, 1916, J. E. alludes to some feelings of helplessness, and though alleging that his general health is good, he acknowledges shaken nerves and real need for rest.[1] Health is mentioned again in a letter from Davis to Dr. T. B. Ray (the Board's "Foreign Secretary"—perhaps equivalent to a vice president for overseas operations). Davis writes from Lamar, Colorado, and comments, "I am feeling 'no-account.' " And with implications of how deep the fatigue/depression has been, he says, "I am rallying... and beginning to feel a little more like myself." J. E. also admits that while he wants to get back to the *Expositor* work (perhaps doing it from the furlough location of Colorado), he recognizes his "need to be a good way from the turmoil of the work for a few months yet."[2] Another letter to Dr. Ray, dated September 6, reports improvement but confesses, "I was so run down... but am feeling so much better now that I have hope of getting over it and being ready for the fight again..."[3] Three weeks later, in another letter to Dr. Ray, Davis says, "The cool bracing weather of the mountains has done much for me, and I am getting eager to get to work again..."[4] And just before leaving Denver for his first visit to El Paso, J. E. writes to Dr. Ray: "I want to work... am feeling so much improved. I am anxious to get back on the firing line..."[5] Although specific documentation is less available, the likelihood is that Mary Davis suffered as severely as her husband the downside of their return from Mexico. Probably only the Lord knows how close the missionary cause came to losing the Davises at this very low point in their careers. But in the providence of God, they were not lost. Other missionaries came into the picture to help, at least temporarily, keep the publications ministry alive (the names of George Brewer—an ABHMS missionary–, G. H. Lacy, and W. F. Hatchell surface in correspondence), but fortunately Mary and J. E. Davis did recover strength and vitality sufficient to face "starting over"—in El Paso.

Where? Although El Paso had been mentioned as a possible (temporary) printing site for *El Expositor* (and other publications) even before Davis left Mexico, correspondence would seem to indicate that by the time J. E. and Mary got to Tampa and began communications with the Foreign Mission Board, the preferred site was New Orleans. Missionary George H. Brewer was apparently there, and the first plan forwarded to doctors Love and Ray seems to have included a recommendation for location in New Orleans.[6] Dr. Love, in his letter to Davis, dated July 31, 1916, makes a rather strong case for Barcelona, Spain, as the next site for the Spanish publications ministry. But in the end, El Paso was the choice. As strength and calm returned to his body and spirit, J. E. apparently arrived at this tentative selection. In a letter to Dr. Ray, dated September 6, he writes: "I think that finally you will just about decide to locate the plant in El Paso, and [I] feel that for the present at least we can do better there."[7] It did not work out for Davis to attend a Mexican Mission Meeting, held in San Antonio (Texas), in early September, but he did travel from Denver to El Paso around the first of October, and writes Dr. Ray his first letter from that city on October 5, 1916.[8]

Davis would have arrived at El Paso's impressive Union Train Station, opened with considerable ceremony on March 1, 1906. Its elegant red brick structure had been designed by architect Daniel H. Burnham, of Chicago, who had also drawn the plans for the Union Station in Washington, D. C. Outstanding features of the El Paso Station included a bell tower with a spire six stories high, located on the building's northeast corner. Its interior included a main passenger waiting area with a second floor balustrade. Some thirty trains a day were attended. Another attraction of the depot was the Harvey House restaurant, where "Harvey Girls" served excellent food on fine china and linen, with courtesy and promptness. The Union Station was a symbol of what the dusty border village that was El Paso in the 19th Century had become in the opening decades of the 20th.[9] With a population of approximately 70,000, El Paso was already "the largest American city on the Mexican border and the city most closely in touch with the Mexican situation."[10] 1915 had set a record for building permits in the city, exceeding $3,000,000, and increases in population made both residential property and business space woefully in short supply.

The great Elephant Butte Dam, a hundred miles north on the Rio Grande, was almost complete and had already begun to allow a supply of water for irrigation that was putting thousands of new acres under cultivation and serving as a magnet for new population. As a hub of rail transportation, and as a city with an "unsurpassed water supply for domestic purposes," low tax rates, a commendable municipal government, and "front rank" educational facilities, El Paso was "not looking for a slump." It was billed as "one of the best-paved, best-lighted cities in the country."[11] Hospitals included Providence and Hotel Dieu; nearby Ft. Bliss had as its post commander none other than Brigadier General John J. Pershing. The State National Bank was still being presided by one of its aging founders, Charles Morehead. A few years later, he would be succeeded by Charles Bassett, son of O. T., one of Morehead's partners when the bank was founded in 1881.[12]

This city became Davis' choice for "the temporary location" of Casa Bautista de Publicaciones and in an interesting chain of events, he brought the Foreign Mission Board (and the American Baptist Home Mission Society) to agree.

What? As Davis answered the Where?, he really addressed the What? question also: CBP would continue, as it had been from its inception in Mexico, to be bifocal: a publisher who opted also to be a printer. Dr. Love, in a letter to Davis dated July 19, 1916, had specifically raised the possibility of the ministry being a publisher without being a printer, even pointing out that the Baptist Sunday School Board, in Nashville, Tennessee, did not own or operate presses.[13] Other examples of this strategy existed.[14] However it appears that Davis' experience had convinced him that there was value in linking the two: publishing and printing. Probably factors like the kind of publications principally involved (i.e., dated curriculum and dated denominational periodicals/news magazines) and the size of the print runs for a very limited constituency argued strongly in Davis' mind that controlling the print schedule (by way of owning and operating the presses) was vital to maintaining this kind of program. Books had importance, but their production was decidedly secondary, and their printing was essentially used as "filler work" between dated periodical schedules. (Such would be the pattern for CBP for many years.) The possibility of producing some operating subsidy by way of doing commercial work loomed continually as a viable and attractive strategy to Edgar Davis. Ross recounts how CBP opened its shop in El Paso on North Campbell street:

> "Working on his own impulse, Davis, who was then living in Denver, went to El Paso the first part of October to confer with the other missionaries of the Mexico Mission who were temporarily located in that city. Upon investigating the cost of having Spanish publications printed in commercial shops, he found that it would be very difficult to get the American printers to bid on his work, partly because they did not have the type faces necessary for printing in Spanish, and partly because they had all the work they could do in English printing. Davis contacted several Mexican printers, but they were not equipped to produce the quality of work he desired, and, too, their prices were very high. Finding these conditions, Davis then tried to rent a printing plant on a temporary basis but found that this would also be very expensive. He then decided to purchase a small shop, which consisted of two small presses, a stitching machine, a paper cutter, type, and other small items. The plant cost $900, of which Davis paid $500 from the regular appropriation provided by the Board for operating expenses, and gave his personal note for the balance, to become due on January 1, 1917. The Board later appropriated $900 of the Judson Centennial Fund to cover the cost of the plant."[15]

When? The purchase of the shop in El Paso essentially answered the When? question also: Now. Immediately. October 1916. The intent was not to miss a single issue of *El Expositor* (the Sunday School quarterly for youth and adults). And this goal was met. The 1915 issues show to have been done in León; the 1916 issues list both León and Santa Julia, D.F. (Mexico) as editorial and/or production sites; but the first quarter 1917 issue gives an El Paso address (P. O. Box 667) and contains Davis' brief announcement and explanation of his move to the border city as an arrangement necessary to continue the publication of *El Expositor*.

Why? Comments in correspondence address this issue: T. B. Ray's letter to Davis, dated October 26, 1916 contains the gentlest of reprimands for not consulting the Board before purchasing the small plant in El Paso, but concludes by affirming Davis, his business sense, and his response to an emergency.

Dr. Ray writes: "I think it is quite clear you have taken the right step in El Paso, in reference to the Publishing House. We can [now] go ahead with that work... We certainly need literature for the spreading of the light... May God watch over you and keep you in good physical as well as spiritual trim."[16] Some months later Davis writes Dr. Ray and discusses their mutual concern "about the Mexican situation." Davis' dedication to the publications ministry is unswerving: "... We are going to need literature as never before..."[17] Minutes of the Meeting of (FMB) Missionaries to Mexico, held in El Paso, in July 1917, also speak of "the great opportunity" for both literature distribution and publication. The Mission recommends that such work "be continually pressed."[18]

How? To imply that the ministry was ever adequately capitalized would be entirely misleading, certainly not when it began operations in El Paso. Davis frequently foresaw "bankruptcy" looming. But a combination of basic support from the Foreign Mission Board, SBC, plus some support from the American Baptist Home Mission Society, of New York,[19] and a trickle of income from commercial work and retail sales, apart from another trickle of subscription income from the periodicals, curriculum materials, and books, provided the financial resources for the relaunch of Casa Bautista de Publicaciones in El Paso.

What followed were over eight years of work at the North Campbell Street address; thirteen years of work at the Myrtle Avenue address, and from 1938 on (till the end of the Davis years and beyond) at the location on the Franklin foothills, in the northeast outskirts of the city.

Over Eight Years at the 519 North Campbell Street Address

These years comprise the period from October 1916 until March 1925. The story of the acquisition of the small shop at the North Campbell address has already been told. Pictures of this location show it as a kind of small store front building. Though the equipment acquired was sufficient for publication of *El Expositor* beginning with its issues for 1917, one can easily detect an inferior quality when compared to the printing that had been done in Mexico. Davis wanted to address this issue as quickly as possible. Though J. E. did not move his family from Colorado to El Paso until September of 1917, he evidently did considerable editorial work in Denver and made occasional trips to El Paso to keep things going as smoothly as possible. G. H. Lacy was the missionary in charge when Davis was not physically present in El Paso.

In the summer of 1917, Davis, with FMB approval, made a lengthy trip to Mexico and secured the shipment of the press that was still in Santa Julia (a suburb of Mexico City). His letter of August 12, 1917, to Dr. T. B. Ray, in Richmond, was written from El Paso, but was done on CBP stationery that carried its previous "provisional address" in Santa Julia. In it J. E. shares the good news that the Mexican authorities have given permission for the press to clear customs in Piedras Negras, thus leave Mexico and enter the United States. He thinks that by the date of the letter, the press will be in shipment from that point of entry toward El Paso, on the American side. Davis comments: "The whole trip to Mexico has been successful in every aspect. Having this press will significantly add to the capacity and the quality of the printing being done in El Paso."[20] In a sense, this was the tip of the iceberg, for Davis across the years sought to upgrade constantly the shop at the North Campbell Street address. A year or so later, the press left in León was also brought to El Paso. During these years correspondence reflects Davis' negotiations with Board officials to finance acquisition of linotype machines, paper cutters, wire stitchers, and other equipment to upgrade quality and produce more efficiently.

Ross' report of these years is as follows: (Except when ellipsis marks signal slight condensation, Ross' text is transcribed verbatim; however some endnotes are added to document or enrich the quoted material.)

"Davis went to El Paso the first week in January 1917 to check on the work and do what was needed to keep the publication work going... He remained in El Paso for only two months this time, returning to Denver the first week in March.

"Lacy continued to direct the work of the Publishing House until Davis finished his furlough. Under Lacy's leadership a new periodical, El Mensajero Bautista (The Baptist Messenger), was started on May 1, 1917, with Agustín Vélez, Josué Valdés and Josué Bautista serving as the editorial staff. Only fourteen numbers of this paper appeared; it was later suspended to make way for the reappearance of El Atalaya Bautista in January 1918.

"Davis returned to El Paso in June 1917 to take over the management of the Publishing House. Lacy, who had been serving as interim director, transferred to Saltillo, Mexico. There, with the help of Missionary A. B. Rudd, he established the Mexican Baptist Theological Seminary.

"In a meeting of the Mexico Mission, held in El Paso June 20 and 21, 1917, many problems relating to Spanish publication work were discussed. The Mission recommended to the Board: (1) that the Publishing House be located... in El Paso, with such machinery and equipment to be brought from Mexico as needed,[21] and (2) that the American Baptist Home Mission Society be invited to cooperate in the publication work in El Paso. The Board took no action on the first recommendation, but was willing to proceed with the second. After months of negotiations, the Home Mission Society agreed to cooperate in a financial way with the work of the Publishing House, in view of the fact that this House served the Spanish literature needs of the areas where the Society had mission work, and therefore appropriated $2,000 toward the work of the House for a year, with the first payment to begin April 1, 1918.

"Following the meeting of the Mexico Mission, Davis and Missionary J. H. Benson went to Mexico to arrange for the shipment of the press stored in Mexico City, along with some miscellaneous equipment, and to sell, if possible, some of the supplies in the City and in León. About a month was required to attend to these matters. By July 30 Benson and Davis were back in the States. Davis went on to Colorado early in September and moved his family to El Paso.

"Upon Davis' return to El Paso, he began to reorganize the work and to make plans for renewing some of the suspended publications, principal among which were El Atalaya Bautista and Nuestros Niños... Davis felt that he should revive as many of the suspended publications as possible without further delay. With the arrival of the press from Mexico City, and with the purchase of a new linotype machine, for which $2,927.50 were granted in August 1917, the Publishing House was in a position, mechanically speaking, to expand its publication activities. Therefore, El Atalaya Bautista was launched, as a weekly denominational newspaper, for the second time on January 3, 1918, and Nuestros Niños reappeared on January 6 of the same year...

"Additional equipment was added to the plant through grants from the Foreign Mission Board. In September 1917, a melting furnace for linotype metal was purchased at a cost of $150, and 500 pounds of metal was secured for $80. In September 1918 the Board appropriated $400 for a paper cutter, and the following month an additional $400 were granted for a wire stitcher. All of these appropriations were made from the Judson Centennial Fund.

"The American Baptist Home Mission Society continued its financial support until May 1920. This support, which had lasted for two years, was terminated primarily because of a policy disagreement between Davis and the Society. Davis seemed to have an inclination toward controversy with other religious groups, especially the Roman Catholics, and the Society requested 'that the controversial element be avoided to the utmost degree possible in publications which we help support.' Davis' position was stated thus, 'I have tried to edit papers for Mexico for many years, and I find it utterly impossible to avoid controversy... We feel that we must expose error, and we are conscientious in it. We cannot do otherwise.'[22]

"The task of directing the work of the Publishing House proved too much for one man. In order to give Davis some relief, the Mexico Mission in June 1919 asked for the transfer of J. S. Cheavens from Eagle Pass, Texas, where he was directing the mission work in the neighboring Mexican state of Coahuila, to El Paso. After the transfer was effected in August, Cheavens became editor of El Expositor Bíblico and assisted Davis with other editorial work of the House.

"Additional editorial help for the House was secured as the result of a contact made with Mrs. A. M. Gordiano through the Home Mission Society. Mrs. Gordiano, originally from South America but at the time living in New York City, was employed to edit Nuestros Niños, Revista Juvenil (a new Sunday school publication for young people ages thirteen to sixteen), and Tarjetas Ilustrativas (Sunday school lesson picture cards for children ages four and five). The two last named publications were launched the first quarter of 1920.

"Tarjetas Ilustrativas was readily received in all the Spanish-speaking countries. For the first quarter 1920, 500 copies were printed, 1,500 for the second quarter, and 2,000 for the third quarter. It was hard for the House to meet the demand for these lesson cards.

"The circulation of the other periodicals continued to increase, and by 1920, it reached the following amounts: El Atalaya Bautista, 1,750 weekly; El Expositor Bíblico, 4,000 quarterly; Nuestros Niños, 4,000 weekly; and Revista Juvenil, 1,000 quarterly.

"With the expanded activities of the Publishing House in the field of periodical literature, the load of the work became increasingly heavier for Davis and his health showed signs of breaking in the spring of 1920. Because of this, Davis offered his resignation as missionary of the Board on April 21, 1920, after fifteen years of active service. He was encouraged by the Board not to take this drastic step, but rather to take another furlough and see if he could regain his strength and calm his nerves. Davis wrestled with the decision through the summer months, and finally decided to take a furlough beginning September 1, 1920. J. S. Cheavens, although in poor health himself, consented to take the direction of the Publishing House in Davis' absence. Davis did not feel that Cheavens should take this heavy responsibility in his condition. 'It would be like committing suicide to undertake it,' Davis predicted.[23] Time was to prove this to be a rather accurate prediction. Nevertheless, there was no one else to do the work, and the Board had no other course but to ask Cheavens to assume the directorship of the House.

"Davis left with his family for Kansas City to begin his furlough in September 1920, and Cheavens directed the work of the plant until January 23, 1921, when at the age of fifty-two, with seemingly many useful years before him, he laid down the battle of life.

"Following Cheavens' death, the Board named Frank Marrs and W. F. Hatchell, missionaries of the Mexico Mission, to direct the work of the Publishing House until Davis completed his furlough. Both Marrs and Hatchell had served in Mexico until being forced to leave during the revolution, and were now living on the Mexican border and directing the field work in the northern states of Mexico. Neither had experience in printing, but with the help of C. D. Boone, plant foreman, they were able to keep the work going until Davis returned in June of the same year.

"In the meeting of the Mexico Mission held in Chihuahua June 23, 1921, a resolution was passed urging the Board to decide on a permanent location for the Publishing House. A committee, composed of

J. E. Davis, Frank Marrs, and W. F. Hatchell, was appointed to investigate several possible locations for the House.

"After this meeting, Davis went to León to dispose of the rest of the equipment and supplies and, at the same time, sell his home there. The house was in ruins, but he was able to realize a little from the sale of the land. Before returning to the States, Davis proposed to the Board that he go by way of San Antonio and New Orleans to investigate conditions there relating to the possible location of the Publishing House in one of these two cities. He was advised by the Executive Secretary of the Board, however, that the investigation would not be worthwhile at the time in view of the fact that the Board had not yet settled the more fundamental question of 'whether we are going to make this house an international house, and as to whether it is to be located in the United States at all.' The Board had never acted on the previous recommendation from the Mexico Mission that the Publishing House be...[24] located in the United States.

"Returning from León, Davis continued on to Colorado to move his family to El Paso. They arrived in El Paso the latter part of August 1921, and Davis again assumed full directorship of the House. His administrative duties were soon lessened, however, by the appointment of C. D. Boone, then serving as plant foreman, as a regular missionary of the Foreign Mission Board. Boone, a native of North Carolina and an ex-student of Wake Forest College, assumed responsibility for the mechanical department and assisted in securing commercial work for the House.[25]

"El Atalaya Bautista, then edited by E. G. Domínguez, continued to increase in circulation in Mexico and the southwestern part of the United States. By 1922 the total circulation of the seven periodicals had reached 20,000 per issue, as compared to the circulation of 2,000 enjoyed ten years previous by the two periodicals then being published. These seven periodicals were being sent to seventeen countries outside the United States during the early part of 1922, and to nineteen countries the following year.

"There was a further expansion of the periodical literature of the House in January 1923 with the acquisition of La Revista Homilética (The Homiletical Review), a monthly magazine originally published in Valencia, Spain, by missionary Eric Lund which had been suspended during World War I. Lund, who later served for a time as a missionary in the Philippine Islands, was living in California at the time. Davis worked out an arrangement with Lund whereby the Publishing House would revive this publication, all rights of which were transferred to the House. Lund served as editor under the supervision of the editorial department of the Publishing House. This magazine filled a great need among the Spanish-speaking pastors for homiletical materials and suggestions on better ways to carry out their pastoral ministry.

"The Publishing House had operated for several years in very cramped quarters, without room even for an office for the director. In December 1922, to alleviate this situation somewhat, Davis rented a house across the street from the plant. Here he located his office, and used the rest of the house for book and paper storage. The two buildings occupied by the House were located at 519 and 522 North Campbell Street.[26]

"The first efforts toward a training course for Sunday school teachers and officers were put forth in 1922. Davis realized that 'the time is at hand when we must give more attention to the training of our teachers and workers in the Sunday School.' He planned for the translation into Spanish of the books in the Normal Study Course prepared by the Sunday School Board of the Southern Baptist Convention... All [the seven basic] books were available in Spanish by 1924, most of them being manufactured by the Publishing House. A Spanish version of the 'King's Teacher Diploma' from the Sunday School Board was printed and awarded to those completing the requirements of the Sunday School Study Course plan...

"There also existed the need for training course books for workers in the B.Y. P. U. (Baptist Young People's Union). The first step in meeting this need was the publication in Spanish of The New B. Y. P. U. Manual by L. P. Leavell...

"The work of the young people's unions was given a boost in January 1923 with the launching of Revista para la U. B. de J., a quarterly magazine with program helps for young people's meetings, with E. G. Domínguez serving as editor. This magazine underwent a number of changes as it sought to adjust to the changing program of work in the young people's unions...

"The mechanical department of the Publishing House was strengthened the latter part of 1924 with the purchase of a second linotype machine at a cost of $5,046 and a new paper cutter for $1,874. These two machines were paid for out of income from commercial work. There were fifteen to twenty employees during 1924, which, along with the good equipment, provided the House with the best working force and machinery it had ever been able to afford.

"All along the Publishing House was cramped in its quarters on North Campbell Street, and even with the additional rented house across the street there was still an urgent need for more adequate facilities..."[27]

1925 would finally bring a solution to this problem.

As one contemplates this period of CBP's century of faithful service to God and His people, several general facts or features—some of them might be called accomplishments—stand out. Consider the following:

1. Uncertainties. Uncertainty had been a fact of life during the "six lean years" in Mexico, from 1911 to 1916. And uncertainties did not end with the Davis' departure from Mexico. The word itself crops up in correspondence between J. E. Davis and T. B. Ray, Foreign Secretary of the Mission Board in Richmond.[28] Uncertainties concerning the "permanent location" of the Publishing House. Uncertainties concerning Davis' health. Uncertainties about the Publishing House's intended audience and sphere of influence. Uncertainties about its publication program. Uncertainties of other types. All reared their heads. Despite the planning that went on and the proposals that were fielded, each day and each decision was a walk of faith and a risk of life. J. E. Davis could have certainly identified with the apostle Paul when he exclaimed: "...We were pressed out of measure, above strength, insomuch that we despaired even of life... but... we should not trust in ourselves, but in God..." (2 Corinthians 1:8, KJV). Uncertainties were real, but somehow God supplied the needs and the work continued.

   2. Growth. Despite the clouds of uncertainty, the period brought notable growth in the publications ministry. Much of this must be attributed to the determination and dedication of J. E. and Mary Davis. J. E. expressed his willingness to be offered up, if need be—that the ministry might survive.[29] And in one of the few surviving letters of Mary Davis, she also writes: "I am more than glad that I have been able to be of some use... My whole heart is in the success of this work. No sacrifice I can make would be too great..."[30] Helpers—editorial and technical—made important contributions, and growth was achieved. All involved merit sincerest thanks.

   3. De facto international status. As an outcome of its growth, Casa Bautista de Publicaciones achieved a kind of de facto international status that in and of itself became a factor to be reckoned with. And the Casa's international ministry was linked to its location in El Paso, Texas. Users and readers—institutions and individuals—came to identify "El Paso" with "Casa Bautista de Publicaciones." Far away users in Chile, Argentina, and elsewhere in the Spanish-speaking world, might not have had a clue as to the geography of Texas or the specific location of the city of El Paso, but they came to know that was the name of the place where Casa Bautista de Publicaciones was located. "El Paso" and "CBP" became synonymous terms. As this gradually occurred, despite the lack of official FMB strategy or blessing, it became a fact, a generally accepted fact, a recognition given by the evangelical population and by ecclesiastical structures, in both the United States and the Spanish-speaking world. As early as June 1921, Davis insisted with T. B. Ray that the Foreign Mission Board locate CBP permanently in the United States and give it the international character which, he asserted, "it already has."[31] Dr. Ray replied, very diplomatically, encouraging Davis to find encouragement in the present opportunities for the "Mexican Baptist Publishing House," however the decision might go regarding its being recognized as an "international house."[32] But by 1925 CBP had achieved international status, even without Board planning or approval.

4. A "permanent" location. The close of this period brought achievement of a "permanent" location for the Publishing House that was used for the next thirteen years (roughly twice as long as the first building bought for CBP in León). In theory, the Foreign Mission Board might have still looked on it as a "temporary location." In practice, the purchase of the building at 800 Myrtle Avenue in early 1925 gave CBP still firmer rooting in El Paso—with both property and equipment that would serve for several years.

5. Efforts to get the Board to appoint a Business Manager Though Davis' insistence—one is tempted to call it a "campaign"—for the Board to provide more adequate space for CBP in El Paso bore fruit at the close of this period, his similar insistence for the Board to appoint a Business Manager did not see fruit till two years later. Nevertheless the period did bring some relief to J. E. in administrative tasks. This happened especially with the appointment of C. D. Boone as a missionary, to direct the mechanical department.[33] Also it must be registered that Mary Davis, after her major surgery in the summer of 1922, improved in health sufficiently to do again what she had occasionally done in León: become the acting Director—in El Paso, perhaps Business Manager would be the more appropriate term—during some of J. E.'s retreats out of the area for both improving his health and accomplishing his writing tasks especially for the *Expositor Bíblico*.[34] In this way, J. E. and Mary found ways to complement each other that helped him maintain his health and make his editorial contributions, at the same time giving her an opportunity again to be involved personally and directly in the work.

6. Treatment accorded Davis by FMB leaders. Still another impressive feature of this period that must be registered is the very patient and gentle pastoral treatment accorded to J. E. Davis by doctors J. F. Love and T. B. Ray of the Foreign Mission Board. W. R. Estep explains the somewhat curious leadership pattern at the Foreign Mission Board, following the death of R. J. Willingham in December 1914. Willingham had been the Board's executive leader since 1893. Several years prior to his death, he had enlisted William Henry Smith, from the pastorate of First Baptist Church of Columbus, Georgia to be an assistant secretary. Eventually Smith's title became "Corresponding Secretary," though he was still considered an associate to Willingham. Meanwhile J. F. Love came to the Board in 1914 as "Home Secretary." And T. B. Ray, after pastorates in Kentucky and Tennessee and service with the Sunday School Board, was brought to the Board first as "Educational Secretary" but later became "Foreign Secretary." Smith and Love and Ray were apparently functioning as somewhat of a triumvirate in leadership at the Board, following the death of Willingham, when the Southern Baptist Convention of 1915, in the name of efficiency, chose to amend its constitution and directly elect Love "Corresponding Secretary" (i.e., the executive officer). Smith resigned shortly thereafter.[35]

Thus during Davis' crisis period of leaving Mexico and setting up in El Paso, he is found relating to T. B. Ray, as Foreign Secretary, and J. F. Love, as Corresponding (i.e., Executive) Secretary. And the feature or characteristic being highlighted here is the patient, gentle, pastoral treatment both of these executives accorded missionary Jones Edgar Davis. Davis' correspondence is generally to Dr. Ray, as Foreign Secretary. But occasionally, he desires to "go to the top man," or does so on occasion when Dr. Ray is on an extended foreign trip to other areas of the Board's overseas work. Davis sometimes uses what must be classified as harsh, intemperate, or emotional language. But doctors Ray and/or Love seem somehow to always respond with patience, understanding, and genuine love. An example is Dr. Ray's reply to Davis' not so veiled threat to resign, in April 1920, if more Board support (personnel and equipment) is not forthcoming. Health problems seem to be played like trump dominoes. But Dr. Ray replies: "Hold on now! Hold on! Don't be in too big a hurry! Is it quite certain that you have come to the time when a resignation is the thing needed? Perhaps; [but] it will be better if you will take a furlough and give yourself a chance to recuperate... I have been hoping that you could get away and take some rest... I believe that we need you in that Publishing House. You have shown yourself a genius and such geniuses are hard to find... The sphere of the House has been greatly enlarged and its opportunities and abilities were never as good as now... [Consider] the possibility of asking for a furlough. It might be... you would feel [in time] so recuperated you would be unhappy unless you were back in the Publishing House doing the work you are so well fitted to do. What do you think...?"[36]   Similarly, Dr. Love, replying to Davis in a letter dated September 27, 1921, has to give a negative answer. But the tenderness and diplomacy with which it is given is noteworthy. Love writes: "I have this morning your letter of the 22nd and have read it with care, deep interest, and with sympathy for you... It is fair to say... that the Board will be utterly unable to grant much of what has been asked by the respective missions... There is not the slightest probability that our receipts will be sufficient to meet these estimates... without involving the Board in a debt which would most seriously hurt all our work... We... as well as you are victims of circumstance... I should like to see you relieved of unnecessary discomfort and unfavorable conditions... I should find very distinct pleasure... in knowing that by anything I or the Board could do, you had been given the most favorable condition under which to prosecute your important department of the Mexican work... Yours with warm regards, J. F. Love, Corresponding Secretary."[37]

Thirteen Years at the 800 Myrtle Avenue Address

A summary of this period could be given in these phrases: A new "permanent" home at 800 Myrtle Avenue; A banner year, followed by a period of retrenchment; A business manager is named at last; The Great Depression forces further retrenchment, but the Publishing House survives and begins to grow again; Possibilities of another new "permanent" home—to be shared with the Mexican Seminary. Each of these aspects is now explored with at least summary detail.

> ***A new "permanent" home at 800 Myrtle Avenue.***—-The truth is that J. E. Davis had had his eye on this building for almost five years. As early as June 1920 Davis reports to T. B. Ray that "the Knights of Columbus... have a splendid building right back to back with the First Baptist Church... a fine building that could not be built today for the money they want for it... $35,000 or $40,000... [which] can be paid in four or five yearly payments... this is just what I want... it will give us a prestige we need; it will put us on the map. Why wait longer?... I feel the time has come..."[38] A little more than a year later, Davis writes Dr. J. F. Love (Ray being absent from Richmond for an extended trip to the Orient). In a three page, single spaced letter, Davis presents his arguments: 1. "Our present location is now absolutely inadequate..." 2. Renting appropriate and adequate additional space will be difficult and expensive. 3. The Knights of Columbus building is still for sale. It is well located, "a magnificent building" which would "be large enough for many years..with... little or no remodeling... In my way of thinking there is no better place for the House than El Paso, and there is no better house for us in El Paso than this Hall..." 4. The price is reasonable. Perhaps $30,000 to $35,000... A fifth point in the letter is Davis' proposal to buy a lot and build for CBP, if purchase of the Knights of Columbus building cannot be worked out.[39]

The First Baptist Church eventually bought the building from the Knights of Columbus and began to use it as educational space. The price was $40,000 which the church began to pay as periodic notes came due to various K of C members who had together provided financing at 8%. The matter disappears from Davis' correspondence (but not from his prayers or thoughts). J. E. accepted realities. He put into place measures for more intensive use of the store fronts at 519 and 521 North Campbell and may have eventually secured 523.[40] He had earlier rented a house across the street at 522 North Campbell. But his letter to T. B. Ray on January 1, 1923 includes the report that the city's First Baptist Church and the Central Baptist Church have decided to merge and build a new facility at a new downtown location.[41] Davis saw these events as presenting again the opportunity to acquire for the Publishing House the building at 800 Myrtle. The matter surfaces again in correspondence during the year.[42]

Despite the general optimism and prosperity that are thought of in connection with "The Roaring Twenties," the Foreign Mission Board was not necessarily enjoying unencumbered advance.[43] Though both J. E. Davis and G. H. Lacy appear to have had some contact with First Church during 1924 regarding the building, Dr. Ray sent a telegram to J. E. Davis on October 16, 1924, stating:

"Board unable make special appropriation now either for purchase First Church Building or new linotype..." In a letter to Dr. Ray, dated October 20, 1924, Davis reports that First Church is willing to lease the building to CBP and that he has carefully gone over the building to detect the considerable adjustments that will be necessary for Casa to advantageously use the facility.[44] But in a letter to Davis, dated October 23 (which probably crossed in the mails with the one from Davis to Ray, dated October 20), Dr. Ray reports that though the Board received the proposition to buy the building from First Church, it simply "could not consider it, because it did not have the money." But, he adds, "I hope [we] will not finally lose the opportunity to secure this building..." And he suggests the possibility that First Church simply allow the Board to assume the mortgage balance of approximately $23,000. By December 27, all parties have been consulted, and Davis reports to T. B. Ray: "We have a tentative proposition now from the First Baptist here to cede us their equity in the Hall, which is $17,000, leaving $23,000 on the building... We would do well to take it and remodel it for our work... It will be worth that to us—and more."[45] By mid-February, the purchase was consummated, and on March 5, Davis writes Dr. Ray using stationery that shows "800 Myrtle Avenue" as the Casa's address. Necessary remodeling was accomplished for a cost of about $1,000, and by March 11, Davis reports to Dr. Ray: "We are moving now." By the 21st, he could write: "We have moved, and are all still alive..., [and added:] Tomorrow I will be 52 years old. Never was in better trim... Never did more and better work than now. Praise the Lord..."[46] The next nine months brought more motive of praise to the Lord.

A banner year, followed by a period of retrenchment. –Although the term is not found either in Davis' correspondence or in Ross' chronicle, Ross writes that, according to the report given by Davis at the end of 1925, the year "was the most favorable in the history of the Publishing House until that time... The annual appropriations from the Foreign Mission Board had gradually increased, going from $7,500 in 1923 to $12,000 in 1924, exclusive of grants for capital expenditures." 1925 brought some retrenchment in Richmond (due to debt and decreased revenue), and the Board was only able to provide the same amount it had in 1924. Nevertheless, 1925 was the year when the Publishing House "reached new heights in production and distribution of literature... Expanded facilities... greatly increased the potential and efficiency of the plant... The House ... printed 50,000 tracts, 16,750 books, 53,000 Sunday School quarterlies, 1,045,000 Sunday School leaflets, and 221,000 copies of *El Atalaya Bautista* and *La Revista Homilética*... a total of 10,917,500 pages of Spanish literature, besides the commercial work which totaled $12,940. The net worth of the Publishing House, exclusive of building, was $57,000."[47] It had been indeed "a banner year!"

But the banner year was followed by what became a whole period of retrenchment that included the rest of the 1920s and half the decade of the '30s.

Historians generally date the Great Depression from the Stock Market Crash in October 1929. But in Southern Baptist circles, the agricultural problems of the '20s brought a collapse of the Seventy-five Million Campaign, and serious difficulties were confronted by the Foreign Mission Board—and all its related work—from 1926 on. The Board had to reduce its contributions to the Publishing House. Production—despite the new facilities—was curtailed. In 1926 book production dropped by more than 50%; no tracts were printed at all; total pages dropped by more than 30%; and the number of employees was cut from twenty-two to eighteen. The rest of the decade brought ups and downs, culminating in the disastrous slide of the Great Depression.[48]

A business manager is named at last.—-While on furlough in 1920-21, Davis asserted to Dr. Ray: "I cannot go back to that work alone and hold up very long." He proceeds to make the case for two missionary men to be assigned to the Publishing House: one to be Business Manager, and one to be Editorial Secretary. Davis prefers for himself to be named to the latter post.[49] And at that moment, Davis proposed Solomon Ginsburg, of Brazil, for a four-year commitment, despite Ginsburg's lack of experience in Spanish-speaking countries or with the Spanish language. Later there was consideration of naming C. D. Boone as Business Manager, but this never happened. Davis did keep the matter on Dr. Ray's agenda, but it was not until 1927 that J. H. Benson, veteran of service in Mexico since 1906, was named Business Manager. He served in this capacity until 1934.[50] Benson was reassigned from the Coahuila-Chihuahua field in Mexico, and with his naming as Business Manager, Davis "served as director of the editorial department."[51] As of February 1, 1934, J. E. Davis reassumed the general directorship of the Casa as well as shouldering a heavy editorial load.[52]

The Great Depression forces further retrenchment, but the Publishing House survives and begins to grow again.—-Sometimes the proportions of disastrous events are almost immediately detected, as with the terrorist attacks to the World Trade Center buildings, of 9/11/2001. But sometimes the effects of cataclysms take more time to assimilate. Such may well have been the case of the Stock Market Crash of 1929. By that year, the Casa Bautista de Publicaciones was enjoying its "new" facilities at 800 Myrtle Avenue, and was well equipped for its work, in spite of its difficult financial condition. That year "its equipment consisted of three linotypes, two cylinder presses, two job presses, one folding machine, two power paper cutters, and bindery equipment."[53] Most of the equipment had been purchased out of the income from commercial work. And during 1929 and 1930, the Publishing House was able to maintain its nine periodicals, but two of these (*El Atalaya Bautista* —a monthly since July 1927— and the B. Y. P. U. quarterly by then called *Temas para las U. B. de J.*) had to be suspended in 1931, for lack of funds. Practically all book production was suspended. Tract production and distribution was very sporadic.

A bright spot during the Depression years happened in 1930 when William Jewell College granted to J. E. Davis an honorary Doctor of Divinity degree. The Commencement Exercises where held on Thursday, May 22. Four other distinguished alumni received similar honors, including fellow missionary J. W. Lowe whose long ministry had been in China.[54]

In the main, those years brought dark days, very dark days. Davis' letter to Dr. Ray in February 1931 summarized this low point in CBP's history: "Last week and this not a press moved, and the future is about as drab for our publications as it could be... [but] I think we have not yet reached the bottom."[55] In both finances and leadership, the Foreign Mission Board was itself in the throes of "the Great Depression."

Finances had been problematic since the mid-twenties with the relative failure of the Seventy-five Million Campaign. Leadership had suffered also. Estep writes: "Less than two weeks before the Southern Baptist Convention convened on 16 May 1928 in Chattanooga, James Franklin Love died. For some time his heath had not been good. The burden of the board's worsening financial situation, his incessant travels on behalf of the missionary effort of Southern Baptists, and, at the last, the defalcation of the board's treasurer[56], all had taken their toll... Upon the death of the corresponding secretary [Love], the responsibility of his work became that of his associate, T. B. Ray."[57] But if Ray had no strong enemies on the Board, he apparently lacked strong friends to sponsor his being named Love's successor. With the title of foreign secretary, he was asked to perform the duties of executive secretary while the board searched for a permanent successor. A committee recommended Solon B. Cousins, a member of the board and pastor of the Second Baptist Church of Richmond. He was elected unanimously but declined. The committee turned to George W. Truett, who also declined; then to J. B. Weatherspoon, but he did not accept. Thence to J. W. McGlothlin, who also turned down the post. Then the Committee went back a second time to both Truett and McGlothlin, but without success. Finally on October 2, 1929 (twenty-seven days before the Stock Market Crash), T. B. Ray was elected. It thus befell Dr. Ray to try to lead at a most difficult time.

T. B. Ray had been a key friend of missionary Davis—and of Casa Bautista de Publicaciones—across the years. In the end, he became another victim of the Great Depression. No "quick fix" was found especially for the financial problems of the Board. In 1932, Ray was asked to take again the position of foreign secretary while a committee searched for a new executive secretary. Davis wrote Dr. Ray in December 31, 1932 and in his customary frank way, said: "I am thinking of you in your trying situation there. I suppose it will not be the easiest thing in the world to do, to again play 'second fiddle' in a way, after years of directing the destinies of the Foreign Mission Board, but with grace sufficient, we can put ourselves [aside], make ourselves of secondary consideration. After all, I feel that you will not rank any lower in the estimation of the missionaries who have known you and learned to love you as a true yokefellow... you will always occupy in my heart a very warm corner. I shall never forget how you have manfully stood by the men and women out at the front. I shall never cease to appreciate the kind and encouraging letters you have always written, even when the stress of circumstances must have almost broken your heart."[58] The Board finally elected Charles E. Maddry as its new executive secretary, and he took office on January 1, 1933. In less than a year T. B. Ray was forced into retirement, though given the title of "Emeritus Secretary," perhaps to soften the blow.[59] On October 30, 1933, Davis wrote a letter to Dr. Ray that must be regarded as highly reflective of the sincere and long-term friendship that had existed between these two men. The letter also speaks volumes about Edgar Davis. Early in the letter, Davis writes: "I feel that it is an honor and a privilege to express to you my personal regrets at your separation from the work you identified yourself with so completely and for so many happy years. I hope you will understand that I for one appreciate you and your great work in connection with our Foreign Mission Board." And after comparing their ages (Davis was only five or six years younger) and making small talk about both Publishing House work and Davis' additional pastoral/missionary ministries, J. E. finishes the letter with a key paragraph which reads: "Well, remember that Davis—hard-boiled as he is, and often a contender for things that he thought would be better than what his brethren thought—knows and loves T. B. Ray, and always will. And I don't mean maybe either. My prayers are for you...."[60] Dr. Ray lived less than four months, passing away on January 15, 1934. He "became a victim of the depression and of the loss of confidence of his peers."[61] He had lived and labored through the period of rising expectations to face the results of diminishing returns.[62] It was the end of another chapter in Casa's relationships with its sponsoring Board. And it opened a new one with Dr. C. E. Maddry.

During the Depression years, the House benefitted greatly when Miss Sarah Hale, of Monterrey, Mexico, asked the House to publish on contract a number of books she had translated into Spanish. The arrangement began in 1932. "Without this work the House would have had to reduce further its staff and leave much of its equipment idle."[63]

As Ross reports, "Apparently the worst of the crisis had passed by the end of 1935, and once more the House had survived the test, this time of depression instead of revolution... Davis' report for 1935 ended on this high note: 'As 1935 closes, the outlook is better than it has been for many years... All of this makes us hopeful for 1936 and for all the years to come. To God be all honor and praise.' "[64]

Possibilities of another new "permanent" home—to be shared with the Mexican Seminary.—A sometimes complicating factor for J. E. Davis—and the other missionaries to Mexico who had been forced to the border because of the revolution—was the presence in El Paso of personnel of the Home Mission Board, SBC. But El Paso was in the United States! HMB personnel had every right to be here! Davis reported to T. B. Ray in February of 1920 that tensions had been resolved and personnel of the two mission Boards were ministering in good harmony.[65]

One of the grand ministry projects of the Home Mission Board, for El Paso, was a Tuberculosis Sanatorium. (Let it be remembered that in this era and in the absence of antibiotic drugs, sunshine was considered the best remedy for this disease. And El Paso offered plenty!) The Southern Baptist Convention, meeting in Washington, D. C., in May 1920, received the following as part of the HMB Report: "Our Sanatorium for Tuberculosis at El Paso has been in operation for more than a year. At the annual meeting last June [i.e., 1919], our Board projected plans for the institution on the basis of $1,000,000 for the next five years, $500,000 for buildings and equipment and $500,000 for endowment... After extensive examination of various sanatoriums and diligent search for the most capable architects, the Board chose the firm of Messrs. Richard E. Schmidt, Garden & Martin, Chicago, Illinois,... first rank... architects in the line of tuberculosis sanatoriums.... On final approval of the plans, the Board authorized the construction of the first unit... at a cost of $200,000, which we hope to have finished in time for next winter's patients.... This with the 140 acres of land and improvements[66] valued at something like $75,000, given by the El Paso people, will put us well on the way towards the establishment of a great institution that shall bring relief to thousands who are suffering from the white plague, the greatest foe to man's health in our fair land. We are fortunate in having as superintendent, Rev. H. F. Vermillion, who is admirably suited to this great task."[67] The "first unit" was completed toward the end of 1921 and put into service. "Financial difficulties soon developed...."[68] The relative failure of the Seventy-five Million Campaign forced the Home Mission Board to issue bonds in 1924. Difficulties continued, but the sanatorium was kept in operation until October 1937, when it was closed.[69] Its closure created the possibility of a new "permanent location" for the Casa Bautista de Publicaciones.

According to Ross, Dr. J. B. Lawrence, executive secretary of the Home Mission Board, SBC, and Dr. R. S. Jones, field representative of the Foreign Mission Board, SBC, both attended the annual meeting of the Baptist General Convention of Texas in November 1937. There these men met to discuss a possible exchange of properties that the two Boards owned in El Paso. They reached a tentative agreement which was ratified by the respective mission Boards shortly, and the early months of 1938 brought implementation of the exchange: The former Sanatorium building would be jointly occupied by the Publishing House and the Mexican Baptist Theological Seminary (which had been functioning in San Antonio after anti-religious laws in Mexico made its continuation in Saltillo impossible). J. G. Benson (Business Manager for the Publishing House from

1927 to 1934) was serving as president of the Seminary. The Publishing House building on Myrtle Avenue would be used for a Home Board ministry among the Chinese people of El Paso.[70]

The relocation brought for the Casa the end of an era, and the beginning of another.

From 1938 Onward at the Location on the Franklin Foothills

A new "permanent location," a successor to J. E. Davis, the establishment of an advisory committee, and growth amid the complications of ministry during war are phrases that give handles for analyzing this period of Casa's century of service.

A new "permanent location."—The new location did not have a precise street address: it was outside the city limits! Eight miles from downtown, on the highway toward Alamogordo, New Mexico. Later, in 1953, the area would be annexed to the city; "Alamogordo Road" would become Dyer Street,[71] and in 1960 an extension to Alabama Street would finally give another access to city thoroughfares and allow the Casa's physical address to become 7000 Alabama Street, as it is today. But in 1938, when the Publishing House occupied the building, directions were mere approximations. Of course, the Sanatorium had become fairly well known, and "the former Sanatorium" became, in effect, the address.[72]

Ross reports: "In preparation for setting up the new plant, an old Miehle press was traded in on a new Kelly No. 2 press. It arrived on January 26, 1938, and was installed in the newly acquired building."[73] This press served for many years.

Davis' correspondence with Dr. Maddry during 1938 focuses on many details related to completing the installation of the Publishing House in this location. The building had to be fumigated. Some hospital equipment and furnishings had to be sold. (Some would be used by the Publishing House or by the Seminary.) A more satisfactory solution for the water supply was visualized but the actual digging of two wells was delayed until the next year. Some repair and remodeling had to be done. It was like March 1925 all over again! Gradually the move was accomplished and the ministry settled in to its new quarters.

One year after occupying the new location, the Davis' younger son became superintendent of the printing plant. Ed (full name, James Edgar) had helped with a variety of tasks in the printing plant since his boyhood: arising early to light the fires under the melting pots for the linotypes, cleaning the machines, and otherwise helping get things ready for the day's work. Under the guidance of his father, he learned more as he grew older, finally becoming an expert linotype operator and a successful printer. He had good business judgment and helped the Casa obtain commercial work that kept the presses occupied between literature runs. One of these jobs was a monthly medical journal edited by the American College of Chest Physicians called *Diseases of the Chest*. Under Ed's personal supervision, this project continued for many years. He served as print shop superintendent until near the end of 1954.[74]

The Davises eventually occupied an apartment on the southwest corner of the building. From their second floor living room window, the big central patio was visible. Gradually the Publishing House and Seminary staff sought to restore it to some of the beauty the architects had originally envisioned for this area. The embellishment brought Dr. Davis an opportunity to enjoy his hobby of gardening. Burton Patterson specifically remembers Dr. Davis' interest in cultivating dahlias along a north-to-south flower bed in "the big patio." It was adjacent to the door to the building that was closest to Dr. Davis' office. Burton remembers Dr. Davis, in the evenings after business hours, working his dahlias. "He kept them weeded, watered, and fertilized... I remember him out there on his knees working the soil around his flowers... [And]... they grew huge. He evidently was a good gardener."[75]

A successor to J. E. Davis. —-J. E. Davis reached sixty-five, the normal age for retirement, in March 1938. Permission was granted for him to continue as long as his heath permitted, but it became imperative that a successor be found, especially in light of the iron-clad policy of the time which considered seventy as a maximum age for retirement. Providentially, Frank W. Patterson and his wife, Pauline, became candidates for service at the Casa Bautista de Publicaciones, and were appointed on February 9, 1939. Patterson's background and specific service will be surveyed in the succeeding chapters. It is noteworthy here to register Dr. Davis' reaction to their being named. In a letter to Dr. Maddry, Davis wrote: "I am glad you have appointed a couple with this work in view. They will have much to learn. They should understand that they will have to get the language, and get it well. They will then have plenty to learn to get a grip on this work that has expanded so much that it is a job. Fortunately I am still strong and hope to be helping out here for a long time to come, especially with writing. I have a lot of that I want to do, and then I have an ambition to just keep on writing the lesson commentary for several years, even though you should retire me."[76] He was obviously anxious for Frank and Pauline to get a good foundation in the Spanish language. Never one to mince words, he registers his desire to see more rapid progress in a letter to Dr. R. S. Jones dated November 9, 1939. By that date Patterson was in Mexico City studying Spanish and had written Davis a letter–and in Spanish. But J. E. judges: [The letter] "is pitiful. He [Patterson] is working hard however... Let us hope that all of them [the reference is to several new missionaries studying Spanish] will turn out OK."[77] Fortunately it can be stated that Frank and Pauline did, in fact, get both missionary experience and language proficiency during their nearly two years in Mexico City. By January, 1941, the Pattersons were back in El Paso beginning their work at the Publishing House. Davis continued as General Director; Patterson eventually served as Business Manager. But a successor had been found and was "in training." A smooth transition would take place when the moment came.

The establishment of an advisory committee. —-Ross correctly points out that it was in connection with all the details related to the exchange of properties and the remodeling of the former sanatorium building, that Dr. Davis himself proposed the naming of "a local advisory committee," to assist in the operation of both the Publishing House and the Mexican Seminary. As the plan was approved, Dr. Maddry clarified that the Foreign Mission Board had every intention to staff and conduct both ministries but that it did appear appropriate for "the State Board, the Home Board, and the local El Paso Baptists to appoint an advisory committee to work with us. This will make for good will and better cooperation."[78] Though this structure may be seen as a precursor to a later International Advisory Committee, or even the Casa's now longstanding International Board of Trustees, Ross opines that "the very nature of the committee seemed to predict its doom."[79] It had no executive authority. It does not appear to have really represented the Home Mission Board or the State Mission Board. It was composed mainly, if not exclusively, of local Baptist leaders selected by Dr. I. L. Yearby, then pastor of the First Baptist Church of El Paso (and included Yearby himself). Though officially named by the Foreign Mission Board in December, 1938, the committee, almost from the start, did not feel that it received due cooperation from the administration of the Publishing House; and the Publishing House administration felt the Committee easily overstepped its authority and "meddled" in the affairs of the House. Though it at least existed on paper for several years, it was finally dissolved in 1946, the year the Seminary moved back to Mexico.[80]

Growth amid the complications of ministry during war. —War clouds gathered all during the decade of the thirties, and open conflict broke out in Europe by the end of that period. Japan and China had already been at war, and the Japanese attack on Pearl Harbor, December 7, 1941, brought the United States into the conflict that became World War II. El Paso had been "a military town" since the middle of the 19th Century. Ft. Bliss had been an important training center as early as the time of World War I. With the outbreak of WW II, El Paso's role in the military build-up increased. The Publishing House was located near Ft. Bliss, and even lost some of its property during the War due to the enlargement of the base. Without Alabama Street (not built until 1960), access to the plant actually channeled through an annex to the Fort. As young men left for war service, either as volunteers or draftees, help became more difficult to secure and maintain.[81] Disturbances in Europe and Asia had repercussions in Latin America; mailing problems were accentuated; increased costs and the limitations on paper and other supplies for productions "non-essential" to the war effort made life difficult for the House. Demand for commercial work declined. Withal, the Casa Bautista de Publicaciones survived another test and continued its ministry despite the complications of war.

The spring of 1943 brought two events that were indeed significant to the publications ministry:

(1) On March 12, the Foreign Mission Board announced that "the debt is all paid." In debt over a million dollars a decade earlier, the debt had finally been paid—and with interest. The Board could now look forward to expansion as soon as war conditions would permit.

(2) And on April 1, Davis, having reached the mandatory retirement age during March, was retired after thirty-nine years of active service. According to a special concession from the Board, J. E. and Mary were given a retirement salary equal to that of an active missionary and his editorial work was allowed to continue. Frank Patterson's role was changed from that of Business Manager to (General) Director.

It was again, the end of an era—and the beginning of another.

Endnotes

1. Letter, Davis to J. F. Love, dated July 25, 1916; IMB Archives.

2. Letter, Davis to T. B. Ray; August 29, 1916; IMB Archives.

3. Letter, Davis to Ray, September 6, 1916; IMB Archives.

4. Letter, Davis to Ray, September 26, 1916; IMB Archives.

5. Letter, Davis to Ray, September 29, 1916; IMB Archives.

6. A copy of the plan itself has yet to surface in IMB Archives, but see allusions in letters from Davis to Love and Ray, dated July 15, 1916; July 25, 1916; and letters from J. F. Love to Davis, dated July 12, 1916; July 20, 1916; July 31, 1916; IMB Archives.

7. Letter, Davis to Ray, September 6, 1916; IMB Archives.

8. See letter, Davis to Ray, October 5, 1916; IMB Archives.

9. See "Union Depot Witnessed Growth of El Paso," p. 16 in Borderlands, a Supplement to the El Paso Times, produced by the students of El Paso Community College, published as Vol. 22, for 2003-2004, early summer, 2003.

10. Worley's Directory of El Paso for 1916, Dallas: John F. Worley Directory Company, 1916, p. 47.

11. Ibid.

12. See Borderlands, pp. 4-5.

13. See letter, Love to Davis, July 19, 1916; IMB Archives.

14. See Poe, Missions for, p. 129, where the case of mission presses in Burma is mentioned.

15. Ross, Sowing the Seed, p. 62; see also letters, Davis to J. F. Love, dated October 13, 1916, and T. B. Ray to J. E. Davis, dated October 26, 1916; IMB Archives.

16. Letter, T. B. Ray to J. E. Davis, October 26, 1916; IMB Archives.

17. Letter, Davis to T. B. Ray, March 14, 1917; IMB Archives.

18. Minutes, Mission Meeting, June 20-21, 1917, El Paso, Texas, pp. 3-4; IMB Archives.

19. See letter, Davis to T. B. Ray, August 12, 1917, which mentions the recent visit to Davis in El Paso of two high-ranking representatives of the New York Society; IMB Archives. Poe has visited the archives of the American Baptist Historical Society, both in Valley Forge and in Rochester, and has copies of certain documents that reflect this period of joint support of CBP by both mission agencies (FMB, SBC; and ABHMS of what was then called Northern Baptists, later American Baptist Churches).

20. Letter Davis to T. B. Ray, August 12, 1917; IMB Archives.

21. Ross reads "located permanently," but

the Minutes actually read: "that the Printing Plant be temporarily located at El Paso, Texas, and such machinery and equipment be brought from Mexico as is needed, and can practicably be brought out." See Minutes, Meeting of the Missionaries to Mexico, held in El Paso, Texas, June 20-21, 1917; IMB Archives. In 1921 the Mission did recommend that "the permanent" location of the Publishing House be determined; see Minutes, Meeting, June 21-23, 1921; p. 5; IMB Archives.

22. See letter, Davis to J. F. Love, dated April 29, 1919; IMB Archives.

23. See letters, Davis to T. B. Ray, June 29, 1920; July 19, 1920; July 30, 1920; and August 9, 1920; IMB Archives.

24. Ross reads "permanently;" but see endnote 21.

25. As Ross also records: "Another member of the production staff deserving special mention was Ricardo Mireles... He first came to the Publishing House as an apprentice." This may have happened as early as 1920; and "except for a three year period in the middle twenties and a brief interval during World War II, Mireles served continuously with the House until 1959." During his tenure, he worked with CBP in three different locations and under several different plant supervisors. But as a pressman, "Mireles was capable of putting out work inferior to none." (See Ross, Sowing the Seed, p. 126.) As late as February, 2004, Nancy Hamilton discovered that some of her neighbors were descendants of Mireles, and that the family had conserved rather accurate "traditions" and "family anecdotes" concerning Mireles' long-term association with the Baptist Spanish Publishing House. Example: During the two-year stint that Ricardo's son Carlos worked at the Publishing House in the mid-fifties, he and Ed Davis, plant supervisor and son of CBP's founder, would play Chinese checkers at the lunch break.

26. It would appear more precise to say that the Publishing House occupied three buildings, since from the outset it had had both the 519 and 521 spaces on North Campbell, as both photographs and letterheads attest. These small "store fronts" show to have had separate entrances but probably were not over 20 to 25 feet wide and somehow connected inside. It was apart from this small "double space" that Davis rented the building across the street at 522 North Campbell.

27. Ross, Sowing the Seed, pp. 79-88.

28. See letters, Davis to T. B. Ray, July 25, 1921, and Ray to Davis, July 23, 1921; IMB Archives.

29. See letters, Davis to T. B. Ray, August 3, 1921 and September 29, 1923; IMB Archives.

30. Letter, Mrs. J. E. Davis to T. B. Ray, February 15, 1923; IMB Archives.

31. Letter, Davis to Ray, June 27, 1921; IMB Archives.

32. See letter, Ray to Davis, July 23, 1921; IMB Archives.

33. See Ross' summary above; and letter, Davis to J. F. Love, January 2, 1922; IMB Archives.

34. See letters, Davis to T. B. Ray, October 17, 1922 and December 14, 1922. In the latter letter, J. E. calls Mrs. Davis "a good manageress."

35. Estep. Whole Gospel, pp. 187-199.

36. Letter, T. B. Ray to J. E. Davis, April 26, 1920; IMB Archives.

37. Letter, J. F. Love to J. E. Davis, September 27, 1921; IMB Archives.

38. Letter, Davis to T. B. Ray, June 29, 1920; IMB Archives.

39. Letter, Davis to J. F. Love, September 22, 1921; IMB Archives.

40. At least one set of letterheads gives the CBP address as 519-523 North Campbell; see letter, Davis to T. B. Ray, dated November 15, 1924; IMB Archives.

41. See letter, Davis to T. B. Ray, January 1, 1923. The new building was eventually built at 805 Montana Street.

42. See letters, Davis to T. B. Ray, March 10, 1923 and December 21, 1923; IMB Archives.

43. See Estep, Whole Gospel, pp. 194, 199, 207,concerning the Board's debt problem; see also letter, T. B. Ray to J. E. Davis, dated October 18, 1923, where Ray explains to Davis that the Board owes Richmond banks $1,344,000 and how arrangements have been made to borrow another $700,000.

44. In fact, Davis, at this moment, seems to prefer buying a lot "down the valley" and building a facility specifically for CBP. See letter, Davis to Ray, October 20, 1924; IMB Archives.

45. Letter, Davis to T. B. Ray, December 27, 1924; IMB Archives.

46. Letters, Davis to T. B. Ray, March 11 and 21, 1925; IMB Archives.

47. Ross, Sowing the Seed, p. 89.

48. Ibid., pp. 90-92.

49. See letter, Davis to T. B. Ray, February 8, 1921; IMB Archives.

50. This according to Ross, Sowing the Seed, pp. 90 and 67. Curiously, Patterson, in A Century of, p. 227, credits Benson with service in Mexico from 1906 till 1918 and at the Publishing House from 1921 to 1942.

51. Ross, Sowing the Seed, p. 90.

52. See letter, Davis to C. E. Maddry, February 5, 1934; IMB Archives.

53. Ross, Sowing the Seed, p. 91.

54. See Commencement program, from the Curry Library, William Jewell College Archives. The campus newspaper for Wednesday, May 7, also announced that Davis would give "the Missionary Address" on "Sunday evening."

55. Letter, Davis to T. B. Ray, February, 25, 1931; IMB Archives.

56. See Estep, Whole Gospel, p. 208, regarding the $100,000 swindle by the Board's treasurer George N. Sanders.

57. Estep, Whole Gospel, p. 209.

58. Letter, Davis to T. B. Ray, December 31, 1932; IMB Archives.

59. See Estep, Whole Gospel, p. 214.

60. Letter, Davis to T. B. Ray, October 30, 1933; IMB Archives.

61. Estep, Whole Gospel, p. 214.

62. Ibid.

63. Ross, Sowing the Seed, p. 92; see also pp. 117-118 on Miss Hale's death in 1952 and on her general contribution to evangelical literature in Spanish.

64. Ibid., p. 93; see also SBC Annual for 1936, p. 213.

65. See letter, J. E. Davis to T. B. Ray, February 20, 1920; IMB Archives.

66. Apparently this term "improvements" included the building that was incorporated into the east end of the hospital complex. It had been built by a "country club" organization about the time of the First World War and included a beautiful fireplace and hard wood dance floor. This area served as the main conference room until the new office addition was built in 1982.

67. SBC Annual, 1920, pp. 373-374.

68. Encyclopedia of Southern Baptists, vol. 2, p. 1431.

69. Ibid.

70. Ross, Sowing the Seed, pp. 96, 97; see also SBC Annual for 1938 pp. 180, 256; Minutes of Foreign Mission Board, December 9, 1937; letter, C. E. Maddry to J. E. Davis, December 2, 1937; letter, R. S. Jones to Davis, March 15, 1938; IMB Archives; and Viola Campbell, He Leadeth Me, Private Publication, 2003, pp. 15-16.

71. For a number of years, the Casa would use 6700 Dyer as its street address, though its physical entrance was about a quarter of a mile west of the intersection of Dyer and Ellerthorpe, where Ellerthorpe deadends into the Publishing House property.

72. Mailing address for some of these years was maintained at P. O. Box 211; in 1941, it changed to Box 1648; and sometime in the 1950s to P. O. Box 4255, as it is today.

73. Ross, Sowing the Seed, p. 97.

74. Ross, Sowing the Seed, pp. 99, 100.

75. Letter from Dr. Burton Patterson, February 17, 2004.

76. Letter, Davis to C. E. Maddry, February 11, 1939; IMB Archives.

77. Letter, Davis to R. S. Jones, November 9, 1939; IMB Archives.

78. Letter, C. E. Maddry to Davis, December 25, 1937; IMB Archives.

79. Ross, Sowing the Seed, p. 99.

80. Ibid.

81. Ross notes that the number of employees averaged only thirteen in 1942, in contrast to nineteen the previous year. See Ross, Sowing the Seed, p. 102.

Chapter 3

The Frank W. Patterson Years—Part I

A historic video in the library of the Casa Bautista de Publicaciones serves as an excellent link between the Davis Years and the Patterson Years. Siegfried Enge secured the video from a local photographic lab, around 1995, converting it from an eight millimeter home movie shot probably in 1941, Patterson's first year of resident service in El Paso. It is "silently bilingual," in that no sound was recorded (the technology likely did not yet exist for home movie cameras) but posters done in both Spanish and English announce the purpose and follow the sequence of the content. The purpose is announced: [To show] How the *Expositor Bíblico* is published. After panoramic views of the Casa's buildings (the former tuberculosis sanatorium), the viewer is introduced to the Davises, then Frank Patterson,[1] followed by a step by step presentation of the writing, production, and mailing of *El Expositor*. Final takes show a world map and a poster that highlights some eighteen countries where *El Expositor* is being used. This "silent home movie" converted into a video essentially turns back the clock more than sixty years and allows us to relive a special moment of transition from the Davis Years to the Patterson Years.

As signaled in the previous chapter, Dr. Davis reached mandatory retirement at the end of March 1943. On April 1, Frank Patterson received a telegram from C. E. Maddry of the Foreign Mission Board officially naming him (General) Director and installing him by long distance. There was no ceremony or elaborate passing of the baton, but reality hit home. "The Patterson Years" began.

"And Who Are the Pattersons?"

By 1943 J. E. and Mary Davis had become fixtures in evangelical circles of El Paso and nearby areas, having lived and ministered there for more than twenty-five years. But as Frank and Polly Patterson assumed leadership at the Publishing House, it would not be difficult to imagine church leaders or business contacts reflecting lack of acquaintance and asking, "And who are the Pattersons?" The question serves well here to introduce more specifically these VIPs in the Casa's century of service.

Fortunately there are abundant sources for "getting to know" this dedicated missionary couple. Two brief biographies exist of Frank,[2] each with a section concerning his wife Pauline. Dr. Patterson's personal files and private papers have been made available for this project, and the Publishing House library has a full collection of published materials in which the Pattersons have participated.

From this rich variety of resources, we learn that Frank[3] was born to Otis Harvey and Myrtle Patterson, in Alva, Territory of Oklahoma, on July 6, 1907.[4] The event occurred at home, at about 2:30 p.m. with Dr. G. N. Bilby and nurse Miller attending. Birth weight was 8 fi pounds (which doubled before he was four months old). He cut his first tooth at five months, skipped completely the "crawler stage," and walked upright a month before he was one.[5] Though apparently Frank was off to a healthy start, both double pneumonia and whooping cough attacked his little body before his second birthday, leaving him debilitated to the point that the doctor predicted: "If he lives he will probably be a weakling the rest of his life."[6] He started to school at age six, but during the harsh days of winter, Frank sometimes had to be absent rather than risk his health. With serious effort, however, he always managed to pass his grades. At eleven, Frank was still not strong, but he was ambitious and showed plenty of initiative. With a small steel wagon, he delivered packages for shoppers at the town square and began to save his money "for something important."[7] From this work he gained the attention of a Mrs. White who ran a local print shop and published a weekly paper. She offered Frank work there, to help in various miscellaneous tasks. With parental permission, he accepted—and began his career in publications. Besides sweeping the shop and cleaning the equipment, he learned to melt the lead that the linotype used. He also learned to set type, operate the big press, and run the new folder Mrs. White bought. He even dreamed of being an editor, deciding content for the paper, like Mrs. White did. Frank spent so much time at the print shop that his friends teased: "You must have ink in your blood."

One year, during the summer, Frank took a paper route—and later a second route (one in the morning, the other in the afternoon). It was hard work, and required lots of walking (which he gradually accelerated to a jog). But little by little the exercise built his body, to the point that his lifelong health and longevity were the envy of many!

Frank's sixth grade teacher asked her pupils, "What do you want to be when you grow up?" Patterson wrote: "I want to be an editor and a preacher." And in the providence of God, that's just what happened.

Active Christian parents had taken Frank to church since his childhood, but during his early teen years, a summer revival was held in a big tent and involved all the churches in town. Frank gave it special interest, and after a visit with his pastor (a distinguished looking man with white hair), he made his public profession of Christ. "I accept Jesus as my Savior," he told the preacher at the invitation time. Two years later, Frank said to his pastor, "Now I am ready to be baptized." And he was, into the fellowship of the local Baptist church. Active service with youth of the church followed.

Actually within Frank's growing-up years, his family lived in several northwest Oklahoma towns: Alva (where he was born), Waynoka, Shattuck, back to Alva, then back to Shattuck. It was in Shattuck, during his last years in high school that "big decisions" concerning his career and his college studies were made. A visiting preacher helped Frank confront squarely his call to Christian ministry. Shortly, he acknowledged before the church, "God has called me to preach, and I am ready to answer the call."[8] A historical booklet published by the First Baptist Church of Shattuck, in 1957, recounts: "Frank Patterson, a freshman at Oklahoma Baptist University,... preached in the morning service, September 7, 1924. He was licensed to preach at the conclusion of the service."[9] A sentence in the next paragraph reads: "Frank Patterson [was] ordained in August 1925." His age: 18 years, 1 month. A few weeks later (in September 1925), Frank expressed his Christian pilgrimage up to then in a poetic fashion. In five four-line stanzas, he contemplates his lost condition, his salvific encounter with the Lord, and his desire to give back a life of service to the Savior. Not even a high school English teacher would be overly impressed with the poetry as verse, but the sincerity of a young believer, recently ordained to preach, does stir emotions, even profoundly. The last two stanzas read:

> "You paid the debt, You saved my life,
>   You made me as I am;
> You lifted me from out the mire,
>   You've helped me be a man.

> "Lord, take my all; I want to walk
>   The path my Savior trod.
> I want to live as Jesus lived,
>   And keep my hand in God's."[10]

College studies at OBU represented another challenge. Frank's savings were wiped out in a bank failure just before he was to enter, so he delayed his start, found another job, and eventually got to Shawnee. During his first year, he worked for food at a sandwich shop, slept on the screened-in back porch of the shop owner, and barely made ends meet. For his other three years, Frank worked in the university print shop. By operating the presses and linotypes, he covered his college expenses—and gained more invaluable experience for his eventual dual career in preaching and printing.

Frank W. Patterson was graduated from Oklahoma Baptist University with a Bachelor of Arts degree in the spring of 1928. During his time there, he had been a member of the "missions volunteer band," even though he had not yet experienced a clear "call to missions."

The opportunity came to use his college education by teaching and directing teachers. So for a year, Frank served as the principal of a three-teacher school near Perryton, Texas (and really not far from Shattuck and the other northwest Oklahoma towns where he had lived). Though he liked the work, he came to feel it was time to prepare himself further for the preaching ministry to which God had called. In the fall of 1929, he enrolled in Southwestern Baptist Theological Seminary, in Fort Worth, Texas. That's where Frank Patterson met Pauline Gilliland.

Pauline (Polly, for most of her family, friends and colleagues) was an attractive young woman who was also beginning her seminary studies. She had been born to a devout Christian family in Tioga, Texas, on December 14, 1906. The family prospered and moved into Dallas, where Polly had grown up listening to the preaching of Dr. George W. Truett, acclaimed pastor of First Baptist Church in that city. She became a Christian early in life, was baptized by Dr. Truett, and became a dedicated disciple and an avid student of the Bible.

When she entered Baylor University,[11] in Waco, Texas, her financially secure family did not have problems in paying for her education. In fact, she was one of the few girls on the Baylor campus in the 1920s who had her own car! A Stutz-Bearcat. But prosperous times can vanish overnight, and her beloved family experienced serious financial difficulties during those years.

Somewhere along the way, Polly received from God a definite call to missions. Perhaps it happened under Dr. Truett's preaching in Dallas, or when a missionary visited that historic church. Maybe the call came at Baylor, where she had been a member of the "volunteer mission band" (as Frank had been at OBU). And in fact, it was at a meeting of the "mission band" on the Seminary campus that Frank and Polly first met!

Roberta Ryan, probably using memories taken directly from her interviews with both the Pattersons, tells the story like this:

"At a meeting of his mission band one night, [Frank] saw a young woman across the room. 'That's the woman I'd like to marry,' he told himself. 'Who is she?' he asked a friend. 'That's Pauline Gilliland, from Dallas,' his friend answered. 'Her friends call her Polly. She's a missions volunteer, you know.' ...'You must introduce me to her,' [Frank] said."[12]

Friendship blossomed into serious romance. During the courting period, they discovered that their paths might well have crossed in the Texas Panhandle. For following Baylor, Polly had been a teacher at Rock School in the Panhandle area, on the Britt Ranch, a Texas sized spread of about 18,000 acres. She had boarded with the Tom Britt family, owners of the ranch, and they had helped her enormously during her teaching time there. The Britts had made available horses to ride, had helped Polly ford swollen creeks during the rainy season, and in other ways had taken good care of "the teacher." She could have stayed there a long time, but Polly, like Frank, had a call from God. Seminary preparation seemed to be the next necessary step.

Before Frank was graduated from the seminary in 1932, he asked Polly to marry him. "Yes," was her answer, "but I must work a year and pay back the money I borrowed to come to the Seminary." So for the next year or so, Polly worked for her brothers in their business in Dallas, and Frank went back to Oklahoma where he studied at the University of Oklahoma[13] and pastored two small churches.

The wedding took place at the Gilliland home, in Dallas, September 7, 1933. Among Dr. Patterson's personal papers two brief letters to him from Polly have been found, with dates shortly before the wedding. Love, commitment, and excitement abound in the words and between the lines. Their marriage ceremony was performed by Dr. H. E. Dana, Frank's very favorite professor at the Seminary. (And the one who would later attract him to do doctoral studies at Central Seminary in Kansas City, where Dr. Dana had moved.) Frank stood beside the preacher in the spacious living room of the Gilliland home, and he watched Polly smile as she walked slowly down the curved stairway, with its beautiful wooden banister. Each promised... "till death do us part." And that only came almost sixty-seven years later, when Polly went to be with the Lord on March 27, 2000.

What immediately followed the wedding was a period of pastoral service in several Oklahoma towns. In Spiro, Frank bought a printing press and began to print a church bulletin or paper that church youth delivered to every home in town!

The Spiro press accompanied the Pattersons when, in 1935, they moved to Nashville, Arkansas, for Frank to be pastor of the First Baptist Church there. Records show that "Brother Patterson" was an effective and evangelistic pastor wherever he served. (In Spiro he baptized one hundred and fourteen people in his twenty month pastorate there.[14]) A surviving memento found among Patterson's personal papers is a poster announcing a revival of "Eight Great Days" at the church in Nashville. It contains a photograph of the rather impressive church building (small town gothic with an educational annex), along with the smiling faces of Pastor F. W. Patterson and the guest evangelist, Dr. Chester Swor, Dean of Men at Mississippi College and a popular youth speaker of the time. The meeting is announced as "Sponsored by [the Church's] Young People for People of All Ages."

While pastor of this church in Nashville, Frank experienced his call to "printer/preacher" missionary service. It happened like this: At a meeting of the Woman's Missionary Society, the leader distributed to each lady present a prayer request she had clipped from the *Royal Service* magazine. When it was her turn, Polly read the request she had been given and prayed for God to supply the need. But her heart skipped a beat when she did, for the request read: "A missionary printer is needed in Argentina." At home she shared the request with Frank. It wasn't hard for him to get the point: Polly had been a mission volunteer since college days, and Frank had always said, "I'll go anywhere God wants me to go..." Was this God's sign to the "preacher/printer"? They prayed together. Polly prayed especially hard: "Lord, if you need us in Argentina, help Pat to know..."

That autumn the Pattersons attended the Arkansas state convention of Baptists. They listened with special attention to a report given by Dr. R. S. Jones of the Foreign Mission Board. After the service, Polly chanced to meet Dr. Jones on the sidewalk. "Did you ever find a printer for Argentina?" she asked. "Why do you ask... How did you know?" responded a surprised Dr. Jones. "My husband is a printer as well as a preacher..." Polly replied. "Tell him to meet me tomorrow afternoon at three o'clock... I want to talk to him," Dr. Jones said. And Frank did.

The result of the visit with Dr. Jones was "a call to missions" for Frank. Not to Argentina—but rather to El Paso. (The urgency there lay particularly in Dr. Davis' approaching retirement.)

Frank was sure this was God's leading. But Polly had trouble with the idea of being "foreign missionaries to TEXAS!" The couple prayed much, and began to make plans—but Polly's doubts remained. She asked God for a sign. It came—in God's own timing. The sign Polly requested of the Lord was the conversion of Edna, a young lady to whom Polly had often witnessed, and the only member of Polly's Sunday School class who had not yet trusted Christ. The time approached for the Pattersons to travel to Richmond, Virginia, for their missionary appointment proceedings, but Edna had not yet become a Christian. On Sunday before the couple was to leave for Richmond, Polly did not feel well and stayed home from church. It was a dreary, rainy day, and she doubted that Edna would even have attended services that day. But when pastor Patterson got home at noon, he bounded to Polly's bedroom, sat down, and said with a grin, "Guess what? Edna accepted Christ as her Savior today." Polly was ecstatic! God had answered her prayer. If asked in Richmond whether she could be "a foreign missionary in El Paso," her answer would be "Yes!"[15]

It was. So was Frank's. All Board requirements were satisfied, and they were appointed missionaries of the Foreign Mission Board, Southern Baptist Convention, February 9, 1939. (It was an appointment that would last thirty-three years!)

Upon return to Nashville, things happened fast. Frank sold his press to a friend. Household goods were shipped to El Paso for storage. Good-byes were said to beloved church members and neighbors. Final sermons and lessons were given. Preschooler son Burton was brought up to date on the new missionary adventures that were coming soon. (Burton had been born while Frank was pastor in Spiro, Oklahoma.[16]) By the last days of March the family of three had left Nashville, visited friends and relatives in Oklahoma, done the same in Dallas, and had arrived in El Paso for their first visit with the Davises and their first impressions of the Casa Bautista de Publicaciones. After a few days on the border, Pat and Polly (as they were familiarly called) left for language study in Mexico City. There they spent the rest of 1939 and all of 1940. After four months of private language tutoring,[17] "both attended classes at the University of Mexico, and [Frank] received the Master of Arts degree in 1940"[18] in Spanish literature. As Ross observes, "While in Mexico City, they had opportunity to gain experience in the mission work of their local church [First Baptist, Mexico City], and in Vacation Bible School work in other parts of Mexico."[19] At the end of 1940, the Pattersons returned to El Paso and made ready to begin their work at the CBP, in early January 1941.

These are the Pattersons! Praise God for both of them!

And What Did They Do at the Casa Bautista?

Dr. Davis gave Frank a variety of editorial and administrative tasks during his first year. Then, beginning in January 1942, Patterson became Business Manager. As such he "was responsible for hiring workers, purchasing supplies, and making reports. Between jobs, he squeezed in time to write and edit Sunday School lessons and to help in the print shop." [20] Experience—in quantity and variety—came fast!

Polly's tasks at the Publishing House were slower in developing, but gradually they did materialize, and in fact they grew continually across the years. She, like Mary Davis, made multiple contributions to the Casa's ministry. Since her literary career blossomed during the second half of "the Patterson Years," more detail will be given in the next chapter.

Then came that fateful day in the spring of 1943 when Dr. Davis was retired and Frank was named (General) Director.[21] He had had over four years of acquaintance with Dr. Davis and slightly over two under his direct tutelage, when this transition occurred. Such was both providential and decidedly helpful.

In August 1993, during the administration of J. T. Poe,[22] Dr. and Mrs. Patterson visited the Publishing House again, and "don Francisco" (as Spanish-speaking friends often addressed him) gave a message at the weekly chapel service for Casa personnel. The message, given in good Spanish (though Patterson was by then 86 years old), was entitled "Cosas que aprendí de los fundadores de la Casa Bautista de Publicaciones" (Things I learned from the founders of the Baptist Spanish Publishing House). After retracing briefly the Casa's history, Dr. Pat listed five things "he had learned" from J. E. and Mary Davis, the House's founders. An English digest of his points is as follows:

1. From the outset [the Davises] gave themselves wholeheartedly to the task, willing to sacrifice possessions and even life itself, for fulfilling their mission from God. Their example is a continual challenge.

2. With courage and with faith, the Davises persevered against all kinds of obstacles. (Here Patterson mentioned that Davis' life motto, from his youth, had been: "Perseverantia omnia vincit"—Latin for "Perseverance defeats whatever comes.")

3. Davis was a man of great faith. Davis' example in trusting God to supply urgent needs is worthy of our emulation.

4. The Davises were an industrious pair. Neither had a lazy bone in his/her body! May we follow in their train.

5. Dr. Davis was a prolific writer and a fervent evangelist. His writing career included books and magazines (especially *El Expositor Bíblico*) and was almost exclusively done in Spanish, but his preaching career included evangelistic meetings in both languages (English and Spanish), and was highly blessed of God in many places.

Patterson concluded his message asserting, "I give thanks to the Lord that He allowed me to walk in the shadow of this great servant of God. I learned from him, and served like him in both editorial and administrative functions in El Paso for twenty-seven years."[23]

It makes an interesting exercise to consider these two men, J. E. Davis and F. W. Patterson who led the Casa during almost two thirds of its century of service, so different yet so similar. Differences in temperament stand out. Davis called himself "hard-boiled."[24] Patterson has recounted to the author how he confronted Dr. Davis early in his resident service with the comment circulating in missionary circles in Mexico that Davis was "a bear." Patterson, of equally firm convictions but of milder temperament, resolved to love "the bear"—and learn from him. The differences in temperament were outshone by their similarities—in experiences, as preachers/printers/editors; in theological perspectives; in talents; in missionary vision and commitment. Both saw the potential of print for the furtherance of the gospel. Both were committed to keeping the Casa Bautista alive to serve the churches and extend Christ's kingdom. And they succeeded—for the glory of God!

Who Else Came to Help?

In December, 1965, Roberta Ryan wrote a press release to celebrate the Pattersons' "Quarter of a Century" of resident service in El Paso. In the piece, she commented that "The Pattersons' arrival at the Baptist Spanish Publishing House in [late] 1940 doubled its missionary personnel... Dr. and Mrs. J. E. Davis... gladly shared their responsibilities with the new recruits. For two more years the four missionaries labored side by side with ten employees: writing, editing, setting type, printing,... selling, mailing, promoting and administrating."[25] Gradually the staff—of both missionaries and employees—grew. Indeed, during the course of the first dozen years of the Patterson administration, a good number of workers came to help. The following must be recognized and introduced, if ever so briefly. (The year of their arrival is signaled in parenthesis):

James W. and Catherine McGavock (1945). J. W. was named Business Manager on June 21, 1945. Though veterans of more than twenty years of missionary service in Chile, when the McGavocks were named for the Publishing House they were already in El Paso, for they had been transferred to the Mexican Baptist Theological Seminary (still sharing the former sanatorium building with the Publishing House) a year earlier. McGavock's coming to the Casa Bautista de Publicaciones "was in answer to the great need for a man with experience in mission work to dedicate himself to the business administration of the House and the promotion of sales in Latin American countries."[26] McGavock's work allowed Patterson to dedicate most of his time and effort to the editorial and printing areas. Mrs. McGavock was later named editor of *La Hora de los Cuentos*, a new periodical launched in April 1947 and designed to be used with children ages four to eight, during Training Union. She also edited a simple collection of handwork patterns for children's activities that has been in continuous circulation for over fifty years![27] Some time before the McGavocks' retirement in November 1953, together they made a four-month tour of South and Central America, visiting evangelical book stores in twenty-three Latin American countries. Their search for better ways through which the Publishing House could serve in all these areas was reflected in considerably increased sales in 1952, 1953, and succeeding years.

Alfredo and Olivia Lerín (1946). Like the McGavocks, the Leríns were already in El Paso when they began their association with Casa Bautista de Publicaciones. Like the McGavocks, they had been serving with the Seminary. But when the Seminary returned to Mexico in 1946 (to the city of Torreón), the Leríns accepted Patterson's invitation to become employees of the Casa in its editorial department. The Leríns' interesting life and ministry, their effective and long-term contribution to Baptist work in general and the Casa's work in particular would merit its own book! Here space can be given to register only the major outlines of who they were and what they did.

Olivia Sara was from a major pioneer Baptist family, that of don Samuel Domínguez, of Saltillo, Coahuila, Mexico. She was the youngest of several children, all of whom made their mark in the world. Her brother Efraín had worked with Dr. Davis in the early 1920s. Olivia had received her education in the Normal School for Teachers (Colegio Roberts) in Saltillo and later studied at Southwestern Seminary, in Fort Worth. She had taught in the Colegio Anáhuac in Chihuahua, in the Instituto Madero in Saltillo, and in the Mexican Theological Seminary, during its sojourns in Saltillo, San Antonio, and El Paso. During her years at CBP, she edited several of the Sunday School materials for children, helped edit general magazines, translated books, and wound up her active career there as director of the Sunday School Department.

Alfredo was near her equal in his own capacities and contributions to the work. Though not from an evangelical family, as Olivia had been, his religious interests blossomed early. At age eight he became an altar boy in a Catholic church in his home city of Puebla. Noting his abilities, the priests even talked to his parents about sending him to Rome, when he was older, to prepare for the priesthood. Instead he became a student at Howard School, an American Baptist school in Puebla, where Biblical influences and studies led him to become an evangelical Christian of the Baptist denomination. His Sunday School teacher gave him a Bible and even expressed her hope he would eventually become a preacher. He did. In Saltillo, he studied at the Baptist normal school and at the Mexican Baptist Theological Seminary. And in Saltillo, he met Olivia Sara Domínguez. As in the case of Frank and Pauline Patterson at the Baptist Seminary in Fort Worth, friendship blossomed into romance, and Alfredo and Olivia were married on August 22, 1936. Later, both attended Southwestern Seminary in Fort Worth. Alfredo's association with Casa Bautista de Publicaciones lasted for slightly more than twenty-five years of active service. (Retirement came December 31, 1971; death finally overtook him February 10, 1997, at the age of 94 years. Olivia preceded him in death on October 7, 1996, at the age of 86 years.)[28] During his years at the Publishing House, Alfredo served as a general language consultant, a lesson writer for *El Expositor Bíblico*,[29] and editor of various periodicals, among them, *Revista Evangélica, El Pastor Evangélico*, and *Sal*.

Hiram and Charlotte Duffer (1948). While their arrival in El Paso was dated from August 1948, they had been appointed a year earlier to serve with the Publishing House, but, like the Pattersons, first went to Mexico City for language study. Duffer's task, as requested by the Mexican Mission, was to work in the Publishing House but with a view to promoting religious education in the Baptist churches of Mexico. A magazine was planned to help do this promotion, and upon arrival in El Paso, Hiram assumed responsibility for Training Union materials and in January 1949 started *El Promotor de Educación Cristiana*. Simultaneously he served as Royal Ambassador Secretary for Mexico and directed institutes and encampments in that country.[30]

Margaret McGavock (1949). Margaret was the daughter of James and "Kitty" McGavock, and thus had grown up as an MK (missionary kid) in Chile, speaking Spanish from her childhood. She had been educated at Carson-Newman College, in Tennessee, and at the New Orleans Baptist Theological Seminary. Prior to her missionary appointment, she had taught Spanish at Carson-Newman and worked briefly as an employee at the Publishing House.

Though her service as an appointed missionary was brief, before her marriage in El Paso, she continued as an editorial employee after marriage. Her contribution to Training Union materials for early youth and later to a new magazine for Christian families is remembered as substantial. Margaret also wrote a twelve-page PR brochure for the Casa in 1949, probably soon after her missionary appointment. The brochure was entitled "The Light Shineth Afar" and functions like a panoramic snapshot of the Publishing House at that moment.

Hoyt and Marie Eudaly (1952). Again one would wish for book length space to present this colorful and effective missionary couple. A chapter was given to Marie—and Hoyt—in a volume about Missouri missionaries that was published by Woman's Missionary Union, Auxiliary to the Missouri Baptist General Association, in 1956.[31] From this and other sources we know that Marie was born to Bertha Mae and Russell "Dick" Sadler, December 22, 1911, at Appleton City, Missouri. She attended high school in Garden City and Amsterdam, Missouri, and secured her college education attending several schools, including Central Missouri State Teachers College, where she was graduated in 1936, with majors in Education and English. Always active in church and activities for Christian students, Marie taught school for several years and in various Missouri towns, but eventually felt led to apply for a scholarship at Southwestern Seminary, in Fort Worth. Refusing to sign a teaching contract even before a scholarship confirmation arrived, her faith was severely tested. But faith won the day! At Southwestern, she was given a work scholarship and managed to stay at the Seminary for a full year. Opportunities opened up for educational service in West Texas churches and eventually with the Training Union Department of the Baptist General Convention of Texas. It was in connection with these activities that she met a big (young) man from a very small town: Hoyt Eudaly, from Grandfalls, Texas.

By then Hoyt (born in Pecos but raised in Grandfalls) had finished his college studies in business at Texas Tech, in Lubbock, and was owner/manager of a grocery store in Grandfalls. Always active in church, with special attention to Mexican mission work and to Training Union, Hoyt eventually arranged for the Training Union worker he had met at the state convention (Marie) to spend two spring months in 1941 working in Hoyt's home association (Pecos Valley) that included Grandfalls.

Fellowship in church work opened the door to romance. Marie is quoted in the Missouri WMU book as philosophizing about their courtship: "We met as mature Christian young people. As we worked in Training Unions [of the Association], we discussed our hopes, ambitions, future plans and how much we wanted to do for the Lord. Without many formal dates, we came to a deep mutual understanding and felt the leadership of the Lord in bringing our lives together."[32] They were married November 22, 1941—at the Texas State Training Union Convention, held that year in Fort Worth. Dr. W. L. Howse read Scripture and the ceremony was performed by Dr. George Truett and Dr. Douglas Hudgins. Since the bride's father had recently passed away, Dr. T. C. Gardner, Training Union Department Secretary for the BGCT and Marie's boss, gave the bride away. Her earlier application for missionary appointment to Africa was put on hold, and when war broke out the following month, Hoyt entered military service with the Coast Guard. Marie served in churches where Hoyt was stationed during the war years and gave birth to their first son, whom they named Dick. After the war, Hoyt felt led to enter Southwestern Seminary in Fort Worth. Missions—perhaps to Latin America—seemed in the offing.

In April of 1948, the Eudalys were appointed to serve with the Publishing House, with a specific view to replacing McGavock as Business Manager, whose retirement was approaching. But in what must be considered an unusual chain of events, they were sent directly to Mexico for a year of field work in South Mexico, then to language study in Medellín, Colombia, thence back to Mexico for a two year stint on the faculty of the Mexican Baptist Theological Seminary, in Torreón. Finally, in August 1952, they arrived in El Paso and began resident service there, Hoyt as Business Manager, Marie as editor for *La Hora de los Cuentos*. Eventually, during the next twenty-five years, a variety of tasks at the Publishing House came their way. In addition to editing curriculum materials, Marie wrote several books for children, some in Spanish, others in English. Hoyt eventually finished a doctor's degree in Religious Education at Southwestern Seminary, and Marie fulfilled the residence requirements for the same degree. After a reorganization in 1958, Hoyt served effectively as the Director for the Distribution Division, leading the House to new heights in the circulation and use of its publications. He traveled widely and in some circles was better known than the General Director. Instead of proceeding toward retirement, Hoyt and Marie spent their last years of active missionary service in Nicaragua and in El Salvador, specifically filling in for missionaries on furlough. Their next assignment was to have been Venezuela, but health problems kept that from happening. Officially they were transferred back to the Publishing House so their retirement could appear from there. Marie preceded Hoyt in death by about two years. Hoyt died July 25, 1997. Both are buried in Grandfalls. Their contribution to the Casa's century of service is indeed notable and remembered with gratitude.

Wilson and Jimmie Ross (1953). The transfer of this couple from Mexico to the Publishing House was, in good measure, intended to compensate for the transfer of the Hiram Duffers from El Paso to Mexico the previous year. Both Wilson and Jimmie were native Texans whose college and seminary training had been done at Hardin-Simmons University and Southwestern Seminary. Wilson had received the Bachelor of Divinity (the standard theological degree at the time) in Fort Worth and had served as pastor of churches in both Oklahoma and Texas, prior to their missionary appointment in March 1950. (Later he completed Master's degrees both at the Seminary in Fort Worth and at Texas Tech in Lubbock.) Jimmie had experience as church secretary in both Abilene and Fort Worth. In contrast to both the Pattersons and the Duffers who had done language study in Mexico City, the Rosses were part of a large group of missionaries who learned Spanish at a new institute in San José, Costa Rica. (Really it was a rebirth of the Institute in which the Eudalys had studied when it was located in Medellín, Colombia.)

Following language study, the Rosses were located in Chihuahua City, in northern Mexico where they were responsible for a student home in that city and for field evangelism in three large states (Chihuahua, Sonora, and Coahuila). Fulfilling the purpose of the transfer, Ross was given the responsibilities Hiram Duffer had borne (general direction of the Training Union publications, the editorship of *El Promotor de Educación Cristiana*, and the chairmanship of the new International Committee of Religious Education, which Duffer had organized). In the course of the years, Ross showed a variety of skills in both editing and administration, but especially administration. Consequently his jobs tended to evolve in the direction of general business affairs, finances, and property management. He is remembered especially for his effort to organize and staff the Publishing House library, which now is named for him.

Jimmie, though not given active responsibilities at the time of their transfer, came to have charge of the correspondence course section of a program for preparing Sunday School teachers and Training Union workers. She set up files on persons receiving awards, after completing correspondence studies, and awarded appropriate diplomas and seals. Later she gave a number of years to the Library and is remembered especially for that work.

Early retirement for Wilson and Jimmie was provoked by Wilson's ill health in 1988, when colon cancer first incapacitated this missionary veteran and then took his life on September 1, 1989. Jimmie continues to make her retirement home near some of their children, in Fort Worth.[33]

Jack and Laura Disselkoen (1954). Jack was a Chilean by birth, a Dutchman by ancestry, and an American by choice. Laura (Laly, to friends, family, and colleagues) was an MK (missionary kid) raised in Chile, daughter to J. L. and Tennessee Hart, long-term Baptist missionaries in both Argentina and Chile. Family skepticism met Laly's choice to be married to this high-strung son of Dutch immigrants, raised in the south Chilean city of Valdivia, but the marriage turned out well. After several years of family life in Chile and after the birth of three of their four children there, Jack and Laly decided to emigrate to the United States. In Chile, Jack had worked for British companies and spoke English with a combined British-Spanish accent. Upon arrival in the United States, the Disselkoens initially resided in Kentucky. But through circumstances that must be seen as providential, they established contact with Frank Patterson and Hoyt Eudaly, and were employed early in 1954. Jack's duties were those of "office manager" in the business department and also those of property management. Laly divided her time between business office tasks and writing for the *Revista para Uniones de Primarios*. Even in the early years of their service with Casa Bautista, Ross detected that "their wide knowledge of the Latin American people [was] an invaluable asset to the Publishing House in its dealings with customers in all the Spanish-speaking countries."[34] During many years, letters to customers signed by Laura Disselkoen were probably more common than any other signature of CBP staff. Both worked until retirement, and Laly still makes her retirement home in El Paso. (Jack passed to his heavenly reward in October 2000).

Clifford Smith (1955). The end of an era occurred when in 1954 health concerns forced Ed Davis to resign as superintendent of the Casa's print shop.[35] A Davis had occupied leadership roles at CBP for fifty years; Ed himself had worked at the Publishing House since the early 1920s. A replacement for Ed was found in the person of Clifford Smith who for eight years had been superintendent of Bison Press at Oklahoma Baptist University. A graduate of OBU, he (like Patterson) had worked at the campus press during his college years and later had served as editor and publisher of weekly newspapers in three Oklahoma towns. He came as an employee, bought a home on Volcanic Street, only a couple of miles from the Publishing House building, and effectively directed the printing operation for many years. His wife Aleene continued her career as a public school teacher, but in El Paso.

Carroll Gillis and Alfred C. Müller. The help of these men represents special cases that nevertheless need to be remembered. Missionary Müller was assigned to field work in north central Mexico, but in 1948 he was living in El Paso, and though never officially assigned to the Publishing House, he gave a part of his time to editing books there. At that time, the Publishing House missionaries were still a part of the Mexican Mission.

The case of Carroll Gillis is equally special. A highly educated teacher (including the Th.D. degree from Southwestern Seminary), he and his wife were appointed for Argentina in November, 1937, where Gillis taught in the Baptist Seminary. But in November 1948 he was assigned to the Publishing House with the specific task of writing a set of Biblical commentaries that could be used as textbooks. Because of certain family factors and with Board approval, he chose to live in California and do his writing there. He did attend mission meetings in El Paso, and perhaps visited occasionally for orientation. Gillis resigned as a missionary of the Foreign Mission Board, effective October 1, 1956, but worked an additional year, on contract, to finish the series of commentaries on the Old Testament. (The originally planned volumes on the New Testament in this series were never written.) The arrangement was unusual, to say the least, but Gillis' contribution to Biblical literature in the Spanish language merits remembrance.[36]

What Were the Major Accomplishments of Patterson's First Dozen Years as General Director?

To some extent the answer to this questions lies, like the perception of beauty, in the eyes of the beholder, but the following list of ten items is submitted for the reader's consideration:

1. Survival! The first task of any administration may be regarded as survival: If the ministry goes under, it has no further ministry! When this task is compounded by the wartime problems of materials scarcity, personnel unavailability, and shipping and communications complications, survival— never easy— may be next to impossible. Davis knew the trail; he had kept the Casa alive despite the Mexican Revolution, World War I, economic ups and downs, and the Great Depression. Finally it befell him to deliver the Casa to Patterson's hands—in the midst of another World War! J. E. had seen the looming specter of bankruptcy time and again. Patterson would know it too. There were moments when Frank and Polly Patterson almost singlehandedly kept the Publishing House open and "up and running." But it happened. Ross correctly observes, "The Publishing House faced a postwar era with its work on a firm footing and ready to advance with the new opportunities as the countries of the world turned again to peaceful pursuits. The House had come through [the war] with renewed strength and vision... ready to reach for new heights."[37] Survival was an achievement.

2. Recognized international status. Davis had insisted repeatedly that the Foreign Mission Board recognize officially the international status of CBP, which by 1925 it had, in practice, achieved. Achievement in practice, by way of international service, continued (thirty-four countries and territories were listed in a 1954 report). Both Dr. Love and Dr. Ray were apparently reluctant to take this step. But "new laborers plow new furrows." And at the meeting of the Mexico Mission, held in San Antonio, Texas, May 15-16, 1942, Dr. C. E. Maddry (the Board's Executive Secretary since 1933) himself proposed that both the Seminary and the Publishing House be known as Latin American institutions instead of Mexican institutions. There likely was some discussion of this suggestion, but apparently the Mission accepted it and named a committee (J. E. Davis, H. H. Muirhead—seminary president—, and F. W. Patterson) "to work out a name for the Publishing House and Seminary which would identify them as Latin American institutions."[38] Unfortunately, IMB Archives show Mission Minutes for the years 1943 and 1944 as missing, though it may be that wartime travel restrictions kept the Mission from meeting those years. The Mission did meet again in El Paso in early May 1945. By this time, C. E. Maddry had retired and Theron Rankin (missionary to China since 1921) had recently been elected Executive Secretary. He chose Everett Gill, Jr., to be Secretary for Latin America. Both men were in El Paso for the Mission meeting of 1945. The Minutes show no specific reference to the Committee to study names for the Seminary and the Publishing House. However, what happened is that the Seminary remained a Mexican institution, and the following year was moved back to Mexican territory (to Torreón, though Toluca was considered). And the Publishing House name was never changed from Casa Bautista de Publicaciones. It is noteworthy that Dr. Gill, the Secretary for Latin America, did lead in the creation of two "international" Baptist seminaries (in Cali, Colombia and in Buenos Aires, Argentina) and did give, in practice, "international" recognition to Casa Bautista de Publicaciones, partly by the structural innovation detailed in the following paragraph.

3. A Mission independent from the Mexican Mission. Ross gives the following account: "The Publishing House was given a new status in January 1950 when the missionaries connected with the House, who had formerly been a part of the Mexico Mission, organized into a separate mission called the El Paso Publishing House Mission. The first step leading to this separation had been a recommendation by F. W. Patterson, director of the House, to the Mexico Mission in its regular session, June 23, 1947, to the effect 'that the separation of the Publishing House and the Mexican Mission be discussed and some definite recommendation be made.' The Mexico Mission, in turn, had passed the following resolution: 'That the Publishing House be a separate institution in budget and missionaries but that it be related to the Mexican Mission in an advisory capacity.' The Foreign Mission Board, acting on this resolution, and upon the recommendation of Gill, secretary for Latin America, had separated the Publishing House budget from that of Mexico in October 1947, and in 1949 had declared the missionaries of the House a separate mission, directly responsible to the Foreign Mission Board. On January 9, 1950, the Pattersons, the McGavocks, the Duffers and Margaret McGavock met to organize the separate mission, with Patterson elected president and Miss McGavock elected secretary."[39] Reasons given for the division were (1) that the Publishing House actually bore the same relation to each of the Spanish-speaking mission fields as it did to Mexico, (2) that the budget of the Mexico Mission had to carry the financial burden of the House, though it was not exclusively a Mexican institution, and (3) that the Publishing House administration could better carry on the work of the House through a local body than through the Mexico Mission, since it was always somewhat at a distance.[40] Whatever the reasons for the new structure, the effect was to give the Publishing House the official international status its leaders had long desired. An additional effect was to give it direct access to the Foreign Mission Board leaders, apparatus, and finances, an advantage perhaps only topped, among mission institutions of the time, by the European seminary established at Ruschlikon, Switzerland. The local mission, in fact, became for the Casa a "governing body," almost like a board of trustees, for the next twenty-five years. It must be admitted that these were some of the best years in the

Casa's century of service. While some missionaries chaffed at this collective administrative function, others saw it as comparable to a good-size family enterprise. All "family members" were equal "stake-holders," but the day to day operations required members to structure themselves, somewhat hierarchically and with assigned tasks, to function with efficiency. In time, the structure was deemed outmoded and was replaced; but in 1950, and years following, it brought decided benefits.

4. Amplification of the Casa's product line. Current vocabulary prefers to speak of the "resources" which the House offers its constituents, rather than its "products;" good arguments can be made for this emphasis. But in the '50s, it was more usual to speak of the Casa's "productos, artículos, u obras" (products, articles, or works). Catalogs of the period used categories like "libros, himnarios, folletos, cursos educativos, periódicos, útiles" (books, hymnals, tracts, study courses, periodicals, supplies). If one surveys the "general catalog" of 1942 (the year before Frank Patterson became General Director) and the catalog of 1953-1954 (toward the end of the dozen years being surveyed), it is obvious that new products have been added.[41] While some titles published originally in León have been maintained (such as Harvey's *La Iglesia: Su Gobierno y Ordenanzas*, Vedder's *Breve Historia de los Bautistas*, and Neal's *Manual para Obreros Cristianos*[42]), numerous new titles have been added (like *La Fe del Nuevo Testamento*, by W. T. Conner; a condensed Spanish version of *Pilgrim's Progress*—edited by Hiram Duffer—; and a hymnal entitled *Himnos Favoritos*). The number of periodicals, principally for use in the educational activities of local churches, has grown, and a rather considerable list of "Books from other evangelical publishers" is now included as a service to Casa customers. Despite limitations during a good part of these dozen years, individuals and churches were offered a growing variety of publication resources (to use the current term) for conducting their local ministries.

5. New equipment. Ross gives considerable detail to equipment acquisitions of this time frame. "A used offset press was purchased in 1945 to be used primarily in reprinting books. This was the first step in rebuilding the printing department which had suffered from the inability to replace obsolete equipment and secure parts during the war years. Orders were placed for new equipment totaling around $12,000."[43] Both repairs to viable equipment and replacement of obsolete machines became priorities in 1946. Orders were placed for new presses and new bindery equipment. Additional space also opened up that year when the Seminary vacated some ten thousand square feet in its move back to Mexico. "Book production... was given a boost in 1948 with the purchase of a new offset press."[44] Print totals for books doubled within two years. Then, in 1950 "a new Miehle 41 letterpress, valued at $25,000... was purchased... through a gift from the Woman's Missionary Union of Texas... [It] was capable of printing twice the number of pages produced by the other [letterpress] then in operation... In addition..., a new...Baum folding machine [was added]. Also, the lino-type department was moved and enlarged... [All this] led to a new surge in book production in 1951."[45] A pattern developed of using letterpress for new products and offset for reprints, but as offset printing loomed as "the coming thing" (the technology of preference) even for new products, the offset department was strengthened in 1956 with the acquisition of a 24-inch camera and plate-mak-ing equipment. Both additional space (enclosure of a patio) and additional equipment (a Crawley Rounder-Backer, a new gang stitcher and trimmer, and other lesser pieces), in 1955, made the Casa's bindery department the only com-plete book bindery in El Paso. From this postwar renewal of the print shop came continual increases in almost all areas of production.

6. Increased distribution. The increases in production were necessary because distribution was continually growing. According to Ross, "a remarkable increase in sales was experienced between 1953 and 1956. Eudaly, business manager of the House, reported an increase of 250 percent during this short period. He estimated that more religious materials had been distributed [by CBP] from 1950 to 1956 than in the forty-four preceding years. From 1948, when the first adequate figures were available, until 1956, approximately $597,000 worth of religious materials were sold. The average sales by 1956 were running approximately $130,000 annually."[46] As Eudaly himself might exclaim: "Praise God!" Hoyt's analysis of reasons for this growth included the following: (1) The number of Spanish-speaking Baptists was growing. (2) More of these are interested in reading and more of those who are reading are using more mate-rials per person. (3) More denominational and non-denominational groups are using CBP materials. (4) More advertising is done. (5) More book stores and other outlets are now available. (6) The Casa's stock of materials is more com-plete and thus allows orders to be readily filled. (7) The Casa has gained a repu-tation through the years as a provider of sound evangelical materials.[47]

7. Staff growth. When the Pattersons arrived in El Paso at the end of 1940, there were two missionaries and about ten employees at the Casa. With the Davises' retirement in 1943, and J. E.'s death in 1944, the missionary staff was back to two. During some moments of the war years, employees probably dropped to less than ten.[48] But from the arrival of the McGavocks, things began to go in the other direction. By the end of 1953, there were eight missionaries and thirty-three employees. "This number represented an increase of sixteen over a five year period. Further increases in the number of employees were noted each succeeding year, and at the end of 1956 the Publishing House staff numbered six missionaries and about forty employees."[49] The Pattersons, like the Davises, were hard working missionaries, and they never ceased their labors. But they were no longer alone!

8. Appropriate recognition of the Davises. Sometimes new leaders are anxious for predecessors essentially to disappear and be forgotten. Often true in the political realm, it can also happen in churches or Christian institutions. But this was not the style of Frank Patterson's leadership, and the courtesies and recognitions extended the Davises stand as a credit to Patterson and to his administration. The list of these courtesies and recognitions began with Patterson's recommendation that Davis, after retirement be accorded full salary and be used as a writer for *El Expositor Bíblico*.[50] Such an arrangement was put into effect, and the quarterly issues of *El Expositor Bíblico* up through the third quarter of 1944 show Davis' name as principal writer and editor. Both Wilson Ross and Roberta Ryan report that when Dr. and Mrs. Davis boarded the train to go to Missouri for some doctor-recommended rest in April 1944, J. E. promised F. W. he would be back in a few weeks to write the lesson comments for the *Expositor* (probably referring to those for the fourth quarter)[51] But on that trip, Dr. Davis became acutely ill, was hospitalized in Independence, Missouri, and expired there on June 4. The *Expositor* for the fourth quarter bears the name of F. W. Patterson as "redactor responsable" (responsible writer). Patterson wrote and published, complete with a photograph, a tribute to Davis on page 2 of that issue. Personal friendship, professional recognition, and sincere sadness blend in Frank's words. He concludes recalling Davis' blunt but encouraging promise to treat the Pattersons as he would his own son and daughter, to prepare them, as best he could, for the day when he would lay down his labors. Patterson confesses, "I never thought that the day of his leaving would come so soon, and I feel a strange vacancy in my heart for the man who had been a part of this institution for almost forty years. Nevertheless, realizing both the magnitude of the task and my own inadequacies, with help from the Almighty One, we will move ahead along the very path this titan of faith marked out so clearly."[52] In another tribute, published in *Revista Evangélica*, Patterson concluded, "... the Lord has called his faithful servant, and the celestial writer has written *finis* to the last chapter of an exceedingly noble and fruitful life."[53]

Still another dimension of Patterson's courtesies to the Davises had to do with special recognition to Mrs. Davis (who continued to make her retirement home in El Paso) on occasion of her eightieth birthday, November 18, 1953. A reception was given in her honor, and portraits of her and Dr. Davis were unveiled. Her "speech" was characteristically modest. She said it was J. E. who did all the work; "I just 'tagged along.' " The following year, when the Casa converted a large front porch into a chapel, the portraits were hung there and the chapel was given the name "Davis Memorial Chapel." Although space in the new building, constructed in 1982, became a new chapel, it too carries the name "Davis Memorial Chapel."[54] The Davises' portraits now hang with those of other General Director couples, in the Wilson Ross Memorial Library (just down the hall from the chapel).

9. A new "advisory committee." The creation of a "local advisory committee"—and its essential failure— has already been recounted.[55] A new "advisory committee" was created in 1950, under the leadership of missionary Hiram Duffer. It was not a rebirth of the old committee, with which Dr. Davis had frequently tangled. In fact, no "meetings" were envisioned nor did the committee pretend any administrative functions. Its name suggested its area of work: International Committee of Religious Education. Duffer, by mail, invited one person from each Spanish-speaking country (or from each convention of Baptist churches, when two or more conventions existed in a country, as was the case in Cuba) to form "an advisory committee" to consult, suggest, give counsel concerning study course materials and other matters related to the field of religious education. The committee's first project was to formulate a new study course curriculum for training both Sunday School teachers and Training Union workers. This was accomplished in 1951, and a revision to the course was accomplished later to be put into effect January 1, 1958. The Minutes of the 1950 Meeting of the Mexico Mission reflect the visit of Hiram Duffer and his comments about the new committee being formed. The Minutes record: "As far as possible they are seeking nationals to work on the Committee..."[56] The committee was undoubtedly created with Patterson's approval and serves to show again his interest in relating the Casa appropriately to the fields it sought to serve.

10. Recognized authorship. This achievement could be considered personal rather than institutional, but it had implications for the institution as well as the person. Reference is to the fact that in his first dozen years as General Director, Frank Patterson proved himself to be a writer/author/editor of the caliber of J. E. Davis; at least equal, perhaps superior. Yet Patterson, like Davis, did not join the Casa's staff as a recognized writer—either in English or in Spanish. But just as Davis became a clear communicator in written Spanish, and both wrote, translated, and edited, so did F. W. Patterson. From that fourth quarter 1944 issue of *El Expositor Bíblico* on, Patterson's Biblical expositions— in Spanish—were found there (he had undoubtedly made some contributions to *El Expositor* earlier, but they are hard to identify). The 1953-1954 general catalog lists Patterson's first full book. Title: *Manual de Finanzas para Iglesias* (A manual for church finances). Helping churches in the practical area of church finance became one of Frank's specialities. Various other titles would follow.[57] It was another dimension of his call to be a publications missionary, and he fulfilled it well.

After a dozen years at the helm, there was good reason for Frank Patterson---and all the Casa family---to sing the Doxology! "Praise God from whom all blessings flow..." These had indeed been good years for the ministry of gospel publications in Spanish, and more were yet to follow.

Endnotes

1. Mrs. Patterson's absence is probably to be explained as having to do with care of Burton, still a small child when the couple returned from language study in Mexico City.

2. The Claim Staker, by Roberta Ryan (published by Convention Press in Nashville, Tennessee, in 1977), and El Intrépido Francisco, by Mary J. Stewart (published by Casa Bautista de Publicaciones, in 1979).

3. Frank's son Burton supplies this interesting detail concerning the middle name that eventually came to be used. Burton says that Frank was not given a middle name at birth. Much later, "when signing in for military service, a middle name was required. Frank chose Willard, put it on his service records and used it from thence forth." Letter from Dr. Burton Patterson, February 17, 2004.

4. Oklahoma became a state just a few months after Frank was born; the date was November 16, 1907.

5. See a "Baby Book," kept by Frank's mother Myrtle, and found among his personal files and memorabilia.

6. Ryan, The Claim, p. 10.

7. Ibid., p. 11.

8. Ibid., p. 20.

9. "Yearbook of the First Baptist Church, Shattuck, Oklahoma, 1957." Private publication, p. 6. Found among Dr. Patterson's personal files and private papers.

10. Probably unpublished. Found, written in longhand, signed and dated by F. W. Patterson, among his personal files and private papers.

11. Her son, Dr. Burton Patterson, supplies the interesting detail that Polly, following a pattern for "the brighter high school students" that was "not unusual in Dallas in the 1920s," took some of her "final high school courses at SMU.... Mother did so," writes Burton. "We have her grade cards. These courses transferred to Baylor." See letter from Dr. Burton Patterson, February 17, 2004.

12. Ryan, The Claim, p. 22.

13. Son Burton says that "it was during his studies at the University of Oklahoma that [Frank] joined the Reserve Officers Training Corps and was a Chaplain." See letter from Dr. Burton Patterson, February 17, 2004.

14. Ryan, The Claim, p. 27.

15. Ibid., pp. 28-32.

16. Burton's birth actually took place not in Spiro but in Fort Smith, Arkansas (less than 20 miles from Spiro); the date was August 11, 1935.

17. Ryan, The Claim, pp. 47-48.

18. Ross, "A History of," p. 109.

19. Ibid.; see also SBC Annual for 1939, p. 200.

20. Ryan, The Claim, p. 49.

21. The date was April 1. Twenty years later, in a letter to Dr. Frank K. Means, dated April 5, 1963, Patterson, who says he is answering a letter from Means, dated April 1, comments: "I am reminded that that is an anniversary date at our home. Polly and I had our first date on April 1, 32 years ago [i.e., 1931]; we entered Mexico on April 1, 1939, and I became the active manager of the Publishing House on April 1, 1943..."

22. See chapter 9.

23. See unpublished manuscript of chapel message for August 11, 1993, found among Patterson's personal papers. A recording of the message also exists and is found in the Publishing House library (T-617).

24. See letter, J. E. Davis to T. B. Ray, October 30, 1933; IMB Archives.

25. See press release by Roberta Ryan, dated December 15, 1965; copy found among Patterson's personal papers and files.

26. Ross, Sowing the Seed, pp. 106-107.

27. Title: Actividades Manuales para Niños. El Paso: Casa Bautista de Publicaciones. There have been at least twelve printings.

28. See Marie Eudaly's press release concerning Lerín's retirement, dated January 13, 1972; copy found among Frank Patterson's personal papers; see also Olivia

Lerín's privately circulated biographical article entitled "De monaguillo a predicador del
evangelio," undated; see also Ross, Sowing
the Seed, pp. 110-111.

29. Especially when the lessons fell in the
Old Testament; normally Patterson wrote
the New Testament lessons, and Lerín the
ones from the Old Testament.

30. See Ross, Sowing the Seed, p. 112.

31. Mary Tudor Walsh, Assignment: Light
Bearers. Woman's Missionary Union, Auxiliary to the Missouri Baptist General Association, 1956, pp. 154-158. Curiously neither J. E. nor Mary Davis are included in this
compilation of biographical sketches.

32. Walsh, Assignment, pp. 155-156.

33. See Ross, Sowing the Seed, pp. 122-
123; also, press release by Mary Speidel,
Foreign Mission Board news staff, dated
September 6, 1989.

34. Ross, Sowing the Seed, p. 125.

35. Ed's retirement further affected the
Casa by bringing to an end the income producing contract work on the medical journal,
mentioned earlier.

36. In 1991 a second edition of the complete set was issued by Casa Bautista, emphasizing its range, namely the Old Testament. See Carroll Gillis, El Antiguo Testamento: Un Comentario sobre su Historia y
Literatura, vols. 1-5. El Paso: Casa Bautista
de Publicaciones, 1991.

37. Ross, Sowing the Seed, p. 108.

38. Minutes of the Mexico Baptist Mission,
San Antonio, Texas, May 15, 16, 1942, pp.
1, 3; IMB Archives.

39. Ross, Sowing the Seed, p. 115; see
also Minutes, Mexican Mission, June 1947,
pp. 1, 2; IMB Archives.

40. Ross, Sowing the Seed, pp. 115-116.

41. See catalogs for years mentioned,
author's private collection; also found in the
library of Casa Bautista de Publicaciones.

42. See chapter 1.

43. Ross, Sowing the Seed, p. 108.

44. Ibid., p. 114.

45. Ibid., p. 117.

46. Ibid., p. 129.

47. Ibid.

48. Frank's son Burton remembers that
"during the war years some of the printers
and binders were drafted, and others volun-
teered. Little Burton was pressed into service. I gathered the signATures for the
Sunday School quarterlies on the bindery
end. And in the printing end, I started out
melting the used type from the linotypes and
pouring it into molds for the bars that went
back into the linotypes. Jim McGavock was
a few years older than I was, and he mowed
the Casa's lawns and pruned the trees, etc.
When you say the missionaries 'worked
hard,' you must know that it was with more
than their brains. Brawn was included."
See letter from Dr. Burton Patterson, February 17, 2004.

49. See Ross, Sowing the Seed, p. 122.
The 1954 "Annual Report" from El Paso to
Richmond mentioned "Eight missionaries
and 37 employees..."

50. See Ryan, The Claim, p. 50, where
Davis' response to Patterson's invitation is
said to have been: "I want to keep writing
and working for the publishing house as
long as I live." See also Minutes of the
Mexico Baptist Mission, May 15, 16, 1942,
where the Mission officially recommended
that the Foreign Mission Board "authorize
the employment of Dr. J. E. Davis... [at] the
Publishing House, after his retirement in
1943, making the necessary appropriation
which together with retirement pay would
equal the salary formerly received," Minutes, p. 2; IMB Archives.

51. See Ross, Sowing the Seed, p. 104,
and Ryan, The Claim, p. 51.

52. F. W. Patterson, "El Dr. J. E. Davis
Deja su Pluma," El Expositor Bíblico, Tomo
LI, Número 4, (Fourth Quarter, 1944), p. 2.

53. Revista Evangélica, VIII (1944), p. 241.

54. Ross, Sowing the Seed, p. 120.

55. See chapter 2.

56. Minutes, Mexico Mission, July 3, 1950,
p. 10; IMB Archives. See also Ross, Sowing the Seed, pp. 116-117.

57. The card catalog of the Publishing
House library contains reference to a dozen
or more works by F. W. Patterson.

Chapter 4

The Frank W. Patterson Years — Part II

At the beginning of what providentially became the second half of Frank Patterson's three decades of resident service with Casa Bautista de Publicaciones, in El Paso, he might well have used a figure sometimes employed to illustrate the beginning and the expansion of the world-wide Baptist movement. The figure is found in a small volume entitled *We Baptists,* which was put together by various members of the Study Commissions of the Baptist World Alliance, during the quinquenium of 1995-1999. James Leo Garrett, Jr., served as the editor-in-chief of the project. W. R. Estep was probably the original author of chapter 1, titled "Baptists: A Global Community of Faith." It is in this chapter, in a section called "The Movement Expands," that Baptist growth is described in the following way: "Baptist historians often use the illustration that England was the puddle into which the stone fell, and the ripples spread first within Britain, then to America, and eventually throughout the entire world."[1] If the figure is appropriate for the Baptist movement at large, it is also true for many Baptist institutions, like Casa Bautista de Publicaciones. In the Casa's case, Mexico would have been the puddle of origin, with the ripples extending then to many parts of that largest of Hispanic countries. From there ripples continued to spread to all the Hispanic world. This was what happened by the time BSPH completed its fiftieth year.

A Golden Anniversary

In the mid-1950s it was obviously time to celebrate the Casa's half century of service. But, curiously enough, it was not so clear when to do it. If this sounds confusing, a good part of the blame has to rest with the founder, J. Edgar Davis. Davis had obviously given thought to the question, "When did the Casa Bautista de Publicaciones start? How old is it?" Stickler for detail that he was, Dr. Davis apparently dated the House from the year he had begun to use the name "Casa Bautista de Publicaciones" to designate this ministry of publications and printing. Such must have happened in the year 1908.[2] A CBP catalog from 1942, when Davis was still General Director, opens its presentation of the House with these words: "Esta Casa de Publicaciones se estableció formalmente a prin-cipios del año 1908, en León, Gto., México."[3] (English translation: "This Publica-tions House was formally established at the beginning of 1908, in León, [state of] Guanajuato, Mexico.) It is noteworthy that the Casa's first book was issued in 1907, but under the logo of "La Imprenta Bautista" (The Baptist Printery). Nevertheless, it was common knowledge that the Davises had been in Mexico since December 1904, that some printing had been done in Toluca in 1905, and that the operation had functioned in León since early 1906.

In the mid-50s, with Davis no longer present to insist on the 1908 date, the question was revisited as the Fiftieth Anniversary approached. The response that achieved consensus at that time was to consider 1906 "the birth year." Thus the celebration of fifty years of service was done in 1956. This dating held for another ten years, and the Sixtieth Anniversary was celebrated in 1966. But by 1980 the consensus shifted, and Casa leaders declared that the baby had been born in 1905. In the Davises' kitchen. In Toluca.[4] Never mind that the child didn't receive its official name till a few years later. (After all, many organiza-tions and not a few individuals have undergone name changes, but without changing their "date of birth!") Hence 75, 90, and 100 years have been (or are being) celebrated in 1980, 1995, and 2005. But the Fiftieth got celebrated in 1956. And F. W. Patterson was General Director.

Ross reports on the celebration as follows: "The year 1956 marked the Fiftieth Anniversary of the Publishing House. The first item had been printed in its location in León, Mexico, on January 12, 1906. To publicize its Golden Anniversary, a special letterhead was issued as well as an illustrated brochure on the work of the House. These were widely distributed, and words of greeting were received from many parts of the world. The net worth of the House had reached $400,000, exclusive of buildings. This was a remarkable increase over the thousand dollar plant established in León and more remarkable still when it is noted that this figure had doubled in the four preceding years. The average annual increase for the fifty-year period had been $8,000, but by 1956 the annu-al increase was approximately $75,000."[5]

If the celebration activities seem a bit low key, such was likely occa-sioned by two factors: (1) Casa personnel found themselves simply too busy making history to do much in celebrating history,[6] and (2) a considerable num-ber of absences of key personnel occurred during the mid-years of that decade, making a celebration more difficult. Really all the absences amounted to leaves for pursuing advanced studies. From the fall of 1954 till the late summer of 1955, the Pattersons took their first full furlough after fifteen years of sacrificial service at the Casa. Frank pursued doctoral studies at Central Baptist Theol-ogical Seminary in Kansas City. He had been initially attracted there by his favorite professor at the Seminary in Fort Worth, Dr. H. E. Dana.[7] Patterson continued his plan to study at Central, even though Dana had died unexpectedly and prematurely in 1945. During 1956, Frank and Polly were back in El Paso, but he was burning the midnight oil writing a doctoral dissertation, which was subsequently accepted in time for graduation in May 1957.[8] During Patterson's absence from El Paso, Hoyt Eudaly functioned as acting general director, and Wilson Ross served as acting editorial director.

The Rosses themselves took a leave from mid-1955 till mid 1956, when Wilson pursued studies in Southwestern Baptist Theological Seminary in Fort Worth and at Texas Technological University in Lubbock, Texas.[9] His M.A. thesis for the studies at Texas Tech later became the basis for his book *Sowing the Seed in Spanish.*[10]

Then in August, 1956, the Eudalys left El Paso for a furlough of study in religious education, at Southwestern Baptist Theological Seminary in Fort Worth. Hoyt was able to complete all the required resident studies for a doctorate in Religious Education. Later he wrote a dissertation concerning educational leadership in Latin America, and was graduated with the D.R.E. in 1959. Though his dissertation was never published, his studies and his doctoral research served to give him considerable clout in circles dealing with religious education, both in El Paso and elsewhere. They also enlarged his influence as a Casa representative.

If the Golden Anniversary Year (1956) got a bit less attention than it really deserved, it nevertheless constituted the threshold of a decade and a half of notable growth in service to God and His people in the Hispanic World.

A Period of Evangelical Expansion in Latin America

It was impressive to Frank Patterson that Baptist mission work in Latin America had undergone something of a resurgence beginning in the mid-1940s. Research concerning this phenomenon had been his first choice as a dissertation topic. In a letter to Frank Means, recently elected Secretary for Latin America of the Foreign Mission Board, Patterson outlined his interest in "The Resurgence of Baptist Missions in Latin America after 1940." He wrote, "My thought has been to outline the establishment of Southern Baptist Work in Mexico (1880), Brazil (1881), Argentina (1903), Chile (1917). Then two problems would have to be worked out: Why no further territorial expansion in Latin America on the part of the FMB until 1943, and why the resurgence shortly after 1940 that has resulted in opening work in Colombia, Venezuela, Ecuador, Peru, Paraguay, Guatemala, Honduras, and Costa Rica?" Further, he proposed to explore "modification of method and to some degree shift of emphasis..., and seek to evaluate the results thus far." He says that preliminary ideas have been assembled into "an outline of theories and probable reasons and contributing factors to be explored."[11]

It is clear that Patterson saw himself and the Casa Bautista de

Publicaciones as a part of that "resurgence." "Advance" was the operational word in Richmond, at the Foreign Mission Board; and it was in El Paso also. Frank Patterson's leadership at the Publishing House for the next fifteen years may be characterized as responding to a philosophy of expansion and of intensified service to a growing evangelical community in Latin America. Among his personal papers two folders contain notes or manuscripts of presentations F. W. made in a variety of venues concerning "Publication Work" (as a missionary method) and "Publishing House Task and Work." Still another file contains "Literature Articles." A sampling of these presentations reflects the operational philosophy of the Casa's General Director for this period.

In an address to the student body at Southwestern Baptist Theological Seminary, in Fort Worth, Patterson spoke on "The Place of the Press in Modern Missions." Citing the Biblical examples of Paul and Luke and the modern examples of William Carey and his printer William Ward, Frank emphasized: (1) The purpose of the press, (2) the privilege of the press, and (3) the power of the press. He illustrated the purpose of the press (..."to help spread the gospel...") by recounting Gutenberg's dream when a voice warned him that his invention would fall into the hands of wicked men who would use it to spread falsehood and evil. In the dream, Gutenberg was at the point of destroying his invention when another voice bade him persist in the completion of his printing press, with the consolation that God would make it the fountain of good among men and give right the final triumph in all the earth. The "privileged character" of the press was described in terms of its ability to go where missionaries could not go, enter homes where the missionary would not be invited, and stay even when the missionary might be asked to leave the field, all the while speaking its mind freely, even when a preacher saying the same might be imprisoned. The "power of the press" was acknowledged to be either for good or for evil, to mold opinion and to shape character for the better or for the worse. Though true that "vicious influences of printed filth and untruth run on in successive harvests of evil," Patterson declared: "I thank God that we have truth on our side... [and] missions must keep pace with the age in which it operates... The work [of Christian publications]... is not easy..., but it is highly needful. If the Lord calls,...[we must] answer..." And all Christians should remember to pray regularly for those whom God has called into this work.[12]

A Spanish version of this message was apparently presented to the Hispanic Baptist Convention of Texas, and a slightly condensed version (in English) was given at a Foreign Missions Convocation, at the Ridgecrest Baptist Assembly, in North Carolina. Patterson always adapted to his audience and presented illustrations related to the Publishing House that would be of interest to his hearers.

Another presentation is entitled "Iron Preacher Goes Abroad." In this one, Patterson introduces the figure, saying "the printing press is frequently dubbed...'the Iron Preacher.' And," he says, "seldom does a missionary enter a new field of service that he does not find that the 'Iron Preacher' has already been there." He gave specific examples of how publications from El Paso had preceded and to some extent facilitated the new advance of the gospel in several Latin American countries. Extending that theme, another message is entitled "Literature Enlightens Latin America." Frank begins by asserting, "Christian literature is absolutely essential to the march of Christianity. Missions and journalism have walked hand in hand down through the centuries."

Still another presentation carries the title, "Sharing Our Faith Through the Printed Page." In it Patterson asserts: "Christian literature has for nineteen centuries played an important part in sharing Christ with a lost world, in establishing churches, and in strengthening them." Evidence shows that "the printed page accelerates mission progress." Recognizing problems continue to exist, Patterson nevertheless declares that missionary publication work can help prepare and distribute literature in the language of the people for Christian indoctrination, establishment of churches, cultivation of national leadership, and stimulation of indigenous mission work.

In an address to missionaries gathered to visit the Publishing House and learn of ways CBP materials could enhance their ministries, Patterson spoke concerning "Our Task and Yours." Emphasizing the partnership between on-the-field missionaries and those serving in publication agencies, he noted that production must be complemented by adequate distribution. "In distribution and teaching people how to use the materials effectively, we must cooperate... Only thus can the literature ministry accomplish its purpose; only thus can we together build Christ's kingdom."[13]

Found in these same files are two papers actually presented by Wilson Ross, but obviously representing the philosophy espoused by Frank Patterson. One, entitled "Kingdom Growth Through Printed Materials," was presented to a Field Missions Conference held in Cali, Colombia, in June, 1963. The other was entitled "The Publishing House, A Partner in Mass Communications;" it was presented by Ross at a Mass Communications Conference, held in Mexico City, in March of 1965.[14]

To a remarkable degree, Frank Patterson was able to see this philosophy of expansion applied and realized during his tenure as General Director. And as his predecessor had done, he always strove to keep the Publishing House's plans and projections anchored to its Biblical base.[15]

In 1969—only one year prior to leaving the general directorship—, Patterson wrote the following summary sketch of the operations and ministry of Casa Bautista de Publications: "A staff of 82, including 22 missionaries, publishes literature used in 41 countries. Net worth, including buildings, is $2,000,000. Production reported in 1969 was: 3,416,509 copies of 31 periodicals; 567,773 copies of 57 book titles; 5,600,000 tracts; 2,000,000 booklets and miscellaneous pieces. A 17,000 square foot production area built in 1960 sparked advance. In 1962 the first of 14 wholesale deposits was established. In 1966 the Publishing House celebrated its Sixtieth Anniversary, printed a marked New Testament, and convened an Advisory Committee representing 15 countries. Twenty-eight Crusade of the Americas items, including 2,000,000 copies of a marked Gospel, were produced in 1967-69."[16]

Allusions or implications in this summary sketch are found to staff, new ventures, special projects, and a highly productive relationship with the Foreign Mission Board. These factors are now explored with some additional detail.

An Expanded Staff from Many Countries

As implied in Patterson's 1969 summary, Casa staff generally got divided into two categories: "employees" and "missionaries." The Casa itself provided salary for the "employees." "Missionaries" were supported by the Foreign Mission Board, SBC. At the moment Frank wrote his summary, he reported a total of 82, of which evidently 60 were employees and 22 were missionaries. While space limitations make it impossible to give a biographical sketch of all who participated in the Publishing House's ministry between 1956 and 1970, efforts are made here to highlight briefly those who served at department or division rank and those whose long tenure warrants mention. The list is organized according to the year service with the Casa initiated.

1956. Marta Nuñez Peña began in 1956. Marta Nuñez was a recent graduate of the Colegio Comercial (Business College) in Ciudad Juárez, when she became an employee of Casa Bautista de Publicaciones. After some six years of work at CBP, she married Ricardo Peña, and took time out to have a family. But she returned for a two year stint in 1969 and again in 1976 and continued until retirement in 1991. During the years, she gave secretarial collaboration to Wilson Ross, Hoyt Eudaly, Olivia Lerín, and Ananías González. Her pleasantness and efficiency are remembered delightfully!

1957. Judson and Dorothy Rose Blair. Judson was born in Argentina and raised there, where his parents were missionaries. He married Dorothy Rose Sullivan in 1946, and three years later they were named missionaries to Argentina, where they served with the Seminary in Buenos Aires. While on furlough in 1956, they were invited to consider work with the Casa Bautista, in El Paso. Their transfer was approved in October 1956 but their arrival occurred in 1957. Blair first headed both the Music Department and the General Book departments; later he was named Director of the Editorial Division. Still later Judson became the Director of the Production Division and finally gave time as Special Consultant to the General Director. Dorothy Rose served as editor of several publications and contributed especially to Christian dramatic materials. They retired in mid-

1989, after some forty years of missionary service, thirty-two of which were spent in Publishing House ministry.

1958. José Amézaga, Edna Mae Franks Brantley, and Dorothy Hicks Pettit all began their work at the Casa in 1958.

In lamentable but unrelated cases, both these missionary women, serving in Chile, lost their first husbands (Ruben Franks and Marlin Hicks) to fatal illnesses, during the year 1957. Both had children still at home. Signals were apparently given that the Foreign Mission Board might be willing to transfer them to El Paso, rather than insist that they return to an overseas ministry. On January 30, 1958, the El Paso Mission voted to request their transfer. The transfers were approved and both women arrived in El Paso before the July 1958 Mission meeting.

Tasks were assigned to Edna Mae in editorial functions and with the Publishing House library; and to Dorothy Hicks in areas that included art and advertising. While Edna Mae was undoubtedly sincere in expressing feelings of divine leading toward El Paso,[17] the length of her service there was of short duration, owing to her marriage in 1960 to Maurice Brantley, a widower of missionary service in Africa. They have been long-term residents in Tucson, Arizona, where Maurice has been active as both a teacher and a pastor and Edna Mae as both a teacher and a pastor's wife.

In contrast to Edna Mae's experience, Dorothy Hicks' time as a missionary at the Publishing House, with responsibilities in the Art Department, continued till 1968, when she married Rev. Max Pettit, a former missionary to the Orient. She and Max have made their home in El Paso (where he has worked both as a teacher and as a pastor), and Dorothy continued at the Publishing House as an employee until her retirement in 1985. Even after that she has been an occasional volunteer, always in the area of art. Her contribution to the Casa's ministry has thus been lengthy and notably productive. For purposes of this book, she has shared a memory from her last year in Chile and another one from her early years in El Paso. "My last year in Chile," she writes, "I was named director of Vacation Bible School work for that country. This meant planning and cutting mimeograph stencils for printing the materials for the churches. This occupied the time of one missionary completely! No VBS materials were then available from the Publishing House in El Paso. Then one of my first assignments after arriving at the Publishing House in 1958 was to help prepare VBS materials! I thought of how the preparation of those materials was 'freeing up' the time of missionaries in all of the countries where they were planning Vacation Bible Schools for their churches. It was a good feeling!" Still another memory Dorothy has deals with Dr. Patterson's "good eye for checking work prior to printing." She writes, "If he spotted a line which was not just right in a 'paste-up,' he very tactfully would say, 'I think something may be a bit off.

Double check it, please.' He was the type of person that inspired you to do your best."[18]

José Amézaga came to work in typesetting and page formation in February 1958. By his own words, he came for two weeks (to fill in for someone) but stayed for forty years! In the course of those years (before retirement April 1, 1998), he lived through many, many changes at the Casa, especially in his area of typesetting and page formation. Technology in the industry was revolutionized—going from manually operated linotypes that used lead, to linotypes activated by punch-cut tapes, to electronically set "cold type," to computer generated laser-set type, and finally to "desk top publishing" that put a computer—instead of a typewriter—on every editor's desk.[19] The whole organization celebrated "José Amézaga Day" on April 14, 1993, to recognize José's thirty-five years of service with the Casa, and retirement did not come until five years later.

1959. Alvin J. Meek, Merle B. ("Boots") Lee, Aida Carrasco Medrano, and Blanca E. V. Martínez began working at the Publishing House during 1959.

When Blanquita retired thirty years later, she said: "During my life this was my first and last employment, and I wish to sincerely say that I am very grateful, first to the Lord and then to those who employed me, for the great privilege of cooperating in a small way in the marvelous work of spreading the word of God."[20]

Aida Medrano could almost write the same words, since she began working at the Publishing House, following graduation from Jefferson High School, in El Paso, and one year's training at a local business college. After her marriage to Raúl Medrano, also a CBP employee at the time, she took time out to have a family, but returned, and in the course of the years has worked under supervisors like Jack Disselkoen, Jimmy Hartfield, J. T. Poe, Cecil Thompson, and Jesse Bryan. At this writing, she still has retirement at arm's length!

Merle B. ("Boots") Lee came as Binding Department supervisor from the OBU Press in Oklahoma, to work under his former director there, Clifford Smith. (Smith had become the Casa's plant superintendent in 1955.)[21] And when Smith retired, "Boots" Lee became his successor, serving till his own retirement at the end of February 1987, a total of 28 years service.

Alvin J. Meek[22] was employed as supervisor of the building and grounds department. He and his wife occupied an apartment in the building that had originally housed the boiler which supplied steam heat for the Tuberculosis Hospital. Tunnels still existed that connected the steam pipes to the main building, but the large smoke stack had long since been taken down. (An old picture in the Publishing House library shows it once felled.) "Mr. Meek" brought a varied background in handling machinery and equipment, as well as heating/cooling and construction experience. He made a valuable addition to the Publishing House staff for a decade or more.

1960. Toxie White, Hilda Navarrete Kaplan, and María Luisa Cayetano Porflit began to work at CBP in 1960.

Toxie White represented a reinforcement for the distribution division. He was employed to direct the shipping department. Toxie, a native of Corpus Christi, a military veteran, and a graduate of Bob Jones University, had been active in Hispanic mission work in Texas for a number of years. In addition to his work at the Publishing House, he served as pastor of a Hispanic Mission, during his years in El Paso. His wife Louise survived an automobile accident that took Toxie's life, some years after retirement, and she continues to be an active supporter of Casa Bautista de Publicaciones, from her residence in Dallas.

Hilda began on May 2, 1960. Her initial assignment was as Receptionist, a position she occupied for a full ten years. A Chilean by birth and training and a fairly recent immigrant, she added a South American smile to her pleasant voice and efficient attention during her years as receptionist. Subsequently she was transferred to the Publicity Department, where she worked first under the supervision of Laly Disselkoen and later under that of Josie Smith. In the course of the years she married Harry Kaplan, also an employee of the Casa. Gradually the breadth of her experience in sales and promotion came to the fore. In May 1995, a "Hilda Kaplan Day" was observed by the entire staff in recognition of Hilda's thirty-five years of service to this publications ministry. She retired at the end of 1996, but she and Harry continued to reside in El Paso. Death overtook her in 2000. She is remembered for her excellent work and dedication to the CBP ministry.

María Luisa was part of the Cayetano family from Torreón that Viola Campbell related to so closely, both in Torreón and later in El Paso.[23] María Luisa studied at the Baptist Seminary in Torreón, graduating in 1956. For a time she did mission work in Mexico. But after the family's move to El Paso in 1960, she became an employee of the Casa (her mother, Mrs. Evangelina Cayetano was also an CBP employee for a few years in the '60s). María Luisa married Elbin Porflit, also an employee of the Casa, in 1966, and both of them continued to work here until their retirement in December 1999. As essentially a life-time proof reader, not many of the Casa's publications failed to pass by her careful revision. Her total of thirty-nine years in CBP service has rarely been exceeded!

1961. The rather long list of new staff that arrived in 1961 includes these: Roberta Ryan, Joe and Eleanor Poe, Viola Campbell, Matthew and Dora Jean Sanderford, Orlando and Josefina Pérez, and Elbin Porflit.

Roberta Ryan was a veteran of sixteen years mission service in Chile when she was transferred to El Paso along with a line of W.M.U. publications at the beginning of this year. Roberta edited the lead magazine for women, *La*

Ventana. Service in this area continued for Roberta until 1980. A tireless editor and a writer of notable skill, both in Spanish and in English, she worked from 1981 till her retirement at the end of 1986 as an editor in the General Books Department.[24]

Joe and Eleanor Poe arrived in El Paso in April 1961, after three years of missionary field work in Chile, to start what would turn out to be a long period of resident service with Casa Bautista de Publications. Joe's first decade of service was with the Sunday School Department of the Casa. As a Registered Nurse, Eleanor's work in El Paso really blossomed a dozen years later with her founding of the El Paso Baptist Clinic, a "volunteer labor" she is still directing![25]

Viola Campbell was another veteran missionary, who had served with the Home Mission Board, SBC, working among the Chinese people in El Paso. Then, under the Foreign Mission Board, she had essentially been Dean of Women at the Mexican Baptist Theological Seminary when it jointly occupied with the Publishing House the former Tuberculosis Sanatorium. Viola had moved to Mexico, with the Seminary, in 1946, and taught Religious Education and Church Administration there for some fifteen years. In 1961 she was transferred to CBP to head up the Vacation Bible School Department. Her "Reflections" are delightfully recorded in a small volume published posthumously and entitled *He Leadeth Me.*[26]

Matthew and Dora Jean Sanderford came to the Publishing House from a decade of missionary service in Uruguay. As Hoyt Eudaly's associate in the Distribution Division, Matthew had much involvement in the establishment of "the deposit system" in several countries. Subsequently he presided the Merchandise Accounting Division and became the Casa's point-man in the area of computation and computer-generated information. He oversaw the installing and programming of different computer systems that served the Casa's information needs between 1964 (first computer-related system) till the Sanderfords' retirement in early 1987. Dora Jean worked variously in the Missions Department and in the Casa Library. At retirement, the Sanderfords moved to Horizon City, a suburb of El Paso, where Matthew, always the preacher, served as pastor of the local Baptist church. Later they moved to Waco, which had been Matthew's "home town" and where Dora Jean still lives; Matthew was called to his heavenly reward in January 2004.

Orlando and Josefina Pérez were Cuban nationals that Judson Blair interested in coming to the Casa, in part to escape the repressive Castro regime which had recently come to power. Initially Orlando served as Blair's associate in directing the flow of materials being processed by correctors and editors. Later he worked briefly as director of the Advertising Department. Josefina worked for many years as a reader in the corrections department. Orlando was ordained as a Baptist pastor during his years in El Paso. Orlando preceded his wife in death and is buried in El Paso.

Elbin Porflit was another international who joined the Casa staff in 1961. Elbin's home country was Chile. His home city was Valdivia, where he did his schooling, including commercial studies. During his youth, he got around on a motorcycle and enjoyed employment with various companies and organizations including the Sociedad Evangélica Bautista (Baptist Evangelical Society) of Chile, which was the official name for the group of Southern Baptist missionaries in that country. At the Casa, Elbin was employed as an accounting associate to Jack Disselkoen (another Chilean!), but in time Elbin became director of the Credit and Collections Department in the Finance Division. Work at the Casa became a family affair after his marriage to María Luis Cayetano in 1966. The length of his service in this ministry speaks to his loyalty and to his own appreciation of the publications ministry.

1962. Abel and Coy Lee Pierson, and Ann Swenson were assigned to work as missionaries with the Casa de Publicaciones in 1962. But none of the three were strangers to missions nor strangers to El Paso.

Abel and Coy Lee Pierson had been appointed missionaries of the Foreign Mission Board in 1944. Abe had actually been born to missionary parents in Mexico, but did college and seminary work in the United States, marrying Coy Lee Childress in January 1929. After almost a decade and a half of mission work among Hispanics in New Mexico and California, the Piersons were appointed to serve with the Mexican Baptist Theological Seminary (functioning then in El Paso) in 1944. They returned to Mexico with the Seminary in 1946 and served in that country (sometimes at the Seminary in Torreón, sometimes in field evangelism and student home work in Chihuahua) until their transfer to the Publishing House in 1962. For a dozen years (their retirement came in 1974), Abe directed the General Church Materials Department and Coy Lee assisted in the Missions Department.

Ann Swenson was also, like Abel Pierson, born to missionary parents, but parents who were serving in Argentina rather than in Mexico. Ann's university studies were done at Wheaton College and at the University of Wisconsin. When Erhardt and Anna Granberg Swenson, Ann's parents, finished their career of service in Argentina, they were attracted to make their retirement home in El Paso. There Rev. Swenson served some time on the staff of First Baptist Church, El Paso, as an associate. For almost three years in the late '50s, Ann lived with her parents in El Paso and worked as an employee at the Casa Bautista de Publicaciones. In 1960 she decided to pursue seminary studies at Southwestern in Fort Worth and subsequently seek missionary appointment. The appointment occurred in 1962, and Ann came back to work at the Publishing House, this time as a missionary and in charge of the Student Work Department. She founded *Ancla* magazine for students, edited many materials for this important segment of Latin American population, and continued at the Publishing House till 1980, when she took a responsibility especially for student ministries in Mexico.

1963. Adolfo and Emelina Robleto. Having served as a pastor, an editor, and a writer in his native country of Nicaragua and in the neighboring Central American country of Costa Rica, don[27] Adolfo Robleto and his family (wife, Emelina, and their only daughter and four sons) arrived in El Paso in December of 1963. He worked as both an editor, a translator, and as a department director. Together Adolfo and Emelina edited the *Hogar Cristiano* magazine for several years. After serving as an Associate in the General Book Department, don Adolfo directed the General Church Materials Department and later the Church Administration and Pastoral Leadership Department until the fall of 1981, when he "retired" from the Publishing House and accepted work with Accelerated Christian Education, Inc., of Lewisville, Texas (a Dallas suburb), to direct their Translation Department. In a letter which signaled the intention to conclude his work with the Casa Bautista de Publications, don Adolfo finished with this Bible verse: "But none of these things move me, neither count I my life dear unto myself, so that I might finish my course with joy, and the ministry, which I have received of the Lord Jesus, to testify the gospel of the grace of God" (Acts 20:24, KJV). Returning to El Paso in 1987, he became pastor of the Iglesia Bautista Internacional and served until the end of 1993. He passed to his eternal reward on Good Friday, 1994, at the age of 77 years. Emelina continues to make her home in El Paso. During his lifetime, don Adolfo authored some eighteen books,[28] most of them published by the Casa Bautista de Publicaciones.

1964. Thomas W. and Cornice Hill. Tom and "Connie" were transferred to El Paso from missionary service in Costa Rica in the summer of 1964. They had been appointed in October 1956 for service in Venezuela. During their language study year of 1957, conditions in Venezuela made their going there somewhat problematic, and a need emerged in the Central American country of Costa Rica that they were invited to fill. Tom was born and raised in South Carolina. He did college work at Furman University and theological studies at the New Orleans Baptist Theological Seminary, including the Th.D. program, finishing in 1956. He married Cornice Winter in 1954. "Connie" was a native of Mississippi, a graduate of Mississippi College, and was studying at the New Orleans Seminary when she and Tom married. Tom's responsibilities in El Paso began with his directing the General Book Department. He was the first missionary to come to the Publishing House having already completed an earned doctor's degree. During the Crusade of the Americas years, Tom authored the book *Cristo la Única Esperanza* (Christ, the only hope) which figured as the theme of the Crusade. Tom became the third General Director of Casa Bautista.[29]

1965. Laura Beamer. Laura began in January of this year and worked as an English language stenographer under the supervision of Jack Disselkoen. She was really bi-lingual, but her second language was German. She had escaped the Nazi regime as an adolescent and lived with relatives in England prior to her marriage to an American soldier stationed there. Through the years her service to the Casa grew, and she was director of the Personnel Department at the time of her retirement in 1990.

1966. Tom Hegwood. In August of 1965 a new Miller TPJ Press was installed. By early 1966 Tom Hegwood was on the job as a full time pressman to operate the TPJ. Tom was a bivocational pastor with ties to both Louisiana and Mississippi. Coming to El Paso for him (and his family) was almost like going to a foreign land! But they made the transition well, and in addition to his Publishing House work, Tom served as pastor of Kemp Street Baptist Church during most of his years in El Paso. In Clifford Smith's Production Division Report in the spring of 1967, he praised Tom's productivity and commented that the volume of print output for the year being reported on was "close to an all time high."[30]

1967. José Martínez and the Kenneth Evensons began their work with the Publishing House in 1967. Martínez worked in the Shipping Department while it was still being supervised by Toxie White. His work in that department would last almost twenty years and would be done under several different department supervisors. Officially he retired in 1985, but in 1988 when recognized as the Employee of the Month, he was still at it! He and his wife Amanda were parents to a large family. Originally from Parral, Chihuahua, Mexico, José became an evangelical Christian at the tender age of ten years. He felt that his work at the Publishing House (though the pay was less that what he had earned previously both in Arizona and in California) made a contribution to Christ's Kingdom. That kind of satisfaction was important to José, and to other Casa workers as well.

Ken and Mary Ann Evenson were natives of Oklahoma and Michigan, respectively, but were persons of international experience by the time they came to El Paso. Married in 1954, both were graduates of Grand Canyon College, in Phoenix, Arizona. During seminary studies at Southwestern, in Fort Worth, Kenneth was pastor in Powell, Texas, where their twin daughters were born in 1955. After missionary appointment in 1957 and their required period of language study in Costa Rica, the Evensons served in Uruguay. Transfer to El Paso came in 1967 where they served slightly more than ten years. Ken directed the Art Department, and Mary Ann contributed in numerous ways, part of the time in the General Book Department. In 1978, they returned to Uruguay, but are remembered with high esteem for their notable contributions to the publications ministry during their time in El Paso.

1968. Mary Jo McMurray Wilburn. Mary Jo and her first husband Jesse Daniel McMurray were native Oklahomans who married the year of her college graduation, 1942. Studies at Southwestern Baptist Theological Seminary followed, where Dan was graduated shortly before their missionary appointment in 1945. The McMurrays did their language study in the country of their service: Uruguay. Dan and Mary Jo served in district field evangelism, pastoral ministry, and some school administrative work for almost twenty-three years. While on furlough in 1968, Dan suffered a heart attack and died. Subsequently Mary Jo was invited to serve at the Publishing House in El Paso. Her work with women in Uruguay easily linked to the Missions Department at the Casa Bautista. Subsequently she became Librarian and served efficiently there until her retirement in 1988. After retirement Mary Jo married Bob Wilburn, widower to her sister. She succumbed to declining health in May 2002.

1969. Yolanda Rosales Oseguera began in the month of February. Like several other Casa related personnel, Yolanda was a member of the Primera Iglesia Bautista of Ciudad Juárez. In fact, she had been converted there at the age of fifteen and baptized by longtime pastor Mateo M. Gurrola. Her tenure at the Publishing House lacked only a little getting to a total of twenty-five years, when she retired in early 1993. At that time she was director of the Customer Service Department, in the Marketing Division. When recognized as "Employee of the Month," she acknowledged that reading was her favorite pastime. (Now that's an appropriate pastime for a publishing house employee!)

1970. Edward and Gladys Nelson. This talented couple came to direct the Music Department and did so for some eighteen years. Both had a background of military service as well as university and seminary training in music. For Ed that included the doctorate in Church Music from the New Orleans Baptist Theological Seminary. A lasting achievement of their service was the development of a new hymnal (*Himnario Bautista*), first published in 1978, but still in print.[31] Since retirement they have lived at the Baptist Memorials Center in San Angelo, Texas, where for a number of years they were neighbors to F. W. and Pauline Patterson, who also made their home there. When recognized as "The Employee of the Month," in May 1988, Gladys registered her favorite hymn as "Great Is Thy Faithfulness" (Spanish version, "Grande Es Tu Fidelidad," number 230 in the hymnal she and Ed worked so hard to produce).

New Ventures

Among the new ventures that must be highlighted are (1) new periodicals, (2) W.M.U. publications, (3) the deposit system of distribution, and (4) a reentry into Scripture publication.

(1) New periodicals. —January 1957 brought the discontinuation, after twenty years of continuous publication, of *Revista Evangélica*. But in its place, two new periodicals were launched: *El Pastor Evangélico* and *El Hogar Cristiano*. Their titles pretty much indicated their target audiences: evangelical pastors, and Christian homes (i.e., families). *El Hogar Cristiano* was begun with a quarterly print run of 3,000, but by the end of 1961 the circulation had grown to 7,600 per quarter. Circulation of the magazine for Christian families generally continued to rise during the Patterson years, but circulation of *El Pastor Evangélico* soon leveled off at about 3,000 per quarter. Still another periodical that was begun in 1957 was *Historias Infantiles* (lesson cards for two- and three-year-olds). Mrs. Patterson was the editor.[32] *Sal* , a magazine of missionary materials for evangelical men, was launched in the first quarter of 1962. *Guía para Maestros de Niños,* which had been launched in 1955 to serve all the teachers of children through age twelve (grouped into four departments), underwent major changes in 1964 when a "Teachers' Edition" was launched for *Heraldos del Rey,* the curriculum material for Bible classes of children nine to twelve years of age, and a book (really an "annual") was published for teachers of nursery age children (birth to three years). Beginning in 1964 *Guía para Maestros de Niños* subsequently served for teachers of only two groups, "Párvulos" (ages four and five) and "Principiantes" (ages six to eight). *Ancla,* the material specifically targeted toward students and young professionals, was launched in 1966. Curriculum materials for Training Union continued to evolve into a fully graded line of six quarterlies.[33] *Verdad,* a periodical evangelistic tract, *Respuesta,* a "soft sell" general interest periodical, intended for evangelistic outreach, and *Nueva Vida,* a more directly evangelistic four-pager with some "cartoon-like" presentation, were also added during Patterson's last decade. The result was that thirty-one periodicals were being published and distributed in totals that annually superceded three million copies by the end of Patterson's time as General Director.

(2) W.M.U. Publications. —Though this "new venture" might have been included under the category of "new periodicals," it seems preferable to highlight it separately, for it truly did represent innovation for the Casa. CBP had been born with a burden for Sunday School curriculum materials, and the Publishing House came to be identified widely as the source for such. To mention *El Expositor Bíblico* was to imply its publisher, Casa Bautista de Publicaciones. The two were almost synonymous. While the Publishing House had made some effort to publish materials specifically for women,[34] a line of women's materials emerged from the leadership of missionaries Mary Moore and Lou Ellen Hawkins in Chile and Argentina. By the mid-fifties, a trunk line magazine (named *La Ventana*) for Woman's Missionary Union (in its Hispanic incarnation) was being published as a monthly in Santiago, Chile. Some other missionary materials for girls and younger children were also being published there, and a missionary magazine for boys was being done in Argentina. Its title was *El Escudo*. All these publications were being subsidized through the Foreign Mission Board and its missions in Argentina and Chile, with considerable initiative and insistence coming from the Baptist women of North America. The complications of such a system, particularly for the aspects of production and distribution involving various countries, caused the idea to emerge that the whole program, including personnel and funding, be transferred to the Publishing House in El Paso. Such a plan was approved by the International Committee for Women's Publications in Latin America (Spanish name: Comité de Publicaciones Femeniles Bautistas Hispanoamericanas) when it met in Rio de Janeiro, in June of 1960. The approval came despite an understandable reluctance on the part of women leaders in both Chile and Argentina to "lose their magazines."

All affected parties ratified the plan, and in 1961 missionary Roberta Ryan (who had been leading the program in Chile, following Mary Moore) was transferred to El Paso and the Casa began publishing all the missionary materials, with the issues that corresponded to the third quarter of 1961. (*La Ventana* was continued as a monthly until 1969 when it became a quarterly. The first issue published in El Paso was for July 1961.) Graded missionary materials for girls were published in *La Estrella*; for boys, in *El Escudo*;[35] for young children, in *El Rayito*; and for the leaders of missionary organizations for young children, in *El Rayito, Edición para Consejeras*. In 1968, a magazine for young women was added, entitled *Resplandor.* This new program, now with its location in El Paso, gave the Baptist churches of Latin America basically one source for all their curricular needs, in a very complete program of "religious education" for the local scene: Bible study, membership training, and missionary education. In the future, it would be looked at as perhaps too heavy for all churches to carry, but at the time it was considered desirable and in some quarters almost mandatory for fully rounded "Baptist churches." The influence of what at the time was considered normative for Southern Baptist churches in the United States can hardly be missed.

(3) The Deposit System of Distribution. —Hoyt Eudaly saw the potential for increasing distribution of CBP publications by involving the various Baptist Missions of Latin America. Some of these already sponsored one or more book stores. Hoyt wanted the Missions to buy a reserve stock and thus serve church and individual needs more immediately (without having to wait for materials to arrive from El Paso) and even function as wholesale outlets from which other bookstores in the various countries could secure Casa products.

During the July 1961 Mission Meeting, attended by both Dr. Frank Means, Area Secretary for Latin America, and his "Field Representative" for Mexico and Central America, James Crane, the idea emerged of "deploying" a good portion of the Casa inventory, basically on consignment to the several Missions of the hemisphere, in order to achieve higher levels of use and more efficient attention to needs. On September 15, 1961 the Mission's Executive Committee met and heard a report given by Frank Patterson entitled "Deployment of Stock of the Baptist Spanish Publishing House for an Expanded Literature Ministry." After establishing the rationale for this program, the report detailed the "Plan and Responsibilities." In summary, the Publishing House offered to consign to the Missions (related to FMB, SBC) "an adequate stock of our books to be held in deposit for wholesale distribution." Basically a partnership was established with the Publishing House supplying the stock and the Missions supplying personnel and space for local operations. A modest "extra margin" was built in to the plan "to help defray the expenses involved" for the Missions. The plan was approved and offered to the Missions.[36] Before Patterson concluded his administration, fourteen such "Deposits" came to exist. At the time, the system was easily the envy of other evangelical Spanish publishers. And the result was increased circulation of Casa publications during all the remaining Patterson years. It was truly an achievement for its time.

(4) A Reentry into Scripture Publication. —Though it often goes unnoticed, the Casa Bautista de Publicaciones entered the area of Scripture publication during its first decade in Mexico. All the factors that motivated Davis and his associates to enter this arena have not come to light in correspondence or available documents. What is clear is Davis led CBP to offer an alternative translation of the New Testament as early as 1916. He chose a lesser known translation from Greek to Spanish, made in the mid-nineteenth century and published with the title *El Nuevo Pacto*.[37] Davis set type and printed the book in León. In the first quarter issue of *El Expositor Bíblico* for 1916, Davis announced that he was printing the Bible text of the lessons from *El Nuevo Pacto*. He offered and recommended that students order a copy of the book recently published by CBP. He explained: "No es más que una fiel traducción del Nuevo Testamento, y lo recomendamos por su corrección y fidelidad al original."[38] (English translation: It is no more than a faithful translation of the New Testament. We recommend it for its precision and faithfulness to the original language.) Apparently several thousand copies were printed in Mexico and gradually brought to El Paso in the Casa's first years there. The 1924 Catalog still lists it as available, as does one from 1933. Eventually it was sold out and apparently demand did not justify a reprint.

A half century passed from the year of the original issue of *El Nuevo Pacto* (1916) and the moment when Frank Patterson led the Casa to reenter the area of Scripture publication. In Dr. Patterson's mind a vision emerged of a niche, in the area of Scripture publication, where the Publishing House could contribute. It would be with a "soul-winner's marked New Testament," using the Reina-Valera revised text that the United Bible Societies published in 1960. Permissions were secured, Patterson directed the project, and printing was done in El Paso. In December of 1966, an edition of 120,000 copies of *El Nuevo Testamento: Edición Camino de Vida* was completed. It was a significant event, and in the course of the years eight or more editions have been done, with the printing sometimes done in El Paso, sometimes elsewhere in the United States, or even in Russia. This event opened the door for the Casa to eventually offer other Scripture publications also.

Special Projects

Four must be mentioned: (1) Building projects, (2) materials for the Crusade of the Americas, (3) the emergence of Editorial Mundo Hispano as the Casa's "non denominational logo," and (4) reorganization(s).

(1) Building projects. These took place in 1955, 1959, and 1960. In 1955, approximately 4,000 square feet of floor space was added by enclosing a paved patio adjacent to the main building on the east end of the large central quadrangle. Ross reports that a special dedication service was held when the bindery department began to function in this space with its new equipment.[39] Special tribute was paid to the Davises and to José Pérez who (with the Davises before him) had bound many books by hand. New equipment and efficient staff made this the only complete book bindery in El Paso at that time.[40]

In 1959 new office space was made available for the distribution division with the construction of a two-story addition to the building on the southeast side, near the front entrance. "The construction provided approximately 3,000 square feet of floor space... [and] was erected at a cost of $14,500."[41]

In 1960, completely new quarters were provided for the production division (which included the bindery department) by closing in approximately 17,000 square feet of the large central patio of the main quadrangular building. Advantage was taken of three existing walls, giving a very economical per square foot building cost. Upon completion, all of the production equipment was moved into it, and this move had the effect of freeing up some 8,000 square feet in the main building, which was re-converted to other uses. "The part that had been the bindery was converted into a periodical shipping room; the area vacated by the presses was remodeled and used to house the newly created service division...; the area vacated by the composition department was used to increase the facilities of the editorial division."[42]

Not included in these "building projects" were other material improvements like securing regular natural gas service (allowing conversion from butane to natural gas) and getting a regular city water connection (allowing dependence on local water wells to be phased out).[43]

(2) Materials for the Crusade of the Americas. -- This hemisphere-wide evangelistic effort was born in the heart of Brazilian pastor Rubens Lopes, and got its launch at the 1965 Miami meeting of the Baptist World Alliance. When Frank Patterson made his annual report to the local Mission, in May of 1967, he wrote: "The challenge of this campaign is quickening; the response from the Latin American fields is heartening; our position in the campaign is strategic. Let every department secretary and every editor [at CBP] utilize their materials to promote this campaign. Keep a calendar of its activities in view: 1967 is the year of spiritual preparation. 1968 emphasizes training in visitation and soul-winning. Many churches will have a Sunday school enlargement campaign. 1969 is the year of revivals with conservation of results and teaching of new converts beginning immediately. 1970 is a year of conservation and follow-up revivals. The Training Union should plan indoctrination of new members."[44]

In his 1969 summary of activities at the Publishing House, Patterson noted that twenty-eight items specifically designed and published to support the Crusade of the Americas had been done, including 2,000,000 copies of a marked Gospel of John.

It appears that all departments of the Publishing House did in fact follow Patterson's request to utilize their publications in support of this massive evangelistic undertaking. Examples include the narrator's script for an interpretive filmstrip that *El Promotor de Educación Cristiana* carried in its second quarter issue for 1968, as well as the good coverage given to the new follow-up materials found in the second quarter issue for 1969. *El Expositor Bíblico, La Ventana,* and even *El Hogar Cristiano* also supported the campaign with appropriate articles, posters, announcements, and in other ways. It became "a magnificent obsession."

(3) The emergence of Editorial Mundo Hispano as the Casa's "non denominational" logo. --To some extent following the trend already perceivable in the United States and Europe in which "denominational publishers" were beginning to use "brand names" or "identification logos" that did not blatantly announce their denominational affiliation (and thus avoid pre-judgment based on factors other than content), the Casa Bautista de Publicaciones began the search for a "non-denominational" logo. When reentry to Scripture publications occurred with the marked New Testament in 1966, the issue came to the fore, lest the product be viewed as merely "a Baptist Bible." The first issue of the New Testament was published with an editorial logo of "Editorial Verdad" (Truth Publishers). The issue continued to be studied and soon a consensus emerged to use the logo "Editorial Mundo Hispano" (Hispanic World Publishers). Gradually its use has increased, though without completely abandoning the use of "Casa Bautista de Publicaciones." "Editorial Mundo Hispano" came to be considered the preferable logo for Bibles (and other Scripture products), "specialty products" (such as calendars and some novelty items), and materials that have a marked degree of circulation in the secular market place, as well as textbooks, commentaries and reference works that easily cross denominational lines. Its use continues to grow. And in the process of the years, two imprints were developed for French language resources: Centre de Publications Baptistes and Editions du Monde Evangélique Francais.[45]

(4) Reorganization(s). —-Someone has said that organizations regularly evolve or change about every two years. Major changes in Publishing House organization have probably not occurred quite that often, but during the second half of the Patterson years, major changes did occur in 1958 and 1960. Patterson had inherited from Davis the tradition of a two-pronged organization (Editorial and Business Administration), and he had continued that pattern during approximately the first half of his long tenure as General Director. But a change that Ross calls "a further refining of the Publishing House organization" occurred in 1958.[46] Three divisions of work were set up, each representing a cluster of departments. The "editorial division" was to be directed by J. Wilson Ross; the "business division," by N. Hoyt Eudaly; and the "production division," by Clifford Smith. "This move served to clarify administrative activities of the publishing House and to provide for further expansion."[47]

Two years later, in 1960, more major organizational changes were made. The work was divided into four divisions, in place of three. These four divisions were: distribution, production, editorial, and service. Eudaly and Smith were continued as directors of the distribution and production divisions, respectively. But Judson Blair was named to head the editorial division, and Wilson Ross was named to direct the service division. Though the new organizational structure proved effective and provided for a further expansion of the work of the Publishing House, it was not without some repercussions for the General Director. In July of 1961, Patterson (just back from a year's furlough during which the Pattersons had spent considerable time traveling in Latin America and Pauline had completed her Master's Degree in Religious Education at Southwestern Seminary), made his report as General Director. In it, Frank comments: "Reorganization was inevitable. It was expected. We had discussed the need for some time. There will be other shifts in organization as we expand. The present organizational set-up of four divisions, with their respective departments, seems to be functioning well. Accomplishments under this set-up during my absence have been outstanding. My heartfelt gratitude for the leadership exercised during the year."

Then he continues concerning a "definition of responsibility:"

"The status of Director of the Publishing House has changed with the evolution of the institution. The plan by which the Director works through an Administrative Committee, composed of division heads, is better than the former plan of frequent consultation with the Executive Committee [of the Mission] as problems arose...

"The [General] Director has responsibility both to the Foreign Mission Board and to the Mission. These need to be defined. He has a responsibility for offering leadership in planning, in eliciting the same from others about him, and of offering some guidance for consideration by the Mission. His administrative responsibilities and executive responsibilities need to be spelled out.

"Regardless of personalities, or who is [General] Director, the Publishing House will function more effectively if: (1) the Director has a mandate of responsibility from the Foreign Mission Board and from the Mission, and (2) if the Mission can agree as to what responsibilities the missionaries working with the Publishing House have to the Director. I recommend that in this annual meeting the Mission attempt to crystallize its thinking at this point."[48]

The Mission subsequently attempted to do what Patterson recommended, and apparently both General Director and individual missionaries were satisfied.[49]

Still another aspect of "reorganization" during the last decade of the Patterson years had to do with a new Advisory Committee. Dr. Davis' experiment with a local Advisory Committee had largely been unsatisfactory.[50] Hiram Duffer's effort to organize an International Committee of Religious Education had produced some positive and ongoing results.[51] And thanks to Wilson Ross, it still existed and was functioning into the late '50s and early '60s, albeit entirely by correspondence (as Hiram had originally envisioned). When the women's materials were transferred from Chile to El Paso in 1961, the new department of Women's Missionary Materials essentially brought with it the Comité de Publicaciones Femeniles Bautistas Hispano-americanas (Committee on Hispano-american Baptist Publications for Women) that had existed to give some international legitimacy to the publication program which had been headquartered in Santiago. The El Paso Mission found itself naming members to both entities.[52] In these circumstances, the idea was born to combine the functions of these two committees and attempt to have periodic meetings.[53] A study group was created with Dr. Frank Patterson as its chairman to consider possibilities. The report of the General Director, rendered to the Mission in May 1963, includes this paragraph: "The committee of which I was chairman has already reported favorably to the Mission on having [an International Advisory Committee for the Publishing House. It] would widen our sphere of contact and strengthen our ties with the Missions and national leaders."[54] Subsequently, with Mission approval and Foreign Mission Board backing, such a committee was formed. Baptist convention entities were invited to name three representatives each (two men and one woman). The first meeting was held in 1966,[55] and a second was held in 1970 just as Dr. Patterson completed his years of active service in El Paso.[56]

A Highly Productive Relationship with the Foreign Mission Board

Frank Patterson's years as General Director were blessed with extraordinarily close, friendly, productive relationships with the Foreign Mission Board, SBC, and its top administrators, especially the Area Secretaries (Frank Means and Charles Bryan) and with Theron Rankin and Baker James Cauthen, the Board's Executive Secretaries during this period. On both personal and professional levels, these relationships opened doors for very notable expansion during the second half of the Patterson years.

The period of Frank Patterson's service as General Director came to a close not because of normal or mandatory retirement (as had been the case with Davis). Dr. Charles Bryan, as the new Area Director for "Middle America and the Caribbean" (Frank Means continued to be the Area Director for South America), came up with the idea that the Pattersons should give their last years of active service (prior to normal retirement) in a promotional and "field service" ministry. Initial reluctance from the Pattersons turned to acquiescence and then enthusiastic acceptance, and Frank and Polly began to plan for the conclusion of their resident service in El Paso which would occur in the fall of 1970.

The Mission, in its early summer session of that year, faced (for it) an unprecedented task: naming a new General Director for Casa Bautista de Publicaciones. Though several possibilities may have been considered, it was Dr. Thomas W. Hill who was named. Patterson was recognized and Hill was installed in a very special program in September, 1970.

✳✳✳

Frank and Polly began an eighteen month stint of residency and field service in various parts of Latin America. They spent six months living in Costa Rica, traveling and ministering in Mexico and Central America. Then six months in Cali, Colombia, doing a similar ministry in the "países bolivarianos" (countries of Northern South American identified with the great liberator Simón Bolívar); and subsequently, with residence in Buenos Aires, six months in Southern South America ("el cono sur;" the southern cone countries) doing the same kind of work. Retirement finally came with their return to the United States in 1972.

For the Pattersons "retirement" was lengthy, active, and highly productive. Frank wrote Sunday School lessons in Spanish (really his first love); authored several books,[57] served as visiting consultant or professor in Brazil and

Mexico (both in Mexico City and in Oaxaca), was pastor of a small church in the southern New Mexico mountains,[58] and (with occasional visits to El Paso) became a living inspiration to current Publishing House staff . Polly finished her earthly career in March 2000; Frank was in frail health when this project was authorized, but still living at the Baptist Retirement Center in San Angelo. It had been hoped that he might survive to see the Casa's Hundredth Birthday. After the first four chapters were drafted, his son Dr. Burton Patterson spent some time with him, reading those pages in Dr. Pat's hearing. Some details were retouched with his input. (Special thanks are due to both these doctors Patterson!) But in the providence of a loving Heavenly Father, Dr. Frank W. Patterson finished his earthly pilgrimage January 20, 2004. Notices, obituaries, and tributes were carried not only in the denominational press and in the *El Paso Times*, but in several newspapers of Latin America. One article was headlined: "Missionary 'legend' left mark on Spanish-speaking world."[59] Indeed he did; in fact his contribution to the Casa's hundred years of history and ministry is really incalculable.

Endnotes

1. We Baptists, Study and Research Division, Baptist World Alliance. James Leo Garrett, Jr., editor-in-chief. Franklin, Tennessee: Providence House Publishers, 1999, p. 3.

2. See chapter 1 where evidence is presented showing that the name was definitely in use by 1910.

3. Catálogo General de la Casa Bautista de Publicaciones, 1942, p. 3.

4. See chapter 1.

5. Ross, Sowing the Seed, pp. 127-128.

6. In the Minutes of the El Paso Publishing House Mission, for a meeting held on August 1-3, 1956, there is the following reference to the Anniversary: "After a discussion of how we could best advertise or take note of our 50th Anniversary this year, it was decided, because of the late date and the heavy responsibilities of each missionary during this year, to publish a small but attractive pictorial brochure to celebrate a half century of service and to print some stationary with a 50th anniversary motif." Minutes, page 8, Publishing House Mission Archives.

7. Dana left Fort Worth to become president of the Central Seminary in Kansas City in 1938. See the article "Dana, Harvey Eugene," by Franklin M. Segler, in Encyclopedia of Southern Baptists, vol. 1. Nashville: Broadman Press, 1958, p 346.

8. The dissertation later became the basis for Patterson's book A Century of Baptist Work in Mexico.

9. He completed the Master's Degree in Religious Education at Southwestern in 1956 and was awarded the M.A. from Texas Tech in 1958.

10. Special thanks are extended to Mrs. Jimmie Ross for her blessing on this project, in which frequent use is made of her deceased husband's material.

11. See letter, Patterson to Frank Means, undated but written from Kansas City, apparently in the fall of 1954. Means' reply to Patterson seems to date the letter on October 15. Means encourages the project Patterson proposes, and, in a later letter dated January 12, 1955, expresses disappointment that approval has not been obtained from Seminary authorities, because "someone else had already done some work on the dissertation subject [Patterson]

had selected." Letters found among Patterson's personal files and papers.

12. See manuscript found among Patterson's personal files and papers.

13. See personal files and papers of F. W. Patterson made available for this project; eventually to be archived in the Wilson Ross Library of Casa Bautista de Publicaciones.

14. Ibid.

15. See another of Patterson's presentations entitled "La Base Bíblica de Nuestra Literatura" (The Biblical base of our literature); found in his personal files and papers. Alicia Zorzoli, long time editor at CBP, says on one occasion she was presenting a conference on Casa materials in one of the Latin American countries, when a woman got up and said, "I buy materials from Casa Bautista de Publicaciones almost with my eyes shut because I know they will represent sound, Biblical doctrine."

16. See a one-half page typed summary, found among personal files and papers, signed by Frank W. Patterson.

17. See letter Frank Means to Wilson Ross, April 7, 1958, where Dr. Means reports that Edna Mae "has a strong sense of divine leadership toward El Paso." Copy of letter found among Frank Patterson's personal files and papers.

18. See Questionnaire Reply from Dorothy Hicks Pettit, received in February 2004.

19. With a bit of understandable nostalgia, José likes to remember "the good years–those, before the computer revolution–when the true Typography techniques were used at the Casa Bautista." He takes pride in having worked under every General Director, save the founder and the present one (meaning Davis and Díaz). Etched in his mind are "the economic problems during some years," but these are superceded by his recollections of "relationships with so many persons that worked at the CBP during those wonderful years." For this "typographer, 'floor man,' department and division director," those friendships made it all worth while. (See Questionnaire Reply received by Poe in February 2004.)

20. See Entre Nos, vol. 12, No. 39, Septiembre 27, 1989.

21. See chapter 3.

22. Jimmie Ross' father.

23. See Viola Campbell, He Leadeth Me, pp. 28-29.

24. Among her works is the biography of Frank Patterson entitled The Claim Staker.

25. See "By Love Serve One Another" by Joe T. Poe, published in 2003 by the El Paso Baptist Clinic, in celebration of its Thirtieth Anniversary.

26. Viola passed to her heavenly reward August 21, 2002, nine months after finishing the writing of her memoirs. The book was published in both English and Spanish in 2003 and distributed gratis as a part of her legacy.

27. "Don" is used here in its Spanish sense: a title indicating respect, used only with the first name of a person, normally not capitalized and generally left untranslated.

28. Titles: Sermones para días especiales, Tomo 1; Sermones para días especiales, Tomo 2; Sermones para el nuevo milenio; 501 ilustraciones nuevas; Catecismo bíblico y doctrinal para el nuevo creyente; Dramas y poemas para días especiales, #1; Dramas y poemas para días especiales, #2; Dramas y poemas para días especiales, #3; El sermón evangelístico y el evangelista; El día del Señor; Mayordomía cristiana de la vida, de la iglesia, del hogar; El mensaje de los bautistas para el mundo; Fundamento y práctica de fe y mensaje bautista; Un vistazo a la doctrina romana: interpretación a la luz del Segundo Concilio Vaticano; Tengo que divertirme... pero, ¿cómo?; Ester se quiere casar; Conozca quiénes son; Qué hacer en tiempos de crisis? During the administration of Joe T. Poe an annual award that bears his name was created; see chapter 9.

29. See chapter 5.

30. See Mission Minutes and Reports, 1966-67, p. 103; held in Mission Archives in El Paso.

31. Published under two titles, Himnario Bautista and Himnos de Alabanza Evangélica, in a variety of formats.

32. Materials for preschoolers in Sunday

School (and Vacation Bible School) became Polly's specialty. The Publishing House Library's card catalog lists her as the author (or joint author) of the following works: Cuadros Ilustrativos: Serie A; Cuadros Ilustrativos: Serie B; Cuadros Ilustrativos: Serie C; Mejor Enseñanza para Maestros de Niños; Animalitos Amigables; La Familia Feliz; Figuras Bíblicas Ilustrativas: Serie A; Figuras Bíblicas Ilustrativas: Serie B; Figuras Bíblicas Ilustrativas: Serie C; Estudios Bíblicos para Niños, Libro del Alumno; Estudios Bíblicos para Niños, Libro del Maestro; Lecciones para Niños de Dos y Tres Años; Manual para el Departamento de Párvulos; 150 Cosas que Hacer con Papel; La Iglesia Ministrando a los Párvulos; Juegos Digitales y Otras Actividades; Santa Biblia para Mí; Programas de Adoración para Niños; and Walk, Eddie!, a total of 19 books.

33. Marie Eudaly became the specialist in children's materials for the Training Union curriculum. She also authored several books.

34. Apart from books, Mensajeras del Maestro, a magazine of programs for women's meetings, was apparently published during 1938, 1939, and part of 1940. The Publishing House library has issues from "vol. I," (1938), all four issues of "vol. II," (1939) and one issue from "vol. III," (1940).

35. Beyond the magazine, some books were also edited. David Fajardo, CBP employee since 1986, recalls: "The first Casa book I ever read was when I was eleven years old and in Royal Ambassadors, in my home church in Ecuador. The book was about J. Paton, a missionary to some cannibal tribes who lived on islands in the South Pacific. The book made a permanent impact on my life. It helped me dedicate my life to the Lord and to His service down to the present. I never dreamed then that I would some day have the opportunity to help publish that kind of book."

36. See Minutes, Executive Committee, Baptist Spanish Publishing House Mission, September 15, 1961; Mission Archives in El Paso.

37. Little is known about the original translator who only signed his initials, "G.N." A Scottish missionary named Guillermo Norton is generally credited with the work.

38. El Expositor Bíblico, Año XXV, Núm 1, (1916) p. 1.

39. See Ross, Sowing the Seed, p. 127.

40. Ibid.

41. Ibid., p. 140.

42. Ibid.

43. As narrated in chapter 10, the new office building erected in 1982, during Aldo Broda's administration, was named "The Frank W. Patterson Building," in honor of this major leader in 'building the House' during its first hundred years.

44. See El Paso Mission Reports and Minutes, May 1967-May 1968; Mission Archives in El Paso.

45. The Casa found it necessary to eliminate its publication of French materials as of the end of 2003.

46. Ross, Sowing the Seed, p. 134.

47. Ibid.

48. See Mission Minutes and Reports for 1961, p. 185; Mission Archives in El Paso.

49. See Mission Minutes and Reports, October 10-11, 1961, when a three page report entitled "Publishing House Missionary Relationships and Responsibilities" was approved. Major sections dealt with "Relationships of Missionaries to Publishing House and its Administration" and "Responsibilities and Relationships of the General Director to the Mission and to the Publishing House." Documents housed in Mission Archives, in El Paso.

50. See chapter 2.

51. See chapter 3.

52. See, for example, Mission Minutes, for 1963.

53. The Women's Committee had occasionally met, but the Religious Education group had never had a gathering.

54. See p. 5 of the General Director's Report to El Paso Mission; dated May 13, 1963; El Paso Mission Archives.

55. Dr. and Mrs. Thomas W. Hill and Mrs. Jimmie Ross have reminded the author that 1966 was also when the Publishing House celebrated its 60th Anniversary Year, very possibly in connection with the first gathering of the International Advisory Committee.

56. See chapter 5.

57. The full list of his works held in the Wilson Ross Library of Casa Bautista de Publicaciones is as follows: Programas para las Reuniones de los Primarios e Intermedios en la Escuela Bíblica de Vacaciones, Libro D; Programas de Apertura para las Reuniones de los Primarios e Intermedios en la Escuela Bíblica de Vacaciones, Libro C; Programas para Cultos de Adoración de los Primarios e Intermedios en la Escuela Bíblica de Vacaciones, Libro A; Baptists Around the World: a Comprehensive Handbook (one chapter by Patterson); Programas para las Reuniones de los Primarios e Intermedios en la Escuela Bíblica de Vacaciones, Libro C; Cómo Escribir para Ser Entendido; Breve Historia de la Obra Misionera Cristiana; Los Evangélicos frente al Siglo XXI; A Century of Baptist Work in Mexico; Manual para la Escuela Dominical; A Little Bird Told Me...; A Short History of Christian Missions; Manual de Finanzas para Iglesias; Jones Edgar Davis of Mexico; a total of 14 works. Not included in this list is his work as editor and chief writer for El Expositor Bíblico for more than a quarter century. The Wilson Ross Library also holds a copy of his Oral History Interview, done by Nell Stanley of the Foreign Mission Board's Jenkins Memorial Library and two other audio recordings done in 1980 and 1993.

58. Mention of the Pattersons' pastoral service in New Mexico calls to mind their remarkable relationships to local churches in the El Paso/Juárez area during their career there. Though they enjoyed some close personal ties with pastors and members of the Grandview Baptist Church in El Paso, they opted for many years to be active members of Primera Iglesia Bautista (First Baptist Church) in Ciudad Juárez. There they not only helped in the main church with its Sunday School, stewardship program, etc. but rendered regular service in its mission program. For at least the last dozen years of their residency in El Paso, they worked with the Monterrey Mission in Juárez. Its services were held in mid afternoon on Sundays. In this very needy neighborhood, Polly came in contact with a paralyzed boy and helped get needed medical attention for him. See her book Walk, Eddie! The mission was organized into a church on one of the last Sundays of 1970, just before the Pattersons left El Paso. The church continues its ministry today.

59. Southern Baptist Texan, February, 23 2004; p. 3.

Chapter 5

Tom Hill at the Helm

As late as April or early May of 1970, Dr. Thomas W. Hill, who with his wife Cornice (Connie to most friends and colleagues) had been serving with the Casa Bautista de Publicaciones since the summer of 1964, had no inkling of the major job changes that lay just around the corner. If someone had said to him, "Get ready, Tom, for the train's a-coming," he probably would have replied, "What train?" The correct answer would have been: "The train that will carry you to CBP's General Directorship." And if some prophetic voice had given him that answer, he likely would have uttered one of his characteristic chuckles and replied in good South Carolina English: "You've got to be kidding!"

But the train arrived.

It did bring surprise to several—including Tom and Connie.

Hill Is Chosen and Installed

The naming occurred during the May 1970 meeting of the El Paso Publishing House Mission. As signaled earlier,[1] the Mission had existed as a separate entity from the Mexico Mission since 1950. With the help of meticulously careful members like Wilson Ross, the Mission, functioning as the governing body of the Publishing House and within its direct responsibility to the Foreign Mission Board, had elaborated a "constitution" and compiled some policies.[2] But it had not put into place any specific policies or procedures for electing a new General Director. It was probably assumed that Dr. Frank Patterson would follow Dr. Davis' example and serve until obliged to retire.[3]

As also signaled earlier (in the closing lines of the previous chapter), the initiative for the surprising chain of events lay not in El Paso but in Richmond; not with the Pattersons (or the Hills) but with Dr. Charles W. Bryan, who in 1968 had been named Area Director for Middle America and the Caribbean. He conceived a plan that he felt would assist the work in his Area, and in that of another Area as well (South America, still under the direction of Dr. Frank K. Means).

101

It must be assumed that Bryan approached the Pattersons first.[4] Apparently their reluctance turned to acquiescence which finally became enthusiasm. Dr. Bryan was in attendance for the Mission meeting and properly took it upon himself to inform the Mission of his plan and of the Pattersons' acceptance. He also signaled the consequent need for the Mission to take appropriate action.

After recovering from the surprise, the Mission proceeded to name a new General Director. During the twenty-five years the Mission functioned as the governing body of the Publishing House, this was the only time it was called on to name a General Director. For Mission officers,[5] it had become the tradition of the group to use secret ballots for all voting, but not to have either nominations or any committee work prior to the election itself. In a sense, all Mission members were candidates for all offices. "Run-offs" among the top "vote-getters" were used as necessary, and normally those who were thus chosen accepted without question the responsibility to which they had been named.

With this "tradition" in place, it seemed appropriate to the Mission to follow it for selecting the new General Director. It apparently was assumed that the new General Director should come from someone already on the scene and involved in the ministry. In one sense, this meant that all Mission members were "candidates." That year, the Mission consisted of the following persons:[6]

Judson Blair	Pauline Patterson
Dorothy Rose Blair	Abel P. Pierson
Viola Campbell	Coy Lee Pierson
N. Hoyt Eudaly	Joe T. Poe
Marie Eudaly	Eleanor Poe
Kenneth Evenson	J. Wilson Ross
Mary Ann Evenson	Jimmie Ross
Thomas W. Hill	Roberta Ryan
Cornice Hill	Matthew Sanderford
Mary Jo McMurray	Dora Jean Sanderford
Frank W. Patterson	Ann Marie Swenson

Assumedly the Pattersons voted in the process, but obviously neither of them were "candidates." The process was complicated a bit by the absence of four Mission members. Joe and Eleanor Poe were temporarily away from El Paso for a "Study Leave," when Joe was advancing toward his Ph.D. in Biblical Studies, at Baylor University. Judson and Dorothy Rose Blair were on a Publishing House representation trip to Spain that unfortunately coincided with the Mission Meeting dates. Mission Minutes do not reflect how many persons received votes, nor how many votes were taken. At some point it was decided that the Mission Secretary for the year, Roberta Ryan, should contact both the

Poes in Waco and the Blairs in Spain and give them the opportunity to vote though they were not physically in El Paso. Such was done.

The process yielded the election of Thomas W. Hill as the third General Director of the Casa Bautista de Publicaciones. A committee was named to plan appropriate program activities both to recognize the Pattersons and officially install Dr. Hill. Dorothy Rose Blair chaired the committee, and the other two members were Kenneth Evenson and Roberta Ryan. Because the International Advisory Committee was already scheduled to meet in September, a date was chosen to coincide with their convocation. And because 1970 was a special Anniversary of the founding of the Foreign Mission Board (the Publishing House's parent organization), it was decided to add to the program a third dimension, namely the commemoration of the 125th Anniversary of the Foreign Mission Board, of the Southern Baptist Convention. The effect was impressive, if somewhat extended.

The program was conducted at the Publishing House, on the evening of September 21, 1970, beginning at 8:00 p.m. A twelve-page bilingual program guided the good-sized audience that assembled in an area of the Production Division room, substantially rearranged for the evening. This included the construction of a circular platform that served as the stage; the program director called it "theater in the round." Probably every folding chair in the building was brought in, and there were still people standing. Instruments were relocated from the chapel, with Linda Douglas playing the organ and J. O. Stewart, Jr., the piano. Wilson Ross presided over the first part of the program. In the course of the evening, vocal solos were presented by Elias Garrido, Jr., Linda Douglas, Judson Blair, John Preston, and Jim Van Hemert; vocal groups—forming either duets, quartets, or quintets—sang (participants included Norma Blair, Martha Blair, Bill Blair, Paul Blair, Kenneth Hicks, Sara Ruth Porterfield, John Preston, and Jim Van Hemert). The Area Director, Dr. Charles Bryan, was present from Richmond and participated with both words of appreciation for Frank Patterson and words of challenge for Tom Hill. The Patterson response included words by both F. W. and Pauline. Tom Hill's acceptance message was upbeat. Dr. Gene Garrison, then pastor of El Paso's First Baptist Church, offered the dedicatory prayer for the new General Director.[7] Some instrumental music (a violin solo by Orlando Perez, Jr. and a marimba solo by Joan Kennemer) provided the effect of a brief interlude before the FMB Anniversary Commemoration part of the program began. This section included choral readings, dramatic monologues, and costumed representations of the FMB's areas of service. The program closed with a poetic challenge to action, a vocal duet by "The Sons of Thunder,"[8] and a final prayer led by Dr. Thomas W. Hill.

It all made for an unforgettable evening!

Nine days later (September 30), Frank Patterson concluded his work in the General Director's office. Tom Hill began his there the next day.

Background for the Task

The most immediate antecedent to Dr. Hill's selection as the new General Director was his half dozen years of service at the Publishing House. The Mission had requested his transfer in 1963 to be "book editor," which organizationally implied being director of the Book Department, in the Editorial Division. With the growth of the work (both at the Casa and in the Latin American countries), it was no longer feasible for Judson Blair or Frank Patterson to carry this load in addition to their other duties. And since the Publishing House was specifically seeking to supply the need for textbooks in the theological seminaries and Bible institutes, it was anxious for the "book editor" to offer to those schools good credentials that would elicit both appreciation for and participation in the textbook publication program. Tom Hill's credentials were indeed very attractive.

He was young (in his mid-thirties at the time he was invited to El Paso), well educated (a graduate of Furman University, in Greenville, South Carolina, and of the New Orleans Baptist Theological Seminary, including his Th.D.[9]), and experienced in theological education. Though appointed to do theological education in Venezuela, circumstances had redirected him and Connie to Costa Rica, following their language school year of 1957. Indeed while in Costa Rica from 1958 to 1964, both Tom and Connie had taught in the young but growing Baptist seminary functioning there.

The Mission's request for the Hills' transfer had won approval from Foreign Mission Board authorities, and the family of four arrived in El Paso in August of 1964. The publications work was new for Tom, but he learned fast. Tom and Connie "won friends and influenced people" during their early years in El Paso. Tom's work was well recognized by Publishing House staff. And his belief in and commitment to the publications ministry was unquestioned.[10]

Thus these six years of service in El Paso were the most immediate antecedent of Hill's selection as the new General Director, but behind them lay other years of study, experience, and dedication to the missionary cause of Jesus Christ.

Tom was born to very godly parents, Thomas R. and Pearl Huggins Hill, in Lamar, South Carolina, on December 10, 1928. Lamar is the county seat of Darlington County and located about fifty miles east of Columbia, the state's capital city. Its population of some 2,000 made it typical of small town America, closely tied to agriculture, as the predominant regional industry. Thomas R. was a farmer, a business man, and a respected leader in town; a deacon and a Sunday School teacher in the local Baptist church. Though confessedly "not a politician," the town elected him its mayor for sixteen years! A man of strict Christian ethic, Thomas R. set a behavioral example for his son hard to equal. "I never knew a preacher or another layman who was a better Christian than my father," Thomas W. still asserts.[11]   Pearl Huggins Hill was also a dedicated Christian. She directed the Cradle Roll ministry of their local church for thirty years! Thomas W. confesses that one of his earliest memories in life is of his mother singing the Christmas carol, "Away in a Manger." Her influence and her teaching led Tom to open his heart to Jesus as Savior even before he did so publicly at church. The public confession of Christ did occur, followed by his baptism as a believer, when Tom was about nine years of age. But, surprising as it may seem, God was already at work in Tom's heart and mind to interest him in a career in ministry.

The living example of his pastor (Rev. M. O. Owens, Sr.) who had a son entering the Christian ministry (M. O. Owens, Jr., later a long term pastor in North Carolina) made its mark in Tom's mind. One day he borrowed his grandfather's pocket knife, found a piece of scrap lumber, and carved (prophetically) his name as "Rev. Thomas W. Hill."[12]   And this was before his baptism! Indeed God does work in marvelous ways his wonders to perform.

Though initially Tom had not liked school, his childhood interest in the Christian ministry became a specific call from God and motivated him to conquer his natural timidity ("In Training Union, I gave a part"—his first public speaking) and to accept the challenge of post high school studies. He left home to study at North Greenville Junior College,[13] subsequently transferred to Furman, also located in Greenville, and was graduated in 1949 with a major in history. A philosophy professor at Furman, Dr. A. E. Tibbs, had earlier taught at the Baptist Seminary in New Orleans. He suggested to Tom that he do his theological studies in New Orleans, and that was precisely what happened.

During his Furman years, Tom did some work in mission Vacation Bible Schools in different parts of the state of South Carolina. This was his initiation into "missions work," but his specific call to foreign mission service came during the seminary years. It occurred on a Missions Day, when the featured speaker in chapel was Dr. Everett Gill, Jr., then serving as Secretary for Latin America, of the Foreign Mission Board, SBC. "I offered myself for missionary service that day," Tom recalls.[14] And in the providence of God, his field turned out to be Latin America. Dr. Gill did not live to see the Hills' appointment in October 1956; but when that happened, he probably smiled down from heaven.

New Orleans Seminary was important for Tom in other ways apart from his academic preparation; it was there he met Cornice Winter who became his wife and life partner in ministry. Connie was a native of Mississippi. She had been born near Grenada, Mississippi, to a couple that represented blended backgrounds. William Wyatt Winter (Connie's father) was of both German and Choctaw descent, and her mother, Lela Wilson Winter, was of Scotch/Irish descent. With these interesting ethnic strains, it is little wonder that Connie felt "I've come home" when in 1990 she and Tom went to Germany to give pastoral leadership to the Bethel International Baptist Church, in Frankfort, for some five years. They discovered that the family name "Winter" is quite prominent in Germany as well as in the Netherlands and in Scandinavia. William Winter, of Grenada, Mississippi, was a violinist and had his own band. He often entertained his family with his instrument. Sometimes the children were put to bed with the violin strains of "Pop Goes the Weasel!" William's rendition always included making one of the strings go "Pop!" Delighted children then embarked for dreamland.

Though not practicing Christians, William and Lela lived within walking distance of the Hardy Baptist Church, near Grenada, and they offered no objections when Cornice began attending church there. She was attracted by a good number of older children and younger youth that she knew at school. At the age of eleven, she made a public confession of faith in Christ and was baptized into the fellowship of the Hardy church. Church youth activities during her teenage years included Sunday School and Training Union, and also participation in the Young People's Speaking Contest, a national competition among Baptist youth. Participation in the contest at the state level did not produce a blue ribbon, but second place did serve to encourage Connie in her search for God's direction in her life. She says, "I always wanted to be a teacher,"[15] perhaps with a specialty in religious education for elementary age children. During her high school years, in Grenada, two different teachers counseled her to go to Mississippi College, a Baptist school in Clinton, a suburb of Jackson (the state's capital). In God's providence, it worked out for this to happen. She majored in Modern Foreign Languages, but got a teacher's certificate in Elementary Education, and managed a minor in Library Science!

During her college years, she had the opportunity of attending a Foreign Missions Conference at Ridgecrest Baptist Assembly, in North Carolina. Among the speakers of the week, Connie gave special attention to Mrs. Ellen Dozier, a missionary to Japan. With missions interest having been triggered in this way, Connie wrote a term paper for an English class, back at college, on "Japan as a Mission Field for Baptists."

Following college graduation, Cornice accepted a teaching position in the Natchez, Mississippi public schools. "Teaching got in my blood, and I loved it," Connie (still the teacher) yet declares.[16] Nevertheless the feeling lingered that God had something else for her, perhaps a role in "religious elementary education," perhaps in missions—in Japan, or elsewhere. Additional study at the New Orleans Baptist Theological Seminary might help to get clearer directions from the Lord. She tendered her resignation in Natchez and planned to go the seminary. Her school superintendent, a devout Christian himself, was reluctant to see her take this step. "You don't fit the mold of a missionary," the school official commented. Finally, he said to Connie, "Go, but if things don't work out, call me; I'll make a place for you back here." It was with that "reserve plan," then, that she went.

Her first impressions of Seminary were not too positive. "I probably won't stay but one semester," she may have thought. She was encouraged to continue by Dr. Eugene Patterson of the faculty. Then she chanced to meet Thomas W. Hill, from South Carolina. Tom was still unmarried and had attracted the attention of more than one of the single female students, who in addition to finishing their education were hoping to find a life partner. Tom was already doing graduate work and had changed the focus of his studies after that "call to missions" when Dr. Gill was the chapel speaker. Friendship blossomed into romance, and Thomas W. Hill and Cornice Winter were married at the Woolmarket Baptist Church (where Tom was pastor), on May 25, 1954.

Tom, who had begun his preaching and pastoral ministry while still a student at Furman, [17] continued such during his New Orleans years. From 1953 to 1956 he was pastor of the Woolmarket Baptist Church near Biloxi, Mississippi. During these same years he was completing his graduate studies at the Seminary in New Orleans, where the dissertation topic had to do with specific training for service in overseas situations. Connie helped him tabulate replies from a questionnaire instrument he used with missionaries, particularly in Latin America. One week, three replies came from missionaries in Venezuela. Each one, but without contact or consultation among themselves, suggested Tom and Connie seek appointment for Venezuela and lead a program of theological education. God seemed to use this idea, and they did indeed seek appointment from the Foreign Mission Board. An opportunity came to go to Africa with an independent though very evangelical mission effort. The invitation was appreciated but not accepted.

In effect, 1956 brought three major events: the birth of their first child,[18] the successful conclusion of Tom's graduate studies,[19] and their appointment for missionary service—to Venezuela![20]

Yes, the background for service as General Director of the Casa Bautista was there. Now the opportunity came, and with God's help, the new General Director would deliver.

Visions for the Remaining Years of the 20th Century

The events of May probably took Tom Hill by surprise; but by October 1, when he actually began to function as General Director, there had been time for prayer and reflection to the point of allowing Dr. Hill's dreams and visions for the Publishing House during the remaining years of the twentieth century to begin to take shape. Input from the International Consultative Committee, which met during the same week he was officially installed, undoubtedly made some contribution. One of Tom's early projects as General Director was to have a personal conference with each Publishing House staff member, no matter what their rank. Very likely some helpful ideas were gleaned from this interchange.

Other sources existed: prayer, personal observation and study, suggestions from missionaries and mission administrators, and requests from individuals and organizations in the various Hispanic countries. Gradually his dreams jelled into these nine areas (now listed and briefly explained):

(1) *Emphasis on publishing materials that were originally written in Spanish, more than on translations.* In retrospect, this may have been "good missions and poor business," but it loomed as legitimate strategy for reinforcing the efforts to make Baptist life in Latin America an authentic and indigenous expression of Christ's presence and not merely a transplant or reflection.

(2) *More commensurate recognition and remuneration for authors creating materials in Spanish.* In the years following the Great Depression and World War II, the Casa had made some progress in recognizing and remunerating national authors. But it was still mainly symbolic. Even gifted and prolific national authors like Arnoldo Canclini, of Buenos Aires, found it next to impossible to make a career of free lance Christian writing in Spanish. Tom determined the Casa should do better by national authors.

(3) *A more specific effort to address contemporary issues in the Hispanic world context, always from a careful evangelical and Biblical perspective.* This was part of Hill's philosophy that CBP should be on the cutting edge of bearing a broader witness to the whole Hispanic world. He felt that the time was ripe for evangelical Christians in Latin America and Spain to speak relevant words to issues that earlier hadn't even existed. And since the Hispanic world represented such a young population, he took special interest in materials that targeted youth, especially students—tomorrow's leaders in formation. *Ancla* magazine–and the whole thrust of the Student Materials Department, under the direction of Ann Marie Swenson–got Hill's full support.

(4) The creation of a series of Bible commentaries, written in Spanish. They would be designed to provide for the Spanish-speaking world practicality and exegetical richness comparable to what the Barclay commentaries had done for the English-speaking world. Without knowing it, here Tom connected with an unrealized dream of J. E. Davis.[21] Unfortunately, the dream was still on the drawing board when Tom Hill left El Paso; but it got reincarnated a decade later as a series to be known as the *Comentario Bíblico Mundo Hispano*. Of the twenty-four volumes projected, at this writing fourteen are in print. By the centennial year (2005), the project should be further along toward completion. Tom Hill will be happy![22]

(5) An increase in the publication and distribution by CBP of the Holy Scriptures. In his book *Rivers of Ink,* Hill recognized that "there is an explosion of Bible publication in Spanish."[23] He wanted the Publishing House to be "in the forefront of this explosion," for "gospel witness through Bible publication and distribution is at the heart of the missionary task..."[24] During Dr. Hill's tenure as General Director, new printings were made of the soulwinner's New Testament that Dr. Patterson had designed,[25] arrangements were concluded with the Lockman Foundation for CBP distribution of the *Biblia de las Américas,*[26] and decisions were made that would lead to Casa's first publication of complete Bibles.

(6) Major attention to the development of a new Baptist hymnal and to the publication of indigenous Latin American Christian music. With the coming of Dr. and Mrs. Ed Nelson,[27] Tom was able to see considerable progress toward the realization of this dream, though its complete fruition came to pass during the administration of his successor, Aldo Broda. The publication of "indigenous Latin American Christian music" was addressed and partially accomplished, but such is, of course, an ongoing task.

(7) An increase in the publication and distribution of what Hill called "marketable Christian products" that did not fit regular book or magazine formats. N. H. Eudaly supported this thrust, and sometimes synthesized the rationale by saying, "Specialty products have ministry, attract customers, and produce income." Hill encouraged viable development of calendars, greeting cards, plaques, and specialty booklets that sometimes involved international partnerships coordinated by Angus Hudson in London.

(8) Penetration of "the secular market" with Christian materials. Great hopes were pinned on "an outreach magazine entitled *Respuesta* (Answer)... the first effort at evangelization through secular channels. Designed to be sold on the newsstands, *Respuesta* has been sold experimentally in certain magazine racks... and is widely used by evangelical Christians in door-to-door visitation. It is also placed in waiting rooms of medical and other professional offices. Its sale by individual church members sometimes brings spectacular results."[28] Hill recognized that "the vast potential of *Respuesta*" to some extent depended on its becoming a monthly publication, instead of a quarterly one, and that it needed "a broad base of advertising and distribution." Further, he lamented that "these requirements demand financial resources not presently available to the Publishing House."[29] Though the magazine was published for 30 years and undoubtedly was used by God to achieve much good,[30] the really adequate resources for its massive distribution never became available, and it was discontinued after 1994. Some book products targeted "the secular market," but with only limited success.

(9) Entrance into the publication of Christian and missionary materials in languages other than Spanish. Hill's vision was that of converting an "all-Spanish publishing house" into a "multilingual" venture. He saw limited advance in this direction. A "Multilingual non-Spanish Department" was established within the Editorial Division. Missionaries Weldon and Joyce Viertel were assigned to the Publishing House to develop, for primary usage in the Caribbean, "theological study books designed for guided individual and group study."[31] Though originally written in English, French translations were projected. The House actually printed some booklets in Dutch for use in Surinam. "Armed," as it was in the early 1970s, "with the latest electronic typesetting and printing equipment," Hill felt that the Publishing House was "in a position to extend its ministry as needed in the preparation, printing, and distribution of materials in other languages."[32] With characteristic optimism and faith, Thomas W. Hill was sure that without forgetting or forsaking its rich history of service, the Publishing House's "greatest hour" lay ahead.

Major Developments and Issues of the Era

In Hill's memory, some of these "developments and issues" that appeared on the scene (generally uninvited) were positive in their impact toward reaching his goals and dreams for the Publishing House; others were decidedly negative. But all were factors to be dealt with. This is Tom's list, with very brief commentary.

(1) The emergence of competitive evangelical Spanish publishers. Earlier CBP had enjoyed a dominant position among evangelicals as publisher (in Spanish) of both doctrinally sound curriculum materials and a variety of books. Alternative sources barely existed. Suddenly, it seemed a plethora of publishers entered the field. Some were tied to denominations (like Editorial Vida, to the Assemblies of God; and Casa Nazarena, to Nazarene churches) but others like Moody Press, Editorial Caribe, Logoi, and CLIE, from Spain, sought clientele irrespective of denominational lines. While fraternal gatherings and organizations gave opportunity for friendly contact, day to day operations brought a competition that became fierce. CBP struggled to adapt to this environment.

(2) The aggressive steps taken by the Baptist Sunday School Board to become a major publisher and distributor of Spanish materials. As early as during Dr. Davis' years in Mexico, the appeal was made for the Baptist

Sunday School Board to help the Publishing House minister in Spanish. Help, largely in the form of gratis permission for translations and access to the International Sunday School Lessons outlines, was received during the Davis and Patterson years. But during the decade of the 1960s, pressure built (from both Home Mission Board personnel and leaders in states with considerable Hispanic populations) that the Sunday School Board itself provide materials more denominationally specific to Spanish-speaking Southern Baptists. An early result was *Fe Bautista*, a Spanish Training Union quarterly that was produced by CBP for the Sunday School Board, according to agreed upon specifications. The pressure continued to build and eventually impacted dramatically the administrations of Aldo Broda and Bob Tucker.[33]

(3) Liberation theology. Earlier it seemed that evangelicals had the pertinent message for the poor and marginalized segments of Latin American population. Liberation theology appeared on the scene from Roman Catholic clerics and theologians, and seemed to upstage the gospel as offered by evangelicals. Essentially it caught evangelicals off guard and obliged them to rethink their theology and the pertinency of their message for the poor and marginalized. CBP also was essentially caught off guard and only later got help from thinkers like missionary Bob E. Compton and nationals like Abdías Mora and Roberto Gama.[34]

(4) The dramatic growth of Spanish-speaking evangelicals and the "broader markets" this growth brought. To some extent it was this growth that gave viability to all the new publishers that emerged. But since Pentecostals, not Baptists, were at the vanguard of this growth, the consequences for a Baptist house like CBP were not the most desirable.

(5) Changing product demands. One dimension of these changes had to do with product attractiveness. One might have assumed that Latin American evangelical book and magazine buyers would pay more attention to the content than the cover; but such was not always the case. The truism had been expressed by McLuhan: "The package is the product." Casa always seemed to be playing catch-up in the packing of its products. Apart from attractiveness, the growing Pentecostal majority among Latin American evangelicals sought products compatible with their approaches and traditions,[35] some of which were problematic for a publishing house linked with Baptists.

(6) Long-range planning techniques with their organizational implications. Planning was an administrative function fully recognized by Dr. Hill and other leaders at CBP. But the How of planning often remained puzzling or enigmatic.[36] A thorough but complicated planning technique that had been developed by Dr. W. L. Howse and his staff at the Baptist Sunday School Board attracted the attention of Area Director Charles Bryan and his Associate, Dr. Clark Scanlon. Under their direction it was strongly recommended, almost made mandatory, to the Missions and missionary institutions of Middle America and the Caribbean. When Dr. Howse retired from BSSB, his services were contracted by Dr. Bryan, and El Paso became his base for consultatory services to the region. Both the El Paso Mission and the Publishing House (as an institution) learned how to use this planning approach. Such had not necessarily been on Tom Hill's agenda; it became another "development and issue" to be sized and tailored as much as possible to CBP. In the long run, it helped him accomplish his goals for the Casa.[37] The organizational implications that came with this technique brought the most thorough reorganization of the Publishing House since the realignments of 1958-60.[38] For the Mission, it brought the end to its function as governing body for the Casa and the initiation of a Board of Trustees, none of whose members would be Publishing House staff.

Personnel Changes during the Tom Hill Years

Among the major personnel changes that occurred during the years Dr. Thomas W. Hill was the Casa's General Director are the following:

New missionaries that came (the list is alphabetical by surname; the year of arrival in El Paso is given in parenthesis):

Dan and Betty Alice Carroll (1973). Dan and Betty Alice came with twenty years of missionary experience in Argentina and in Jamaica. In Argentina, both had taught in the International Baptist Theological Seminary, in Buenos Aires; and in Jamaica, they had fostered education work in the churches. In El Paso, Dr. Carroll[39] would serve especially in the areas of planning, related to the General Director's office; and Betty Alice would use her theological training to contribute as an editor of theological materials and in the editing of English language materials, aimed especially for the Caribbean. They served with the Publishing House until retirement in 1989. They have made their retirement home in Waco, Texas, though they are natives of West Virginia and North Carolina, respectively.

Walton and Lorena Chambless (1973). These "Southeasterners" (Walton was a native of Georgia; Lorena, of Florida) came with the attractive background of business and mission administration, both in the United States and in Mexico. Walton also had served a two year stint in the U. S. Marine Corps. Their work in Mexico, where Walton had been the Mexico Mission's business manager, had spanned a decade; and though they had resigned in 1972, they were reappointed in 1973 for work with the Publishing House, where Walton directed the

Distribution Division. Lorena, a talented artist, served in the Art Department at the Publishing House, among other things, designing a number of book covers. In 1977 they were transferred to Chile, where for a number of years they were active in the literature ministry in that country.

Jimmy and Sussie Hartfield (1975). The Hartfields were another couple that brought to their work at the Publishing House field experience in the Republic of Mexico. Both were natives of Mississippi; both had done their college work at Mississippi College (as had Connie Hill); and their seminary training at New Orleans Baptist Theological Seminary (as had both Tom and Connie Hill). Their appointment by the Foreign Mission Board had come in 1960 and their language study in Costa Rica, during 1961-62. Once in Mexico, Jimmy worked with the national Baptist convention in the promotion of religious education among other tasks. This work occupied them in the capital (Mexico City), or in Guadalajara, or in Querétaro. Upon transfer to El Paso, Jim served as director of the Product Development Division. Health problems brought a change in their assignment in mid-1979.

Lewis and Jo Lee (1971). These Texas natives (like Polly Patterson, of earlier years[40]) agreed to become "foreign missionaries in El Paso." Lewis, a native of Dallas, had been educated at Baylor University and Southwestern Baptist Theological Seminary in Fort Worth. Jo began her college work at Howard Payne College in Brownwood, Texas, near her home town of Anna, and taught school during their years of pastoral service in Goodlettsville, Tennessee. Missionary appointment for this couple came in 1960, and they overlapped in language school with the Hartfields in 1960-61. Their field of missionary service was Peru, where Lewis directed the Baptist Bible Institute, in Trujillo, beginning in 1967. Earlier they had done evangelistic work in Chiclayo and in Lima. While on furlough in 1970, Lewis advanced toward his Doctor's Degree in Religious Education at Southwestern Seminary. The couple was invited to El Paso for Lewis to direct the Sunday School (e.g., Bible teaching) Department. It seemed to fit perfectly with the studies he was just completing.

Weldon and Joyce Viertel (1972). This couple was mentioned in relation to Dr. Hill's desire to lead the Publishing House into "multilingual work." Weldon and Joyce were first appointed missionaries of the Foreign Mission Board in 1959. Their field was the Bahamas, where both were involved in theological education and religious education promotion. Though they resigned (in good part, for Weldon to pursue Ph.D. studies at Baylor University) in 1968, they were reappointed in 1970 for service in Barbados. In 1972, they were assigned to work at the Publishing House in El Paso, preparing materials that would be used in Barbados and other locations (first in the Caribbean, then elsewhere) for training pastors and other congregational leaders.[41] Following their years in El Paso, they served in similar materials preparations in the Philippines. Later they had a similar assignment for preparation of materials to be used in the Middle East, during which time they made their residence in Cyprus. In active retirement, they are still writing and active in ministry from their home in Tyler, Texas.

Major employee changes:

A. D. Lagrone. A. D. was a native of Central Texas and at some point had been a member of a church pastored by Matthew Sanderford.[42] The Sanderfords and the Lagrones had kept in some contact, though life's ventures had led the Lagrones to Boise, Idaho, where A.D. was employed as a commercial pressman. When the need arose to increase production in El Paso by way of a partial night shift, Sanderford recommended contact with Lagrone. Though possibilities of missionary appointment were explored, he came as an employee to be a press-man—and worked ten years there! The good Lord led him and his wife Ruth into a children's home ministry for some three years, but he returned in 1985 as Director of the Pre-Press Department—and worked a dozen years there! He served for a total of twenty-two years prior to his retirement toward the end of May, 1997. He was another colleague who merits the accolade: "Well done, good and faithful..."

Federico Mariotti was from one of the many Italian families who migrated from Italy to Argentina after World War I. He grew up in a Buenos Aires neighborhood and responded to the gospel in an open air service conducted by the Constitución Baptist Church whose pastor was a Spanish emigré (and ex Roman Catholic priest) José María Rodríguez. Mariotti became active in his church and in Argentine convention circles. He remained so until the decision he and his wife Cecilia made to follow their daughter (also named Cecilia) to the United States. Eventually they settled in El Paso, and he—already semi-retired—renewed his acquaintance with Judson Blair at CBP and inquired if part time work might be available. Though primarily a businessman in Argentina, he was an avid reader, a self-made "literato" (man of letters[43]), and a sometime translator for the Junta Bautista de Publicaciones (Baptist Publications Board) in Buenos Aires.[44] Judson hired him, and for some five years he was Poe's "right hand man" in the Book Department. "He was definitely an asset to our ministry," asserts his former boss.

Josie and Fred Smith. Names sometimes give instant (and correct) identification; sometimes they don't. By name one would hardly identify Bernardo O'Higgins as the important figure he was in Chile's struggle for independence; nor would José Antonio Navarro likely be chosen as the name of a cohort of

David Crockett and Sam Houston in Texas' battle for independence from Mexico. And "Mr. and Mrs. Fred Smith" might not be quickly identified as an Argentine couple who began a long association with Casa Bautista in the mid-1970s. But life is full of such surprises! Fred came from British stock; and Josie was the daughter of missionaries Tom and Lou Ellen Hawkins who gave a long career of missionary service in Argentina, dating from 1921 to 1962. Providential circumstances brought this "long distance move," with Josie coming in 1973 and Fred the following year. Josie first worked in the Art Department, but became secretary to the General Director in 1974. After some five years in that post, she was named director of the Publicity Department and worked there essentially another ten years. And all the while she carried a variety of editorial responsibilities with missionary magazines or the outreach piece *Respuesta*. Even in retirement, Josie has been a constant resource person for free lance editorial or translation work. Fred began his work in June of 1974 in the Shipping Department and served for some 17 years as director of that department, finally retiring in 1993. The Smiths have made their retirement home in El Paso.

Abdías Mora was a Chilean who came from a Baptist family in rural south Chile, but who was able to get a good education at the Colegio Bautista in Temuco, and at the Baptist Seminary in Santiago. But educational aspirations led him to immigrate to the United States where he studied at the Baptist Institute in San Antonio, Texas, and subsequently at Southwestern Baptist Theological Seminary in Fort Worth. There he completed the Bachelor of Divinity degree and later did doctoral studies at Brite Divinity School of Texas Christian University, also in Fort Worth. After seminary studies, he accepted the pastorate of a Hispanic congregation in Artesia, New Mexico. It was from Artesia that he came to El Paso as an Associate in the Book Department, in 1975. In 1976, he accepted an invitation of the school in San Antonio to return there as a professor, with speciality in the area of theology. His time at CBP was limited, but while there he and Poe gave good "Chilean leadership" to the department.

Norma Cayetano Armengol. In 1968, while the Book Department was under the direction of Dr. Thomas W. Hill, a need presented itself which was addressed by a project employment of a UTEP student who was from a family already related to the Publishing House. Mrs. Evangelina Cayetano and her family had been good friends of Viola Campbell in Torreón. When the family came to El Paso, they related to the Publishing House, and Mrs. Cayetano worked there briefly. One daughter, Maria Luisa, became a regular employee of the Casa and has already been presented.[45] A younger daughter, Norma, graduated from high school in May 1967 and began her college studies at the University of Texas at El Paso that fall. Petite of stature but tall on energy and other capabilities, Norma showed special talent in languages. These were the skills in which Tom Hill was interested, and in 1968 Norma performed the work Tom needed. From that, she became a part-time employee for general office tasks or to assist in editorial work in the General Church Materials Department (presided then by A. P. Pierson), the Vacation Bible School Department (presided by long term family friend Viola Campbell), or the General Book Department (presided by J. T. Poe[46]). Though her formal studies were in linguistics,[47] her skills in office administration attracted both Jim Hartfield, as a division director, and Aldo Broda as a General Director.

Married in 1970 to José Armengol, they became parents to three children, Samuel, Arturo, and Sussie. Though Norma took time out to have her family, she never really left the Publishing House. And since 1986, she has been the secretary to the General Director: Aldo Broda, Robert Tucker, Roberto García-Bordoli, Joe T. Poe, Ted O. Stanton, and Jorge Enrique Díaz. During these years, she has performed so many administrative functions and handled so many logistical arrangements, that it must be doubted if ANYONE knows more about the Publishing House than Norma Armengol! At times she has carried duties in the Public Relations Office, attached to the General Director's suite. Her tenure, her efficiency, her willingness to help, her general and specific knowledge of the Publishing House and its ministry are legendary! Her work with the Board of Trustees—making logistical preparations for their meetings, preparing the materials for their sessions, handling the issuing of Minutes, and the conservation of their records—puts Trustees, both of the Casa and of its Foundation, in Norma's debt as well. When the Casa celebrates is 100th anniversary, Norma will have been a part of more than a third of that history. She has helped to make it! (Thank you, and God bless you, Norma!)

"God Leads His Dear Children Along"

The title to this concluding section of the present chapter seems to connect with the last musical element in the triple-header program during which Tom Hill was installed as CBP's General Director. Both have to do 19th century gospel songs that reflect experiences and desires in the pilgrimage of a Christian life. At that inauguration program in September 1970, the last musical element was a duet by John Preston and Jim Van Hemert ("the Sons of Thunder"). What they sang was a P. P. Bliss gospel song entitled "Let the Lower Lights Be Burning." The words utilize the figure of trimming the lights in the Father's lighthouse to help tempest tossed sailors make it safe to heavenly shore. It was intended to reconfirm individual and institutional missionary commitment to keep on doing this, as the Foreign Mission Board had been doing for 125 years and as the Publishing House had been doing since its founding in 1905. The closing prayer of that program emphasized precisely that kind of commitment and was led by Dr. Thomas W. Hill, the Casa's just installed General Director. He stepped to the helm, at the call of his brethren, and faithfully guided the destinies of the Baptist Spanish Publishing House during six challenging years, 1970 to 1976. Some of his dreams and visions were achieved, though not all (owing, at least in good part, to the "developments and issues of the era," which he himself identified).

Then in 1976 it was time for Tom and Connie to sing, "God Leads His Dear Children Along."

Probably most colleagues assumed and would have preferred for Hill's tenure "at the helm" to last as long as Patterson's had (27 years). It didn't. Sometime during 1976, Dr. Keith Parks, at the time director of the Mission Support Division, of the Foreign Mission Board, in Richmond, invited Tom to accept the directorship of the Communications Department, a unit within Dr. Parks' supervision. After considerable heart searching and prayer, Tom and Connie felt led to accept. Their perception of God's leading was—and continues to be—summarized in this statement: "The Lord doesn't reveal things full blown, but He leads–one step at a time."[48] Our job is to follow—also step at a time.

Goodbyes were said in El Paso, with that regular bittersweet mixture of sadness at farewell and joyous anticipation of what God has awaiting. Tom and Connie were off on the next leg of their greatly blessed and highly variegated lifetime missionary pilgrimage to the whole world!

The Casa's new Board of Trustees faced its first major challenge: finding and electing a new General Director. They did not leave the House without a functioning leader. Wilson Ross was named as Interim General Director effective immediately upon Tom's departure, and he served a full year in that capacity. His quiet, patient, careful leadership for that period evokes grateful remembrance and ongoing recognition. He handled two jobs (Division Director and General Director) throughout the next twelve months. He did it gracefully, productively, and successfully. Thanks to Wilson Ross, the Casa was in good shape when the new General Director arrived.

Endnotes

1. See Chapter 3.

2. Later Dr. Dan Carroll would codify these with considerably more detail.

3. At this point obligatory retirement at 70 was still being practiced; and service past 65 required annual review.

4. See the closing section of Chapter 4 for more detail about Bryan's plan.

5. Thomas W. Hill was serving as Mission president in 1969-70.

6. The list is alphabetical, by surname.

7. Later, First Baptist Church contributed funds for a new desk chair for the General Director.

8. An epithet current at the time to refer to the impressive "James and John" duet from

El Paso's First Baptist Church: Jim (James) Van Hemert and John Preston, Ministers of Music and of Youth, respectively, at that church.

9. He was the first Publishing House staff member to do resident service in El Paso who brought an earned doctorate as he began his work there. Carroll Gillis had an earned doctorate from Southwestern Seminary, but Carroll never did resident service in El Paso. Also, while Davis and Patterson received the title during their tenure as General Director (Davis, an honorary doctorate from his alma mater William Jewell; and Patterson, an earned doctorate from Central Seminary, in Kansas City), Hill was the first General Director to bring to task an earned doctorate as he began his work.

10. In 1974, during Hill's years as General Director, he was invited to make a presentation to new FMB missionaries at Calloway Gardens, Georgia. His fifteen page presentation was titled "The Utilization of the Printed Page in World Missions." In it he not only gives his own convincing and strongly stated rationale for the printed page in world missions, but he reflects the then prevailing philosophy of the Foreign Mission Board, SBC, by quoting two of its main leaders: Baker James Cauthen and Winston Crawley. Dr. Cauthen is quoted thus: "The effectiveness of any educational process depends on several factors. Literature is one of the most important." Dr. Crawley is quoted as asserting that a Mission must do at least three things: promote the establishment of local churches, provide leadership training for nationals and assure the provision of a literature program for the people it serves. See "The Utilization of the Printed Page in World Missions," prepared by Thomas W. Hill for Southern Baptist Foreign Missionary Orientation, Calloway Gardens, Georgia, 1974; unpublished; copy made available by Hill for this CBP centennial book project.

11. Interview with Dr. and Mrs. Thomas W. Hill, done by Joe T. Poe, in Ruidoso, New Mexico, on October 25, 2003.

12. Though apparently not given great importance by the family at the time, a portion (with the words "Rev. Thomas W.") was found years later at the Hills' home in Lamar and became a treasure that now hangs in Tom and Connie's home in Ruidoso, New Mexico.

13. A small but significant Baptist school, where two other missionaries serving at the Publishing House (Roberta Ryan and Viola Campbell) had studied.

14. Interview, October 25, 2003.

15. Ibid.

16. Ibid.

17. His first pastorate was with a mission in a needy neighborhood of Laurens, South Carolina; the mission was sponsored by the Hunterscourt Baptist Church of Laurens.

18. A daughter, born in Gulfport, to whom they gave the full name of Cynthia Paige, which was shortened, even from childhood, to "Cindy." Their second daughter was born in Costa Rica. Her name is Crystal Patrice.

19. The degree was awarded by the New Orleans Seminary in July 1956. His dissertation bares the title: "A Critique of the Training of Southern Baptist Foreign Missionaries."

20. As signaled earlier, their appointment occurred in October 1956.

21. See Chapter 1.

22. Hill is the author of the exposition on Second Corinthians, in this series, which appears in Volume 20, first published in 2003.

23. Thomas W. Hill, Rivers of Ink, Nashville: Convention Press, 1977, p. 53. This was the mission study book for adults used by Southern Baptists that year in the promotion of world missions and the Lottie Moon Christmas Offering for Foreign Missions.

24. Ibid., pp. 53, 54.

25. See Chapter 4.

26. The Spanish counterpart to the New American Standard Version. During Hill's time in El Paso, only the New Testament was available in Spanish.

27. See Chapter 4.

28. Hill, Rivers, p. 50.

29. Ibid, p. 52.

30. See Hill, Rivers, pp. 51-52 for a success story from Ciudad Juárez, Mexico.

31. Ibid., p. 55.

32. Ibid.

33. See Chapters 6 and 7.

34. Efforts were made to attract both Gama and Mora to the CBP staff during Dr. Hill's administration as General Director. Though it never did work out for Dr. Gama to come on staff, Dr. Mora did serve a couple of years. See section on staff changes during Hill's years.

35. Such included, but was not limited to, the praise oriented worship format.

36. Dr. Hill brought Sid Reber, Vice-president for Management Services, from Richmond to El Paso for appropriate planning and organization consultations in 1971.

37. It provided the convincing background for making several important personnel changes and in securing various new missionaries.

38. See Chapter 4.

39. Dan's D.R.E. was from Southwestern Baptist Theological Seminary. Dan and Betty Alice met while doing undergraduate work at Carson-Newman College in Tennessee, from which both were graduated in 1949.

40. See Chapter 3.

41. Weldon finished his Ph.D. at Baylor in 1976.

42. See Chapter 4 regarding Sanderford and his coming to the Publishing House.

43. His writing skills are represented in his book El Supremo Renacimiento which the Casa published (under the Mundo Hispano imprint) in 1973.

44. One of the books he translated and which the Argentine Baptist Publications Board published was C. E. Matthews' book Every Christian's Job.

45. See chapter 4.

46. Poe particularly remembers a complicated "paste-up" and editing job that involved both Norma Armengol and Betty Alice Carroll, namely the work on a new edition of Petter's Greek concordance that was completed and published in 1976 under the title La Nueva Concordancia Greco-Española del Nuevo Testamento.

47. She was graduated from UTEP in 1971.

48. Interview, October 25, 2003.

Chapter 6

Aldo Broda Leads

The account of Aldo Broda's years as General Director of the Casa Bautista de Publicaciones must begin with the story of the Board of Trustees that named him. As indicated in the closing section of the previous chapter, it can be considered the first major decision of that Board. It put to test a new system of governance for the Baptist Spanish Publishing House. In various ways, it was the beginning of a new era.

The Board of Trustees was new and small. The first minutes are dated April 15-19, 1975 and labeled as those of a "Preliminary meeting" of the "interim trustees" of the Baptist Spanish Publishing House. The trustees present were "A. Clark Scanlon (field representative for Middle America), Don R. Kammerdiener (field representative for Eastern South America) and William W. Graves (field representative for the Caribbean)."[1] The minutes further explain: "The field representative for Spanish Western South America was named area secretary for that area in the April meeting of the Foreign Mission Board. When his successor is named, he will form a part of the Board of Trustees."[2] Dr. H. Robert Tucker was the person named to this position in July 1976, and he began to function on the Casa's Board in November of that year.

A second meeting of the "Interim Board" was held in Miami on June 10, 1975. Besides Scanlon, Kammerdiener, and Graves, two FMB Area Secretaries were on hand (Dr. Charles W. Bryan, Area Secretary for Middle America and the Caribbean, and Dr. J. Bryan Brasington, Area Secretary for Western South America) plus Dr. Thomas W. Hill, General Director of the Publishing House. Organizational and staff concerns dominated the meeting in light of planned reorganizations to be effected January 1, 1976. Other meetings of this Board were held in Panama City, Panama, August 29, 1975, and in El Paso, December 3-5, 1975. By this time, key positions for the new organization had been staffed, including V. Walton Chambless for the Distribution Division, and Jimmy J. Hartfield for the Product Development Division.[3] Progress toward internationalization of the Board was discussed. By May of the next year, when the Board met again and in El Paso, only Chile had responded to the invitation to name a trustee for the new "International Board;" other countries eventually followed suit.

With this new governance Board and using the Program Base Design as its planning technique,[4] nothing less than a complete "re-invention" of the Publishing House was being attempted. When Dr. Hill felt led to accept a Richmond position with the Foreign Mission Board in the fall of 1976, the vacancy he left gave the Board an opportunity to complete its "re-invention." At this time, the Interim Board was still functioning, now with Bob Tucker as its newest member. Fortunately, for purposes of this book, it has been possible to secure input from three of the original members of the Interim Board.[5] Dr. Don Kammerdiener, retired Executive Vice President of the International Mission Board, shared most interestingly by way of a letter. Postmarked December 4, 2003, the letter reads as follows:

"The field representatives who selected Aldo [Broda] were well aware of the significance of the decision. I went to the meeting with the desire to nominate Bill Graves. I even consulted with Dr. Means to see how he would feel. His response didn't mean too much to me at the time, but later I remembered his words. He said, 'If the group should decide to propose one of the field representatives, I would have no objection.' I later realized that he hadn't commented directly about Graves.

"It seems that others were also talking to Dr. Means. When we met...,[6] Bill said that he could not accept the post. The other three members insisted that I should accept the challenge. They indicated that Means had given his approval. I was overwhelmed at their decision and made a serious mistake. I told the group that my inclination was to accept the offer, and that I would return to Buenos Aires to discuss it with Meredith and to pray about the matter. I said that if they hadn't heard anything from me after the weekend, that I would take the position. Returning to Buenos Aires I discussed it with Meredith. Her response was that she would be happy with whatever decision I made. Within 24 hours we decided to go, and we literally started the process of cleaning out medicine cabinets. It was while I was starting that process that I felt a clear word from the Lord telling me not to go. The message I received was twofold. First He made it clear that I didn't know anything about publishing and would be a failure in the job. Then the same voice said, 'Why are you thinking about this when the person best prepared in Latin America is Aldo Broda.' He was already deeply involved in the publishing of evangelical books and knew the business inside out. Furthermore he was a man of deep spiritual convictions and of solid integrity.

"I contacted the members of the Board and refused the job. We agreed to meet again in Miami to continue the search. I felt some confirmation in the fact that none of them attempted to change my mind. Maybe they had been hearing from the Lord also. We met in

Miami and almost immediately came to the conclusion that we ought to pursue the possibility of Aldo Broda. At this point I am not certain who first proposed Aldo, but I think I was the one. The fact is that it found unanimous acceptance almost at once. Our only hesitation was the fact that the Publishing House had never had a non-missionary as director. We didn't know how the Foreign Mission Board would react. Therefore we spent a considerable amount of time in preparing to persuade Charles [Bryan].[7] We even assigned different members of the group to present [matters] to Charles. Then we called Charles and asked him to come to Miami to talk to us. We never got to persuade him. He had been listening to the same voices we had heard and had gone so far as to clear with Dr. Cauthen[8] the possibility of electing a national. Our time with him was very brief. Without any voice in opposition we agreed to contact Aldo and extend the invitation.

"The rest, as they say, is history. My conviction is that this near miss on my part was the prelude to one of the most significant roles I played during my 40 years with the Board."

Dr. A. Clark Scanlon, now retired as former missionary, mission administrator, and research consultant, wrote a more formal reply. It must be included here too:

Election of N. Aldo Broda as General Director

December 9, 1976

"The moment for naming N. Aldo Broda as General Director of the Baptist Spanish Publishing House appeared to me then as now to be God's timing—His chairos.

"A number of historical events had prepared the stage for the historic decision the Interim Trustees were about to make:
- A long and solid foundation had been laid by missionary general directors working beside Spanish American counterparts in a collegial and fraternal relationship of mutual respect and appreciation.
- The publishing house for decades had made a significant contribution to the founding of and development of Baptist work in the Spanish-speaking world. Many of its writers, friends, and distribution channels were there.
- The international Advisory Committee met periodically with publishing house personnel to evaluate materials, identify literature needs and prepare themselves for a ministry of literature evangelism.
- Many countries in Spanish America and Spain had produced

outstanding Baptist leaders both of national and international stature capable of leading international organizations.

"The recent creation of an international Board of Trustees composed of rotating representation from national Baptist conventions, missions, and regional field representatives of the Foreign Mission Board, SBC made the way easier to choose the best person for the job, whether missionary or not. The FMB area leadership had given their affirmation for the Interim Trustees to go beyond missionaries in looking for the best candidate.

A Changing of the Guard

"In the fall of 1976 Dr. Thomas W. Hill, the third general director of the publishing house had resigned to take the position of Secretary for Communications at the home office of the Foreign Mission Board in Richmond, Virginia.

"With Wilson Ross, an experienced and capable missionary as Interim General Director, the Interim Trustees, William Graves, Donald Kammerdiener, Clark Scanlon and Robert Tucker turned to the tasks of preparing for the installation of the new international Board of Trustees and to the selection of a new General Director.

"The first part of our meeting took place at the publishing house in El Paso, November 16-18. It dealt with the reports of the various division and department directors and related matters and ended. It ended by seeking their input on the qualifications for a general director and suggestions of possible candidates.

"Because of assignments of the trustees on the east coast, the second part of the meeting took place in Miami, Florida on December 9. Its main purpose was the consideration of a general director. In the past the process had been to select the best missionary available for the assignment. Among the interim trustees both William W. Graves and Donald R. Kammerdiener could have served in the post. But God moved in a different direction. Both removed themselves as candidates. Each had lived in Argentina, been part of Baptist life there and worked beside Aldo Broda. They both recommended him highly.

"Since the publishing house had exerted a profound influence on my life and missionary career in Guatemala and the rest of Middle America, I felt a keen sense of responsibility in chairing this session. Churches and conventions in Guatemala, Honduras and Costa Rica, during their founding and development, had all benefited from literature and workshops led by personnel from the Casa Bautista. I taught my first Sunday school lessons from El Expositor Bíblico, the flagship of its Bible teaching magazines. From its books and periodical literature I learned much of my religious vocabulary.

"I had known personally and counted among my friends Thomas W. Hill (the third director) and Frank W. Patterson (the second director) who had followed the founding pioneer, J. Edgar Davis.

"The climate was favorable for naming a Spanish American Baptist as the General Director of the Baptist Spanish Publishing House. Reviewing the minutes of that historic meeting I recall a number of traits that caused me and my colleagues unanimously to ask Brother N. Aldo Broda to become the fourth General Director of the Baptist Spanish Publishing House.

- He was an outstanding leader in the Christian literature ministry in Argentina. In that capacity he had been the director of the Baptist Publishing Association in Argentina. Beyond that fact, Christian literature was his passion.
- He was a committed Christian with a rich Baptist heritage. His father had been a pastor and a Bible colporteur.
- He had business acumen and financial expertise. He used this perspective to advocate stewardship both in Argentina and in many parts of Latin America.
- He had been an active member of the international Advisory Committee of the publishing house. He understood and loved its mission and ministry.

"Later, as I met his family and saw his service as General Director, my appreciation and admiration for him grew and affirmed God's wisdom in the selection."[9]

Dr. Tucker gave his "Amen" to all that Kammerdiener and Scanlon wrote, without adding more detail from his own memory.

Motion 65, of the Trustee Minutes (from the meeting held in Miami, December 9, 1976) reflects the landmark decision in simple terms: "Que la Junta invite al señor N. Aldo Broda de la Argentina para la posición de Director General de la Casa Bautista de Publicaciones." [English: That the Board invite Mr. N. Aldo Broda, of Argentina, for the position of General Director of the Casa Bautista de Publicaciones.] Further details are given in the minutes concerning how the invitation would be made, what salary and benefits would be offered, and how contractual and legal details would be handled if Aldo accepted.

The invitation was made, and Aldo (and his wife Dora) did accept. Broda recalls that the invitation arrived on his fifty-third birthday. What a present! He also confesses that in that time frame he had felt very outdone that the invitation for the Argentine Convention to name a member to CBP's "International

Board" (that would hold its first meeting in 1977) stipulated that no employee of another publishing house was eligible. This eliminated Broda, since he was director of the Argentine Baptist Publication Association (earlier called the Argentine Baptist Publications Board). Aldo had been a member of the CBP International Advisory Committee that at its meeting in El Paso, in 1974, had recommended an international governance board for the Casa. Deep down, he had aspired to be a member of that Board when it was created, then felt "ruled out" when the invitation carried the "conflict of interests" stipulation. Now, instead of being named a member of the Board, he was being asked to become General Director of the Casa! "I never forgot that lesson," he confesses.

"At first," Aldo comments further, "my wife and I didn't know what to do. [To accept] we would have to leave many years of labor in the Christian work of Argentina, leave our children, and others. Go to a country that although we had visited there was still unknown to us in many aspects. At first, our heart-answer was to say no. But then the Lord gradually convinced us, and we accepted. What an error it would have been to say no! Subsequently, during our years at the Casa, the good Lord was so near to us, His help was so evident... it would have been a crime not to accept His sovereignty, [represented in the invitation]."[10]

Elsewhere, Aldo has shared how much the publications from El Paso have meant to him and his family.

"The Casa is an entity that has been a part of my life really since my infancy; and it still is. Its materials gave orientation to my parents also—and with the passage of time, to my descendants as well. My wife had the same experience with her family.

"How did this happen? This way: I was born in 1923, and already at that date, Casa materials had influenced and were continuing to influence my family. So from my childhood years, CBP materials have impacted my life. I remember delightfully the Sunday School materials we children used, and how from them we learned to know God better as Creator and to discover His plan of salvation and redemption.

"My parents served churches with pastoral leadership, but they didn't have the opportunity to train at a seminary. Really at that time Baptists in Argentina were just beginning to try to develop a theological training school. But thanks to my parents' dedication to the Word of God and to their practical use of materials from Casa Bautista, they were able to forge their pastoral skills and to develop better their ministry. It would really be impossible to imagine my family apart from the influence on it by the Casa Bautista. Of all the CBP materials, Dora and I feel most indebted to how the Sunday School materials have helped us know the Word of God.

"Of course I must also recognize that Casa books, beyond the Sunday School materials, have helped me to know still better God's Word and also to be challenged to take my place in the Lord's work.

"My parents, my brothers, and my own immediate family have all derived inspiration and help from CBP materials. Along with myself and my wife Dora, our three daughters have imbibed the message of God, from the Bible and from the publications of CBP. Now my grand-children are drinking from the same fountain. I am, at this writing, 79 years old; and still I can be found, every Sunday, sharing a Sunday School class with others of my age group—and being helped in our study by curriculum materials from Casa Bautista.

"That which I share as personal—and family—experience, I have seen, through the years, duplicated in thousands upon thousands of believers in all parts of Hispanic America: Lives have been blessed through the help of books and materials published by Casa Bautista de Publicaciones."[11]

Baptist Spanish Publishing House could not have had a General Director more convinced of the value of its ministry. Nor one more convinced that his opportunity to lead this work had been given him by God Himself.

Goals for the Broda Years

In a communication with the book's author, Aldo has given a list of what he now remembers as the most important goals he had for the Casa during the nearly nine years he served as its leader. These are as follows, though not necessarily in order of priority or importance: 1. To develop and take full advantage of the knowledge and capacities of the administrative staff. 2. To provide for all personnel better equipment to do their work. 3. To increase sales. 4. To improve interpersonal relations. 5. To build a new building in response to the ministry's needs and to update the older building. 6. To improve relations with entities such as the Foreign Mission Board and the Sunday School Board, both of the Southern Baptist Convention. 7. To improve salaries of CBP personnel.[12] These goals are now briefly commented and reported on.

1. To develop and take full advantage of the knowledge and capacities of the administrative staff. Aldo's personal efforts to train staff especially took the form of periodic "charlas" (talks, addresses) to administrative personnel. The Publishing House library contains sound recordings on at least three of these.[13]

2. To provide better equipment for all personnel to do their work. Broda fully recognized that productivity is related to the equipment a worker has at his/her disposal. As long as the Publishing House continued in the printing business as well as publishing, he wanted the print shop to be "first class." Thus new printing and binding equipment were somehow acquired.[14] But apart from mechanical equipment for the Production Division, Mr. Broda wanted office workers to have the equipment that would enhance their productivity also. An incident that clearly illustrates this deals with acquisition of the first "desktop computer" for CBP staff. José Morelos had been employed to be the director of Reprints and Contract Production. Morelos, a Colombian by birth, had come straight from university studies in New Jersey and was somewhat aware of the approaching wave of personal computer equipment. He convinced his supervisor, J. T. Poe, that a desktop computer would increase his productivity. The year was 1979; and up to that point "the computer" was considered the exclusive territory of the data processing department under Matthew Sanderford. Broda listened to Poe and Morelos make the case for acquisition of a Commodore 32 for about $3,000. Undoubtedly with some reservations, Aldo nevertheless bent the rules to allow financing within available budget and gave clearance for the acquisition. In successive years, it was literally amazing the work Morelos got out of that early day desktop! Broda's decision to allow such a purchase represented his commitment to providing equipment for higher productivity.

3. To increase sales. Wilson Ross served as Interim General Director during the last months of 1976 and until Aldo Broda arrived in 1977. When he made his report to the Trustees in May 1977, he reported that 1976 sales reached a total of $897,339.95.[15] This is the floor on which Aldo Broda built. The reports for 1980 (essentially, Aldo's third year to lead), the total for "net sales" given to the Trustees was $1,950,344.72.[16] The "net sales" total reported to the Trustees for 1982 was $2,240,931.99.[17] The 1983 total dropped considerably, explained by Dr. Jesse Bryan, Director of the Distribution Division, as the result of economic circumstances in Latin America and the new arrangement for distribution in the United States by way of the Sunday School Board, SBC.[18] 1984 totals dropped again though very slightly,[19] but the 1985 total almost got back to the two million level.[20] This was Aldo's last year to have the full leadership role. Nevertheless 1986, year of the "co-regency" or "shared leadership" between Broda and Bob Tucker, produced a surprising rebound with total net sales slightly exceeding $2,500,000.[21] To say the least, Aldo's years of leadership did see substantial growth in sales.

4. To improve interpersonal relations. Aldo Broda made no claim to be an industrial psychologist, but he was concerned with interpersonal relations within staff. On January 25, 1979, Aldo gave an address to CBP personnel which he specifically called a "Charla sobre Relaciones Humanas" (A Talk about Human Relations). And he gave it the subtitle: "La Gente Es Importante" (People Are Important). It was the second in a series of talks that expressed his philosophy for a Christian enterprise like CBP. In the presentation, Mr. Broda emphasized that besides the assets an enterprise can report on its balance sheet, both its history of service and its "human capital" represent other assets that must be cared for. His philosophy essentially emerged from the Golden Rule, which he quoted from Matthew 7:12, to which he added appropriate Proverbs (like 15:1; 15:18; 15:32; 16:28; 18:19; and 18:24). He offered ten practical guidelines for applying these Biblical concepts to "our workplace." A third section of the "charla" contained extracts from three important articles on the art of administration and the importance of human relations. The General Director concluded with an appeal for good interpersonal relations to be one of the Casa's hallmarks.[22]

5. To build a new building in response to the ministry's needs and to update the older building. This goal may not have been absolutely new, but it quickly took on new life during Aldo's years of leadership. The need was both psychological and practical. The psychological or symbolic dimension in good part related to the prolongation of Alabama Street which dissected the Publishing House property on the west side. Opened in early 1961, it gave the House a new street address: 7000 Alabama.[23] But as one entered the Publishing House campus from Alabama, it was hard to find "the front entrance." The building seemed to have no "front," certainly not on the Alabama side! It needed a better image, and on its west side! The practical dimension was not absent: growth and expansion during the second half of the Patterson years, and during all the administration of Tom Hill was continuing. Even with the enclosure of patios that had occurred during Dr. Patterson's time,[24] staff and attendant operations (warehousing, shipping, etc.) had grown to utilize all available space in the facility. And continued growth was assumed! The goal of a new building seemed totally appropriate.

6. To improve relations with entities such as the Foreign Mission Board and the Sunday School Board, both of the Southern Baptist Convention. Aldo's heart—as big as Argentina—and his love for and loyalty to the Baptist family clearly show in his expression of this goal. And he was an excellent ambassador for the Casa Bautista de Publicaciones. But it was much easier for him to deal with the Foreign Mission Board than the Sunday School Board. It had to do with language. To this day he feels his major problem lay in failing to learn English adequately. "It was a tremendous mistake," he comments. In hindsight, he says that before assuming the job in El Paso, he (and Dora) should have been given some time to learn fully the English language. "We asked for it," he says, "but because of the urgency to take over the leadership role, it was not allowed."[25] In his relationships with the Foreign Mission Board, Broda could generally find a Spanish-speaking administrator (like Kammerdiener, or Scanlon, or Graves), and deal with them. But in negotiations with representatives of the Baptist Sunday School Board, this was much more difficult. A specific incident has lodged in Aldo's mind concerning one of the tough negotiating sessions, in El Paso, with representatives of the Sunday

School Board (and Foreign Mission Board). After some tense exchanges, Broda sought out Dr. Morton Rose, one of the SSB reps, at a break moment, and asked him (perhaps just making polite conversation—and probably in broken English) concerning Rose's family background. Dr. Rose told Mr. Broda that he was of Italian extraction. Broda says he then commented to Morton: "So that's why you are so hard headed! You come from the same stock as I do!"[26] Aldo's perception was that the two "hard headed 'Italians'" found common ground—ethnically if not linguistically, and promptly produced a solution for their disagreement. Broda remembers: "That very afternoon we signed an agreement."[27]

7. To improve salaries of CBP personnel. Aldo's goal responded both to his innate Christian generosity and to his high standards of fairness. His efforts to accomplish this goal are easy to document: During his some nine years as General Director, modifications to the Casa's wage and salary scale were presented at least ten times to the Trustees for approval, almost always upward.[28] The context of the modifications, to be sure, was a period of relatively high inflation (and high interest rates) in the United States. These factors may have puzzled Broda, since they were still amazingly low by Argentine standards. His quip to the author one day has lingered in the mind: "I wonder if I can manage in a non-inflationary economy." Admittedly it was a new experience–and a challenging one.

Accomplishments during the Broda Years

Aldo's list of memorable accomplishments has four matters that can easily be recognized as important happenings. (The other four items on his list turn out to be more impressions than events or tasks accomplished.[29]) Among the achievements that stand out in Aldo's memory are these: 1. The celebration of the Casa's 75th Anniversary (in 1980). 2. The publication of the RVA Spanish Bible. 3. The building and inauguration of a new 30,000 square feet building. 4. The arrangement with the Baptist Sunday School Board to distribute CBP products in the United States.

These "victories" now warrant brief comment:

1. The celebration of the Casa's 75th Anniversary (in 1980). If the 50th Anniversary had been slightly underplayed,[30] such was definitely not the case for the 75th. The Diamond Jubilee was celebrated in good style. For one thing, a whole graded series of books was published to help individuals and churches participate in the celebration.[31] Aldo reported that concluding the celebration, which had been in its planning stages since before his coming to El Paso, brought a certain sense of relief—mixed, to be sure, with satisfaction that the Casa had arrived to this point in its history and that growth and expansion were continuing to come at an almost dizzying pace. The Anniversary festivities reached their climax during the fall Trustee Meeting, November 17-24 and included a special Thanksgiving Service on Friday, November 21, held in El Paso's First Baptist Church.[32] Earlier the same day, a new printing press and new bindery equipment were dedicated; and a ground-breaking ceremony was conducted for the new office building. Historical exhibits and contemporary displays were set up, and over 500 visitors came for Open House hours held on Friday, Saturday, and Sunday afternoon. Denominational periodicals, like *Luminar Bautista*, in Venezuela, and *The Commission*, in the United States, carried ample reports and informative articles.[33] Aldo's simple statement to the Trustees, in his report, must be understood as celebratory understatement: "We give thanks to God for what we were able to achieve."[34] It had indeed been a very special year!

2. The publication of the RVA Spanish Bible. The Casa's reentry into Scripture publication has been touched on in the chapters related to Frank Patterson's and Tom Hill's administrations.[35] Bible publication was a topic dealt with by even the Interim Board of Trustees.[36] In fact the notion of the Casa's doing its own revision of the Reina-Valera Bible in Spanish was born in a Trustee meeting. The publication of the *Biblia de Estudio Mundo Hispano* was achieved in late 1977, using the RVR-1960 Bible text, with contractual permission from the United Bible Societies.[37] But a variety of factors continued to encourage the idea of a proprietary revision of the Spanish Bible that would give CBP completely free access to a contemporary version of the Scriptures. These factors came together in early 1979 and led to a contract with Moisés Chávez[38] and a missionary transfer for Dr. Cecil McConnell (and wife Mary).[39] Chávez did his basic work from Boston, where he was pursuing advanced Biblical studies; the McConnells arrived in El Paso in late 1980, and began what turned out to be almost a decade of full time work on a new Bible revision, to be known as the Reina-Valera Actualizada. A Gospel of John was published in 1982. Aldo Broda came to feel additional input was needed for the project; and he and Poe worked to enlist a core team of special editors for the New Testament and Old Testament.[40] The New Testament was completed and published in 1986 (Aldo's last year in El Paso);[41] the full Bible finally appeared and was officially launched in May 1989.[42] Aldo correctly remembers the project as belonging to his years as General Director.

3. The building and inauguration of a new building. As indicated in the paragraph on the 75th Anniversary, the groundbreaking for the new office building was held on Friday afternoon, November 21, 1980. Construction of a two story building, containing about 30,000 square feet, was begun the following year. As the *El Paso Herald-Post* reported in an article published on December 4, 1982, the addition contained about seventy-five offices, three conference rooms, and a library.[43] (Perhaps the "chapel" was considered a "conference room" for purposes of the newspaper article.) The building was dedicated in special activities on Friday, December 3, 1982, with the unveiling of plaques installed in the reception area, a dedication service held in the new chapel,[44] and guided tours of the new facilities. On Sunday afternoon, December 5, an additional special ceremony was held to dedicate the new electronic organ, placed in the chapel at the generosity of Dr. Burton Patterson. A concert was given by Mr. David Palací, an Argentine organist—resident in Miami—and a close friend of Aldo Broda. Though at one point it had been assumed the building might have to be constructed in two stages if all financing did not fall in place, monies became available from various sources, and the approximate cost of $950,000 was paid as construction progressed, with no debt accruing after the building was finished.[45] Subsequently the older building underwent considerable refurbishing so that staff housed in that facility would not feel "second class."[46] Aldo's goal, in this respect, was fully accomplished.

4. The arrangement with the Baptist Sunday School Board to distribute CBP products in the United States. To call this arrangement an accomplishment, or a victory, might be considered by some as a slight exaggeration. As a goal, this matter undoubtedly emerged by necessity, not by design or preference. While contact, varying degrees of relationship, and even some "partnership" between CBP and the Baptist Sunday School Board can be traced as far back as Dr. Davis,[47] what happened in the 1980s makes for a very different story. The "arrangement" Aldo refers to has to do with an agreement between these two entities that Baptist Sunday School Board would be the Casa's exclusive distributor in the United States.[48] In theory, the arrangement sounded good: The Sunday School Board, specifically through its own chain of bookstores and its trade publisher Broadman Press[49] and its Holman Bible division, had the potential to carry CBP's product line to many more users than CBP could achieve on its own. But in practice the results never satisfied either BSSB nor BSPH. Prices had to be increased to allow for another level of distribution activity, while net income to the Baptist Spanish Publishing House was seriously decreased. The mainly non-Spanish speaking sales force of Broadman and Holman were at a serious disadvantage to either interpret the products or service Spanish-speaking customers (commercial or retail). Even the "loan" of Laverne and Betty Gregory to the Sunday School Board for promotion of Spanish sales did not bring acceptable levels of circulation. The agreement did keep CBP products from completely disappearing from the USA market; but the bottom line results were not satisfactory—to either party. Eventually the agreement was annulled.

Personnel Highlights during the Broda Years

Very conceivably the Publishing House reached its zenith during the years Aldo Broda was General Director. While this complicates reporting on personnel matters during these years, efforts must be made to at least give the highlights. (To avoid interrupting the narrative flow, this chapter–in contrast to previous ones–uses endnotes to present some detail on new personnel.) Because of the recent reorganization,[50] Aldo essentially "inherited" the structure and the staff approved by the Interim Trustees in their June 1975 Meeting.

The General Director's office included two department level consultants: One for Market Research (N. Hoyt Eudaly); and one for Research and Design (Daniel M. Carroll, Jr.).

The Product Development Division had Jimmy J. Hartfield as its director. The division was subdivided into four sections, each with a section leader plus a cluster of departments.

The Evangelism and Church Growth Section was to be presided by Ananías González.[51] Its departments and directors included: Church Administration and Pastoral Leadership (Adolfo Robleto); Bible Teaching (Olivia Lerín, till 1978; Jorge Díaz,[52] 1979 onward); Church Missions (Roberta Ryan); Church Music (Edward W. Nelson); Church Training (Judson Blair); Student Work (Ann Swenson); Vacation Bible School (Viola Campbell).

The General Products Section had Joe T. Poe as its leader, though he gave most of his time as director of the Book Department. The other department in this section was that of Specialty Products and Procurement, directed by N. Hoyt Eudaly.

The Multilingual Section had Weldon E. Viertel as its leader and only later was subdivided into departments of English and French work.

The Development Services Section had Kenneth R. Evenson as its leader. Evenson also directed the Art Department. If the Evensons overlapped with the Brodas, it was very briefly, for they were transferred back to Uruguay in 1978. Dorothy Hicks Pettit then became the department director for the second time. Other departments in this Section included Editorial Services, presided over by Judson Blair and Photocomposition, directed by José Amézaga.

The Printing Division had Merle Lee as its director and was composed of two departments: Offset Printing, directed by A. D. Lagrone; and Bindery, whose director was Harry Kaplan.

The Distribution Division had V. Walton Chambless as its director. Its departments and directors included: Sales Promotion (vacant); Advertising (Laura Disselkoen); Order Processing (Jack Disselkoen); Shipping (Fred Smith[53]); Customer Accounts (Elbin Porflit).

The Management Services Division was directed by J. Wilson Ross. Its departments and directors were: Internal Services (Rubén Angulo[54]); Information Processing (Matthew Sanderford); Maintenance (Floyd Gremar[55]); Library Services (Mary Jo McMurray).

This list does not contain secretaries, editors, or other workers at below a department head rank.[56] It nevertheless shows the complexity of the Casa's organization and implies a total staff of more than a hundred.

Organizations, like living organisms, never "stay put;" they are forever changing. By 1980, Aldo's organization and staff had changed somewhat.

González's section became the Church Program and Development Division, and an Evangelism Department had been added; Roy Lyon[57] was its director. The Music Department's name had been enlarged to include "Worship;" and the Youth and Student Work Department had a new director in J. Antonio Rengifo.[58]

The other sections of the Product Development Division were amalgamated into a new unit known as the General Products and Services Division, with Joe T. Poe as director. Poe also presided over a new department responsible for Scripture publication, and José Luis Martínez[59] arrived from Spain to direct the General Books Department. Texts and Reference Works were separated from the general book line, and Cecil Thompson[60] came from Argentina to direct this department. Miguel A. Blanco[61] was contracted from his native El Salvador to be director of the Editorial Services Department. Siegfried Enge[62] had also come from Argentina to direct the Specialty Products and Audiovisual Materials Department. José Morelos was the director of a department responsible for Reprints and Contract Production.

Missionary Jesse Bryan[63] now directed the Distribution Division. Missionary Laverne Gregory[64] was director of the Sales Department; Josie Smith, of the Publicity Department; Yolanda Oseguera, of Order Processing.

In the Management Services Division, only one change occurred in department directorships: Donald E. Ivie now headed the Maintenance Department.[65]

To be sure, changes continued to happen during the additional years that Aldo Broda was General Director. By 1985,[66] the organization charts reveal more new names, functioning at the department level or above, and more changes in structure. Bob Tucker was then the Associate General Director.

Of six department directors in González's Church Program and Development Division, only two have been previously introduced. New faces include Steve Ditmore[67] (directing the Evangelism Department), Mary Jo Stewart[68] (directing the Missions Department), Charles Campbell[69] (directing the Church Administration Department), and James West[70] (directing the Christian Development Department).

Cecil Thompson was now the Director of the General Products Division.[71] The Multilingual work was led by Gayle Hogg[72] and Linda Wilson.[73]

Judson Blair functioned as the Director of the Production Division which included both development services (art, editorial services, and photo-composition) and printing (pre-press, printing, and binding). Missionary Peter Stillman[74] directed the Art Department; José Amézaga, the Photocomposition Department; and Miguel A. Blanco, the Department of Editorial Services. M. B.

"Boots" Lee directed the printing "section," with Jesús Carreón[75] and A. D. Lagrone as foremen responsible to him.

Jesse Bryan's Marketing Division had one new face also: José Morelos, who earlier had served in the General Products and Services Division, now directed the Department of Marketing Services, in this division. Other department heads continued as in 1980.[76]

The Division presided by Wilson Ross was now called that of Administrative Assistance and Finances. Two department heads who were relatively new to their jobs in 1985 were: Laura Beamer, Director of the Personnel Department (this structure was new); and Jackie Disselkoen,[77] Director of the Accounting Department.

1986 brought more personnel changes. While in the May report of the General Director to the Trustees does not mention changes or request action naming (or requesting) new personnel, a similar report to the November meeting mentions the retirement of two missionary couples (Matthew and Dora Jean Sanderford, and Charles and Bernadene Campbell). It also advises that extension of service has been granted for two other missionary couples (Judson and Dorothy Rose Blair, and Ed and Gladys Nelson). It also advises of the naming of both Rubén and Alicia Zorzoli as editors and the appointment of Wayne Quarrier as a Production Consultant. Further, P.D. Lee is to be named Director of the Computer Services Department (position held by Sanderford before his retirement) and A. D. Lagrone as Director of the Offset Department.[78]

****

1986 was also a transition year. Aldo was already beginning to work on his new assignment with the Continental Committee on Stewardship. Bob Tucker, whom Aldo had brought as Associate General Director, had been named "General Director Elect" in November, 1985. Thus 1986 was a year unique in the Casa's hundred years of history and ministry, in that two leaders jointly functioned in the General Director's role: Broda and Tucker.[79] They handled it well, and the transition was completed with a public service in November of 1986.

Endnotes

1. See Minutes, of date mentioned, p. 1; CBP Archives.

2. Ibid.

3. Beyond these two divisions, Merle "Boots" Lee headed the Printing Division and J. Wilson Ross, the Management Services Division.

4. And, to a lesser extent, the Operations Manuals of both the Foreign Mission Board and the Sunday School Board.

5. It had been hoped that all four could be consulted, but Dr. William W. Graves passed to his eternal reward in October 2003, before his input could be secured. He and his wife Marjorie were in attendance at a Friends of the Casa Dinner, held at the Green Acres Baptist Church in Tyler, Texas on September 25, 2003, less than a month before his passing. At the dinner, Bill gave a brief but impressive testimony concerning his support of CBP, its ministry, and its Foundation.

6. Kammerdiener writes "in Miami;" Minutes

seem to show the first meeting to have been held in El Paso. The place of the meeting is not so important as its content, according to Dr. Kammerdiener's memory.

7. The FMB Area Director most directly related to the Publishing House.

8. Chief Executive of the Foreign Mission Board.

9. Essay written by A. Clark Scanlon, January 27, 2004; received by e-mail.

10. From notes and comments received by the author from Aldo Broda, by e-mail, early in 2004. Not conserved elsewhere.

11. From Casa: The Partner in Ministry You Need, El Paso: Casa Bautista de Publicaciones, 2004, pp. 17-18.

12. From Notes and Comments, received by the author from Aldo Broda, by e-mail, in early 2004. Not conserved elsewhere.

13. T-218, titled "Conceptos generales sobre la empresa evangélica y sus ejecutivos," given in 1978; T-279, the address about interpersonal relations [see below on Goal #4]; and T-348, titled only as "Charla con el personal administrativo," given sometime in 1981. Four other sound recordings are also found in the library (T-363; T-450, T-454, and T-473) but respond to specific circumstances.

14. See below concerning the new equipment dedicated at the 75th Anniversary Celebration.

15. See Ross' report in the Reports to Trustees, May 1977, p. 8; CBP Archives.

16. Not found in the General Director's report, but rather in the Sales Department report, given by Laverne Gregory. See Reports given to Trustees, May 1981, p. 100; CBP Archives.

17. See Distribution Division Report for 1982, given to Trustees in May 1983, p. 100; CBP Archives.

18. See Reports to the May 1984 Trustee Meeting, p. 102; CBP Archives.

19. See Distribution Division Report, given to May 1985 Trustee Meeting, p. 117; CBP Archives.

20. The specific total was $1,963,062.25, as reported to the Trustees in May 1986; see p. 14g of the Marketing Division report; CBP Archives.

21. The total, as found in Laverne Gregory's Sales Department report, is $2,571,415.80; see Reports to May 1987 Trustees Meeting, p. 95; CBP Archives. It is interesting to note that approximately 80% of the sales were outside the United States.

22. A manuscript of the message is conserved in the Casa library's vertical file; see folder titled "Broda–pictures and newspaper clippings, 1977-1986;" the address is also conserved as a sound recording, under Broda, Aldo, "Charla sobre relaciones humanas–La gente es importante," T-279.

23. Earlier Casa had used 6700 Dyer Street, although it was actually located several blocks west of the intersection of Dyer and Ellerthorpe, really without a specific street address.

24. Including the large central patio that became the production facility; see chapter 4.

25. From Notes and Comments, received by the author from Aldo Broda, by e-mail, in early 2004. Not conserved elsewhere.

26. Aldo's grandparents had emigrated from Italy to Argentina.

27. From Notes and Comments, received by the author from Aldo Broda, by e-mail, in early 2004. Not conserved elsewhere.

28. They were never revised downward; a few times they were put on hold for a mid-year review, when usually they were upped slightly. See Trustee Minutes for all years, from 1977 through 1986.

29. They are expressed by him, in Spanish, as follows: "5. La reiterada información que recibíamos de los países a los cuales servíamos, acerca de personas que llegaban a conocer al Señor por medio de nuestros materiales publicados. Folletos, revistas, libros, Biblias, himnarios. 6. Comprobar la importancia de la página impresa. Experiencia de mi familia con la Biblia". [Here the allusion is to Aldo's Grandmother's experience, narrated in a brief book of his authorship: Recuerdo un Evangelio.] 7. El servicio que siempre le he reconocido a la CBP en todas las iglesias, de estar toda la vida con el creyente: desde niño, joven, adulto, anciano. 'De la cuna a la tumba de la mano de la CBP.' 8. El ministerio de la CBP es imperecedero. Deberá adecuarse a los tiempos, pero su aporte para el ministerio de las iglesias no tiene fin."

30. See chapter 4.

31. For "Beginners and Primaries," Roberta Ryan wrote Las Aventuras de Pelú, the Casa's ministry presented from the viewpoint of a library mouse; for "Juniors," Mary Jo Stewart wrote El Intrépido Francisco, the Frank Patterson story especially told for children; for teenagers, Olivia S. D. de Lerín wrote Envíame a Mí, the story of J. E. Davis geared to its

target audience of younger youth; and for older youth and adults, an adaptation was done of Tom Hill's mission study book, which then bore the title in Spanish of Ríos de Tinta. Hill recognized the very efficient help of Josie Smith in the preparation of both the original English edition and of the Spanish version.

32. Participants included Dr. Leslie Gómez, at the piano; Dr. Ed Nelson, directing congregational praise; and special numbers by the choir and orchestra of Trinity Baptist Church, where Ananías González was serving as pastor. Dr. Frank W. Patterson was officially recognized and given the status of General Director Emeritus; the principal message was brought by N. Aldo Broda, General Director. A reception followed the service in which the Board of Trustees and the Administrative Staff of the Publishing House formed an official receiving line. Though not present to be a program participant, Dr. Keith Parks, President of the Foreign Mission Board, had recently visited the Publishing House and sent his greetings, as did other dignitaries and institutions.

33. See Luminar Bautista, Noviembre 1980, pp. 1, 2 and 3; and The Commission, January, 1981, pp. 18-25. With text and photos by Mike Livingston, the Commission article is especially optimistic: "The future of the Baptist Spanish Publishing House in El Paso, Texas looks very bright..." (p. 18).

34. See General Director's Report for 1980, in the volume of Reports rendered to the May 1981 Trustee Meeting, p. 7; CBP Archives.

35. See chapters 4 and 5.

36. See, for instance, p. 21, Minutes of the Meeting of the Interim Trustees, December 3-5, 1975; CBP Archives.

37. Tito Fafasuli came to the Publishing House in 1976 to replace Abdías Mora (who accepted a professorship in San Antonio). Fafasuli along with J. T. Poe served as General Editors of this Study Bible; Stanley Clark and José Borrás were the Special Editors for the New Testament and Old Testament, respectively. Many others helped to make this publication a reality.

38. Chávez was a Peruvian Biblical scholar whom Poe had met in Costa Rica the year Moisés taught at the Latin American Biblical Seminary. He was a product of the Peruvian Evangelical Church, and a graduate of evangelical schools in his country as well as the Hebrew University of Jerusalem, in Israel. In 1979 he was doing advanced Biblical studies at Brandeis and Harvard universities; later he completed his doctorate from a school in California. He now resides with his wife and daughter in La Paz, Bolivia, and ministers from there.

39. The McConnells were natives of Ohio and Pennsylvania, respectively; and served as FMB missionaries in Chile from 1938 to 1978. They worked in a variety of missionary tasks including directing and teaching at the Baptist Seminary in Santiago. In 1979 he was guest professor at the International Baptist Seminary in Cali, Colombia when Poe interested him in coming to help with the RVA Bible project. Interestingly, Patterson had tried to bring him to El Paso in the 1950s as book editor.

40. Dr. Robert Garrett, then a professor at the International Baptist Theological Seminary in Buenos Aires, and Professor Alfredo Tuggy, of the Evangelical Seminary of Limón, Venezuela, were secured as Special New Testament Editors (Mrs. Tuggy also helped); and Professors José Borrás (Spain) and Oscar Pereira (Chile) were secured as Special Editors for the Old Testament. (Both Mrs. Borrás and Mrs. Pereira also helped.) These, plus Chávez, McConnell, and Poe formed the executive editorial teams which worked periodically in El Paso on a "project basis." Some two hundred consultants were enlisted and participated by mail. A local editorial consultative committee was formed to assist on call.

41. Over a million copies were circulated, many in special "national editions," featuring a special cover to relate that edition of the New Testament to a specific country. The basic edition bore the title Venid a Mí and included evangelistic Bible studies developed by the Casa's Evangelism Department, under the direction of missionary Steve Ditmore. This edition is still in print.

42. See chapter 8.

43. See "Publishing House addition contains offices and library," unsigned article in El Paso Herald-Post, December 4, 1982, p. A-6. A week later, the El Paso Times published an article that mentioned the new building but featured Laverne Gregory, as Sales Director. It mentioned "the publishing house's 140 workers" and reflected its service to "about 40 countries;" see El Paso Times, December 12, 1982, p. 2-B. Both articles were accompanied by a photo of the new building.

44. Still named, appropriately, the J. E. Davis Memorial Chapel.

45. A good portion of the cost of the building was financed with proceeds from the sale of properties west of Alabama Street which were not needed by the Publishing House, the Foreign Mission Board permitting retention of these funds in El Paso for the building project. FMB made available considerable additional capital funding for the project. And very astute funds management by Wilson Ross helped generate interest that completed the cost of the building. Somehow funds for furnishings were also found.

46. The two buildings were connected on both the north and south sides: on the north end, by a room whose floor was a ramp, and on the south end, by an enclosed bridge at the second floor level.

47. See chapters 1 and 2.

48. Its background was the interpretation of then current SBC "program statements" that seemed to prohibit CBP from rendering any service in the United States.

49. By 1980, the Sunday School Board acquired Holman Bible Publishers and eventually combined Holman with Broadman to become "B & H" as it functions today.

50. Put into effect January 1, 1976.

51. Ananías and Nelly came from Argentina in 1978, slightly after the Brodas arrived. They continued to minister with the Publishing House until early March 1997. Ananías served as a Division Director from 1980 on. Under his supervision, new curriculum designs were implemented for both Bible teaching and Vacation Bible School. Nelly served as an editor in her early years with the Publishing House, and from 1985 on as a department director (Youth/Student; Vacation Bible School; Christian Education). They have made Houston their "retirement" home.

52. As the present General Director, Díaz will be presented in more detail in chapter 11.

53. An Argentine of British extraction, Fred (and wife Josie) emigrated to the United States in 1974; Fred served as director of the Shipping Department from 1976 until retirement in 1993. He had a total of nineteen years service with CBP.

54. Rubén was of Chinese-Mexican ancestry. He became a Casa employee in the 1950s. An active member of Primera Iglesia Bautista Mexicana (First Mexican Baptist Church) of El Paso, he eventually was ordained as a Baptist pastor and served a congregation in Ysleta (a suburb of El Paso) for several years. In retirement, he and Elizabeth (also a long-time secretarial employee at CBP) have made their home in Ft. Worth, near one of their daughters (Margarita) who is married to Matthew Sanderford, Jr. Elizabeth preceded Rubén in death in March, 2004.

55. Floyd Gremar succeeded Alvin Meek; he and his wife Pat (a Registered Nurse) also lived in the apartment near the old steam boiler building, on the northeast corner of the campus. He worked with the Publishing House from August 1973 to June 1979.

56. It is interesting that several employees who began their work with the Casa during the Broda years at a below department head rank are still serving with CBP, some of them now as department heads or equal rank. Among these are: Vilma M. de Fajardo, Velia M. Hodge, Exequiel San Martín A., Violeta Martínez, Jorge Rede, Eleazar Peña, Carlos Santiesteban, Gilberto Pérez, Carol Ann Martínez and Mario Martínez. Velia Hodge has a humorous recollection from the Broda years: She says that Yolanda Oseguera received delivery at the Publishing House of some bedding sent by a relative in California. Before getting the mattresses sent on to her home, Mr. Broda happened to pass by, saw the bedding at Yolanda's office door, and sardonically asked, "Is this lady moving in?"

57. Roy and his wife Alma Ruth were veteran missionaries when they were transferred to the Publishing House. Appointed in 1952, they first served in Mexico (1952-1966) and then in Venezuela (1966-1979) where he had been the founding president of the Venezuelan Baptist Seminary in Los Teques from 1970 till their transfer to El Paso.

58. Missionary Ann Swenson had been transferred to Mexico, but continued to reside in El Paso and was active in student ministries in Ciudad Juárez as well as in other work elsewhere in the country. The Rengifos, subsequently named as FMB missionaries, have served in both Costa Rica and in Mexico; Tony succumbed to leukemia in May 2004.

59. Martínez was a graduate from both the Baptist Seminary in Spain and the International Seminary in Ruschlikon, Switzerland; he had given pastoral leadership to churches in Spain and came recommended by José

Borrás, Baptist leader and professor in Spain. Both Martínez and his wife Violeta became long time employees of CBP.

60. Cecil and Jean Thompson were appointed FMB missionaries for service in Argentina in 1956. Both taught in the International Baptist Theological Seminary of Buenos Aires until 1977, when they were transferred to serve with the Publishing House in El Paso.

61. Blanco was a pastor in his native country, but brought newspaper experience plus linguistic acumen and proofreading abilities that were a definite asset to CBP.

62. Siegfried and Donna Enge were appointed FMB missionaries for Argentina in 1966, arriving there a year later after language study in Costa Rica. Their ministry in Argentina was centered in the city of Mar del Plata, where they lived until transfer to the Publishing House in 1977. Though a professionally trained nurse (and a long term volunteer at the El Paso Baptist Clinic, directed by Eleanor Poe), Donna discovered her editorial skills and helped with projects in the Bible and Commentaries Department and later with the English materials in the Multilingual Department.

63. Jesse and Beverly Bryan were appointed for missionary service in Spain in 1965. They did language study in Valladolid, Spain, and subsequently ministered in general evangelism, but Jesse eventually became the manager of the Baptist Book Store (Spanish: Librería Bautista) in Spain and Director of the Casa's Deposit Operation there. Though some earlier contacts had broached the possibility of service in El Paso, it was not until the Bryans returned from Spain because of Jesse's bout with thyroid cancer that they had peace about leaving their beloved Spain to minister with CBP. They were transferred to El Paso in 1977. During 25 years of work there, Jesse served as a sales representative, then a department director (Sales) and, for many years, as a division director (Marketing, and later Finance). He also gave a brief time as Director of the Office of Communications, related directly to the General Director. Jesse had no further problem with cancer during these years, which has often made him ponder if the illness was just God's way of "getting us where he wanted us." Beverly helped reactivate the Volunteer Program during the administration of Joe T. Poe. From their retirement home in Longview, Texas, Jesse continues to serve on the Board

of the Baptist Spanish Publishing House Foundation.

64. Betty and Laverne Gregory are both natives of Missouri. They were educated at schools in that state, and both are graduates of the Southern Baptist Theological Seminary in Louisville, Kentucky. They were appointed for missionary service in 1958. Though their original plans called for work in Chile, during their language study year in Costa Rica, they were invited to become resident missionaries there, where they were active especially in religious education promotion and literature distribution work from 1958 until 1974. In 1974 they were transferred to Mexico, where they lived in Ciudad Satélite (a suburb of Mexico City) and continued with essentially similar ministry emphases to what they had done in Costa Rica. Their relationship with Casa Bautista continued to grow, and in 1979 they were transferred to El Paso to give full time to the literature ministry. Laverne is author of a booklet on the deaconship (El diácono: servidor de Cristo en la iglesia local–published by CBP in 1973–)and a manual of literature evangelism (Evangelice con la página impresa –published by CBP in 1975–). Betty always worked closely with Laverne. They were active in the Casa's ministry until retirement, and even afterward took an ISC assignment for a couple of years. They make their home in San Angelo, Texas.

65. Ivie succeeded Floyd Gremar in 1979, who retired because of health problems. Ivie was actually Gremar's brother-in-law. A big man, in every sense, he had already survived open-heart surgery. But he worked hard for some fourteen years, finally retiring, as had Gremar, for health reasons. He and his wife Sue now make their retirement home near Albuquerque.

66. Aldo's last year to shoulder the general directorship alone, 1986 being a time when he and Bob Tucker essentially shared the general director's role.

67. Steve and Shirley Ditmore were appointed FMB missionaries to Peru in 1964. After language study in Costa Rica, they served in Piura and in Lima until transfer to the Publishing House in 1981, where Steve directed the Evangelism Department and Shirley served as a children's music editor until their retirement in 1993.

68. Missionary Mary Jo Stewart had served in Ecuador prior to her transfer to the Pub-

lishing House in El Paso. Her appointment had occurred in 1974, her language school year in '73-'74, and her service in Ecuador, with a specialty in women's work, from 1974 to 1978, when she was transferred to El Paso.

69. Charles and Bernadine Campbell were another missionary couple who brought lengthy Argentine experience to their work at the Publishing House. Having been appointed in 1953, they served in various capacities and in several cities until their transfer to the Publishing House in 1981. Their service in El Paso was of fairly short duration, but effective and sincerely appreciated.

70. Missionaries James and Bobbie West, like Bob and Meg Tucker, brought field experience from Venezuela. Appointed in 1969, they arrived in Puerto Ordaz in 1971 following language study in Costa Rica. They were transferred to the Publishing House in 1981. During their El Paso years, interest developed in Chinese work, and since 1992 the Wests have served in Hong Kong.

71. At this point in time José Luis Martínez continued as director of the General Book Department; Poe was giving full time to the RVA project in the Bible Publication Department; and the non-Spanish "Multilingual Department" functioned with Gayle Hogg and Linda Wilson editing in English and in French.

72. Gayle Hogg came as Weldon Viertel's associate in 1977. When Viertel left for missionary labors elsewhere, Hogg became head of the English work. He continued with very considerable output, till 1985.

73. In March 1982 Linda Wilson was employed to head the French work. Linda came with journeyman experience in French-speaking Africa and with extraordinary skills in the French language. (She had completed a Master's Degree in French at the University of Indiana.) Her production (sometimes as translator, sometimes as editor, sometimes as both) was constant and remarkable across some 17 years. Emphasis was primarily on French versions of the Viertel series of decentralized theological studies, but various other productions were done including Survivor's Kit for New Believers and Experiencing God. Linda eventually married a French-speaking Chadian, Neaouguen Nodjimbaden. In October 1995,

"Nodji" was employed as an additional editor in the French Department. With essential defunding of this program by IMB, Ted Stanton found it necessary, at the end of 1999, to keep only "the native speaker." And with complete defunding and inadequate income from sales to justify continuation, Jorge Díaz found it necessary to eliminate completely the French program at the end of 2003.

74. Peter and Jennie Stillman were appointed directly to serve with the Publishing House in El Paso, he in the field of art. They arrived, after language study, in 1984. In what seemed like a very unusual turn of events, they transferred in 1989 to Indonesia.

75. Carreón was a long time pressman in the CBP print shop, serving from August 1975 until the print shop was closed in May 2003.

76. See above. Elbin Porflit's department is now called "Credit and Collections." Elbin takes pride in remembering that he was the only director of this department for the years it existed as such. He also takes delight in having obtained first place recognition years later (still presiding this department), in a competition with other department supervisors concerning job comprehension.

77. Daughter of Jack and Laura (Laly) Disselkoen, Jackie had grown up "on the hill," when her family occupied an apartment in the northwest corner of the Publishing House building. Following college studies at Hardin-Simmons in Abilene and seminary studies at Golden Gate in California (and a period of administrative and accounting work at the Seminary in Mill Valley), she returned "home" to work for the Publishing House, until cancer cut short her life in 2003.

78. See Minutes, Trustee Meeting, May 1986, pp. 42, 42a, 42b,43; and Minutes, Trustee Meeting, November 1986, p. 43; CBP Archives.

79. Symbolic of the two wearing the General Director's "hat," Aldo and Bob served as joint chefs at a hamburger cookout for all Casa personnel. The vision of them, with white aprons and tall cooks' hats, functioning at the grill is a scene etched in Velia Hodge's memory—and of all those who were present. It was a living figure of servant leadership. "And we all had a good time!", remembers Velia.

Chapter 7

Bob Tucker's Pastoral Approach

Upon being named Associate to the Area Director for Western South America,[1] H. Robert Tucker became a member of the COP Board of Trustees. The naming actually occurred in July 1976. The Tuckers moved to Calif, Colombia and began to work for the Area, in early 1977. But Bob began to function on the COP Board in November 1976. He served as president of that Board for three years during 1981, 1982, and 1983. In May, 1984, he was asked to resign his position with the Area staff in order to be named as Associate to Aldo Broda, then serving as General Director of Casa Bautista de Publicaciones. And in November 1985, Tucker was named to become General Director, upon Aldo Broda's "retirement."[2] 1986 was really a transition year, with both Broda and Tucker sharing leadership roles, Broda as "retiring General Director," and Tucker as "General Director Elect." As indicated in the previous chapter, Broda was gradually picking up responsibilities for a "Total Stewardship Campaign" to be directed toward the continent-wide Baptist constituency in Latin America and managed by an international committee of which he would be the executive. A combined service was held on November 20, 1986, to officially recognize and conclude Aldo Broda's work as General Director and install Dr. H. Robert Tucker in that position. The date was set to coincide with the fall meeting of the International Board of Trustees.

The service was held in the spacious sanctuary of First Baptist Church, El Paso. Dr. Leslie Gómez, of the Casa's Music Department, played a prelude on the church's nine-foot Steinway, after which Dr. Ed Nelson led the congregation in singing "A Dios Demos Gloria" (To God Be the Glory). The opening prayer was offered by Rev. Omar Pachecano, then Director of Missions of the El Paso Baptist Association. After a period of both welcome to all present and greetings from representatives of organizations (local, national, and international), the program was divided into two main sections: one of recognition and thanks to Aldo Broda, and the other of rites to install Dr. Tucker. In the recognition and thanks to Broda, Rafael Altamirano, trustee from Paraguay and president of the Board for 1987 spoke words of thanks. J. Wilson Ross brought similar words from the perspective of Casa personnel. Mr. Broda himself responded.

140

In the installation section of the program, former General Directors Thomas W. Hill and Frank W. Patterson were present and participated. Dr. Tucker himself brought a message (in both English and Spanish), Carlos Caramutti, trustee from Argentina and secretary for the Board, offered a prayer of dedication, and Jennie Stillman, missionary, wife of the Casa's Art Department Director and professionally trained soprano, sang "The Lord's Prayer." The congregation concluded by intoning the Doxology, and all present were invited to a reception to greet both the Brodas and the Tuckers. It was a very special event in the life of Casa Bautista de Publicaciones as the fifth General Director was installed.

A Pastor at the Helm

Probably no other General Director has had a smoother transition than Bob Tucker into the role of top leader at the Baptist Spanish Publishing House. It is likely more difficult for Dr. Tucker to isolate his years as Associate from those as General Director; they all tend to fuse. And they all have the flavor of a shepherd. Tucker frankly says, "I saw myself as a pastor."[3] His call to a leadership role on the staff of the Publishing House evidently had the background of certain tensions that had been generated among the personnel. Tucker saw himself as shepherding a "flock" of highly trained, highly skilled, and highly motivated staff people, who, unfortunately, had sometimes allowed their own vision of the ministry and its accomplishment to create relationship problems. "Bridges" between individuals and groups were needed. If such situations existed internally, they were exacerbated by similar, or even more complex, problems in the Casa's "external relationships," especially within the Baptist family. Again, a "pastoral approach" seemed to be needed.

Tucker was a pastor at heart and had been since his call to the Christian ministry during his sophomore year at college, while studying at Texas A. and M. University (where he had assumed to become a chemical engineer). God had other plans, plans which had been gradually unfolding since Bob's birth to a committed Christian couple in Athens, Texas. Though his father, a doctor of chiropractic, joked about his "three baptisms" ("I was christened as a Catholic, sprinkled as a Lutheran, and finally immersed to become a Baptist," he used to say), Bob's memory of his father is as an active deacon of First Baptist Church of Athens. His mother, though raised as a Presbyterian, had also become a Baptist and was equally active in First Church, Athens. Bob says his mother, in fact, started the church nursery after the birth of her baby boy in March of 1934.

Probably part of Mrs. Tucker's purpose was to see that her son, born with a "clubfoot" defect, got appropriate care when he was at church. The attending physician at Bob's birth warned the parents that the little boy might never walk. Bob's father was determined that normal development would come, and as a chi-

ropractor by profession, he massaged little Robert's foot every day. His efforts
and prayers produced the desired results: Bob came to walk—and without a
limp! Today even close friends perceive no problem from what might have been
a life-long disability.

Thus "raised in the church," it is not surprising to learn that Bob accepted Jesus as personal Lord and Savior at the tender age of eight years. "I gave my
life to the Lord," Bob says, and during the "junior years" that followed he felt
attracted to service as a Christian missionary, especially after hearing a representative from Africa speak at a summer church camp.

The teenage years brought other interests and provoked his decision to
begin studies at Texas A. and M. after high school graduation in Athens. The
career choice never quite brought peace to the heart of this young Christian,
and finally he acknowledged God's clear call to ministry–the pastoral ministry.
Baylor University seemed a more appropriate place to prepare for that work, and
Tucker transferred to Baylor for his last two years of university studies.

At Baylor, Bob met Margaret Sue Roberts. Margaret (Meg to most family,
friends, and colleagues) had been born in Anson, Texas, but the family had moved
to another West Texas town, Tahoka, where she had been graduated from high
school the same year Bob had, in Athens. Meg was the daughter of active
Christian parents and, like Bob, had become a believer by personal choice, early in
her life. She remembers that it was during family devotionals that Paul's "confession" in 1 Timothy 1:15, where he declares: "This is a faithful saying, and worthy of all acceptation, that Christ Jesus came into the world to save sinners; of
whom I am chief," came home to her. God used these lines from His Word to con-
vince Meg of her own need for Christ, and she opened her heart to the Savior. It
was the beginning of a life-long Christian pilgrimage—which still continues!

Margaret Sue Roberts and Harold Robert Tucker, Jr., were married on
June 24, 1955, following their graduation from Baylor.

Robert had already begun his pastoral ministry, attending, on weekends,
a mission congregation of his home church in Athens. He and Meg continued
to serve this congregation during his years at Southwestern Seminary, which
began in the fall of 1955. The couple lived in Fort Worth, where shortly Meg
became a teacher in the public schools of that city. Bob attended classes at the
Seminary during the week, and both would make the weekend trips to Athens
to serve their flock.

When Meg had to interrupt her teaching work for the approaching birth
of their first child in late 1957, Bob added to his schedule employment at a local
aircraft factory on "the swing shift," from 3 till 11 p.m. And when the young
couple lost this first child, shortly after birth, they became the objects of the
very real and supporting love of their flock. It was a particularly special experience that they have never forgotten.

During those seminary years, Bob again felt attraction to missionary service. Contact was made with the Foreign Mission Board. But because of Meg's hearing problem policies in place at that time occasioned a negative response from the Mission Board. A case of strep throat during her childhood years had left Meg with rather severe hearing loss. Even today she lives with the problem, but says, "I could have been left blind or crippled; I'll take the hearing loss."

In response to that "closed door" for overseas service, the Tuckers explored possibilities of "pioneer missions" in areas where Southern Baptist churches were few or non-existent. A specific opportunity to explore possibilities in Ohio came via a visit of Dr. Ray Roberts to the Seminary chapel in Fort Worth. The result was that the Tuckers became "Texas missionaries to Oregon, Ohio" and started a church there. Their home churches in Athens and Tahoka helped support "our missionaries" in Ohio. And during their five years there, a son (Robert Mark) and a daughter (Kay Elaine) were born in 1959 and 1961, respectively. Meg taught in the Ohio public schools during most of their time there.

Then, the possibility of overseas missionary service resurfaced. A layman at their church told in Training Union about a couple who were giving much of their time to teaching missionary children, overseas. The idea came to Meg that perhaps she could be a teacher of MKs (as she had taught in Fort Worth and in Ohio) and give Bob the opportunity to be the "overseas church planter" he wanted to be. New contact was made with the Foreign Mission Board, SBC, and somewhat to their surprise the policies that had so quickly closed doors in 1958 had been changed! Their application was not only received; they were appointed in near record time! After being named for missionary service in Venezuela in the spring of 1963, they entered Spanish language study in San José, Costa Rica in August of that year.

Their first couple of years in Venezuela were spent in church planting work in Maracay. Then they were named to go essentially as "national missionaries" to Anaco, in eastern Venezuela, to help start Baptist churches in that whole area of the country. Some two years were spent in very productive labors there. Their second daughter (Karen Beth) was born while they served in Maracay, and their twin sons (Philip Alan and John Vincent) were born in Anaco.

In 1969, Bob and Meg had the opportunity to be on the founding faculty of a new Venezuelan Seminary, which was opened in the Caracas suburb of Los Teques. As Academic Dean, Bob taught whatever he could not get someone else to teach, but especially majored in Christian education. Meg also taught in the field of Christian education. In addition Bob was the pastor of a new church in Los Teques, and he also had special responsibilities for establishing and administering the Seminary's extension centers, known collectively as SEMPEX. These came to number over a dozen and connected with leadership training for new congregations that were being established all over Venezuela. Bob and colleague Roy Lyon (president of the Seminary) collaborated in writing a short book on starting new missions.[4] Students in the extension centers were expected not only to know the theory but also actually to participate in starting new work. During these happy years, Bob initiated his doctoral studies in the field of Christian education at Southwestern Seminary in Fort Worth. His major professors were Dr. LeRoy Ford and Dr. Jim Williams.

Special Ties between COP and Baptists in Venezuela

When the time came for the Tuckers to relate specifically to Casa Bautista de Publicaciones, they took extra delight in recalling the historic ties between the Casa and the Baptist work in Venezuela.

Bob managed to allude to this relationship in his doctoral dissertation: "The start of Baptist work in Colombia, Guatemala, and Venezuela was greatly facilitated as independent evangelical groups used Baptist Spanish Publishing House literature."[5] Then he footnotes Wilson Ross's attention to these same developments.[6]

Correspondence is on file to show J. E. Davis' interest in Venezuela and his desire to visit that country in the last few years of his long period of service at the Publishing House.[7]

The Tuckers' service with the Publishing House brought all this history back into focus.

The Pastor Remembers

In connection with CBP's 90th Anniversary celebration in 1995, Dr. Tucker wrote a summary remembrance of his time as General Director of the Publishing House.[8] More recently, he was interviewed for this centennial book project.[9] To a surprising degree the two reviews coincided in content and emphases. Such being the case, it has seemed more than appropriate to use here Bob's own words, to look back at his years in the General Director's office; these follow:

"Quantity and quality don't mean the same thing. Although I did not serve many years as General Director of the Casa Bautista de Publicaciones (there's the 'quantity' angle), the time that I did serve there was a source of great joy and blessing in my life (there's the 'quality' factor). And being a part of the COP family was something that extended considerably beyond the time I served as General Director. To begin with, and as both a church planter and a national promoter of Christian Education for the Baptist National Convention of Venezuela, I leaned heavily on the materials published by Casa Bautista and thus had great interest in the ministry of the Publishing House. As a participant in the founding of a new Baptist Seminary for Venezuela and its program of extension studies, I reviewed proposed textbooks for publication and I promoted the publication of others. In the new Seminary, we became part of a program of extension training, and that included sales and promotion of appropriate books.

"Once named as the new Associate to the Area Director for Western South America, I learned that I would become a part of the Publishing House's Board of Trustees. I even had the privilege of serving as its president for three years, during which time I became deeply involved in the ministry and in the planning and policy making process related to the publications program. After some seven years 'on the Board,' I was asked to resign in order to accept the position of Associate General Director, working with brother Aldo Broda, then the General Director. I should acknowledge, I guess, that the publications ministry came to seem very much different and more complex, from the point of view of staff personnel, instead of from the viewpoint of a board member. It had been relatively easy to vote about matters related to policies and plans, but it was something different to make them work. When brother Aldo retired, I was asked to occupy the important post of General Director.

"Many challenges raised their heads in those days. The first priority was 'to create a good work team.' Indeed this had been one of the principal reasons that I had been asked to come to El Paso. With God's help I felt that my gifts would help me achieve what was needed.[10] It was not an easy task. There seemed to be more 'chiefs' than 'Indians.' Balance was needed in an institution like COP. I still remember the wise counsel of one of my colleagues and good Latin American friends, that came in a moment when I was trying to solve literally everybody's problems. 'Bob,' this friend said to me, 'there were problems here before you came, and there will be problems when you have gone. You can't solve the problems of everybody. Don't try! We need for you to help us see 'the big picture.' Most of the problems that folks have, they themselves will have to solve.' He was right, and I told him 'Thank you.' I needed the reminder.

"One of the things that Meg and I really enjoyed during our time in El Paso was inviting Publishing House staff (and their spouses) to our home for a dinner. We divided the total invitation list into groups of about thirty people. And each occasion was unique. The only 'constant factor' (if my memory doesn't fail me) is that it rained almost every time we had a group come! Now that's something for El Paso!

"In our day to day work we put in some new procedures that helped to enhance internal communication and thus reduce internal friction. I had never worked with so many capable and highly trained people in one place. It was a challenge!

"Another innovation was that the 'management team' (called in those years the 'cuerpo administrativo' or 'administrative staff') began to have annual retreats to study, pray, and communicate with each other. Good experiences resulted. I still remember the first time we did one of those retreats. Upon returning, we realized that we had caused a good amount of confusion. This was because all the administrative personnel had gone on the retreat; and when an emergency came up, nobody knew who was in charge or how to handle the emergency! (The next year, we made sure that a system was in place to handle such situations. 'We live and learn...' as the saying goes.)

"Perhaps the principal worry during those years was that of 'the debt' that continued to grow. And it seemed that the harder our efforts to reduce it, the greater it grew. When administrative personnel from the Foreign Mission Board visited or when trustees arrived for meetings, their first question was always: 'Bob, how's the debt?' I regularly responded: 'It's fine—growing every day!' Only God knows how many hours Wilson Ross and I talked—and prayed—and traveled, seeking solutions to the situation. There were weeks when cash receipts were less than the payroll; but it seemed that just in the nick of time, when payroll checks were to be cut, some client/customer would pay all or part of his debt to us. And we covered minimum needs. These experiences served to force our faith to grow—but they were hard on our nerves!

"I will always remember the sincere concern that Wilson and other members of our administrative team had as we tried to keep in view the needs and best interests of all our personnel, during those difficult times. The truth is that 'debt' was not the problem; it was 'cash flow.' We were developing a new line of curriculum materials for Bible study and discipleship, along with the launch of a new revision of the Bible. These were very costly projects.

"Still another 'opportunity' had to do with our contractual relationships with the Baptist Sunday School Board (now known as LifeWay Christian Resources). It was their conviction that the rules of the Southern Baptist Convention gave them the exclusive rights to publish and distribute all Southern Baptist materials in the United States. Since our House was an arm of the Foreign Mission Board of the Southern Baptist Convention, it was the Sunday School Board's position that COP ought to cease and desist from selling anything in the United States. Such sales had come to represent a significant portion of income to sustain our ministry. Now we lost that, since the Foreign Mission Board essentially accepted the position of the Sunday School Board. And since a good part of our annual operating budget as well as a significant portion of our personnel came from the Foreign Mission Board, the Casa as such had few if any viable options. (I recall a favorite saying of later friends in Canada that describes how the Canadians often feel in their relations with the United States: 'It's like a mouse getting in bed with an elephant!')

"One day, I received a telephone call from the president of the

Baptist Sunday School Board. The conversation lasted an hour or more! When we finished, I had two reactions: (1) I was glad that he called, which meant that they were paying for the call! And (2) I was glad we were already friends before the call, because the exchange got hot enough that had that mutual respect not already existed, I'm not sure we would have been friends after the call.

"With the best of intentions, many suggestions were offered—sometimes radical ones—like the suggestion that we 'declare independence' from the Foreign Mission Board, or the one that we be absorbed into the Sunday School Board. But in the end, we agreed to a relationship which specified that the Sunday School Board would be our exclusive distributor in the United States. Things could have turned out worse; but perhaps a better solution existed that we didn't find. I felt that 'the elephant' had abused 'the mouse' (to use the Canadian figure), but there didn't seem to be any other alternative. Fortunately, the circumstances changed a few years later.

"Another 'challenge' we faced had to do with getting dated curriculum materials to the churches on time. I discovered one thing with absolute clarity: Shipping dates don't wait! It was like racing cars. Everybody was going as fast as they could, but we seemed to lack a program that would allow us to print all our products as needed. When we put off reprinting out-of-stock general products in order to print dated curriculum materials, we lost customers. And when we stopped printing dated curriculum materials to reprint out-of-print general products, we missed shipping dates—and thus we began to get back dated materials that had arrived late. My office needed a revolving door to handle the traffic of those coming to consult (and often complain) of problems either with some phase of the literature production or distribution. We had problems running out our ears! And all this was further complicated by the untimely illness of our director of production, M.B. 'Boots' Lee. He had directed the Printing Division successfully for several years, but illness now affected his work. Eventually, we solved the problem, at least partially, by adopting an annual program of publication. The first time we tried it, it took almost the whole year to put it into practice! Gradually, we were able to refine the process, and make it work better. With the help of God—and everybody working together—some order was brought out of what was close to chaos.

"To give us a clearer sense of direction and of mission, I began to use the phrase: 'Hasta la última iglesia.' (Out there— to the very last church.)[11] I used the phrase for the first time when Aldo Broda passed to me the gavel, symbolizing the passing of leadership as General Director. The phrase seemed to make a point. I hoped that with this emphasis we would be signaling our intentions to meet the literature needs of every Hispanic church, however small, however isolated. And in relation to this theme, we conducted in several countries leadership workshops concerning our publications. Even yet, I occasionally receive personal letters from people who participated in those training events, giving testimony of how they were impacted and how they have, since then, given much of their lives to the literature ministry.

"Still another aspect of work in those years—somewhat related to our desire to be there for every last church—was our competition to design a new logo for the Casa that would capture our intended image and mission. I believe the House is still using the logo that came out of that effort.

"Yet another facet of work was our attempt to involve more persons in planning for the future of our ministry and how to improve it. Unfortunately, this effort was only partially realized before God led me elsewhere. But it is obviously important for an organization to know where it is going; and it is equally important for individuals to see where they are going—as individuals—and how they fit into the total picture.

"Another major change had to do with our system of computerized information. The equipment we had been using became obsolete, and there was no way to update it. Thus we contracted with a company to reprogram our whole operation (with reference to computerized information). And we bought some new equipment, that in one sense was smaller than what we had but in another sense had newer capacities. I confess that I really didn't know how difficult it would be to integrate a new system. We had meeting after meeting with the key persons to discuss the process. I also failed to anticipate how many kinks would have to be eliminated from the new system, as we worked with good customers who had gotten double billed or whose payments had not been credited properly. It was a time when each day I went to the office with some heaviness of heart, knowing full well I would have to deal with some more customers who were seriously upset! But once again, the personnel came together, under heavy circumstances, and slowly we began to see the light. In retrospect, I can say it was great to work with a good team, even when not everybody was of the same opinion about what needed to be done.

"One of the most exciting projects that I inherited from the previous administration was that of a new revision of the Reina-Valera Bible. It was a giant project that involved Bible scholars from many parts of the world. Some of them came to El Paso to work directly on the projects for brief, agreed-upon periods of time. I thus had the opportunity to make their acquaintance and become their friends. Dr. J. T. Poe and his team invested hours and hours, studying the manuscripts in the original languages, apart from consulting a variety of other Spanish translations. We all shared great joy when the first printings of New Testaments from this project arrived,[12] and we could begin to distribute them. Voices of strong opposition surfaced, especially from Miami, that expressed the thought that we had erred in some editorial decisions and had, in effect, not been faithful to what they considered to be the most reliable manuscripts. I received various letters which I had to manage with the care of one handling branding irons. But the Word of God prevailed.

"I am very grateful for the privilege I had to work with persons of such talent who love the Lord and love the ministry of the Casa Bautista de Publicaciones. It was a blessing to work for about three years with Aldo Broda, who had first invited me to be his associate, with special attention to the area of finances.

"When I consider the fact that all this happened in such a brief time, I marvel. Of course it was really the Casa Bautista family that made it all happen. And that 'family' merits the credit for whatever positive results that came about. I will accept responsibility for the things that didn't quite come out as we would have liked. I know that it fell as a surprise to a good many when I left the Casa, and many kindly expressed their sadness at our farewell. Deep down, I felt that most of what had been asked of me had been accomplished and that it was time now for someone to lead who had more administrative background than I.

"I do believe that one of the things that I regretted more than almost anything else was failing to realize that Wilson Ross was as sick as he was when I resigned. Everybody seemed to think that I knew, but I didn't. I doubt I would have felt free to leave if I had known he was dying of cancer. But God has the power to take the most difficult circumstances and fulfill his will. He's done it time and again in the history of the Publishing House—and he'll continue to do it."[13]

Key Personnel Changes during the Tucker Years

Since personnel changes up through 1986 have been registered in the chapter concerning Aldo Broda's administration, what will be presented here are changes that occurred during 1987 and the first half of 1988, the specific time Dr. Tucker functioned as General Director, without association to his predecessor Mr. Aldo Broda.

The General Director's report to the May 1987 Trustees' Meeting concerning personnel does not propose new namings that required Trustee approval. It does mention "provisional namings" that had been authorized by the Trustees' Executive Committee and the Minutes reflect that all those provisional designations were confirmed on an ongoing basis. These included: José Amézaga to be Associate Director of the Production Division; Ricardo Solís[14] to be Director of the Bindery Department; Samuel Shaw[15] to be Director of the Church Administration Department; Jorge Díaz to be (again) Director of the Bible Teaching Department, and Ernest McAninch[16] to be Associate Director of the Sales Department. Most of these namings had to do with new or modified assignments for people already working at the Publishing House, either as missionaries or as employees.

The report does list several persons who have retired since the last meeting of the Trustees: Aldo and Dora Broda; Roberta Ryan; and Matthew and Dora Jean Sanderford. Among those whose have resigned there appears the name of Merle B. "Boots" Lee, Director of the Production Division, whose resignation was provoked for health reasons, as alluded to in Dr. Tucker's own memories (above).[17]

Undoubtedly the most important personnel change had to do with a new Associate General Director. During the year of "co-regency" (1986), Dr. Tucker and the Trustees' Search Committee had considered various candidates but had recommended Dr. Roberto García-Bordoli, who had been elected by the Trustees in their November 1986 Meeting.[18] As an Argentine and a resident of Buenos Aires, considerable time was required for him to actually arrive and begin to work in El Paso. But he was present for the May 1987 Trustee Meeting. More attention will be given to him and his wife in the chapter concerning his administration.[19]

The November 1987 report from the General Director to the Trustees, regarding personnel, contains additional significant information. It reports the retirement of Charles and Bernadene Campbell (retirement date given is May 31, 1987). Charles had been serving as Director of the Church Administration Department, with Bernadene as his associate.

The report also advised of the departure of Dr. Bob E. Compton and his wife Peggy who had been working in the Text and Reference Works Department.[20]

In addition, the report announces the arrival of Rubén and Alicia Zorzoli[21] whose invitation to come as employees had been voted by the Trustees in November 1986,[22] with Rubén essentially to assume the editing responsibilities that Bob Compton left and Alicia to assume editing tasks in the General Books Department, essentially those that had been left vacant by Roberta Ryan (whose retirement had occurred December 31, 1986).

Wayne Quarrier, whose invitation had been issued in November, is also announced as having begun to work as a special consultant to the Director of the Production Division. Quarrier was recruited specifically by Dr. Tucker, who had gotten acquainted with Wayne as a deacon in the El Paso church Tucker was serving as interim pastor. Wayne's background in manufacturing and his availability made him an attractive addition to the Casa staff. While he first served as a Production Consultant, he later served as a Division Director.

Another important personnel decision at the November 1987 Trustee Meeting had to do with the naming of Rafael Altamirano as a Regional Sales Director. Altamirano was completing his term as a Trustee member from Paraguay and was actually the president (for the second year) of the Board. Though a citizen of Paraguay, Rafael had studied at the International Baptist Theological Seminary in Buenos Aires and had been employed by the Argentine Baptist

Publication Board during some of his seminary years. He had married an Argentine and had served churches in both Argentina and Paraguay. His university studies in both Brazil and Paraguay had been in business administration. Altamirano's experience and education made him an ideal candidate to enhance the Casa's distribution program in southern South America. Unfortunately, cancer cut short his life and his career, ending both in 1995.

The November report also indicates that Ernest McAninch and his wife Lee Ann had been incorporated as associates in the Sales Department (being led by Laverne Gregory). Ernie and Lee Ann had been serving as missionaries in El Salvador, with principal responsibilities for directing the COP "Deposit."[23] Lee Ann was a highly efficient administrative assistant. Both served effectively until they chose to leave for other work, in 1993.

The Personnel Report to the Trustees in May 1988 mentions the resignation of Samuel Shaw (to accept a pastorate in Las Cruces, New Mexico). The date was January 1, 1988. The Report also advises of Josie Smith's retirement as Director of the Advertising Department as of May 31, 1988, and recommends the naming of Jorge Rousselin, a Guatemalan serving in the Art Department, as Interim Director of the Publicity/Advertising Department. (An attachment from Dr. Jesse Bryan, the Director of the Distribution Division, indicated that by November it should be clear if Rousselin fit the job well enough to be named permanently.)[24]

Unquestionably the most delicate personnel issue to be dealt with at this meeting (May, 1988) was the unexpected resignation of Dr. and Mrs. Tucker from their Publishing House responsibilities and their departure for further missionary service in Canada. A Search Committee was named.[25] Dr. García-Bordoli, who had only been in El Paso since around the first of January, was not only the Associate General Director, but became the de facto interim.

The Trustees included in their program a dinner with the Tuckers on Tuesday evening (May 17) to recognize them, thank them for their services at Casa Bautista, and pray God's blessings on them as they began "a new career" at the Canadian Baptist Seminary in Calgary. The personnel of the Casa honored the Tuckers in a special chapel service the week following (May 25) including a luncheon. An atmosphere of sincere gratitude and friendship prevailed. The Tuckers, who left shortly for Canada, wrote these words for the next issue of *Entre Nos*: "The word 'thank you' is sometimes not sufficient to express all the emotions that one feels. This is what has happened to us in wanting to share the love and deep gratitude we have for each of you. You have given us support, friendship and affirmation during our years here. Your efforts to carry forward this ministry have been great. And you have worked very hard these last few days so that we could have an unforgettable farewell. Even though these words have their limitations, we say them again: 'Thank you very much for everything.'"[26]

Endnotes

1. The Area Director was Dr. J. Bryan ("Breezy") Brasington, Southern Baptist missionary to Peru, 1955-1970; Field Representative for the north field of Spanish South America, 1970-1975; and Area Director for Western South America, from 1975 on.

2. See Minutes, COP Trustees, Motion number 19, November 1985; COP Archives.

3. Interview with Dr. and Mrs. Tucker, October 1, 2003.

4. Title, Cómo comenzar una misión nueva, published by the Seminary in Los Teques, Venezuela.

5. Harold Robert Tucker, Jr., "Curriculum Preference of Selected Latin American Baptist Pastors Toward Two Bible Study Series," Unpublished dissertation submitted to the faculty of the School of Religious Education, Southwestern Baptist Theological Seminary, July 1984.

6. Ross, Sowing the Seed, p. 151.

7. See, for example, letter from Davis to Dr. C. E. Maddry, of the Foreign Mission Board, dated June 12, 1942; and letter from Maddry to Davis, dated June 23, 1942; several additional letters in this period show the interest Dr. Davis had.

8. Published, in Spanish, in Entre Nos, Vol. 18, Number 38, September 27, 1995.

9. Interview done by Joe T. Poe, in Ruidoso, New Mexico, on September 30, 2003.

10. Gloria Williams-Méndez, who has worked full time in the Art Department since 1983 (earlier as a free-lance collaborator) and is its present Director, remembers an incident that illustrates Bob Tucker's "pastoral approach:" "I'll never forget," Gloria writes, "the time that Brother Tucker came into the Art Department for something or other. He looked over and saw me working at my light-table and said, 'Well done, thou good and faithful servant.' It made me feel both humble and proud."

11. David Fajardo, long time COP employee and whose experience in his native country of Ecuador included churches in cities and towns but also those in isolated rural areas, says Tucker's "slogan" really made an impact on him. He could identify with the figure and wanted to help achieve the goal.

12. The New Testament of the RVA project appeared in the spring of 1986. Its principal edition was called the Nuevo Testamento Venid a Mí. It is still in print.

13. Entre Nos, Vol. 18, Núm. 38; 27 September, 1995. English translation by J. T. Poe.

14. Solís, the son of long time COP employee Velia Hodge, was employed for the Bindery Department in the Production Division in 1985. He learned this work very well, became director of this department, and served there till the closing of the print shop in 2003.

15. Sam and Ruthie Shaw had been serving in the Dominican Republic prior to an automobile accident that almost killed the whole family. IMB accepted their reassignment to El Paso. Sam assisted in launch preparation for the RVA Bible. He left missionary service to accept a pastorate in Las Cruces, New Mexico; subsequently was pastor of First Baptist Church, Tulsa, Oklahoma, and now is pastor of Germantown Baptist church near Memphis, Tennessee.

16. Ernie and his wife Lee Ann were named for missionary service in 1979. After language study in Costa Rica, they were active in the literature ministry in El Salvador for seven years. Transfer to the Publishing House in El Paso came in 1987, where they gave some six years of service.

17. See Trustee Reports and Minutes, May 1987, Reports Section, p. 156; and Minutes, Motion 1; COP Archives.

18. See Report and Minutes, COP Trustees Meeting, November, 1986; Motion number 1; COP Archives.

19. See chapter 8.

20. Bob and Peggy had been resident missionaries in both Colombia and Costa Rica before coming to the Publishing House. Their departure from El Paso was occasioned by Bob's acceptance of responsibilities with the Missionary Learning Center, a training center owned and operated by the Foreign Mission Board, SBC, and located in the outskirts of Richmond, Virginia. Subsequently Peggy became an Assistant in the Middle America Regional Offices at the Board's headquarters in Richmond and served there for a number of years.

21. Rubén is a native of Argentina; Alicia, of Uruguay. They are both graduates of the International Baptist Theological Seminary in Buenos Aires and experienced in the Baptist work of both Southern Cone countries. In addition to pastoral service, both were teaching in the Buenos Aires seminary at the time of their invitation to join the El Paso staff of COP. Rubén recalls the emotions he felt when he first saw the video Junto con ustedes, produced to celebrate the Casa's 75th Anniversary. It contained a testimony of a man whose life had been changed by the COP book Los hombres en su crisis de media vida (Men in mid-life crises). Rubén recalls: "Since I had translated that book for the Casa, I sensed the power of the printed page to reach a person for Christ, although 'evangelism' was not the principal purpose of that publication." In 2004, the Zorzolis are still with COP as subsequent chapters of this book reflect. They are now career missionaries of IMB.

22. See Motion 27, Minutes, COP Trustees, November 1986 Meeting; COP Archives.

23. Essentially a wholesale distribution operation; see chapter 4 concerning the origination of the deposit system. The deposit in San Salvador was closely linked with a major retail book store, which McAninch had also directed.

24. See Report and Recommendations concerning Personnel, page 111 ff., including Attachment F; COP Trustee Reports and Minutes, May 1988; COP Archives.

25. Search Committee members: Harolt Sante, Edgardo Eudy, Benjamín Bedford, Carlos Caramutti, plus Daniel Sotelo as the Board's president for this year. A letter was issued, signed by both Caramutti (Board secretary) and Sotelo, to all Casa personnel inviting recommendations. A similar letter undoubtedly went to Baptist leaders around the continent.

26. Entre Nos, Vol. 11, Núm. 21, June 1, 1988; see also issues for May 11 and 18.

Chapter 8

Roberto García-Bordoli: Our Second Argentine General Director

Dr. Roberto García-Bordoli was elected General Director of the Baptist Spanish Publishing House in May 1989. But he was no stranger: He had been recommended as the Associate General Director by Dr. H. Robert Tucker and the Trustee Search Committee in the Trustee Meeting of November 1986 and elected to that post immediately[1]

Dr. Tucker's memory is that the Search Committee was composed of Dr. Joe Bruce, Rafael Altamirano, and Carlos Caramutti. The Board wanted a national as the Associate, since Tucker was a missionary. And while the Board desired its own committee to function responsibly, it also intended that Dr. Tucker, as the General Director, have a strong voice in the selection process. With a profile in hand and having received recommendations from various sources, the group planned a meeting in Buenos Aires.

Tucker remembers that García-Bordoli "fit the profile" and had good recommendations from persons like Aldo Broda and Carlos Caramutti. He also remembers that, apart from formal meetings and candidate interviews, the search group attended a service (part of an evangelistic campaign) being held at the church where García-Bordoli occupied a leadership role.[2] The group observed how "the candidate" seemed to be well loved and respected by the members of the congregation; Tucker says that in his conversations with some of the members, always in an unofficial way, "they all spoke very highly of him."[3]

Tucker's recollection is that the search group emphasized in their interview with the candidate that their search was for an Associate General Director and that "he should not, if recommended, consider this as a stepping stone to be the General Director." The result was that Dr. García-Bordoli became the group's recommendation to the Trustees, and his election followed immediately.

Dr. García-Bordoli was present for the May 1987 Trustee Meeting (held in El Paso, as usual), but all the arrangements for his visa and his move to El Paso did not fall into place until late that year. He began functioning at the Casa in January 1988. As indicated in the closing section of the previous chapter, when the Tuckers surprised almost everybody in the spring of 1988 by accepting positions on the faculty of the new Canadian Southern Baptist Seminary, in Calgary, and thus substantially refocusing the remaining years of their active missionary career, Dr. García-Bordoli became the de facto Interim General Director for the Casa Bautista. But, again surprisingly, the Board of Trustees did not name him "Interim" but instead created a Search Committee. This approach by the Trustees must have created questions in the mind of Dr. García-Bordoli, if not a tinge of frustration.

He had come to El Paso with the reputation of being as a very successful Argentine professional and as a highly esteemed lay leader among Argentine Baptists.

Roberto Remembers Family History and His Formative Years

Specifically for purposes of this book, Dr. García-Bordoli has shared some very notable aspects of his family's history as well as reflections on his years of study, work, and Christian service before coming to the staff of Casa Bautista de Publicaciones. These are translated and condensed as follows:

"I was born July 9, 1930 in Berisso, Buenos Aires, Argentina, in the home of evangelical believers. My parents were Santos Manuel García Reiriz and Estela Bordoli Benelli. My only sibling was an older brother named Ismael (now enjoying the heavenly mansions). Throughout our childhood, our parents gathered us each night to open the Holy Bible, read a passage, and pray as a family (generally after a brief meditation on the passage).

"My father had roots in Spain, having been born in Castinieiras, that belonged to the municipality of Ribeira, in the province of La Coruña. These are all places in the north of Spain. All the family were fishermen–and had been for generations. And, of course, all the family practiced the Roman Catholic religion. Really it was the only expression of Christian faith that they new–until my grandmother María Benita Reiriz had contact with some evangelical missionaries from England.

"These English missionaries read and preached straight from the Bible; they prayed directly to God; they sang hymns that were simple but meaningful; and they spoke of Jesus as One who was ALIVE. By the grace of God, my grandmother Benita attended some of those humble services and soon decided to give her life to that Christ who lives as certainly as though he had come down from the cross. My grandfather (Juan García Vilar) also became a believer, though not quite as soon as did my grandmother Benita. But when he did, one of his first acts was to quit smoking the old seaman's pipe which he had used all his life. The family preserved as a special story his conquest of the tobacco habit: He called his wife, and together they put the pipe, its accessories, and his supply of tobacco in a little leather bag and stored it on an exposed roof beam in the living room, where grandfather Juan could see it from his favorite chair. 'Why?' he was asked. And his reply was: 'I want to see it every day, to remember how the Lord has freed me from slavery to that habit that was injurious to my life.' He never smoked again, and he lived to 86.

"When my grandmother gave birth to the baby that would become my father (the date was August 22, 1895), very devout neighbors secretly took the baby to have it baptized in the local parish church. When the priest asked for the baby's name, the neighbors didn't know how to reply. They simply declared, 'He's the son of that Protestant woman.' At the priest's suggestion, they agreed to give him the name of 'Santos' (Saints), as a way of attacking the Protestant rejection of (Catholic) 'saints,' since every time they pronounced the boy's name, the family would be speaking of the 'saints.' Surprisingly the mother's reaction was, 'Fine; it's a nice name for a boy who, in my thinking, already belongs to God's kingdom.'

"Other circumstances brought severe trial and even imprisonment to my grandmother Benita for her evangelical faith. The whole family had become believers–and founding members of the Iglesia Evangélica (Evangelical Church) in Castinieiras. But persecution was strong; the clergy prohibited their selling fish in the local market. Other markets had to be found. On occasion Benita refused to kneel before a religious precession. She was jailed for 30 days. Finally the family decided to immigrate to Argentina, in search of those newer and freer horizons that America offered.

"My mother's family had the same motivation when they immigrated to Argentina. They were from northern Italy. Mother's parents were Esteban Bordoli and Teresa Benelli; she was born in Buenos Aires. In her youth she was a faithful Roman Catholic, including weekly confessions and regular attendance at mass. But in her neighborhood, 'the evangelicals' of Iglesia Bautista Sudoeste (Southwest Baptist Church) opened a mission point and began to preach the Word of God and sing gospel hymns. Esteban and Teresa (her parents) began to attend those services. Estela (my mother) felt fear to do so. But Esteban and Teresa were converted and began to live a transformed Christian life. Their home was different. The joy they felt and the love they radiated impacted my mother. She saw that her parents HAD was she had been looking for: assurance of salvation, the certainty of the having Christ at their side each day; belonging to a church where all were brothers in Christ. Bothered by her spiritual uncertainties, she asked local priests for permission to read the Bible. 'If you do, you are condemned' was the reply she received. Finally, she decided to attend a service at the Iglesia Bautista de Vélez Sarsfield (the church which the neighborhood mission had become). The message was preached by pastor Manuel García Reiriz (brother of Estela's future husband), but it was the words of a hymn that really penetrated her heart: 'Hay perdón, por la sangre de Jesus; hay perdón por su muerte en la cruz...' (English: There is pardon, through the blood of Jesus; there is pardon, through his death on the cross...). Soon she realized that this was what she desired. She began to attend the little church–with her parents and siblings–and soon gave her life to Christ.

"In the course of time, the little baby baptized as 'Santos' (the brother of pastor Manuel García) and Estela Bordoli met–at church–, fell in love, and formed that Christian home into which I was born. They were faithful members of the Vélez Sarsfield church, serving as deacons and Sunday School teachers, and opening their home to gospel preaching. This was the environment in which I was raised.

"Not surprisingly, my own religious experiences began early. I attended Sunday School from a very early age ,and with the support of my family and our church, I gave my life to Christ as a young boy. My public decision came at all-city Sunday School rally held in the Goumond theater near the Congress plaza; Dr. Carlos De la Torre preached and challenged those present to give their lives to Christ. I was one among many who responded. Afterward, I used every opportunity in my church to reconfirm my decision. On November 19, 1944, I was baptized by my uncle, pastor Manuel García Reiriz.

"In the years that followed, I sought to be active in my church and prepare myself for whatever service to which the Lord might call. With some frequency I was the preacher for our youth group. (My mother often helped me prepare and even rehearse my sermons.) Meanwhile I continued to advance in my academic pursuits also. I remember my mother saying one day, 'Roberto, I know that you will be a preacher of the gospel; we are praying for you, and I want you to be faithful to God's call.' Gifts from my parents on special occasions were frequently books that would help me advance in Bible study. Most, if not all, were published by the Casa Bautista de Publicaciones. And I also made a collection of the Expositor Bíblico quarterlies which we used to help us in Sunday School, where I was already a teacher.

"With family encouragement, I studied and graduated from the Escuela Superior de Comercio (Commercial High School), the Universidad Nacional de la Plata (La Plata National University), and the Graduate College of Economics of the Universidad de Buenos Aires (Buenos Aires University), obtaining in the process the recognition as Perito Mercantil (Mercantile Specialist), Contador Público Nacional (equivalent of a Certified Public Accountant), the Licenciado en Administración (approximate equivalent of a Masters of Business Administration) and the Doctor en Ciencias Económicas (a doctorate in economics). My professional career included work as an accountant, as a professor in several schools and colleges, and some activity in the general business sector.

"At church, I continued to serve in various capacities: church clerk, Sunday School teacher, deacon, stewardship leader, sometimes choir director, and occasional preacher.

"In my mid-twenties, I found my life partner: Noemí Elena Ballerini, another Baptist Christian who along with all her family were active members of the Iglesia Evangélica Bautista de Berisso, in the Province of Buenos Aires. We were married in 1956. God has blessed us with two children, Mabel and Guillermo. Mabel is a teacher, married to Jorge Gherman, and they reside in Berisso, with their two children, Gerardo Gabriel, now a university student, and Heidi Eileen, a talented teenager. Our son Guillermo finished his studies after we moved to El Paso, in the University of Texas there. He and his wife, Paula Ferreyra, resided in El Paso until 2004 when his employer transferred him to Amsterdam, Holland, where the company has its European headquarters. They have a preschool daughter, and by the time this book is published a second child should have been born.

"My collaboration with the Argentine Baptist Convention was another important dimension of my Christian service. Besides regularly attending conventions, I served on the Evangelism Board, on the Finance Committee, and on the Argentine Baptist Publications Board. It was in this work that I became more closely acquainted with the Casa Bautista in El Paso, since its Argentine distribution channeled through ABAP. I also helped the International Seminary in Buenos Aires with their annual audit for some ten years. Further, I participated on the International Stewardship Commission that Aldo Broda headed, after leaving the directorship of the Casa Bautista.

"In the providence of God, all these strands of experience came together for my work with Casa Bautista de Publicaciones."

What Dr. García-Bordoli Wrote in 1995

In 1995, Dr. García-Bordoli and his wife were serving as missionaries in Spain. But he accepted the Casa's invitation to write some recollections of his years of service

in El Paso. His summary was published in the *Entre Nos* of April 12, 1995. It serves
again here to represent the Casa's eighth General Director. The following English translation seeks to capture dynamically Dr. García-Bordoli's text. Slight condensations are
represented with elipsis marks. Occasional endnotes offer additional detail or clarifica-
tions.

"The Ninetieth Anniversary

"When a missionary enterprise achieves ninety years of life—years that represent constant effort, dedication, and prayers raised to the Lord—we can definitely know that our good God, through His grace and love, has surely given His
protection and guidance to that labor.

"Many, many brethren have given great amounts of time working at, or in
some way collaborating with, the Baptist Spanish Publishing House, but even
more brethren in different corners of our world have supported this ministry in
prayer or have given thanks for the blessing of its influence, felt personally or
collectively, throughout the Hispanic World.

"On the first page of the CBP General Catalog for 1992/93, it says: 'The call
of that missionary vision that inspired the pioneers of our ministry has burned
without interruption since our beginning. It still shines as a proof of the Lord's
loving care over this span of time and circumstance.'

"The effort to make a brief summary of the blessings of God received during a period of time that by His grace we were involved in this missionary labor
requires,... that we acknowledge that in the final analysis it is the Lord Himself
who has done the work; we have only been collaborators or instruments that,
by His mercy and in His love, He has used.

"To mention some of the important accomplishments in the forward movement of CBP also implies... recognizing the work of all the personnel of the
Casa. Each and all, in their daily work places or in the special functions
assigned at some precise moment, have given what they could, helped along
by the power of the Lord Himself, to reach common objectives.

"All that is achieved—all the work done at CBP—is never an end in itself; it
is all a part of Christian missionary outreach—in a word, evangelizing—the
Spanish-speaking world. And today, more than ever, Spanish-speaking people
are distributed practically throughout the world...

"These, then, are some of the blessings for which we prayed and for which
we may still be grateful considering their fulfillment:

"1. Installation of the first FAX machine at the Casa. Done in collaboration
with the El Paso Mission.

"2. Safeguarding the Casa's bank accounts. Deposits were removed from
banking entities that were less secure and placed in banking institutions with
better guarantees.

"3. Conquest of the evangelical Hispanic market inside the United States,
so that CBP could sell its products directly to that market.[4]

"4. The return to the Foreign Mission Board of $100,000 that had been
advanced to the Casa to mitigate the earlier bankruptcy of a Savings and Loan,
in El Paso, where CBP had considerable funds deposited.

"5. Utilization of 'Leasing' arrangements to facilitate industrial equipment
replacement. New photocomposition equipment was thus acquired, making pos-

sible the direct and more efficient preparation of covers for books and magazines, as well as facilitating more rapid development of art work and page layout.

"6. Purchase of some Macintosh computers that permitted editors to work in closer relationship with the new photocomposition equipment that had been installed.[5]

"7. Special training for appropriate personnel, training contracted from El Paso Community College but conducted on the premises, to utilize fully the new equipment recently acquired.[6]

"8. The installation of an 800 telephone line to make for easier attention to the re-opened domestic market in the United States.

"9. Some reduction of CBP personnel, using the system of attrition, that is, not replacing employees who resigned or retired.

"10. Purchase and installation of a new plastic packaging machine for the production facility.[7]

"11. Better equipment for handling correspondence and everything sent out, with equipment, arrangements, and connections to major courier companies as well as the United States Post Office.

"12. Acquisition of a major floor scale, in order to weigh more efficiently and process full skids of materials for international shipment.

"13. Elimination of two 'consultant' offices that earlier had been attached to the General Director's suite; their responsibilities were added to another 'consultant' office that already existed.

"14. Improvements to the roofs of the sections of the older building that housed both the Production Division and all our warehousing space…

"15. A complete updating of the fire prevention system, especially in the production and warehousing areas. To accomplish this, a new water line had to be brought from Alabama Street and a new fire hydrant installed… to meet the Fire Department's specifications.

"16. The abandonment of a costly and inefficient system of Worker's Compensation, sponsored by the State of Texas, in favor of a private system of Accident Insurance…

"17. Creation of the Casa's first 'Safety Committee,' with representation from all areas of the organization. Further, the Production Division Director and the Director of the Personnel Department attended seminars…, to keep themselves—and all personnel—up to date concerning matters of safety in the workplace…

"18. The creation of a committee to deal with the purchase and use of computers. It was called simply 'the Computer Committee.' As a group, it had the purpose to give counsel, in all areas of the CBP organization, concerning the utilization of equipment on hand as well as making an inventory of all CBP computer equipment and giving its opinion concerning computer purchases, and even advising about the redistribution of equipment on hand…

"19. Agreements were reached with academic entities in the city of El Paso, especially with the El Paso Community College, that led to including Casa Bautista de Publicaciones in the programs for foreign professionals and business men. Many… were from Latin American countries…These visitors were given evangelistic materials, New Testaments, a copy of the Bible reading calendar, and other mementos of their visit.

"20. The creation of a self-financing program of medical insurance for CBP personnel. This program helped the Casa avoid what at one point loomed to be an 80% increase in the cost of such insurance and perhaps the reduction of other benefits.

"21. Officially giving the name 'Wilson Ross' to the library of the CBP. Thereby gratitude was expressed to God and to this missionary who carried out important work in various areas of the Publishing House during many years and who specifically fostered the growth of the library.

"22. Beautifying the grounds of the Publishing House, through planting trees and installing watering systems.

"23. Contracting with a local company to protect the Casa against robberies, providing... additional security and systems of quick alert, in case of doubt or necessity.

"24. Updating the air conditioning systems for the production and storage areas at CBP, thus mitigating the summer heat... so typical of the climate of far West Texas. This also helped control premature drying of the glues used in the binding of books...

"25. A complete reorganization of the music library, creating two different sections: a) a section of musical literature, musical collections, hymnals and everything pertinent to literary and musical production; and b) a section of recorded materials, whether on disks, cassettes, or in other form...

"26. The computerization of some tasks in the Wilson Ross Library of CBP. This brought improvement to services offered; attention was also given to CBP's collection of video materials.

"27. In the main entrance area, visual enhancement was achieved by way of installing an attractive rendering of the House's logo on a prominent wall, as well as a map which clearly symbolized a vision of world missions.

"28. Refurbishing the CBP chapel, with new paint, some new lights, and a display of paintings that emphasized the Great Commission.[8]

"29. The unification of two product originating divisions into one. Such accomplished centralization of editorial tasks...

"30. More efficient execution of publication plans so that books and materials came through without interruption, in fulfillment of CBP's mission to the Hispanic world. These plans included:

"a) The launch of the Reina-Valera Actualizada Bible. This involved special events in El Paso and in various other places. The principal launch event took place in a service conducted at the First Baptist Church of El Paso, and included participation by a number of personages related to the Foreign Mission Board and the Middle America Area. CBP personnel and brethren from the city and other places attended in good number.[9]

"b) More editions of the RVA New Testament, totaling thousands of copies which contributed to evangelistic efforts throughout the Hispanic world; there was a growing appreciation for and utilization of its special Bible studies under the theme "Venid a Mí" (Come unto me).

"c) The initial steps toward eventual full publication of the editorial program known as the Comentario Bíblico Mundo Hispano (Hispanic World Bible Commentary).[10] ... It involves some 150 authors and represents the materialization of long present dreams...

"d) The editorial development and launch publication of a new Vacation Bible School curriculum that carried the central theme ENCUENTRO CON JESÚS (Encounter with Jesus).

"e) Publication of the initial volumes of the Bible study program LA BIBLIA LIBRO POR LIBRO (The Bible, book by book) which represents an alternative to our classic series DIÁLOGO Y ACCIÓN (Dialog and action).

"f) Publication of DESCUBRE TU BIBLIA (Discover your Bible) a panoramic Bible study for children 9 to 11 years of age...

"g) La Biblia Computarizada, Bible software to facilitate study of Sacred Scripture with the delightful help of the computer.

"h) To close this summary of our annual programs of production/publication, I am particularly pleased to mention some books for children: The well accepted series PESCADITOS (Little fish), and other series such as PACO Y ANA (Frankie and Ann), the BUHO series (Owl series), AVENTURAS INFANTILES (Childhood adventures), and ALICIA EN EL PAIS DE LA BIBLIA (Alice in Bibleland). All these are treasures of instruction and inspiration that target the future of humanity: children.

"In making this 'backward look' in my memories, I sense the hand of God guiding and inspiring so many brethren that helped to make these publications possible and thus further God's redemptive mission in the world.

"I feel happy to have been able to participate in the editorial efforts of Casa Bautista de Publicaciones, announcing to the world that there is hope and salvation in Christ and carrying to the world the Holy Scriptures that have been given for the blessing and healing of the nations. 'So... my word that goes out from my mouth: It will not return to me empty, but will accomplish what I desire and achieve the purpose for which I sent it' (Isaiah 55:11 NIV). Amen, let it be so."

Major Personnel Changes 1989-1992

In May 1989, several important personnel recommendations were made:

(1) That Alicia Zorzoli be named director of the Missions Department, in light of the resignation of Mary Jo Stewart[11] to take a chaplain's job in an Arizona hospital.

(2) That the Art Department personnel be reinforced with a request for a missionary who would bring professional skills, considering the imminent departure of Peter Stillman.[12] The coming of John Hatton in 1993 eventually filled this need.

(3) That Ernie McAninch be named director of a reactivated Marketing Services Department in the Marketing Division. His wife, Lee Ann, would serve as an assistant in this department.

(4) That Debra Collins be named director of the Library Services Department, given the resignation of Jimmie Ross.[13]

(5) That Max Furr be named director of the Administration and Finance Division as of June 1, 1989.[14]

(6) The Trustees were also appraised of upcoming retirements of three missionary couples: the Blairs, the Nelsons, and the Carrolls.[15]

In November 1989, the report on personnel is more narrative: the projected missionary retirements have taken place; one notable employee retirement has occurred (that of Blanca Martínez, after thirty years of service with the Publishing House); the arrival of Max and Joan Furr is reported, as of June, and the departure of Mel and Suzie Plunk to take another missionary assignment in Costa Rica.

In May 1990, reported personnel changes included these: Jesse Bryan was asked to leave the Marketing Division to become director of a Communications Office related to the General Director's office. Laverne and Betty Gregory have accepted responsibilities for promoting CBP materials in the United States, as these were distributed by the Baptist Sunday School Board. This decision effectively put the Gregorys "on loan" to the Sunday School Board and left vacant the Domestic Sales Department in El Paso. Two retirements were announced: that of María Lozano who had worked with her husband Roberto in the offset platemaking; and Laura Beamer a long time CBP employee who at the time was serving as director of the Personnel Department.[16]

In November 1990, these changes were announced: Gilbert Pérez has been transferred to the Division of Administration and Finances. Gilbert found his niche here and has become a long term employee in this area, now as a director and with over twenty-five years of service with CBP. His transfer responded to the resignation of Rebekah Lee who had been an associate of Matthew Sanderford in data processing. "Beckie" and her family moved from El Paso. At the time this personnel adjustment was likely overshadowed by the announcement that Mr. and Mrs. Hugo Torres-Gómez had arrived in October, transferring as missionaries from their earlier service in Mexico. Hugo would now head the Marketing Division, filling the vacancy left by the internal transfer of Dr. Jesse Bryan, reported in May.[17]

In May 1991, more personnel movements are reported. Cecil and Jean Thompson have retired (as of April 30). Martha Peña is projecting retirement at the end of this month, after many years of CBP service.[18] Aida Medrano and Cecilia González have been given new responsibilities (in the Administration and Finance Division, and in the Art Department, respectively). No new employees or missionary transfers are reported or requested.

In November 1991, no references are found in reports to Trustees of personnel changes. If any occurred, they must have been very minor adjustments in assignments

In May 1992. Though it did not involve a position requiring Trustee confirmation, it is interesting to note that Nancy Valadez was employed to be the Casa's central receptionist in February 1992. In time she married Cary Hamilton and now is seen in the employee lists as Nancy Hamilton. Daughter of Margarita Valadez, a long time employee in Photocomposition and Editorial Control, Nancy has "learned" the Casa in her now more than twelve years of work here and has served as a key administrative assistant in both the Marketing Division and in the Editorial Division. The author–and the readers–of this book owe Nancy a special word of thanks for compilation of the basic information contained in the Appendices. (Thanks, Nancy–"till you're better paid!")

In November 1992, the personnel report to Trustees speaks of two missionary couples who have arrived and begun working at CBP and the internal transfer of another missionary unit already here: Arrivals included Ed and Kathy Steele to work in the Music and Worship Department[19] and James and Mary Nell Giles.[20] The transfer had to do with Steve and Shirley Ditmore who had been serving in the Evangelism and Music departments, respectively. Their new assignment is reported to be with the Sales Department in the Marketing Division. A veteran employee, Bertha Valle, is reported to have resigned in June to begin working with the El Paso center of Howard Payne University.[21]

Post El Paso Service in Spain

In the late spring of 1993, Dr. and Mrs. García-Bordoli left El Paso for Spain. Their missionary service in Spain has evidently been of surprising duration and ministerial satisfaction. Instead of "perhaps two years," the duration that was in their minds when they left for Spain, their ministry there continued until 1998. Roberto himself has given us what happened next:

"At that point we returned to the United Stated, with the intent of residing in Green Valley, Arizona. But the Baptist church of Vall de Uxo, in Spain, requested the International Mission Board that our appointment be renewed. This was done, and we were reincorporated into the Mission of Spain for a two year stint of volunteer service in the pastorate of that church. After this we returned to the United States and took up retirement residence in El Paso, Texas, where Guillermo and his family still lived.

"Another surprise came when the Evangelical Church of Castinieiras and Ribeira invited us back to Spain! I had preached in that church every time I had visited the area (distant relatives still lived there), and now the church called us to serve as pastor. Somehow it seems fitting to come 'full circle.' For this is where my father's family first heard the gospel and grew in spiritual fervor. Where my grandmother Benita was one of the founding members in 1898.

"The church actually has two locations: One (the older) is in Castinieiras where the present stone building was inaugurated in August of 1910, just a 100 yards from the sea. The second location is in the port city of Ribeira, nearer where most of the members now live. Sunday services and other activities are conducted in both locations. We thank the Lord that after so many years we have the opportunity to serve here. Noemí and I feel that it is very special for us to be returning to the place where the gospel of Christ first came to our family. It gives deep satisfaction to feel that my family's prayer and vision has been fulfilled and that the witness brought to Spain by those British missionaries has indeed borne good fruit."[22]

A Farewell Note from Roberto and Noemí

The Publishing House personnel gave the García-Bordolis an appropriate farewell during the chapel hour on December 16, 1992. *Entre Nos* of that same date published these words from Roberto: "The García-Bordoli family wishes each one of the family of the Baptist Spanish Publishing House the Lord's richest blessings.

"During these five years of our ministry in BSPH, we learned to love you and to enjoy the time that our Heavenly Father permitted us to work together for His glory.

"We will pray for the BSPH and its ministry and for all the friends and coworkers that are a vital part of it. At the same time we ask for your prayers for the future of our lives and the time that the Lord puts before us.

" 'I will extol the Lord at all times; his praise will always be on my lips' (Psalm 34:1; NIV)."

Praise and prayer make good concluding notes—whatever the song— and whenever it is sung.

Endnotes

1. Motion number 1, Trustee Minutes, November 1986, p. 2; CBP Archives.

2. He was a lay leader of the congregation; his ordination to the pastoral ministry came later in El Paso.

3. E-mail communication Dr. H. Robert Tucker to Poe, February 27, 2004.

4. This "re-opening" of the domestic market for direct attention by CBP must be regarded as one of the most important achievements of the García-Bordoli years.

5. Though the term does not appear, "desktop publishing" was essentially brought to the Publishing House with the acquisition of these computers.

6. The reference is especially to training in the use of the QuarkXpress software on the Macintosh computers.

7. Many years earlier the Casa identified the need to protect its books in packages of 2 to 10 copies, for protection in the international distribution process.

8. The framed reproductions were of some impressive original paintings found in the entrance foyer of the Foreign Mission Board in Richmond.

9. May 19, 1989, was the date of this event. It was at this public gathering that the Trustees announced Dr. García-Bordoli's election as the Casa's General Director.

10. Dr. García-Bordoli correctly remembers the early development efforts of this ambitious project of an original multi-volume Bible commentary on the whole Bible to have taken place during his administration. By May 2004, fourteen volumes have been published and are in circulation. Manuscripts are on hand for most of the other ten volumes and will be published as finances and other circumstances permit.

11. Mary Jo's resignation is reported to have taken effect, April 15, 1989; see Report to Trustees, p. 88a; May 1989 Reports and Minutes; CBP Archives.

12. The report says the Stillmans will leave El Paso July 31, having taken another missionary assignment that transferred them to Indonesia.

13. The report includes a letter of resignation signed by both Wilson and Jimmie, terminating their responsibilities with the CBP as of May 30. Wilson's health was deteriorating rapidly and it was decided they should move to Fort Worth to be a bit nearer their children. Max Furr was already on hand to assume the leadership of the Administration and Finance Division and his wife Joan planned to help in the library, under Debra Collins' supervision.

14. All personnel recommendations were adopted; see motions 25, 26, 27, 28, and 29, Minutes Trustee Meeting, May 1989; CBP Archives.

15. Projected dates are June 30 for the Blairs, July 31 for the Nelsons, and October 10 for the Carrolls; see Reports and Minutes, May 1989, p. 88a; CBP Archives.

16. See Reports and Minutes, May 1990, p. 133.

17. See Reports and Minutes, November 1990, p. 133.

18. See chapter 4.

19. This couple came with field service in Panama. Both were highly skilled and very productive. Ed's work on the bilingual hymnal was most notable. They served with the Publishing House until 1998.

20. This couple brought a full career of service in Colombia, principally with the International Seminary in Cali, where James had been both a professor and the president of the school. Their time at CBP was brief but productive.

21. See Reports and Minutes, Trustee Meeting, November 1992, p. 59; CBP Archives.

22. The content of this paragraph and of those on pp. 156-158 were taken from an e-mail message, received by Poe, August 1, 2004.

Chapter 9
Joe T. Poe's Administration

Dr. Joe T. Poe, who with his wife Eleanor had been serving in El Paso since April 1961, was 63 years old in December of 1991.[1] This was already one more than the minimum age for Social Security benefits, and he felt a certain relief in knowing that retirement was available, if it needed to be taken. 1992 loomed as an important year for Eleanor and Joe, for in August it would bring their Fortieth Wedding Anniversary. Already a trip to Hawaii was being planned to celebrate the event![2] Since Dr. Cecil Thompson's retirement in May 1991, Joe was giving part time to be Interim Director of the General Products Division, in addition to his ongoing work as director of the Bible and Commentaries Department. A plan was under way to fuse the General Products Division with the Church Program and Development Division, directed by Ananías González. Much time was given to elaborating the recommendations that would go to the Board of Trustees to approve this reorganization in their November 1992 meeting. As a member of the Administrative Staff (then being called in Spanish "el cuerpo consultivo"), Joe was somewhat aware of ongoing tensions between the Trustee Board and the Casa's General Director, Dr. Roberto García-Bordoli; but he assumed these tensions would gradually ease and that the Argentine's tenure would certainly extend beyond the Poes' retirement—whenever that might come.

But this is not what happened.

The November Trustee Meeting produced an impasse between the Board and the General Director. And García-Bordoli's services were terminated.[3] The Board evidently considered the General Director's style of leadership inadequate for the Casa and preferred a change. Once a decision was made, it proceeded to establish a termination date (November 30) and to specify the details of his benefits upon leaving.[4]

Apparently the Board's first plan was to leave the Administrative Staff in charge of operations, with Dr. Poe as its chairman.[5] Dr. Norberto Herrera heard of the plan and felt it would, in effect, leave the Casa with diluted leadership at a time of serious crisis. He sought out Dr. Carlos García,[6] the Board's president, and expressed his concern. The result was that on the following day, the Board named Poe Interim General Director, effective December 1, 1992,[7] announced such to the Casa's personnel, and requested Poe's presence in the Board meetings for the rest of the week.[8] Poe entered what he subsequently called the most intense six months of his missionary career. In May 1993, Joe T. Poe was named General Director[9] and later was installed in a public service, held on November 19, 1993.[10] He served in this capacity until the day following his 69th birthday, that is, until the end of 1997.

An Interim of Almost Six Months

If the whole interim period (December 1, 1992—May 17, 1993) represented "the most intense" time of his missionary career, as Poe alleges, the first month, December (1992), was the intensest of the intense! Everything and everybody clamored for the General Director's attention.

Poe had assured the Board of Trustees he would work closely with the Administrative Staff.[11] According to minutes recorded by the group's secretary, Dr. Norberto Herrera, five meetings of the staff were held in the first three weeks of December.[12] The first priority had to do with leadership for the Marketing Division. Missionary Hugo Torres-Gómez had been directing this work for about a year and a half, but his own discrepancies with the General Director had become a part of the breakdown in confidence between the Trustees and Dr. García-Bordoli. The result was that Torres-Gómez had also resigned during the Trustee meeting, and his resignation had been accepted with a date of December 7. A list of eleven or more names for his replacement were considered in the December 2 staff meeting. Poe asked for counsel from staff members, without making the process an "election." At the meeting on December 7, he announced that his recommendation to the Executive Committee of the Trustees was that Dr. Jesse Bryan be named as Interim Director of this Division, to begin immediately and function until May 1993. With appropriate Trustee clearance, this naming was done, and Dr. Bryan carried two division directorships until May of the next year. Some divisional reorganization was proposed with a view to economy of budget outlay and enhancing sales sufficiently to cover budget needs.

The Casa's budget for 1993 was another priority concern. Projections of resources available were clearly inadequate to cover budget requests. The result required serious downsizing in various ways to keep the Casa's ministry viable. It would take another month or two of diligent work to produce finally an acceptable budget for 1993.

On Day 2 of his Interim,[13] Poe began what became a pattern during his general directorship: an address (generally monthly) to all Casa personnel, in chapel. These were neither sermons nor devotional talks. They were Poe's efforts to be in open communication with the entire Casa staff concerning matters that influenced the total ministry of CBP. Attendance (always voluntary) was good on this Wednesday morning, and Poe began by asking Jorge Díaz, "his pastor," to pray. Then the Interim General Director announced the obvious: "Yesterday, the Casa opened a new chapter in its history. It 'turned a corner.' "[14] Alluding to the recent developments which had left many sad, bewildered, or confused, he asked the entire staff to put the past behind and pull together toward a positive future. Using Romans 12 as a base, he appealed for sacrifice, cooperation, and victory. Specifically Poe reported on plans to staff the Marketing Division directorship (which he called his administration's first priority) and then dealt with the budget crisis for 1993 (the second highest priority). The operational word would be "austerity," for the Trustees had charged the administration with finding ways to reduce the budget (from the total requested by the divisions) by almost a half million dollars. He requested ideas from everyone to help achieve this necessary reduction.

In chapel on January 6, after a brief program intended to connote the warm afterglow of holiday experiences at Christmas and New Year's, Poe introduced his now full administrative staff[15] (Norberto Herrera, Jesse Bryan, Ananías González, Wayne Quarrier, José Amézaga, Jorge Díaz), commenting that altogether they represented 125 or more years of service with the Publishing House. "Together," he said, "we will find solutions to our problems."[16] While emphasizing the need to grow in total sales and in total collections, Poe was again frank to signal coming budget cuts and obligatory downsizing. It was a part of the theme: "Growth in the midst of austerity." He also announced a Special Offer to employees who would be willing to leave their jobs at CBP. It was not "a golden parachute," but it was an effort to be generous and compassionate in a situation that required downsizing. Employees were given until January 28 to respond. Eleven colleagues signed up for the offer; two additional employees were added. The names of all thirteen, caught in this downsizing need, were published in the February 9 edition of *Entre Nos.*[17] Though for some the offer represented an opportunity to sweeten approaching retirement or to make other career moves being considered, by and large it was a bitter pill. But the medicine was taken, and the Casa moved on.[18]

When Poe made his reports to the May 1993 meeting of the Trustees, personnel changes involved thirty-eight names and affected every division of the House's organization.[19] In hindsight it is little short of amazing that the Casa absorbed so much organizational change in such a short time.

One more change occurred at the May Trustee meeting: The word "interim" was dropped from Poe's designation as General Director. What followed was:

"Non-Interim" Leadership for Fifty-four and a Half Months

Soldiers frequently refer to their military service in terms of total months. Poe says he now has greater appreciation and understanding for this custom, following his four and a half years as Casa's "non interim" General

Director. He also admits that in one sense this is the easiest part of this book to write; and in another equally valid sense it is the hardest. His effort has been to report concisely and fairly, without pretending absolute objectivity.

1993—May to December. When the General Director made his report to the fall Trustee meeting held November 16-19, it was obvious that the Casa was still living critical times of "austerity." But the report on goals seemed at least mildly encouraging. Perhaps the two most important innovations had to do with the designation of Wayne Quarrier as director of an Operations Division (that included both manufacturing and marketing) and the initial use of publishing consultant John Huenefeld of Boston, Massachusetts.

Poe had recommended to the Trustees in their May meeting both the structural change and the naming of Quarrier, and such had been approved. Almost immediately the changes were put into effect. In July Quarrier and Poe had made a brief "trouble shooting" trip to Argentina, with the purpose of shoring up distribution arrangements with the Argentine Board of Publications and the Casa's "deposit operation" in that country, which was being directed by Rafael Altamirano. Unfortunately Altamirano was suffering from terminal cancer. Only limited progress was possible.

With reference to the Huenefeld report and recommendations, the Management Team (as the administrative staff was now officially called) had conducted a short retreat to study Huenefeld's analysis. Poe acknowledged to the Board that the document had created some uneasiness among staff, since Huenefeld recommended further restructuring, questioned efficiency of the print shop, and suggested that Casa continue to downsize to a total of fifty or fewer employees.

Obviously much work remained to be done, but this first year of Poe's administration (half as "interim;" half as "non-interim") had shown the possibilities of change in order to safeguard the long term ministry of CBP. When Poe addressed personnel on December 1, 1993, a year after assuming the General Director role, he noted these things, among the accomplishments of the year:

"We have improved the relations between the Board of Trustees and the Administration of the House.

"We have reconstituted collegial leadership at the level of the Management Team.

"We have elaborated a new statement of our purpose or mission.[20]

"We have renewed the Casa's Program Base Design,[21] taking into account the recommendations of publishing consultant John Huenefeld.

"We have clarified our publication plans not just for one year but for three.

"We have opened the Factory Store.

"We have reduced the operational expenses of the Casa to be in line with our income.

"We have reactivated the program of volunteers.

"We have revised our pricing strategies.

"We have sought to set a more solid basis for our commercial relations in key countries."[22]

Many serious and complicated matters were still pending—and Poe was candid to list several still unaccomplished goals in his message. But something of a "turnaround" had been accomplished. The Casa had again survived a crisis and hopefully could look forward to better times.

1994—A better year. This is precisely the term Poe used to describe 1994 in comparison with 1993, when he made his report to the Trustees in May of 1995. Under the heading of "Administrative matters," the General Director reported that the Casa's finances in 1994 were notably better than a year earlier.[23] Though the goal of a "break even year" had not been achieved, the net operating loss had declined, the annual audit (and relations with missionary Rhea Chafin as the Area Office's auditor) showed improvement, and Dr. Jesse Bryan's management of finances now indicated some modest reserves. In the area of personnel, Poe reported that CBP finished 1994 with some sixty employees with attrition expected to help move that figure lower in the ensuing year. At the end of the year, there were also nineteen missionaries assigned to the Casa's ministry. Dr. and Mrs. James Giles had finished their assignment and had moved to retirement in Dallas, but Ronnie and Freida Adams had been approved to come to El Paso from Venezuela and were expected to arrive in early 1995. Eleven other administrative matters were reported on, including another reorganization of the Marketing Division (June 1, 1994),[24] the implementation of a new program of employee evaluations, and some new equipment acquisitions.

In additional sections of his report the General Director dealt with matters having to do with communications and relationships, and miscellaneous matters. These fill five more pages of single space reporting.[25] Consciously or unconsciously, Poe was attempting to keep the Trustees abreast of the variegated and complicated panorama of matters a CBP General Director has to face. Among other things the report alluded to two events or developments that anticipated the Casa's 90th Anniversary: One was a trip Jorge Díaz and J. T. Poe made to the National Baptist Convention of Mexico in July, 1994,[26] and the other was the filming done by Alan Compton and Jim Swierenga in November (1994) for a video to commemorate the 90th Anniversary.[27] Still another miscellaneous matter reported on was the creation of the Adolfo Robleto Award, as a vehicle to recognize and promote some outstanding recently published Casa book.

1995—A celebration year. A committee was created early in 1994 to plan and direct the Casa's 90th Anniversary Year.[28] It was clear from the outset that the celebration would involve the whole year and be conducted in various ways and in various venues. When the full report of the Anniversary Year Celebration was rendered to the Trustees, it contained twenty-three items![29] These are summarized here:

1. The celebration began the first Wednesday of the year, in chapel. There the anniversary hymn was introduced.[30] The General Director gave one of his monthly messages, finishing this time with a classic quote from Dr. J. E. Davis, the Casa's founder: "There is always much to do, and we cannot do everything in a day, but we propose to march forward with the help of God and achieve all that is possible for us." Since it was "a birthday celebration" of sorts, a cake with "90" candles was served to personnel. The celebration year had begun!

2. In the course of the year, organizational elements (departments and divisions) directed chapel programs with a view to helping all personnel understand the total work of the House.

3. In February, opportunities were seized for the General Director to participate in public activities in Guatemala and Costa Rica. These activities involved deposit personnel in both countries and reached out to the Casa's commercial partners as well as to the evangelical public at large. In Guatemala, a write-up later appeared in the denominational news bulletin. In Costa Rica Guido Picado and Melinda Kyzar achieved some television coverage as well.

4. During the EXPOLIT event in Miami, in late April, a celebration breakfast was hosted for distributors, book store managers and selected friends of the Casa, at which time the anniversary video "La Décima" was launched. Among others, Aldo Broda was present.

5. In connection with the spring meeting of the Board of Trustees, held in El Paso the last part of May, a major event was conducted at the Family Life Center of Scotsdale Baptist Church. Apart from a delicious banquet, attended by nearly two hundred guests (including Trustees, CBP staff and their families, former General Directors, CBP retirees, and other friends), a historic drama was presented on the stage of the Family Life Center. The drama was entitled "Comenzó en una cocina" (It all began in a kitchen). The author was Adelina Mendoza de Almanza, a long time Casa staff member. Everything combined to make May 26 indeed a memorable evening!

6. During the Southern Baptist Convention, held in Atlanta during June, two breakfast events were conducted for key friends of the Casa. These events were directed by Russell and Annette Herrington, Ed and Kathy Steele, and Laverne and Betty Gregory.

7. At the Convención Bautista Mexicana de Texas (Mexican Baptist Convention of Texas; now known as the Hispanic Convention), held this year in Waco, Texas, at the end of June, another event was conducted to commemorate

the Casa's 90th Anniversary. Ananías and Nelly González, and David and Vilma Fajardo directed.

8. At the Baptist World Alliance Congress, held in Buenos Aires, Argentina, during the month of July both an exhibit booth, highlighting the anniversary theme, and a breakfast held at the International Baptist Theological Seminary, provided another venue for celebrating the Casa's ninety years. Those representing CBP and directing these events were Jorge Enrique Díaz, Ananías and Nelly González, David Fajardo, Rubén and Alicia Zorzoli, and Marcos Altamirano (son of Rafael, who was by this time very gravely ill).

9. In September, the General Director had the opportunity to travel to Peru and to Venezuela, where opportunities in Peru with bookstore personnel from all over the country and in Venezuela with a retreat of Baptist pastors, the message of the Casa's Anniversary and its ongoing ministry were emphasized. In Venezuela, the Baptist Convention presented Poe with a hand made tapestry which reproduced the 90th Anniversary logo. It now hangs in the Publishing House library.

10. Packets of materials were developed and sent to the various Baptist conventions in Latin America giving suggestions for a "Día de la CBP" (Baptist Spanish Publishing House Day) in the churches, recommended for the last Sunday in October. Reports of positive and practical response were received from various countries.

11. The mayor and city council of El Paso proclaimed December 1 as a day for special recognition of CBP on its home turf. Several representatives of the Casa attended a ceremony when the mayor made this proclamation on November 28.

12. A public service, held in the sanctuary of the First Mexican Baptist Church of El Paso, on December 1 officially brought to a climax the year's celebrations.

Apart from these events as such, another set of vehicles was mentioned in the report. These included:

1. The anniversary hymn "Seamos Lo Mejor," with words written by Mario Martínez, a long time staff member at CBP, and music by Daniel A. Zamora, a talented Mexican who at the time was studying at Southwestern Baptist Theological Seminary in Fort Worth.

2. The anniversary video "La Décima." Produced by Alan Compton, and filmed by Jim Swierenga, with encouragement and financial support by Dr. Joe Bruce, Area Director, the video had been sent to convention and deposit leadership in all the Latin American countries and was widely used.

3. A commemorative Bible, produced in a limited (and numbered) edition. This beautiful edition of God's Word included a page personally signed by all six living General Directors.[31]

4. All former General Directors were invited to visit the Casa at some point in the year. Several were able to accept and spoke in chapel.

5. Missionary John Hatton, director of the Casa's art department, designed a logo for the year that was widely used on posters, magazines, programs, catalogs, calendars, seals, T-shirts, and in other ways.

6. The current General Director wrote a historical article which was published in *El Hogar Cristiano* (one of the Casa's few remaining magazines at this time).[32]

7. The neighboring association of Baptist churches in Ciudad Juárez (Mexico) and surrounding areas invited the General Director to address their annual associational meeting, with emphasis on the Casa's 90th Anniversary.

8. In connection with a Vacation Bible School workshop, Nelly González and Exequiel San Martín visited the First Baptist Church in León, Guanajuato, Mexico, and conducted a service with special emphasis on the Casa's Anniversary, in the place where Davis had directed the House for ten years during its early history.[33]

9. An updated version of a booklet Wilson Ross had originally done for the Casa's 75th Anniversary was published, somewhat late in the year.[34] It carried the 90th Anniversary logo as its cover design.

10. On October 18, the music library was dedicated in honor of Dr. Ed Nelson, who had been the Music Department director for many years. A special service was conducted in chapel, and a plaque was unveiled. Several members of Dr. Nelson's family came from out of town to attend. Though not directly related to the 90th Anniversary as such, it was another event that contributed to the total program of celebration for the year.

11. Special recognition was given to David Fajardo in his promotional efforts through the local Christian television channel (38) and the local Spanish Christian radio station, Radio Manantial.

Though not mentioned in the "Anniversary Report," two additional celebrations were held to recognize thirty-five years of service by two employees. A "Hilda Kaplan Day" was held on May 3, 1995; and a "María Luisa Porflit Day," on October 25. Longevity has been typical among CBP employees; even so, few get to the 35 year level. Special recognitions seemed totally in order![35]

In addition to the extra things the 90th Anniversary provoked, all the regular work of product development, printing (whether in our plant or elsewhere), marketing and promotion had to go on. The one big shadow over the anniversary year was the economic situation in Latin America. As Poe reminded the Board of Trustees in his report of November 1995: "When we met in November last year [1994], we reported with a strong note of optimism that at that point we had slightly surpassed our sales total of the previous year [1993], and were in a solid position to project growth for 1996.[36] One month later, the devaluation of the Mexican peso hit like a coup d'etat, and with its domino effect [in Latin America]—sometimes called its tequila effect— it destroyed that optimism. In May of this year, [1995], we reported that it did not look like there would be growth (in sales) this year, despite our slogan for the 90th Anniversary.[37] This is the way things are turning out. It does not appear that we will even equal last year's sales; in fact, we will do well to finish the year with total sales some 5% to 10% less than last year."[38]

Poe's November report was apparently written in late October. He had a postscript added which told the Trustees that on November 6 he was diagnosed as needing open-heart surgery to remedy four clogged arteries. The surgery was done on November 7. Hours prior to the surgery, he turned the reins of the Casa to the Division Director at the top of the year's "chain-of-command" sequence, namely Jorge Enrique Díaz. Díaz represented the General Director's office during a special retreat between the Trustees and the Management Team[39] as well as during the Trustee meeting, November 29 and 30. Poe received the Executive Committee in his home during those days to signal his recuperation was progressing, and he was able to attend the climactic Anniversary Service on the evening of December 1. And by the first of January, recuperation had come to a point where the General Director was keeping nearly normal hours.

For a 'jillion' reasons, 1995 really was a year worth remembering!

1996—A good year. Poe continued his custom of monthly messages to all Casa personnel, speaking in chapel on Wednesday, January 3, 1996. His announced theme was: "Ideas and Information to Begin the New Year."[40] Some "Ideas" were drawn from five sources: (1) From the day's issue of *Entre Nos*, where Dietrich Bonhoeffer was quoted as saying: "The year that begins will not be without fear, fault, or need. But with all its fault, all its fear and all its needs, it will be a year with Christ. We have begun with Christ and will follow a future with Christ. Day by day the future will begin with him, and that is what matters."[41] (2) From *The El Paso Times* which had carried articles titled "El Paso survives a challenging year" and "Time to pull together." The application to the Casa's life and ministry was more than obvious. (3) From an article by Dr. Jimmy Draper, president of the Baptist Sunday School Board, who attributed a dramatic turnaround in that Board's performance to seven factors.[42] (4) From an article on Christian radio concerning how to balance the concepts of "business" and "ministry." And (5) from the Bible. Brief passages were read from Philippians, Colossians, Isaiah, and Habakkuk. In the Information section of his message, the General Director reported net sales for 1995 as $2,177,667—about ten percent less than in 1994; and total sales income (collections) as $2,243,840—about sixteen percent less than 1994. Some recovery was expected in 1996, but great care would be needed to keep outgo in line with total available resources. Unfortunately this likely would mean no salary adjustments; it was hoped that Huenefeld's recommendation "No hire/no fire" could be practiced. Careful administration and still improved efficiency were the challenges of the year. Among the fifteen goals for 1996, elaborated by the Management Team in October and approved by the Trustees in November,[43] one spoke of increasing the percentage of sales in the United States by at least three percent, pointing toward a goal that such represent fifty percent of the Casa's sales by the year 2000.

On January 17, Paul D. (known to most colleagues as simply, "P.D.") and Brenda Lee were given a "farewell reception" in chapel, and recognized for ten years' service at CBP. In his presentation concerning the Lees, the General Director commented: "The Lees arrived at a time when we needed them badly. Matthew Sanderford was near retirement as the director of the Computation Department, and we badly needed a replacement. P. D. Lee arrived to become that. And Brenda offered to do office work. One of her first jobs was as my secretary in the department that at that time was called Bibles and Commentaries. They leave the work here, but they will continue working–now for the First Baptist Church of Starkville, Mississippi. We will miss them greatly but we wish them the best..."[44] Fortunately, 1996 did turn out to be "a good year." Something very special was done for the May Trustee Meeting. It was held in Miami, in connection with the EXPOLIT trade show and with a gathering of the deposit directors from most of the Latin American countries. The logistics of the Miami meetings were handled by Ronnie Adams, who did an excellent job. "Extra events" even included an "evening cruise" up one of the canals in Fort Lauderdale to a fish feast under a tin roofed dining hall and a delightful outdoor show of family orientated music and comedy. Following the Trustee Meeting, an assembly was held of the Casa's Management Team, the Executive Committee of the Trustees, and the three Area Directors and their Associates, covering all Latin America. Optimism reigned as growth was projected for all Areas and in the Casa's role related to that growth. There was enough hope for improvement in general sales and distribution for the Trustees to authorize the Management Team to revisit the matter of frozen salaries if the situation seemed to warrant.[45]

In his November report to the Trustees, Poe mentioned his trip to the CBA convention, held in Anaheim, California in July, during which the Casa received its first Gold Medallion Award from the Evangelical Christian Publishers Association.[46]

The General Director also reported on a trip to Richmond, accompanied by Jorge Díaz and Norberto Herrera to dialog with representatives of both the Foreign Mission Board and the Sunday School Board. The meeting's purpose, as expressed by Dr. Don Kammerdiener, the convener, was "to discuss the worldwide Spanish literature needs and submit to the respective entities a plan for ministering to the Spanish market more effectively with less expense and duplication of efforts."[47]   While "joint venture" was the terminology used for these discussions, it was essentially clear that the Sunday School Board now saw its publishing role as world wide and would have been interested in swallowing up CBP, if some agreement could be achieved. Poe urged the Trustees to be open to dialog but cautious to protect the interests of Latin American Baptist constituencies, "to whom this ministry belongs, as represented by this Board of Trustees."[48] Given the ninety years Casa Bautista de Publicaciones had enjoyed the support of the Foreign Mission Board, both philosophically and practically, its representatives were ill prepared for the drastic changes in Board support that lay just over the horizon. One can only conjecture whether the outcomes of these conversations would have been different if Board representatives had been more open concerning the reductions in support that may already have been in the making. The reality is that the moment passed, and whatever possibilities existed then no longer exist. CBP must find its ministry, for its second century, essentially without being a "joint venture" with the Baptist Sunday School Board (now named LifeWay), and–more surprisingly–without the patronage of the Foreign Mission Board (now named International).

At the end of the year, Hilda Navarette Kaplan, a Publishing House employee for 36 years, retired, as did missionary Betty Burtis, who had served in El Paso since 1982. Missionaries Bill and Libby Stennett, who had been directing the CBP operation in Miami, also retired. In their place, missionary Eddy Williams was reactivated from previous service in Mexico and a Last Frontier country.

1997—A record year. Goals for 1997, previously presented to and approved by the Trustees in November, were reviewed by Poe in his first chapel discourse of the year with personnel, on January 15, 1997. The very first one said: "To achieve, by December 31, a total in net sales of $2,650,000." The second one was: "To function during the year with healthy finances, in line with the budget approved by the Trustees." Thirteen other measurable and dated goals followed.[49]

By early June, Poe could report to all, in another chapel message, that good progress was being made on goals for the year.[50]

By late summer, quite a number of changes in personnel occurred: Ananías and Nelly González had retired and moved to Houston. A. D. Lagrone retired toward the end of May, after some 22 years of employment at CBP.[51] Missionary Debra Collins resigned, effective June 26, to accept a position on the ministerial staff of First Baptist Church, El Paso. Steve and Barbara Manuel were transferred from missionary service in Mexico, Steve to be director of the Office of Communications and Public Relations. Siegfried and Donna Enge, whose earlier mission work had been done in Argentina, ceased their work with CBP in August, after some twenty years in El Paso, to begin their retirement. Brian and Tina Allen[52] were transferred from the Publishing House to the new Regional Leadership Office in Quito, Ecuador,

On October 8, 1997, Poe brought what he announced would likely be his last message to CBP personnel, in a chapel service, during his tenure as General Director.[53]   Rev. Ted Stanton had already been elected as the new General Director, to begin serving in January. Poe hoped to contribute to a smooth transition in general leadership. His message was entitled "How to finish one chapter in the history of the Casa's ministry and be in optimal conditions to begin a new chapter." His counsel was neither surprising nor particularly innovative, but it was practical and realistic. Sales totals were announced to be close to the targeted goal, "for the first time in several years." Poe counseled, "Don't let up—in this last quarter of the year!... We may even go beyond our goal for the year... Together, we can do it!... Let's don't end 'this chapter' by letting down our efforts. Nor should we allow ourselves 'gossip-like speculations'... Transitions bring uncertainties, but let's avoid speculations and unnecessary fear," he counseled. Rather "let's conclude this chapter with 'a mind to work' (Nehemiah 4:6),... dedication (Romans 12:1-2),... efforts to reach our goals (Philippians 3:14),... and with courage and faith (Joshua 1:7a, 9)... Let's prepare for 'the new chapter' in the Casa's history that is soon to open, with prayer, gratitude, faithfulness, and in honor of those who have gone before... In this process [of transition], may God be glorified, ourselves edified, and our ministry advanced..."

When Jorge Díaz, as Marketing Division Director, reported to the Trustees in November 1997, he signaled that sales for the year were ahead of the goal, and that 1997 could turn out to be a record year. According to the Marketing Division Report to the Trustees in May 1998,[54] the total turned out to be $2,885,395.00. This victory was celebrated in chapel in a service led by Díaz on January 21. "Victory" coffee mugs were distributed to all personnel with the slogan "Thanks to You...Together We Can Do It!" [Spanish: "Gracias a Usted... ¡Juntos Sí Podemos!"] It was a special moment to celebrate "a record year."

A Transition into Retirement

Between Christmas and New Year's, Poe with the help of his brother-in-law Frank McAnear, vacated the General Director's suite, moving his personal files and belongings to offices on the north hall of the older Publishing House building, where he had worked as director of the Bible Publication Department since 1983. The Trustees had assigned him the title of General Director Emeritus, and Ted Stanton, as incoming CEO, had accepted Poe's offer to be a volunteer in the product development division.

Thus in contrast to what might be considered "normal," for retirees to conclude their work and move from the scene, the Poes bought the mission home where they had been living for thirty-five years, and, as Joe likes to comment, "We didn't even clean out the closets!" At the Publishing House, he made the quick transition to a part-time but regular "volunteer."[55] His first editorial assignment was to review the manuscript material on hand for a new Spanish Study Bible. At the time, the project was under Exequiel San Martín's supervision, but when Ted Stanton, the new General Director, named San Martín Director of the Production Division (in early March), Poe's assignment grew to that of a General Editor for the new Study Bible, eventually titled *Biblia de Estudio Siglo XXI*. He was given part-time secretarial assistance in the person of Gladys Echegoyen, and the two of them worked hard on this project to see it to publication in late 1999.

Poe has continued as a regular, part-time volunteer during these years, giving approximately 500 hours annually to Publishing House tasks. As 2005 approaches, he can look back over nearly fifty years of some kind of relationship with CBP. For it was on November 28, 1955, that he wrote his first letter to the Foreign Mission Board, inquiring about appointment for El Paso.[56] "The purpose of this letter," he had written Elmer West, Personnel Secretary of the Foreign Mission Board, "is to relate an experience and an impression concerning our particular place of potential mission service." He related an encounter with a published personnel need in *The Commission* magazine, where in the context of Latin America's total current needs, it was stated: "El Paso Baptist Publishing House Mission" needs a missionary "couple (the man to be book editor)." Poe wrote Dr. West: "A peculiar sense of 'that's my place' came and continues..." On Monday, December 12, Mr. West called from Richmond and invited Joe and Eleanor to a conference with him in Nashville (Tennessee) "this week."[57] On Wednesday, December 14, Eleanor and Joe met with Dr. West and Dr. Frank K. Means, Area Secretary for Latin America, at the Hermitage Hotel in Nashville. Joe wrote this note for his files: "Both Eleanor and I feel encouraged about mission service in general, [the] El Paso position in particular." Appointment procedures moved along, and in October 1956, Joe and Eleanor were among eighteen new missionaries appointed by the Foreign Mission Board.[58] Now, almost fifty years later, they are "still at it." And still thanking God. "His compassions fail not. They are new every morning; great is thy faithfulness."[59]

Joe delightfully recalls that his "call to missions" came at a Pre-School BSU Retreat, in the fall of 1946, when the invitation hymn being sung was B. B. McKinney's song, "Wherever He Leads, I'll Go." God has used the song time and again to help him perceive divine leadership in his pilgrimage of faith and Christian service. Its words still synthesize that basic commitment of a disciple: "Wherever He leads... to do whatever He directs..." For "whoever I am, thou knowest, O God, I am thine."[60]

Endnotes

1. His date of birth was December 30, 1928. Place: Eastland, Texas (100 miles west of Fort Worth). Parents: Paul and Maye Broughton Poe. Personal and family details, both for Joe and Eleanor, may be found in his books Missions for a New Century and "By Love Serve One Another."

2. The trip was made in late June and early July, and in part was shared by Eleanor's sister and husband, Dr. and Mrs. Frank McAnear, who were then serving as ISC missionaries in South Korea.

3. See Trustee Minutes, November 1992, Motion 3, p. 6, CBP Archives.

4. Ibid., pp. 5, 7, 8; CBP Archives.

5. Ibid., p. 5.

6. Peru's representative on the Board and, at the time, a Vice-President of his country.

7. Trustee Minutes, November, 1992, Motion 10, p. 8; CBP Archives.

8. Ibid., Motion 8, p. 7; CBP Archives.

9. See CBP Trustee Minutes, May 1993, Motion 3, p. 5; CBP Archives. Several denominational periodicals subsequently carried announcements of the naming; examples: El Eco Bautista, Mayo-Junio de 1993, p. 12; Luminar Bautista, Junio de 1993, p. 5; The Commission, August, 1993, p. 51; La Voz Bautista, Año 86 (1993), Núm. 2, p. 7.

10. The service was held in the sanctuary of First Baptist Church, El Paso, with participation by various trustees, such as Roberto Velert Chisbert (from Spain), Lemuel Larrosa (from Uruguay) and Alberto Salazar (from Chile). Special music was presented in the form of a duet sung by Delores Robleto and Wayne Quarrier; the principal message was given by Dr. Donald Kammerdiener, Executive Vice President of the Foreign Mission Board; and the Prayer of Dedication was led by Dr. Joe Bruce, FMB's Area Director for Middle America and Canada. A reception followed. The El Paso Times, in its issue for November 19, 1993, carried an announcement of the event and invited the public.

11. When Poe occupied the General Director's suite, at the end of December, 1992, he decided to designate the main office used by previous General Directors as the Conference Room for the Administrative Staff and occupy himself the smaller adjacent space. He placed a hand lettered sign in the Staff Conference Room: "The Team Is More Important than the Coach."

12. See sets of minutes numbered 23 to 27, pp. 53-61; CBP Archives. The Publishing House was closed for a Christmas recess the last ten days of the month.

13. December 2, 1992.

14. Chairs in the chapel had been rearranged to symbolize that "turned corner." Miryam R. Díaz-Picott, CBP employee since 1986, Marketing Division Director since 1999, says the rearrangement impressed her and other personnel. "It surprised us," she says, "and made us think on the need for changes."

15. Still officially called "el cuerpo consultivo" but now described as "un equipo gerencial que funciona;" not surprisingly the term "equipo gerencial" (roughly equivalent to "management team") became the preferred and official name for the administrative staff.

16. See manuscript, conserved by Poe, p. 11; apparently a sound recording was not made.

17. The Entre Nos list is as follows: Sandra Anderson, Martha Ayala, José Martínez, Roberto Marrufo, Roberto Monroy, Aurora Morales, Yolanda Oseguera, Othon Peregrino, Josefina Pérez, Esperanza Rodríguez, Norma Rolón, Elsa Rousselín, Clara Ruiz-Velasco.

18. Apart from these positions that were eliminated, there was a voluntary program of salary reduction, approximately 2%, and Poe later reported that "thirty four of us have participated in that plan of voluntary salary reduction." (See Message, Poe to personnel, December 1, 1993; conserved in recorded form in the CBP Library as T-712.)

19. See pp. 220-221 of the reports and recommendations to the May 1993 Trustee meeting; CBP Archives. Though missionaries Laverne and Betty Gregory are mentioned as having been reactivated from their

pre-retirement category and missionaries Tom and Peggy Sutton are mentioned as arriving and beginning work (along with three new employees in the Marketing and Production divisions), all the others have to do with transfers or persons ending their work at CBP. Missionaries Hugo and Fifi Torres-Gómez and Steve and Shirley Ditmore were among those ending their work with CBP.

20. At this time (December, 1993), the wording approved by the Trustees was: "The purpose of the Baptist Spanish Publishing House is to efficiently publish and distribute the best in literature, music, Bibles, books and other materials to help individuals and churches in reaching the world for Christ and to develop Christians in their walk with the Lord."

21. In effect, this was the last time the Program Base Design technique was used as the Casa's planning vehicle; subsequently an annual Business Plan was used.

22. See pp. 3 and 4, manuscript of Message, Poe to personnel, December 1, 1993; a sound recording is conserved in CBP Library as T-712.

23. At the end of 1992, unpaid bills totaling some $200,000 had to be carried into, and become the first priority of, the budget for 1993. At the end of 1993, there were no unpaid bills; without this carryover burden, 1994 had a better chance from its very start.

24. It was at this point that Wayne Quarrier left the employ of the Casa to move to Pensacola (to open a counseling practice); manufacturing and marketing were separated into two divisions; Jorge Díaz was named as director of the Marketing Division and José Amézaga was named director of the Production Division.

25. See Reports and Recommendations for Trustee meeting, May 1995, pp. 7-11; CBP Archives.

26. The Convention was held in Toluca, where the Casa was born; see chapter 1. Poe was invited to address the convention and used the occasion to launch the Casa's 90th Anniversary.

27. Still another early development for the anniversary was a major article in The El Paso Times that appeared on September 17, 1994 (Section F, p. 1). One of its subheads proclaimed: "What began in a Mexico kitchen

stays strong 89 years later." Its historical summary emphasized that in 1995, Casa Bautista would "celebrate 90 years in business."

28. Members of the original committee, according to minutes of a meeting dated April 27, 1994, were: David Fajardo, J. T. Poe, Tom Sutton, Jorge Díaz, and Betty Gregory. Certain subcommittees were created along the way, and many helped with the kaleidoscope of events and emphases eventually planned and executed.

29. See "Informe de las Actividades Realizadas en Celebración del Nonagésimo Aniversario de la CBP," originally intended to be presented to the Trustee meeting in November 1995, but actually given to the meeting of Trustees held in Miami, Florida, May 15-17, 1996; pertinent pages among the reports and recommendations: 24a-24d; CBP Archives.

30. See below. Its title was a challenge: "Seamos Lo Mejor" (Let's Be the Best).

31. Patterson, Hill, Broda, Tucker, García-Bordoli, and Poe all personally signed a page that was expressed from place to place on three or four continents and then tipped into the Bible, manufactured in Great Britain.

32. See "Casa Bautista de Publicaciones— 1905-1995—90 Años de Servicio," by Dr. José Tomás Poe, General Director, in El Hogar Cristiano, Tomo XXXIX, No. 4 (October-November-December, 1995), pp. 18-19.

33. A home video was made of this service which is catalogued in the CBP Library as VC-151. See also chapter 1.

34. See Noventa Años de Historia y Ministerio, J. Wilson Ross, Revisión y Actualización de José Tomás Poe, El Paso: Casa Bautista de Publicaciones, 1995.

35. 1996 brought two more such recognition events for 35 years of CBP service, one for José Amézaga, and one for Joe T. Poe.

36. Poe probably means 1995.

37. The slogan was "Growing with You."

38. See Informe del Director General, Informes y Recomendaciones a la Junta Directiva, November 1995, p. 3; CBP Archives.

39. The retreat was held in Sacramento, New Mexico, on November 27 and 28, and featured conferences by Dr. Justice Ander-

son, former missionary to Argentina and long term professor of missions at Southwestern Baptist Theological Seminary in Fort Worth.

40. See manuscript of message, conserved by Poe; apparently a sound recording was not made.

41. See Entre Nos, Vol. 19, No. 1; January 3, 1996, p. 1.

42. These factors were identified as: (1) the identification of problems and the quick implementation of solutions; (2) careful administration of budget; (3) fulfillment of deadlines in both editorial and production processes; (4) attention to feedback and efforts to introduce improvements; (5) better cooperation across departmental lines and the development of products that correspond to felt needs and that transform lives; (6) improvements in bookstores; and (7) the will to continue to analyze our operations, even the accustomed and traditional, to continue to innovate.

43. See Entre Nos, vol. 18, No. 42; October 25, 1995.

44. See manuscript of Poe's remarks, conserved by him, dated January 17, 1996.

45. See Motion 25, Trustee Minutes, Meeting May 15-17, 1996; CBP Archives.

46. The book so recognized was Los Evangélicos y la Política by José Luis Martínez.

47. In the "Informe del Director General," dated November 1, 1996, rendered to the Trustees in their November 1996 Meeting, p. 6; see also Poe's specific report on the Richmond meeting, same source, pp. 105-106 plus attachments on pages 107-108 (the attachments include Dr. Kammerdiener's letter in which the purpose is expressed in English); CBP Archives.

48. Ibid., p. 106.

49. See manuscript of chapel message by Poe to personnel, dated January 15, 1997; conserved as a sound recording in the Publishing House library, as T-826.

50. See manuscript of message, conserved by Poe, dated June 4, 1997; apparently a sound recording was not made.

51. 1972-1982; 1985-1997; first as a pressman and later as Director of the Pre-Press Department.

52. The Allens who had earlier served in both Mexico and Kazakhstan were reactivated from "on leave of absence" status in mid-1996 and came to El Paso where Brian served as Associate Director of the Administration and Finance Division. It had been assumed he would succeed to the division directorship when Dr. Jesse Bryan retired.

53. He said that according to his count there had been 46 such messages during the 58 months of his service as General Director (with three more months left to go).

54. Rendered by Díaz, though his own responsibilities had changed to the Editorial Division in the month of March.

55. The January 7 issue of Entre Nos carried a notice that Poe's "new telephone extension is 232," and the January 14 issue included a thank-you-note from Joe and Eleanor for the retirement banquet the Casa personnel had given them on December 18, complete with photographs, cards, and various gifts.

56. Both Joe and Eleanor had been "mission volunteers" since their college days—in Eleanor's case, since even earlier. Joe's first contact with an FMB Personnel Department representative happened in the fall of 1946, a decade before their mission appointment in October 1956.

57. At the time the Poes were giving pastoral leadership to First Baptist Church of Alamo, Tennessee, a small town about 150 miles west of Nashville.

58. Among these were Tom and Connie Hill and Cecil and Jean Thompson, all of whom served several years at the BSPH; see chapters 5 and 6.

59. Lamentations 3:22, 23, KJV.

60. The last line is from Dietrich Bonhoeffer's poem "Who Am I?" Found in Letters and Papers from Prison, New York: The McMillan Company, 1967, pp. 188-189.

Chapter 10

Ted Stanton's Years

Although J. T. Poe had publicly compared his service as General Director to a one term presidency,[1] the years moved along on an acceptable trajectory,[2] and neither personal health issues nor pressure from the Trustees appeared to force him to conclude his directorship. Nevertheless, Dr. Joe Bruce, FMB's Area Director for Middle America and Canada,[3] specifically counseled Poe not to announce his retirement dates too early, lest his leadership be affected negatively, like that of a "lame duck president."[4] Thus it was not until May 1997 that Poe announced to the Trustees that he would conclude his service as General Director at the end of that year.[5] As expected, the Trustees proceeded to name a Search Committee, opting (as it had done in 1992-93) to charge the Executive Committee with this responsibility. This meant that the following people composed the Search Committee: Misael Marriaga, Hayward Armstrong, Frank Johnson, and Victoria Flores.

In contrast to the somewhat generalized custom in the circle of CEOs of North American companies, Poe did not feel he should seek to influence directly the choice of his successor—and he so stated to the Trustees in his Retirement Letter. However, loyalty to outstanding members of his staff did prompt him to make sure three names were on the "possibility list," which the Search Committee compiled. Thus he wrote brief but sincere letters to the Committee asking that Jesse Bryan, Jorge Díaz, and Norberto Herrera be given consideration. He felt strong cases could be made for each of these three men. Dr. Jesse Bryan offered the advantages of lengthy service with CBP in various positions, related to both the Sales/Distribution/Marketing area as well as in the Administration/Finances area.[6] Jorge Díaz offered the advantages of being arguably the most widely known staff member of CBP plus successful and extensive service in the editorial area[7] and successful though slightly less extensive service in the marketing area.[8] Dr. Norberto Herrera offered the advantages of long term service at CBP, with most of that related to administration at both the division level and as a part of the general director's staff, apart from his care to detail as a recognized attorney in Nicaragua, his country of origin, and his years of educational and administrative leadership as founding president of the evangelical university in his home country.[9]

Before the May Trustee meeting ended, the Search Committee reported its plan of action.[10] The precise workings of the Committee were appropriately held in confidence, but by late summer the group had agreed on a recommendation, and a special session of the CBP Board of Trustees was convoked for Miami, Florida, on September 19, 1997. The Committee recommended another very strong candidate that had emerged as both available and very well qualified. He was Ted O. Stanton, a member of the Trustee Board since 1990. Perhaps not since Patterson had a candidate emerged that combined so many elements of background and experience that seemed ideal for the General Director of Casa Bautista de Publicaciones. Ted (like Patterson) seemed to have ink in his blood. Three of his brothers had been active in the printing industry in his home state of Arkansas. Indeed Ted himself had trained to be a printer and had worked as a printer in his youth. God's call to vocational Christian service had somewhat altered that career trajectory, and he studied church music both at Ouachita Baptist University and at Southwestern Baptist Theological Seminary. Following seminary studies, he had served churches in Arkansas, Texas, and Oklahoma, in the areas of music, education, and administration.

In 1961, he had married his high school sweetheart, Mary Frances Ridgell. Mary was also talented in music and had studied along with Ted at Ouachita, where she received bachelor's and master's degrees in elementary education. Three children were born to Ted and Mary: Jeffrey Mark, in 1965; Alisa Kay, in 1967; and Eric Paul, in 1971.

This couple eventually felt called to missionary service, and they were appointed for work in Argentina by the Foreign Mission Board, SBC, in May 1976. After language training during 1977 in San José, Costa Rica, they first lived in Paraná, Entre Ríos and later in Buenos Aires where Ted served for nine years as national worship and music promoter for the Argentine Baptist Convention. He led more than 200 workshops in that field, and numerous workshops and conferences on personal evangelism and discipleship. He was pastor of two churches, periodically taught in various Bible institutes around the country, and served briefly as substitute professor at the International Baptist Seminary in Buenos Aires. Mary was active, both in local churches and in several Bible institutes, in organizing and directing children's choirs, and in leading workshops for children's choir workers.[11]

Ted's administrative and relational skills always blossomed, in whatever setting he labored in. Not surprisingly, the Foreign Mission Board detected these gifts and in 1990 asked Ted to serve as Associate to the Area Director for Spanish South America. From 1990 to 1992 the Stantons continued to make their home in Buenos Aires while traveling and working among all the nine Spanish-speaking countries of the continent. An additional associate, Dr. Hayward Armstrong, was added to the area staff in 1992, and the Stantons moved to Caracas, Venezuela, where their responsibilities then focused on the five northern countries: Venezuela, Colombia, Ecuador, Peru, and Bolivia. Mary's ministry from 1990-1997 was concerned primarily with missionary families and with area staff support.

Ted became a member of the Board of Trustees for the Baptist Spanish Publishing House when he was named an area Associate in 1990. He served as vice president for several years. In this capacity he had formed a part of the Search Committee for General Director in 1992-93. In every meeting of the Board of Trustees, his knowledgeable and wise participation made him well known and deeply appreciated. It was certainly not difficult to see why the Search Committee in 1997 had made him their choice. And he was unanimously elected in that special meeting of the Trustees in Miami.

Plans were made for a special service in El Paso to recognize Joe Poe for his work as General Director and to install Ted Stanton in this position. The event, complete with an elaborate reception, was conducted at the First Mexican Baptist Church, in El Paso, on December 4, 1997.

At the author's request, Ted has written a summary of his years of service with CBP as its General Director. With only such editing as necessary to bring this section into full harmony with the style and structure of this centennial book, Ted's memories are herewith presented as he wrote them. Special typography and indents identify all his material. Brackets are occasionally used to show editorial changes or additions. The effect is like a coffee klatsch conversation with Ted and Mary at their home in the Little Rock, Arkansas, suburb of Bryant. Over coffee, perhaps served by Mary, Ted begins:

Dates of service at CBP

"I was elected by the Casa's international Board of Trustees in September 1997, and agreed to assume the leadership role as of January 1, 1998. Dr. Joe Poe and I had a joint retirement and installation service in El Paso with the entire board present in early December 1997. I served as General Director until November 30, 2001 when Jorge Díaz officially assumed the position upon my retirement. Mary and I had originally planned to work at CBP for about two more years, but [we] decided to retire early due to my continuing heart irregularities, the installation of a pacemaker, countless doctor visits and five periods of hospitalization in El Paso between June 2000 and March 2001.

"During our service at CBP, Mary worked in the Resource Design and Development Division as Editor of Children's Resources. She greatly enjoyed this responsibility not only for the work she was able to do with various books and other children's resources, but also for the opportunity it gave her to become well acquainted with most of the personnel of the Casa.

"Mary was of great encouragement and help to me and to Norma Armengol[12] by assisting in numerous social and hospitality roles at the Casa, both for regularly scheduled activities and on various special occasions.

"My decision to accept the directorship of the Casa at the invitation of the international Board of Trustees brought a flood of memories to my mind as I considered God's providence in my life up to that time. I worked for several years as a part-time printer and a part-time music and youth director to pay my college expenses, and began my university studies in psychology and counseling. I later changed my major to a church music emphasis, where I organized and directed the Ouachita BSU Choir and was eventually appointed Student Director of the Ouachita Choir and the Ouachita Singers. In my senior year, I was elected to 'Who's Who in American Colleges and Universities.' I found my greatest pastime in writing and editing (having been editor of newspapers in both grammar school and junior high), and along with my future wife (Mary) was actively involved in the Mission Band (a missions activity and promotion organization) in Ouachita Baptist University. Upon graduation, I spent two years in active service with the U.S. Army followed by several years of reserve duty. Then for eleven years I had experience on church staffs, including administrative duties in a large church. [All this was before we answered] God's call to missions.

"My background and preparation were at least in some ways similar to those of Dr. Frank Patterson, yet I hasten to clarify that his formal theological preparation went far beyond my own, and his admirable capacities for giving sound leadership in times of crisis make my own pale in comparison. 'Dr. Pat' and I compared notes on several similarities in our lives' stories before I was officially installed as General Director. Following are but three examples: I went through printing trade school and worked my way through college as a part-time printer, and Dr. Pat had printing experience of his own. My life's roots were also grounded in the First Baptist Church of Nashville, Arkansas where Dr. Pat last served as pastor before beginning his career as a missionary. My mother was born and raised near Nashville, and Dr. Pat remembered some of my relatives who are still members of that great church. The third similarity is somewhat humorous, but perhaps significant as well. As a youth and until my sophomore year in college, I raised rabbits commercially in my back yard (reaching a total of about 250 at one point) to pay high school and college expenses, while Dr. Pat raised chickens [on the Publishing House grounds] in El Paso [and sold] eggs [to help meet] expenses.

"A memorable highlight during our four years at the Casa was the privilege of hosting the entire Board of Trustees in our home for a 'home cooked meal' every May and November with only one exception – the final month in 2001 when we were preparing to move – after many household belongings had already been sold or packed. Those dinners which Mary cooked, usually with Norma Armengol's assistance in serving, were a special delight for all of us. We always set up the regular dining table, plus two other small tables in an adjoining room, to accommodate all present. After dinner each time, we gathered in the living room for informal conversation, occasional singing, and an endless round of jokes and 'Who can top this?' humor. By consensus, we usually decided that Leoncio Veguilla from Cuba was the undisputed champion of humor, especially with his seemingly endless 'Pepe' jokes. A close runner-up, however, was Juan Calcagni from Argentina on the night he favored us with the history, background and actual solo singing of several tangos. I'm sure the neighbors sometimes wondered what kind of crowd we were!

Developments and Other Events

"After having served as a member of the Casa's Board of Directors from 1990 until my election near the end of 1997 as General Director, I had a fairly comprehensive idea of the needs, possibilities, difficulties, and general administration concepts in relation to the publishing ministry. However, having general knowledge and limited experience with some aspects of the Casa's ministry and suddenly having overall responsibility for its direction and leadership are two significantly different things, as I quickly learned.

"The constant tension caused by financial difficulties, staffing needs, uncertainties in the international marketing and distribution systems, and rapidly evolving technological changes undoubtedly took its toll on the energy level of employees and missionaries working there. This was an ever-present challenge for the administration.

"I am convinced that one approach which helped to encourage employees and missionaries, and to solidify in our minds the true purpose of the Casa, was the annual 'Spiritual Emphasis Week' with invited outside speakers. Those were days of heightened awareness and spiritual renewal for the great majority of workers, and were remembered long past the final 'Amen' of each session.

"In an attempt to honor the enormous contributions of both Dr. Frank Patterson and his wife, Polly, to the ministry of the Casa, the board approved my recommendation to name the newer building on the west side of the complex the 'Frank and Pauline Patterson Building.' A public worship service in which both the Pattersons shared vignettes of their

Casa experiences consummated the recognition on November 19, 1998, and a beautiful plaque and photograph hang in the main foyer as a memento of the occasion.

"It is significant to note that not long after the building dedication, the Lord called Polly home after a prolonged illness. Soon thereafter, Dr. Pat sold their vacation cabin in Cloudcroft, New Mexico and donated the proceeds to the Baptist Spanish Publishing House Foundation – a gift which helped get the Foundation off to a good start.

Reflections of Appreciation for CBP's Ministry

"On numerous occasions during my tenure as General Director, I heard comments from people all across Central America and South America concerning their appreciation for the Casa's long ministry to Spanish-speaking people. The following personal experience during my years as a missionary in Argentina is but one such testimony of the value of the printed word.

"In the cold regions far south in the Argentine Patagonia, some sheep herders routinely spend long months in isolation with almost no one to talk to except their sheep, dogs, and horses. Such was the case with Mario Choiquehuala, who worked alone on a sheep ranch near Río Grande. Mario looked forward to his occasional visits to the city to stock up on meager supplies and to drink alcoholic beverages for two or three days before he had to return to his isolated post.

"Just after arriving in Río Grande for one such visit, Mario heard singing as he was walking the city streets. The nearer he got to the source of the sound, the more the music attracted him. His curiosity caused him to approach the building and look in. Someone in that small Baptist church welcomed him in and made him feel at home. After enjoying the music, the visitor was given a Gospel of John which had been published by the Baptist Spanish Publishing House. Mario returned home two days later and nothing was heard from him for nearly three months.

"The next time when Mario traveled to Río Grande for supplies, he went straight to the Baptist church and greeted those in attendance with a cheery 'Hello, brothers!' With joy, he shared what had happened in his life since his earlier visit. Alone on that Patagonian sheep ranch, he had read the Gospel of John several times, felt the presence of the Holy Spirit, trusted Jesus as his Savior, and gained enough understanding to look for fellowship with his new brothers and sisters in Christ. The spiritual hunger in Mario's heart was met through his ears as he heard the church singing hymns from a hymnal [published by Casa Bautista], and through his eyes as he read the Gospel of John, also [published by CBP].

"The Casa's ministry had reached all the way to an isolated sheep ranch south of the windy Strait of Magellan which separates the South American continent from the Tierra del Fuego ('Land of Fire,' so called by early explorers who saw many small cooking and warming fires which dotted the sheep ranches of the frigid Patagonia).

Looking Forward

"In looking toward the Casa's second century of service, I am more convinced than ever before of the value of this specialized ministry to the entire Spanish-speaking world. Although we recognize that a number of other languages and dialects are spoken throughout Latin America and Spain, we must remember that by far the dominant and official language of government and business in those same countries is still Spanish. For this reason alone, even if there were no other reason, this publishing ministry in the Spanish language is a key avenue for spreading the gospel through the myriad resources of the Casa. Significant communities of Spanish speakers are alive and well on every continent of the earth regardless of the 'official' language in those countries. These communities whose heart language is Spanish depend primarily upon the resources of the Casa to provide doctrinally sound materials for evangelism, discipleship, church growth, and expansion. I firmly believe the Casa amply fulfills needs for Spanish speakers around the globe, and increasingly so in the United States as well, that no other entity is equipped or prepared to fill.

"My paramount dream for the second century of the Casa's ministry is specifically concerned with the Baptist Spanish Publishing House Foundation. My dream is that the Foundation will grow to such an extent that significant funding can and will be provided for the Casa to enable needed resources to continue to reach the hands of Spanish-speaking people at a price they can afford to pay even if it means the Casa must sell those resources at a subsidized price. The Casa's ministry has always been characterized as just that— a ministry— rather than a money-making business venture as is the case with most other publishing houses. This fact alone distinguishes the Casa from most of her 'competitors' and gives me great pride in remembering that I have had a small part in leading the Baptist Spanish Publishing House.

"In short, I believe in the Casa, and I am determined to do everything possible to see that this ministry continues for many years to come. We cannot afford to do otherwise for the sake of those who depend upon us. The 'everything possible' I refer to, however, includes my personal financial commitment and my personal encouragement to others to join me in the task.

"I have seen numerous changes in the methods, materials, operations, techniques, strategies, policies and procedures utilized by Casa personnel in recent years, including those during which I was leading. Likewise, I fully expect to see many changes in both immediate and long-range outlooks for this ministry. Change is inevitable, and I welcome it!

"Our societies become increasingly more dependent upon electronic means of communication with each passing year, but the printed word has been and will continue to be a primary means of communication for many years to come. At the same time, I believe a great part of the future of the Casa depends upon the ability to employ not only the printed and recorded word, but also the electronically reproduced word through the Internet, CDs, DVDs, mini-DVDs, and whatever vehicle tomorrow's technology may offer. The Casa's ministry is constantly changing in regard to methods, but we must never change from presenting the central message of Christ until He returns!

Difficulties

"Even from the beginning days of my four years at the helm of the Casa, we knew that we were facing serious difficulties concerning finances. We were in the final two years of a declining support in operational funding from the SBC's International Mission Board,[13] and we were forced to make significant changes in our operational structure in order to meet the challenge of becoming a self-supported institution. Our sales had to be sufficient to take up the slack of now-absent subsidy funding from the IMB. This was most difficult, to say the least.

"In addition, the change in the general philosophy for the placement of IMB missionary personnel directly affected the Casa as most institutions related to the IMB (publishing houses, hospitals and clinics, and seminaries) found it more difficult to secure additional missionary personnel. The beginning of the almost singular emphasis directing that almost all missionaries be directly involved as church planters — at the expense of a more balanced emphasis to include many specialties such as discipleship training, theological education, music evangelism, medical missions, publishing houses, etc. — naturally slowed and in some cases made the placement of missionaries for long-term service at the Casa a virtual impossibility. This had never been the case in previous decades, and it was a disheartening reality we had to face.

"Since about 2002, however, we have seen some tempering of this emphasis to allow greater flexibility in assigning missionaries in various disciplines where they have exhibited a commitment to follow God's call. This is, in my opinion, a wise decision as urgent calls have come from all around the world for missionaries to be involved in evangelism through those same disciplines (discipleship training, theological education, music evangelism, medical missions, and publishing houses) which for at least a few years had seemed to many missionaries to have been relegated to a perceived non-essential, invalid role in the overall picture.

"An additional result of the significant reduction in the number of missionaries permitted to work in missionary publishing efforts was related to those who had previously been directly involved in the management and supervision of 'book deposit' operations in Central America, South America, and Spain. One of our earliest changes in terminology during my years at the Casa was my insistence upon referring to 'resource centers' rather than 'book deposits.' I am firmly convinced that everything produced at the Casa is a valuable resource for someone (otherwise, it should not be produced) and that it must be treated as such.[14]

"It must be noted that virtually every 'book deposit' related to the Casa was distinct in some aspects from every other one due to local needs, provisions, and operations. During the significant change in IMB philosophy of missionary personnel placement in 1998-2000, almost every one of the missionaries previously assigned to 'literature promotion' through book deposits was removed from those places of leadership in order to become more directly involved as church planters. This resulted in the necessity for the Casa to assume direct responsibility for personnel, salaries, buildings, equipment maintenance, vehicles, and literature operations for those new 'resource centers.' In some cases, smooth transitions characterized the changeover. In others, the Casa had little or no time to plan for an orderly transition of management and changes were effected within only a few weeks. A natural consequence of so many changes occurring in such a short time was, to say the least, a distressing problem for Casa leadership at the same time that leadership was dealing with multiple changes taking place throughout Central and South America. An ever-present difficulty which will likely never be solved is that of the fragile economies of numerous Central and South American countries. As their economies were bogged down or, in some cases, in violent turmoil, revolution and overnight devaluation, the Casa's finances suffered accordingly. The resource centers were unable to collect from those who owed them, making it impossible for them to pay what they owed in turn to the Casa. This resulted in what was at times a severe cash flow problem. We never missed a payroll, but there were times when special arrangements had to be made in order to pay all our bills on time.

BSPH Foundation

"In years to come, perhaps the only accomplishment which will be considered worthy of mention during my four years of Casa leadership is the realization of my dream which resulted in the establishment of the Baptist

Spanish Publishing House Foundation. Through the advice and cooperation of a number of 'friends of the Casa,' this became a reality in the spring of 2000. Many [Casa friends helped, but special recognition must be given to] the valuable assistance of Dr. Burton Patterson. With Burton's expertise as a lawyer, the Foundation was chartered in Texas as a legal non-profit organization solely for the benefit of the Casa. Founding board members included the following: Dr. Frank Patterson, Dr. Tom Hill, Dr. Bob Tucker, and Dr. Joe Poe (all four of whom were ex-General Directors), Dr. Jesse Bryan, Dr. Mike Gonzales, and Dr. Burton Patterson.

"The entire history of the BSPH reflects God's guidance and blessing, and that history is unquestionably a result of answered prayer from the days of the Toluca, Mexico kitchen publishing operation in 1905 to the present day in El Paso.

"During my years as General Director (just as I am positive my predecessors had also done), I placed a strong emphasis on the need for prayer support from the individual members of the international board of directors. Board meetings were always characterized by earnest prayer for the entire Casa ministry, including prayer for all employees and missionaries working there.

"In the course of one semi-annual board meeting, I planned a 'prayer walk' for the board members around the perimeter of the Casa, followed by an office-to-office prayer time with personnel and board members. As we stood outside near the southwest corner of the Patterson building before beginning that walk, we quietly reflected on God's goodness across the years and marveled at how in his provision he had elected to give each of us a part in the Casa's ministry at that time. As the Holy Spirit touched our hearts, an impromptu singing of '¡Cuán Grande Es Él!' (Spanish counterpart to 'How Great Thou Art') brought tears of joy to every eye and a deeper commitment to pray for the Casa's continuing publishing ministry to Spanish-speaking people everywhere.

"[I would like to conclude by using] a few paragraphs from the chapter on 'Some Things I've Learned as General Director of the Baptist Spanish Publishing House' in a little book I wrote (in my spare time – not on Casa time) entitled A Little Book of Reflections. I finished this just before my retirement and made copies for my family and a few friends.[15]

"This first quote is one which clearly reveals how I feel about my part in CBP history. 'Many years ago, I heard someone remark that each of us figuratively stands on the shoulders of those who have gone before. This truth has been ever before me while I have been the leader of this 96-year-old Baptist Spanish Publishing House. My seven predecessors as General Director, all were visionaries who had broad shoulders, cast long shadows, and left huge footprints of influence along the way. I still feel like a Lilliputian pygmy among giant Gullivers, but I am grateful for the opportunity I have had to serve here among some of God's finest."[16]

[And here are a few more:]

"A few years ago, I would never have guessed even in my wildest dreams that I would be privileged to serve as General Director of this Publishing House. The work itself has at times given me wild dreams, but these were far outnumbered by other dreams come true and overshadowed by exciting dreams for the future. It has been unquestionably worthwhile from my standpoint."[17]

"I've learned that commitment is not determined by a person's job title or responsibility. I have seen various levels of commitment among all levels of our personnel. Commitment is determined by an inner strength and integrity, and some of the highest levels of integrity may be found among those with the lowest levels of salary and benefits. Commitment is a reflection of character."[18]

"I had 'printer's ink' in my blood when I came here, and today I am proud to say it is thicker than ever. There's something about the noise and smell of the print shop which is so attractive that it takes me all the way back to my junior high days even before I began my training in the high school trade printing course."[19]

"I've learned that this ministry is several times bigger than all of us put together, and infinitesimally smaller than it ought to be in relation to needs around the Spanish speaking world."[20]

Sincerest thanks are due to Ted for this delightful remembrance of his and Mary's time of leadership at Casa Bautista de Publicaciones! An appropriate prayer would be that their retirement years may be many and fulfilling in every way.

Personnel Changes during the Stanton Years

Given the financial and personnel factors related to changes in IMB strategies which Ted himself has mentioned,[21] the number of personnel changes from the beginning of 1998 until late 2001 may come as a surprise. Using data from the Trustee Minutes of these years, the following summary is presented:

1998.–At the outset of his administration, Ted Stanton faced close to a crisis in divisional leadership. Upon the retirement of Ananías and Nelly González in early March 1997, Poe had assumed the directorship of the Product Design and Development Division, with the stated purpose of allowing the new General Director the opportunity to name that major member of his Management Team. Long term CBP employee José Amézaga, director of the Production Division, was scheduled to retire at the end of 1997; and Dr. Jesse Bryan, director of the Administration and Finance Division, had given signals that his retirement plans were imminent. Missionary Brian Allen had been brought on board in 1996 as Bryan's associate, with a view to assuming directorship of the division upon Bryan's retirement. But Allen accepted a new administrative post with IMB in their Quito, Ecuador, offices in the summer of 1997, and thus was no longer available by the time Stanton began his work as General Director.

Nevertheless by May 1998 when Ted made his first reports to the Trustees as General Director, his "cabinet" was taking shape. Jorge Díaz was moved from Marketing to the editorial division which was now to be called "Resource Design and Development Division." José Amézaga had been persuaded to stay on briefly (till the end of February) as director of the Production Division, when Exequiel San Martin assumed this post on March 1. Missionary Ronnie Adams was named interim director of the Marketing Division as of March 25.[22]

Other important aspects of the personnel report of May 1998 included the announcement of Rubén and Alicia Zorzoli having been appointed missionaries of IMB in December 1997, the transfer of Miryam Díaz from the Customer Service Department to become the Administrative Assistant to the Marketing Division Director, and the transfer of missionary Keith Morris from El Paso to Miami to direct the Casa's Regional Distribution Center there. Another important transfer moved Violeta Martínez to the Administration and Finance Division where she was to give full time to the "Office of Reprints and Contract Production."[23]

The General Director also summarized requests for new missionary personnel mentioning those previously approved by the Executive Committee of the Trustees: John Bayer (to be Associate Director of the Administration and Finance Division), Greg Massey (to be Director of the Marking Division upon arrival in El Paso, estimated to be August 1, 1998), and Steve Murdock (to be a multi-media strategist in the Department of Resources for Church Growth). Another request was for the transfer of missionary Kirk Bullington, also to serve in the same department as Murdock. This request prospered, and the Bullingtons arrived in the summer of 1998.[24]

By November, Stanton could report on the arrival of the Masseys, the Murdocks, and the Bullingtons, for their respective responsibilities, but was obliged to report the resignation of Ed and Kathy Steele and the retirement of Laverne and Betty Gregory.[25]

1999.–In May the General Director recommended that Jorge Rede, a Casa employee for some twenty years, be named director of the Inventory and

Shipping Department, to fill the vacancy left by George Villafuerte and that two new missionary units be requested from IMB (one as a "furlough" assignment; one in an ISC category) but no names were submitted.[26]

By November 1999 there were clear indications that missionary personnel assigned to the Casa would be diminishing further. Ronnie and Freida Adams returned to Venezuela. They had come to the Publishing House in 1995. Ronnie began his work as Associate Director of the Deposit Department, but upon the retirement of Tom Sutton at this post, Ronnie was named Director of the Department that was subsequently called Foreign Commercial Sales. During 1998 he served for a few months as Interim Director of the Marketing Division. Their departure from El Paso occurred in the early summer.

Steve Murdock resigned as Media Strategist in the Church Growth Resources Department, to accept work among Hispanics sponsored by the Arkansas Baptist Convention.

Millie Douglas took retirement effective November 30.[27] She had been ministering with the Publishing House since the summer of 1982. Her last several years were given to direction of the Factory Store (which opened in 1993) and to very capable leadership of the Casa's Volunteer Program, which secured thousands of hours of volunteer help from local Christians–mainly Baptists–for a variety of routine but very needful tasks, sometimes in offices, sometimes in areas related to production. Following "final furlough," Millie has made her home in El Paso.

Still other retirements that affected long time personnel were those of Elbin and María Luisa Cayetano Porflit. María Luisa had begun to work at the Publishing House in October of 1960. Her country of origin was Mexico and her formal training had been done at the Mexican Baptist Theological Seminary when it was located in Torreón. She worked thirty-nine years as a proofreader, under various supervisors. Even in retirement she has continued to do some proofreading from her home. Elbin was Chilean by birth but came to the United States during his youth. He began work with the Publishing House in 1962. He and María Luisa met as fellow workers at CBP. Elbin worked in various departments, but always related to sales, customer services and/or credit and collections. During his last years, he served as director of the Credit and Collections Department, in the Administration and Finance Division. The Porflits continue to make their home in El Paso.

2000.–Salomón and Gladys Adriana Mussiett took retirement effective June 15 of this year. Salomón served in the music area; Gladys in the curriculum area. Both were respected and well loved colleagues. José Luis Martínez, who had directed the General Book Department for twenty years, retired on August 10. He expressed his thanks for the "love, friendship, and support" he had received from fellow workers at the Publishing House. His prayer was that the good Lord continue to bless the Casa's ministry and its staff, in order for it to continue to make "a significant contribution to the Spanish-speaking world" through its publications.[28] Toward the end of September, Alci Rengifo resigned to accept the position as Manager of Radio Manantial, a Christian radio station in El Paso, related to the powerful HCJB in Quito. Nora Avalos, who had worked for more than eighteen years in the Photocomposition Department and in the Marketing Division in customer services, resigned. She had been a faithful worker for a long time. At the end of the year, Dr. Norberto Herrera retired and returned to Nicaragua to work with his beloved UPOLI. Adelina Almanza also retired at the end of December. She had worked for the Publishing House for 31 years—in a variety of tasks, secretarial and editorial. She was a poetically inclined person with many skills. It may have been a record year for attrition by way of retirements and resignations.

2001.–In May, the General Director reported that toward the end of February both Daniel Rojas and Silvia Ochoa had left the employ of CBP. Rojas had worked for some 20 years in various tasks in the Production Division (as a pressman, then as a bindery worker, and lastly as director of the Pre-Press Department.)

In November, Ted gave his last General Director's report to the Trustees. Concerning personnel, he reported that total employed staff was down to 63, from a figure of 67 at the beginning of the year. Missionary staff was declining also. Stanton reported that Steve and Barbara Manuel had resigned and moved from El Paso; the Kirk Bullingtons had also left El Paso (to return to the Dominican Republic). He noted again the felt absence of Dr. Norberto Herrera who had retired at the end of 2000. His report also mentions the case of Russell and Nadine Wills, who had been in El Paso mainly for administrative work of the local Mission (organization of IMB missionaries assigned to BSPH). The time had come for "their second retirement," and they returned to their home state of Florida, with many good memories of their "mission career" as ISCers, both in Mexico and in El Paso.

A Somewhat Low-Key Conclusion

Ted and Mary Stanton concluded their leadership years at CBP in a somewhat low-key fashion. There was no public "conclusion/installation" service as there had been in December 1997, when Poe was recognized as concluding his General Directorship and Ted was publicly installed to initiate his service in that office. To be sure the Trustees individually and collectively expressed their deep and sincere appreciation to this dedicated couple. And in a joint effort between the Trustees and the Publishing House personnel, a wonderfully warm dinner event was conducted, again converting the chapel into a banquet hall. The event was held on November 15, 2001 and included a simple but meaningful "recognition ceremony." Some trustees (Juan Calcagni and H. Rhea Chafin) and several Publishing House staff (Mario Martínez, Juan Carlos Cevallos, Alicia Zorzoli, and Exequiel San Martín) participated on the program. Both Ted and Mary were given the opportunity to respond. Appropriate gifts were given the Stantons that symbolized the genuine gratitude of CBP staff for their friendship and their service.

With these and many other expressions of appreciation in their heads, the Stantons moved to the Little Rock area in early December. One of their sons (Mark) came to help them. It seemed the right move to make in God's providential care and guidance.

In Ted's last column for *Entre Nos*, he wrote: "After almost four years as General Director, Mary and I are leaving the Baptist Spanish Publishing House to begin our retirement... Our lives are richer, our friendships deeper, our understandings broader, and our commitment to the literature ministry stronger than ever because of this singular opportunity for service which came our way in the course of God's good will.

"As we prepare to leave El Paso, rest assured that we will continue to grow through the experiences we have had here and treasure the friendships we have been privileged to enjoy especially during these past four years.

"We trust that God will enlarge this ministry and multiply its influence for his own honor and glory, and that you will give your best effort every day toward that end. Our parting blessing for each of you is that you might continue to 'grow in the grace and knowledge of our Lord and Savior Jesus Christ. To him be glory both now and forever! Amen.' (2 Peter 3:18 NIV)"[29]

During their November meeting, the Trustees had elected Jorge Enrique Díaz as Ted's successor, and he was to begin his work immediately; a public installation service for Díaz would be held in May of the following year. Jorge inherited the challenge to keep the Casa Bautista de Publicaciones alive to complete its century of service and move into whatever future God would give.

Endnotes

1. See manuscript of chapel message, May 26, 1993; conserved in recorded form in the CBP Library as T-610, in which Poe declared: "All of us recognize that my service in this position will be for a relatively few years. I have compared it to a one term presidency, which in Mexico is limited by law to six years, and in this country, according to other circumstances, to four years."

2. See chapter 9.

3. This administrative area continued to include the Baptist Spanish Publishing House.

4. Though originally a slang expression that referred to a defaulter on the stock exchange, consequently a bankrupt entity, the expression has been legitimized in normal English usage and now almost exclusively refers to "an elected officer or group continuing to hold political office during a brief interim between defeat for reelection and the inauguration of a successor."

5. See pages 3 and 4 of the minutes, Trustee meeting, May 5-9, 1997. Poe's three-page letter to the Board is included as Attachment #1; Motion #6 accepts the communication that includes the dates for Poe's retirement. Poe's letter indicates that he has just informed the Management Team of his plans also.

6. For a brief period, Jesse had also served as Communications Consultant to the General Director.

7. Numerous materials bore his name either as editor or as author.

8. At the time, Díaz was director of the Marketing Division.

9. Indeed Herrera's experience as president of UPOLI, in Nicaragua, meant he had successfully led an organization considerably larger than CBP.

10. See Attachment #2 to May 1997 Trustee Minutes.

11. The fruit of Mary's choir work with children was eventually distilled in book form and published by Casa Bautista de Publicaciones. See El coro de niños: Su formación y programa para el primer año; publication date: 1995. A vocal cassette to facilitate its use is also available.

12. Experienced and highly efficient secretary to several CBP General Directors, including Stanton; see also chapter 5.

13. The International Mission Board had given clear signals in 1996 that its operational subsidy to institutional ministries like the Publishing House would be phased out by the year 2000. 1998 and 1999 would have been "the final two years" alluded to here by Ted.

14. Ted himself offered this note explaining what he called "a personal prejudice:" "I maintain that 'resource center' denotes a place that is alive and well; a place where actual needs can be actively met. Conversely, to me 'book deposit' almost suggests 'a place where books go to die.' Hence, my insistence upon a change in nomenclature which would manifest itself in a fundamental change in philosophy."

15. See Ted O. Stanton, A Little Book of Reflections, Private Publication; the dedication is dated October 2001. It may be found in the Publishing House library.

16. Ibid., p. 11.

17. Ibid.

18. Ibid., p. 10.

19. Ibid., p. 11.

20. Ibid., p. 12.

21. See earlier section on "Difficulties."

22. See Informes y Recomendaciones a la Junta Directiva, Mayo 1998, pp. 85, 86.

23. Ibid.

24. Ibid., p. 90.

25. The Gregorys did continue as Sales Representatives for the Publishing House for several years after their move to the Baptist retirement center in San Angelo, Texas, serving in the category of International Service Corps personnel of IMB.

26. See Informes y Recomendaciones a la Junta Directiva, Mayo, 1999, p. 104. Apparently these requests did not prosper.

27. As with all missionaries "retiring" directly from Publishing House service (since sometime in the 1980s), the technical date for actual retirement from the International Mission Board came later, following a period of "final furlough" (now called "stateside assignment").

28. See Entre Nos, Vol. 23, Núm. 31, August 2, 2000.

29. Entre Nos, vol. Núm. 48, November 28, 2001.

Chapter 11

Jorge Díaz Brings Experience and Vision
for a New Century
Part I

Jorge Enrique Díaz Figueroa[1] was elected to be the ninth General Director of Casa Bautista de Publicaciones, by its Board of Trustees at their meeting in November 2001.[2] Under his administration, the Baptist Spanish Publishing House is observing its Centennial Anniversary. Because the event provides a time for recollections—of a hundred years of service—and a moment for "straining toward what is ahead,"[3] it has seemed appropriate to divide the material related to Díaz's administration into two chapters. This is done not because of length of years served (as was the case for Dr. Davis and Dr. Patterson), but because of the importance of these two perspectives: backward, to know Díaz as a person and the experience he brings, and forward, to project toward what the God of Heaven has for the Casa Bautista de Publicaciones in the years of its second century of service.

This chapter focuses on the first perspective: looking backward with the purpose of getting to know the human being that is Jorge Enrique Díaz and surveying his experience up to his naming as General Director of CBP.

The following chapter (the last in our volume) will emphasize the second perspective: understanding the early years of Díaz's administration with emphasis on a snapshot of the Casa at age 100 and on capturing its projections toward the future. The concluding note will be an appeal for all "Friends of the Casa" to lend their support in its second century of service.

A "Man of Many Lives"

Jorge Díaz was publicly installed as CBP's General Director at a special service conducted in the sanctuary of the Mountain View Baptist Church, in Northeast El Paso, in May 2002.[4] At the appropriate moment in the program, J. T. Poe was asked to introduce the new General Director.[5] In his opening remarks, Poe confessed that he had been concerned about how to develop the introduction. Then, he said, one morning he awoke with the idea to organize his thoughts around the saying in Spanish that a cat has seven lives.[6] Poe explained that while the adage about cats assumes a series of lives, his use of the figure to introduce Jorge Díaz referred to "simultaneous lives." He thus introduced Jorge and his "seven lives:" (1) His life as a man (a human being), (2) His life as a student, (3) His life as a teacher/professor, (4) His life as a preacher and pastor, (5) His life as a writer and editor, (6) His life as a translator, and (7) His life as an administrator.

Poe confesses that though he felt satisfied with the presentation at the installation service, he worried a little that his friend Díaz or others might have been offended with the analogy of a Very Important Person to a small domestic animal. He was frankly relieved (and pleased) when Díaz himself picked up on the "list of lives" to give Poe input for this chapter in the Casa's centennial book. And he called Poe's presentation "interesante, amena y muy bien resumida" (English: interesting, enjoyable, and well put). Thus with Jorge's "blessing" and with input he himself has supplied for this project, the "seven lives" of JED[7] are hereby presented:

1. His life as a man. Jorge was born to José Arturo Díaz Meza and Julia Margarita Figueroa García, in the coastal city of Puerto Barrios, Department of Izabal, Guatemala, on October 15, 1941. He was the second child born to this couple, though the little girl, born sometime earlier, had only survived a few weeks of life. Another boy was born when Jorge was about two. The family then consisted of the parents and a pair of little boys. Jorge says he has never known the exact circumstances in which José Arturo and Julia Margarita met. Julia's father was a pioneer evangelical pastor in Guatemala, don Feliciano Figueroa. José Arturo was not an evangelical believer when he and Julia Margarita married,[8] but he was a hard working laborer, who had learned the tailor's trade and sometimes ran a small store. Unfortunately, José Arturo did not enjoy good health.

When Jorge was only one year old, the family decided to move from the tropical and costal climate of Puerto Barrios[9] to San Pedro Sacatepéquez, in the central mountains of Guatemala—and not far from the region of San Juan Sacatepéquez where Julia Margarita's parents lived. It was hoped that the cooler climate, the mountain air, and other benefits of the area would help the father regain his health. A small grocery store and coffee shop were opened. Jorge's brother, Rubén Arturo, was born here. But the father did not get well. In fact, his health continued to deteriorate, and the already limited resources of the young family were drained completely in medical expenses. Improvement still did not come. Finally, the family businesses had to be closed; and after a lengthy illness, José Arturo died, leaving Julia Margarita with debts and two small children, ages two and four. "It was a moment of extreme poverty," Jorge now recalls.

The mother literally packed all their clothes and belongings into one small suitcase and took the three of them to Guatemala City, where a friend made available a small room: with a dirt floor, no electricity, no running water, and no furniture. Jorge remembers the first moment when he, his mother, and his little brother entered that room. He says they unpacked on the dirt floor their few things; then the mother kneeled, took the two boys in her arms—and began to pray! It is Jorge's first remembrance of prayer. And he recalls his mother's tears that accompanied her pleas to God for forgiveness, for His help, and for His protection upon herself and her two little boys.

God heard Julia Margarita's prayer and, among other things, guided her to unite with the Iglesia Bautista Bethel (Bethel Baptist Church), there in the capital city. The Bethel church had been one of some eight independent evangelical churches that had been formed in the early 1940s. The pastors of these churches met regularly to pray and find mutual support and encouragement. One of them wrote to the Casa Bautista de Publicaciones requesting copies of certain books. Jorge remembers the testimony of one of those original leaders: "We read and studied those books intensely—and from cover to cover!" A short while later, those eight churches declared that their doctrine and practices would be like those of the Baptist churches that they had discovered in materials from the Baptist Spanish Publishing House.[10] Bethel church became a haven for doña Julia and her two growing boys.

Jorge says his memories of those difficult years have a bittersweet flavor. During the week, his mother worked—hard and long—washing and ironing clothes for neighbors and others who needed domestic help, people who could then "help her" with a little money, enough to be able to feed her two sons. Limitations of various sorts, hunger, and poverty were the family's constant companions. Hard work, harsh treatment, and being looked down on were the teachers that forged a young boy's soul and outlook. Jorge says he learned that nothing in life is free; rather everything, absolutely everything, must be won with effort and determination. Not surprisingly, he developed a spirit of independence that in street language meant "Each man for himself!" Monday through Friday was a battle without truce. Jorge recalls: "We—literally—got up from the ground at 5:00 each morning to fight for every opportunity to earn something—with dignity and honesty. But Saturday was different: We cleaned up and put in order our cramped quarters. We bathed and got our clothes ready for church on Sunday."

Saturday afternoons at Bethel Church brought another brighter moment. From about two o'clock in the afternoon till about nine o'clock that evening, children and youth of the neighborhood would become a beehive of life at church for activities the pastor and his wife directed with great love and patience. It was essentially a "missions education program"—without bearing the name. But children four to six were grouped as "Rayitos de Sol" (Sunbeams); boys seven to thirteen were "Embajadores del Rey" (Royal Ambassadors) and youth fourteen to twenty were "Sembradores de la Verdad" (Truth Seeders). Furthermore, though competition (on the street or in school) reigned during the week, at church all were treated as equals! These Saturday sessions created happy memories for Jorge. "Nothing made a greater impact on my life than learning Bible passages and hearing stories of self-denying missionaries like Judson, Carey, Penzotti, Lottie Moon, and others. These became my heroes," says Jorge. "And I dreamed of being one of them."

The pastor was Dr. Adalberto Santizo Román; the congregation called him "don Beto." He was a bivocational minister, supporting his family from his earnings as a blacksmith. Jorge also remembers that at this time, don Beto was going to night school first to finish his secondary education and later to continue his formal training. He eventually completed university degrees from San Carlos University. Sometimes the pastor would organize a youth recreation activity, even though they had to play ball in the street next to the church! In effect, the pastor provided a living model of what it meant to be a father, a minister, a worker, AND a student! To this day, Díaz feels grateful for that model![11]

During a Vacation Bible School in November 1948, God touched Jorge's heart, and with great joy he invited Christ in to be Lord and personal Savior of his life. He was seven years old, but it was a decision that Jorge looks back on and calls it "mature, serious, responsible, and life-determining." Two years later he was baptized into the fellowship of the Bethel Church. By this time Rev. Gonzalo Morales was the pastor.

When Jorge was eleven years old, he made a trip with his grandfather Feliciano Figueroa to visit a circuit of some half dozen congregations in the mountains of San Raymundo and San Juan Sacatepéquez. For the grandfather, it may have been just another of his periodic junkets to these isolated groups of believers. To the young grandson, however, it was a life-changing and unforgettable experience. Jorge remembers that his grandmother Isabel had prepared them a small lunch for a particular day's jaunt. At noon, man and boy stopped a while, to eat and talk, under the shade of some enormous trees. They washed their hands and faces in a nearby brook and drank from its crystal pure running water. Feliciano was a man of the land, a farmer who maintained his family of twelve children—four were still at home when eleven year old Jorge visited—with his crops. But singlehandedly he had founded the circuit of evangelical churches, and he visited them as often as he could, especially during the off seasons from his work on the farm.

According to Jorge's memory, that day, after lunch and in the shade of those magnificent trees but before resuming their journey on foot (three or four hours were still in front of them), the grandfather took out two books from his carrying case or backpack. One was the Bible; the other was *El Expositor Bíblico*, published by the Casa Bautista de Publicaciones. He first opened the *Expositor* to get the Bible passage, then he opened his Bible and read the indicated verses. Again he went to the *Expositor* (as he fondly called the piece) to read the commentary and explanation. There, with mountain tree shade as their temple, the two prayed before resuming their journey. And as they did, the grandfather commented to the boy: "This is the passage I will use tonight to preach and teach the brethren." Really the teaching had already begun! "The Bible, the hymnbook, and *El Expositor Bíblico* were my grandfather's three basic tools," Jorge says. "And they served him well for a ministry of more than forty years!" God used the trip to bless the circuit's congregations. He also used it to give visions to the boy of what he might be doing for the rest of his life: preaching the Bible, singing the great hymns of faith, and helping the Casa to keep on publishing today's *Expositor Bíblico*!

Eventually the boy grew into a man, and in the providence of God "met his mate." She is doña Raquelita Ortiz Hernández. She and Jorge became friends and eventually sweethearts during their years at the Baptist Seminary in Guatemala, though they had actually already known each other as active Baptist youth, participating in church camps or youth rallies. Their courtship lasted six years; marriage came on August 5, 1966. The year the Casa celebrates its centennial, Jorge and Raquelita will observe their 39th Wedding Anniversary. (A very respectable number—and they're still counting!) Over the years, God has blessed them with two daughters: Miryam Raquel, actually born during the time Jorge and Raquelita studied in Cali, Colombia; and Carol Elizabeth or "Liz," who was born a year after Díaz began his service with Casa Bautista de Publicaciones in El Paso. "Behold the man!"

2. His life as a student. The previous section has given a cue that really from childhood Jorge Díaz has been a student. "I continue to be one," he says; "I believe that learning is indeed a lifelong task." A list of his academic achievements proves the point: He is a certified teacher for primary urban education in Guatemala; he was graduated from the Baptist Seminary of Guatemala with the Bachiller en Teología (Bachelor of Theology); from the International Baptist Seminary of Cali, Colombia with the Licenciatura en Teología (roughly equivalent to a Master's degree); and from the National University of Guatemala as Profesor de Enseñanza Media (credential for teaching at the level of secondary education), and the Licenciatura en Pedagogía y Ciencias de la Educación (roughly equivalent to a master's degree in pedagogy and educational science). Additional studies have been done in Costa Rica (Graduado en Estudios sobre Técnicas Educativas), at El Paso Community College, and at BIOLA University in Los Angeles, California.

Sharing some of his memories as a student, Jorge recounts that during his five years of study at the Baptist Seminary in Guatemala, he tried to read at least some parts of almost every book in the Seminary's library. Since he estimates that at that point sixty to seventy percent of those books had been published by the Casa Bautista de Publicaciones, he was unknowingly preparing for his days of leadership at CBP. Furthermore he asserts, "Every textbook used and recommended by the professors at the Guatemalan seminary—and I mean every single one—were books from the Casa. In my trips through the countries of Latin America and Spain, I have come into contact with highly respected pastors, professors, and leaders who have said to me, 'I grew up being fed and achieving my academic formation using books and publications from Casa Bautista.' Instead of responding with a simple 'Amen,' in my heart I am saying, 'Me too! And thank God!' "

The university atmosphere he experienced while pursuing pedagogical studies during the 1960s and '70s was hardly conducive to evangelical Christian faith. "The political currents of those years, among both professors and students, were strongly leftist," Jorge comments. "The popular heroes of the moment were Sandino, Allende, and Ché Guevara." And the School of Humanities (roughly equivalent to Arts and Sciences) was a hotbed of these tendencies. "To be a student or a professor in the School of Humanities [Spanish: Facultad de Humanidades] was to be heavily exposed to the leftist social and political ideas in vogue at the moment. These currents put me to the test," Díaz admits, "and yielded, as results, extra effort on my part to make my preaching, and teaching, and pastoral work more relevant to the real needs and the thinking of my people." He adds: " When a person grows up in the midst of such abject poverty as I did, it is possible to become thick skinned with insensitivity to human need— or to so overflow with resentments and revengeful feelings that bad things can happen. Fortunately, the loving grace of God and the teachings of Jesus Christ combined with prayer and Bible study can make a difference in the life of anyone who humbly submits himself 'to the power of God unto salvation.' "[12] Jorge sought to be that kind of student, and his life shows it.

3. His life as a teacher/professor. Díaz acknowledges: "From my early youth I have felt vocation for, and calling to, teaching tasks. Very probably this is the phase of ministry I feel I know best." And his curriculum vitae would include references that make for an impressive list of teaching services performed:

Professor of Bible in the Baptist Seminary of Guatemala

Founder, director, and teacher of the Extension Studies program of the
Seminary in Guatemala

Adjunct professor of both Educational Technology and Theology in two
different universities of his country of origin: the San Carlos

National University, and the university named for Dr. Mariano
Gálvez

Occasional Professor of Bible and other subjects at the International
Baptist Bible Institute in El Paso as well as similar service at
the Border Baptist Seminary (Seminario Fronterizo) located in
the neighboring city of Juárez, Chihuahua, Mexico.

Speaker at special conferences or continuing educational convocations
for pastors, religious educators, and other leaders in most of
the Latin American countries and Spain, apart from similar
conferences for Hispanic pastors in the United States.

Jorge remembers consulting with seminary teachers in Guatemala, like
Dr. Clark Scanlon and Dr. Charles Allen, concerning his feeling of being called
into the teaching ministry. They encouraged him and indeed began to use him
in certain didactic tasks even before he finished his five years work at the
Guatemalan Seminary. Furthermore, that Seminary was instrumental in providing at least a partial scholarship that made it possible for both Jorge and
Raquelita to study at the International Baptist Theological Seminary of Cali,
Colombia. When those studies were finished and the Díazes returned to
Guatemala, "the only thing Raquelita and I wanted," Jorge says," was to be able
to dedicate ourselves to seminary teaching: she in the area of Christian Education for the local church, and I in the areas of preaching and teaching the
message of the Bible. And we were—and still are—deeply grateful to the
Guatemalan Seminary that gave us that kind of opportunity." The responsibilities at the Seminary seemed always on the grow, but Jorge still found time to
pursue night studies in pedagogy and curriculum planning at the San Carlos
National University. "We look at those years," Jorge comments, "as just doing
what God had called us to do. It was practicing what we had been trained for.
But from the Lord's perspective, perhaps even those years were just another step
in our formation for later ministries that at the moment we didn't dream of." At
least that seems to be what, by God's will, has happened.

4. His life as a preacher and pastor. Jorge's early conversion has
already been mentioned, as also his baptism into the fellowship of the Bethel
Church. An additional note concerning that trip with his grandfather don
Feliciano Figueroa to visit his circuit of congregations in the mountains is that
don Feliciano gave Jorge the assignment to preach at one of their services! The
boy was eleven! But he preached "his first sermon," and five or six years later
did indeed experience a "call" to the pastoral and teaching ministry. His ordination, according to the customs of Guatemalan Baptists at that time, came after
several years of pastoral experience; his age was twenty-five and the year was
1966. A list of his pastoral experience is as impressive as that of his teaching
work:

1959—1961	Student pastor of the Iglesia Bautista de las Playas, Santa Lucia, Guatemala
1962—1967	Founder and pastor, Iglesia Bautista Damasco, Guatemala City
1967—1969	Pastor, Iglesia Bautista Jerusalén, of the Jamundi Barrio, in Cali, Colombia
1969—1970	Pastor, Iglesia Bautista, in San Raymundo, Guatemala
1970—1974	Pastor, Iglesia Bautista Macedonia, Guatemala City
1975—1976	Pastor, Iglesia Bautista Bethel, Guatemala City
1977—1979	Founder and pastor, Iglesia La Familia de Dios, Guatemala City
1979—1980	Interim pastor, Iglesia Bautista, of Canutillo, Texas
1980—1982	Pastor, Misión El Buen Pastor, in Las Cruces, New Mexico
1982—1984	Pastor, Misión Bautista, of Loma Terrace Baptist Church, in El Paso, Texas

1985—present Pastor, Iglesia Bautista del Centro, in El Paso, Texas.

Two things immediately stand out from this list: (1) the good number of churches and missions served—in three countries, and in two of the United States; and (2) the longevity of his present pastorate. By the time the Casa begins its centennial year, Rev. Jorge Enrique Díaz will have completed twenty years of service as pastor at the Del Centro Church in El Paso! Yes, he has life as a pastor! (And it would be next to impossible to compile a list of places where on occasion he has preached—in the countries of North, Central, and South America; in Spain; even in Australia!)

5. His life as a writer and editor. Detail about Jorge's service in this category at the Casa Bautista de Publicaciones will be given in another section of this chapter, but here it is important to note that this "life" began considerably prior to his arrival in El Paso. Sometime in the 1960s, Guatemalan Baptists created a modest "denominational magazine" which was called *Nueva Era Bautista*. And it ought not surprise one to learn that its editor-in-chief during the period 1970 to 1975 was none other than Jorge Enrique Díaz. What may be more surprising is to learn how seriously Jorge was already involved in writing or editing for Casa Bautista, prior to the invitation for him to become a part of the resident staff in El Paso. From 1975 to 1979 Díaz wrote lessons for a young people's Sunday School quarterly, edited by missionary Ann Marie Swenson and published, of course, by CBP. During that same time frame, Jorge served as principal writer and even as non-resident editor for a men's magazine titled *El Obrero Cristiano*. Once in El Paso, his "pen"—already active—became even more productive.[13]

6. His life as a translator. Jorge's own comment is, "Among the 'lives' of 'this old cat,' probably this is one is the shortest"—but it does exist. Díaz acknowledges suffering what all new missionaries face: the task of learning a second language—and learning it well. (He also admits making similar language mistakes, especially in the spoken language, as new missionaries inevitably commit. He too has felt the need for hearers to respond with patience and for all to take such incidents with good humor.) But reading and translation of written materials are well within his range of manageable skills. If either of his two daughters is available, they can come to his assistance, when needed. The Casa has published at least four books where the translation is credited to Jorge Enrique Díaz (and Miryam or Carol Elizabeth). They are: *Cómo enseñar la Biblia, 50 Palabras clave de la Biblia, Tulipanes en Invierno,* and *Modelos para el Proceso de Enseñanza/Apendizaje.* Who knows, future circumstances might call for this "short life" to be reactivated or prolonged more than even Jorge expects! Surprises happen!

7. His life as an administrator. Jorge confesses that his "life" as an administrator has been another of God's surprises. "I never sought these responsibilities," he says, "and frankly felt some surprise when my colleagues saw in me the gifts of administration." But they did! And thus from early in Díaz's ministry he has shouldered tasks that involved administrative skills. The list may not be quite as long as those recounting his teaching service and his pastoral experience, but it is still impressive:[14]

At the Baptist Seminary in Guatemala, at different times and for varying durations, he was:

> Director of the Program of Extension Studies
> Academic Dean for the resident program
> Rector (or president) of the Seminary

At the National University of Guatemala, he was an assistant to the director of the Department of Education, in the School of Arts and Sciences (Spanish: Facultad de Humanidades)

And at the Casa Bautista de Publicaciones, his administrative tasks have included being:

> Director of the Bible Teaching Department
> Associate director of the Church Program and Development Division
> Director of the Marketing Division
> Director of the Editorial Division, and now
> General Director.

"¡Es un gato de siete vidas!" (English: He's a cat with seven lives!) So said Poe in his introduction of the new CEO at the public installation service.

(Jorge himself apparently accepts the analogy.) It has been useful here to show the multi dimensionality of CBP's present General Director. The Casa is fortunate to have this leader to guide it into its second century of service.

A Veteran of More than Two Decades
of Service with Casa Bautista

A summary of these two decades is now offered with specific focus on Jorge's: (1) Invitation to join the El Paso staff, (2) His participation in the Bible Teaching Department, (3) His participation in the Marketing Division, and (4) His participation in the Editorial Division. First, the

(1) Invitation to join the El Paso staff. As Jorge remembers it, it happened on a day in mid-May 1979. He and Dr. LeRoy Ford (prominent professor in the School of Religious Education at Southwestern Baptist Theological Seminary, in Fort Worth) were team teaching a group of seminary professors gathered in Costa Rica from various parts of Central America. The seminar had to do with lesson planning and curriculum design and was being held at a Baptist encampment not far from the San José International Airport. Someone arrived bringing the notice of "an urgent long distance telephone call for Jorge Díaz." He left the encampment (it had no telephone service) and went to the nearest phone booth (about two kilometers away). The call was from Ananías González, a section leader, at CBP, in the division at that moment being presided by J. T. Poe. González said the Board of Trustees had authorized him to invite Jorge to be the director of the Bible Teaching Department, a spot left vacant by the recent retirement of Mrs. Olivia S. D. de Lerín. It was an inoportune moment for Jorge to receive the call, in the midst of inoportune circumstances to give it much consideration. But he promised Ananías he would do three things: First: Pray to the Lord for guidance, "because," he said, "I have never remotely considered this to be on the Lord's agenda for my life." Second: Talk it over with his wife, when he got back to Guatemala. Third: Call Ananías back, after doing the first two things. Jorge fulfilled his promise—and in the end accepted the invitation.

Jorge, Raquelita, and Miryam (who had just celebrated her twelfth birthday) arrived in El Paso on Tuesday, November 19, 1979—to begin a new chapter in their life as a family. Because of mechanical problems in Houston, the plane arrived in El Paso near the stroke of midnight, several hours late. But faithfully waiting, to give the Díazes greetings and their first words of welcome, were Brothers Ananías González and J. T. Poe. "What a moment!," comments Jorge nostalgically; then continues: "Ananías took us to a small motel on Dyer Street where the Casa had made arrangements for us to stay for a few days while we got our bearings and found a house." Really the "house finding" had already begun—by letter. When Tito and Estela Fafasuli had learned the Díazes had accepted Casa's invitation, they took initiative to write Jorge and Raquelita, offering to sell them their house. The reason was that Tito had accepted a position with the Baptist Sunday School Board in Nashville, Tennessee, and they would shortly be leaving El Paso.[15]

The last days of November and the whole month of December brought an intense time of adjustments and new experiences for Jorge, Raquelita, and Miryam. They had to get used to a radically different climate of cold days and very dry air. And Jorge remembers gratefully the different kinds of help they received from their new "family" of friends and associates. Adolfo Robleto helped them find the right school for Miryam. Don Adolfo also coached Jorge in writing checks—in English! At the Casa, Jorge was mentored by various colleagues there. "Roberta Ryan taught me how to measure and edit manuscripts to fit available magazine space," Jorge remembers. "Viola Campbell helped me understand stateside concepts for the educational program of local churches. Adolfo Robleto was my teacher in matters of border customs and culture, apart from sharing some 'trade secrets' of a successful editor. Miguel Angel Blanco taught me how to mark manuscripts, both originals and proofs. José Amézaga helped me learn to choose type, taking into account the target reader group." He was on a quick learning curve, but his gift for quick learning had been exercised many times before! As with many others who have worked at the Publishing House, "we are," Jorge says, "the product of the instruction our colleagues gave us upon arrival." The "invitee" from Guatemala had accepted and was on hand and beginning his "participation."[16]

(2) His participation in the Bible Teaching Department (1980—1992). Urgent and rigid production schedules of the various Bible study quarterlies, edited in the Bible Teaching Department, required that Jorge immediately enter the fray of these editorial tasks. He himself was responsible as editor and principal writer for both editions (for teachers, and for students) of *El Expositor Bíblico*, Casa's trunk line periodical (that Jorge had met as a boy with his grandfather in the mountains).[17] Other writers could be enlisted, but he was responsible for both enlistment and editorial coordination. Quarterlies also existed for children and youth; these had their editors and writers, but everything had to be supervised by Díaz. He was responsible to see that it all happened—and on time! It would have been easy to get lost (or horribly bored) on what seemed like a machine of perpetual motion.

Jorge remembers that even while he was still in Guatemala, Ananías González had mentioned to him the interest at the Casa in developing "an integrated curriculum for the educational ministry of a local church." For years, the Casa had used the so-called Uniform Lesson Series (with Nashville adaptations). The idea emerged to use this series three quarters of the year and to develop outlines for the fourth quarter that would be "propio de la Casa" (original by CBP) to address matters that churches in Latin America seemed to be calling for. The plan was approved and used for some four years in the materials for youth and adults. During this time, the work of the department tended to be divided in three ways: Nelly González coordinated everything related to children's materials; Antonio Rengifo did the same for materials targeting adolescents and youth; and Jorge concentrated on materials for teachers and for adults. During these years Carol Martínez and Marta Briones also helped as editors for children's materials.

Beginning in 1980, an in-depth study was begun of the needs and wants of Spanish-speaking Baptists for their Sunday School materials. Two tracks emerged. One was to offer a thematic program that would lead people to confront the basic matters a Christian believer ought to know about, and to accomplish this during the first five years a person attended Sunday School. The other option was to have a study of the Bible, book by book. It was judged that this kind of survey would need a span of nine years. Following much study, prayer, and consultations, Jorge and his team decided to do first the thematic curriculum, with the idea that later they would do the book by book program. After analyzing all the topics that had been suggested in their surveys, twenty topics gradually emerged that would be the basis of the new plan. It was decided that eight of these topics would be addressed in the materials for preschoolers and for children in grades one to three. Twelve themes would be included for children in fourth to sixth grades; youth and adults would be exposed to all twenty topics in a lesson cycle of five years.

In November 1980 a workshop was held in El Paso, with participation of carefully chosen persons from different parts of Latin America. All were exceptionally capable in the field of religious education. This group designed the teaching program for the children's materials during two weeks of intense work, being sure that all topics had a clear biblical base and were balanced in sequence and depth. The following year (1981) materials for preschoolers and children up through eleven years of age were edited and published for four groups in a new age-graded plan that was being recommended.

During 1983, a second planning workshop was held which essentially accomplished the same work as the 1980 team, but for young people and adults (these were also divided into four newly recommended groups). Materials for the program were developed and published in 1984, so that beginning in January 1985, Baptist churches (and others that wanted to use these quarterlies) had in their hands the first Sunday School curriculum totally designed by and for Hispanics and published by the Casa Bautista de Publicaciones. Díaz says: "I believe this curriculum truly responded to the real and felt educational needs of our churches in the 1980s. And it put the Casa in the vanguard of this aspect of Christian education."

It was the desire of the Publishing House to be able to offer a fully integrated educational program for local churches. Thus missionary James West was invited to join the CBP staff to do for the discipleship materials something similar to what had been done for those used by Sunday Schools. Jim and Jorge and four other Casa colleagues worked very closely to design a program for what came to be called "Discipulado Cristiano" (Christian Discipleship). The basic philosophy in the program was that in Sunday School the emphasis would be on "What does the Bible say?" about each one of the twenty selected themes or topics. The discipleship program would address application: "How to put into practice what the Bible says." The materials began to appear in 1985, so that it could be said then that local Spanish-speaking Baptist churches had access to a completely integrated program for their educational needs. It was in relation to all this activity that several new people were brought to the Casa: Exequiel San Martín,[18] Edgar O. Morales, Jorge and Elsa Rousselin, David and Vilma Fajardo.[19]

Two other responsibilities Jorge bore during these years in the Bible Teaching Department had to do with the Annual Bible Study Book and becoming editor and a regular writer for the magazine *El Promotor de Educación Cristiana*. It should be mentioned that the Casa did not let the Annual Bible Study books immediately go out of print (as was the case for their English counterparts) but collected them into a series which came to be referred to as "The flowers collection" (because all the covers pictured a beautiful but different flower).[20]

In the seemingly never ending list of tasks that fell Jorge's way during these years, still two more ought to be mentioned: One was the preparation of various books to support general concepts and efforts in Christian education. Ananías and Nelly González lent their support and practical help to these projects. Another area had to do with Vacation Bible School materials. During these years, such products were technically part of the responsibility of the Bible Teaching Department. But fortunately for Jorge, Viola Campbell was still carrying the weight of this work. "Miss Viola and I met from time to time," recalls Jorge, "to talk about the tasks at hand. But she was so well organized and knew her work so well that the sessions were more intense learning times for me than supervisory reviews. I still feel—we all should—thanks to God for persons so dedicated to the tasks of Christian education through printed materials as was Miss Viola."

Nevertheless, obsolescence affects even good things. In time (following Viola's retirement), the Publishing House decided to design and publish a new set of materials for Vacation Bible School use. To help do these new materials, Ibelís Guédez was first invited to come on staff; and, after her departure,[21] Peggy Compton was asked to head up this work.[22] After the Comptons' move to Richmond, Nelly González and Carol Martínez accepted this pending project. And it was they who saw it to completion.[23]

By 1990 the department could turn its attention to the Bible book by book program of studies. Some initial meetings with representatives[24] from the Baptist Sunday School Board (now known as LifeWay Christian Resources) gave hope that this project might be done as a "joint venture." Jorge felt encouraged about the possibility, but shortly the signals turned negative. Apparently authorities at higher echelons (in Nashville, in El Paso, or in both) nixed the idea. But the Casa went forward with its own plan, and it was partially completed when Jorge's next "participation" occurred.[25]

(3) His participation in the Marketing Division (1993—1997). Jorge

recounts that during the year end holidays of 1992 he carried a serious prayer burden concerning his work at the Publishing House. A dozen years of work there had been accomplished, and while he felt satisfied with what had been done, he began to feel the need for something new that would completely challenge his creativity and imagination. The feeling grew that it was time for a change, and he began to pray that the Lord would "open a door" for a new chapter in his ministry. The New Year began, and Jorge continued his work—and his praying. "Frankly," he says, "I thought some church, or seminary, or even a different publishing ministry might emerge to give me the opportunity for a change. I didn't make any calls, write any letters, or send out any resumes. I just prayed and waited for the Lord to act. Perhaps it was that deep in my heart I really didn't want to leave Casa Bautista de Publicaciones." One summer day, "my daughter Miryam (who at that time was working as an administrative assistant in the Operations Division) suggested we have lunch together. She also invited Wayne Quarrier, her division director."[26] During their lunch together, Quarrier asked Jorge: "Have you ever thought of doing something different at the Casa, different from what you have been doing?" "Like what?" shot back Díaz, question for question. "Like," Wayne replied after thinking a moment, "like directing our sales efforts in countries where we have no 'deposit' presently functioning." After chatting a bit more concerning these possibilities, all three went back to their work. Some days later, having further matured his thoughts, Quarrier made his case to Poe, then the General Director, to get approval for this "internal transfer." Recovering from his shock, Poe came to accept the plan, and then worked with Ananías González to get his O.K. for Jorge to leave the important work he was doing in Ananías' division. Somewhat reluctantly González consented, taking the attitude, "If it will help sales, we'll make the sacrifice."

Not more than a month after that "life-changing lunch," Díaz had moved to an office in the Operations Division and was struggling to get a handle on his new job: Directing Casa sales in Mexico, Costa Rica, Argentina, and Brazil. "I had never thought," confesses Jorge, "that at some time or other my principal job would be trying to *sell* Casa products! I began to devour books and journals and professional magazines about what good salesmen do. I also got back to that effort of seminary days to read all the books the Casa published. Some I knew well already; others, only by title. But 'a salesman' must know his products!" Some travel opportunities gave Jorge the chance to know personally "our customers." The rest of the matter, "I left to the Lord," he says. But sales in the countries for which he was responsible did begin to show improvement.

In the spring of the following year (1994), Wayne Quarrier finished a course of study in family counseling, which he had been pursuing nights and weekends. He felt led to resign his responsibilities with the Casa, move to Florida, and open a practice as a professional counselor. And it was at this point that, with Trustee approval, the Operations Division was reorganized into two: Marketing, and Production.[27] José Amézaga was named director of the Production Division. And Jorge Díaz became director of the Marketing Division. Jorge remembers vividly the day Dr. Poe called him to his office for a talk about the Marketing area. Poe told Díaz that he had considered several possibilities but had concluded Jorge was the best candidate to recommend to the Trustees (whose spring meeting was rapidly approaching). Poe wanted to make the recommendation with Jorge's knowledge and consent. They talked and prayed. The recommendation was made; the Trustees approved;[28] and Jorge Díaz faced still another new challenge! "It was the beginning of four years of arduous learning and much hard work," comments Jorge. The necessity of extreme "austerity" that Poe's administration had imposed meant that heavy spending on advertising, publicity, or promotional events was impossible. But Díaz mobilized his staff for the task at hand—with the resources available. They adopted a slogan of "Together we can do it!" (Spanish: Juntos, ¡sí podemos!) They adopted a divisional mission statement which read: "The Marketing Division has as its firm purpose to help people know what products we offer, how to use them, how much they cost, where they can be acquired and that we want to serve our customers rapidly and accurately."

Díaz asserts: "Our experience again showed the faithfulness of God. Slowly, sometimes very slowly with increases marked in a few percentage points, sales improved. It was really a joy when we were able to close the year 1997 having met the sales goal that had been set. That was precisely the year that Dr. Poe concluded his time as General Director."

(4) His participation in the Editorial Division (1998—2001). As previously narrated, Ted Stanton began his duties as CBP's General Director in January 1998.[29] Rather soon after arrival, he announced that he would be making some organizational and personnel changes. He asked for understanding and cooperation from all.

In the Marketing Division, there was a climate of enthusiasm since they had just met the sales goal for the previous year. In addition, some internal adjustments, recently implemented, helped give the feeling that 1998 would be a year of splendid possibilities. Then, during the first week in March, Brother Stanton called Jorge to his office and told him that he (the General Director) had decided Díaz should leave the Marketing Division to head up the Editorial Division.[30] Stanton also informed Jorge that missionary Greg Massey would be coming in August to assume the directorship of Marketing, and that in the interim Ronnie Adams would lead the Marketing Division. This would facilitate Jorge's immediate transfer to the Editorial Division.[31]

"This notice from the General Director impacted me to the point of tears," Jorge acknowledges. "When I left Brother Ted's suite, I went to my office, closed the door, fell to my knees, and poured out my heart to the Lord. I could not understand why, when we were just beginning to see the fruit of months of hard work, I should have to walk out and leave it all! But gradually, on my knees, the Lord helped me see some very important angles: (1) Both Ronnie Adams and Greg Massey had solid educational backgrounds and the capacity to carry the load of the Marketing Division much better than I. Both were missionaries, both younger than I; doubtless the change was for the good of the Publishing House. (2) Second, the Bible tells us that we should submit to established authorities, obey them, and pray for them. (3) Perhaps, after all, my spiritual gifts were not so much in the area of administration and attention to detail, as in capturing a vision and looking for new alternatives for Christian work in general; local churches and individual pastors and leaders, in particular. The Lord knows I love to communicate with people and teach them, especially in small groups of those who can then teach others. And (4): The ministry of the House is more important than individuals and therefore must be above personal interests, preferences, and desires. With this thought process, the God healed my heart and put my mind at peace."

Jorge convoked a meeting of Division personnel and, with the General Director present, announced the changes and thanked all for their help and support during his directorship. A week later he was in his new job as Director of the Editorial Division.

Ted Stanton had succeeded in getting the International Mission Board to provide two new missionaries who would function in the Editorial Division, for special tasks. One was Steve Murdock who would be a consultant for electronic communication media (CDs, videos, even radio, television, and other media). The other was Kirk Bullington, who would be a consultant in the area of music and worship. Stanton also had planned for Russell Herrington to become a consultant for materials related to evangelism, discipleship, and church planting movements. The new organization for the division grouped everybody into two departments: One editorial department, and a department for graphic design and quality control. Rubén Zorzoli was to supervise the Editorial Department (which would cluster three work areas: Books—also to be supervised by Rubén Zorzoli himself—; Curriculum materials—to be supervised by Alicia Zorzoli—; and Music materials—to be supervised by Annette Herrington. Russell Herrington was to supervise the Department of Graphic Design, and Quality Control. In addition to reorganizing existing work flow and personnel assignments, the division felt the impact of the retirement of José Luis Martínez (who for almost twenty years had directed the General Books Department). "Fortunately," says Díaz, "we were able to employ Dr. Juan Carlos Cevallos and his wife María Luisa."[32]

Despite these personnel additions (or replacements), Jorge found it necessary to place rigid limits on the number of new titles. "Earlier," Jorge comments, "it had not been uncommon for the Casa to offer up to seventy or eighty new resources[33] during a year. Now it was necessary to limit this number to forty. Thankfully, we seemed to find a healthy balance between editorial and production capacities during the years 1999 and 2000."

Encouraged by the General Director, the Editorial Division began to explore how to respond to the felt need of new curriculum materials for the Sunday School. A select group of pastors and religious educators from various countries was enlisted to help with planning content, lesson design, and carrier publications. Feasibility and cost studies were made, along with projections for return on investment. But just before the Division began to make writing assignments that would lead to production, the Management Team reviewed the financial implications and decided the project should be put on hold, for lack of adequate financial resources to cover all phases of the preparation, production, and introduction. It was a severe disappointment for the Division, but life went on.

Still another disappointing experience had to do the Casa's two remaining periodicals, *El Hogar Cristiano* and *La Ventana*.[34] Editorial Division personnel organized a workshop to develop ways of improving both the quality and the circulation possibilities of the two magazines. *El Hogar Cristiano* had continued its focus on the whole family, in an evangelical context. *La Ventana* offered materials for women including, but not limited to, those women organized into units of Woman's Missionary Union, in its Hispanic incarnation. The workshop faced worrisome issues: declining circulation, fuzzy targeting, and increasing competition. "We wanted to save these publications," comments Díaz, "by improving their design, sharpening their circulation strategy, and improving their pertinence for specific audiences. But when we presented our recommendations to the appropriate echelons of authority, it was decided that both should be discontinued. Neither was recovering costs nor offered adequate promise of regaining their earlier levels of sales." For the Editorial Division, it was another disappointment.

The year 2001 brought the departure of really all three of the "special consultants." Steve Murdock was the first to leave. He accepted a Hispanic-related responsibility with the Arkansas Baptist State Convention.[35] Kirk Bullington was the next to leave. He and his wife Karen felt led to return to the Dominican Republic, from which they had come to Casa some two years earlier. And Russell and Annette Herrington accepted an invitation to teach at the Mexican Baptist Seminary in Lomas Verdes (a suburb or Mexico City), first on a temporary basis which then became a permanent transfer.[36]

Following the retirement of María Luisa Porflit,[37] the opportunity came for Jorge to recommend employment of Hermes Soto, a Costa Rican well versed in the Spanish language, to take her place. His skills were such that responsibilities were amplified to include certain editorial tasks. In December 2003, he left the employ of the Casa to accept the pastorate of a Hispanic congregation in Austin, Texas.

One could argue, with Charles Dickens, that "It was the best of times. And it was the worst of times." For Jorge Díaz, his greatest challenge was coming closer.

Jorge Díaz is Named to Serve as General Director of Casa Bautista de Publicaciones

Jorge clearly remembers that it was in the early days of May 2001 when Brother Ted Stanton informed the Management Team, in a session just prior to the May meeting of the Board of Trustees, that he planned to present his resignation to the Board, owing to the continual health problems that he was suffering. Jorge recalls: "For a year or so we had watched him as he carried the worries of his office and the problems of his health. We had all prayed for him and with him, interceding with the Lord of heaven to improve his health. I perceived," continues Díaz, "that the pressures inherent in the General Director's office are bound to have an impact on the health of whoever carries that job. Pressures, problems, and tensions come from regular work and from unexpected sources. On the one hand, there are the financial worries (inadequate sales, slow pay from some accounts, cash flow requirements to meet payrolls, apart from necessary outlays to our suppliers and providers). On the other hand, there are the needs and wants of those who have been employed and told to produce. Add this to the background of what might be called a corporate climate based on subsidies and personnel dependent on the International Mission Board. All this together can't help but represent a challenge to the physical health of Casa administrators."

Ted Stanton carried forward with his notice to the Trustees in their May meeting; the Board responded by naming a Search Committee.[38] The committee began to function, writing to Baptist entities in Latin America, Spain, and the United States requesting suggestions for candidates that would fill the profile which had been established. A similar opportunity was given to Publishing House staff. Jorge remembers that in its meetings, the Management Team prayed specifically and regularly that the Lord would guide the Search Committee in its important task.

As expected, the Search Committee carried on its work without public announcements or communication leaks. Summer months turned to fall, and the November date for the next Trustee meeting approached. "My big surprise," recounts Jorge, "was that on Saturday prior to the week of the Trustee meeting, I got a call from missionary H. Rhea Chafin, the Search Committee's president, asking me to meet with the Committee the following day! Sunday! And my church was in the midst of an evangelistic campaign! I responded that I could meet between 2:00 and 4:00 in the afternoon. The meeting took place at the Best Western Airport Inn in El Paso, where the trustees customarily were lodged. The questions that were put to me were rather general in nature: What about my conversion, my baptism, and my ministry both in the Casa Bautista and in other circles? They asked me to pray for them and for the work they were assigned to do. Frankly, I left the meeting somewhat relieved, for they had neither offered me the position nor asked me my opinion about other candidates."[39]

But on the following Tuesday morning, not far from noon, Jorge Enrique Díaz was called to the conference room where the Trustees where meeting. There the president of the Board, pastor Juan Calcagni, of Argentina, told Jorge that the Board of Trustees had taken the decision to name him the new General Director of Casa Bautista de Publicaciones. Furthermore, in view of Brother Stanton's plans to move from El Paso in the next few days, the Trustees wanted Jorge to assume the new responsibilities immediately.

Apparently the Holy Spirit had done His work, preparing the soil—perhaps silently, perhaps imperceptibly. The fact is that Jorge Enrique Díaz Figueroa accepted the naming and began his functions. The Casa had its ninth General Director.

Endnotes

1. Figueroa is Díaz's "apellido materno," his mother's maiden name. It is customary in Latin American countries to use this surname in some way. Sometimes it is placed after the father's surname (as Díaz frequently does). Sometimes it is represented in that position but only by an initial letter (like, "... Díaz F."). Sometimes the two family names are connected with a hyphen (as has been done in chapters 7 and 8 for Dr. Roberto García-Bordoli). In Díaz's case, his mother's family had a very important place in his Christian pilgrimage, which this chapter will clarify.

2. See Motion 3, Minutes, Trustee Meeting, November 2001, p. 3; CBP Archives.

3. Philippians 3:13b, NIV

4. The specific date was May 9, 2002. Participants included: Rubén Zorzoli (master of ceremonies); Pablo Zorzoli (congregational music leader); trustees Eloy Coelho (invocation prayer), Juan Calcagni (challenge to the new General Director), and H. Rhea Chafin (dedication prayer); Elvin Porflit, Jr. (special music), and Julie Sánchez (pianist).

5. Poe acknowledges surprise at having received the invitation and says he considered it

an honor to introduce his friend of more than three decades. The service was conducted in Spanish, and Poe entitled his presentation "Conozcamos al Nuevo Director General de CBP."

6. It is interesting that in English, the saying is that a cat has nine lives. Why "Spanish-speaking cats" have two less is anybody's guess! But popular sayings do not necessarily respond to logic or historical explanations!

7. Jorge has the same initials as Jones Edgar Davis, the founder of the Casa.

8. Later, remembers Jorge, José Arturo "confessed his faith in Christ, but time ran out before he could become an active member of some church."

9. A city located on the Atlantic coast of Guatemala, near the fertile banana growing plantations of the United Fruit Company.

10. Jorge says this was really the beginning of Baptist churches in Guatemala, later organized into a national convention for the country. And, he reminds us, essentially the same thing happened in Honduras and certain other places in Central America.

11. Undoubtedly another model that, consciously or unconsciously, functioned very positively for Jorge was his maternal grandfather; see below.

12. Romans 1:16, KJV.

13. See section entitled "A Veteran of More than Two Decades...", below.

14. The list does not mention the "administrative aspect" of being a pastor—but well it might; for such duties do exist as any successful pastor will testify.

15. The Díazes liked the house, and the sale was consummated; it is where Jorge and family still live.

16. The word choice is from Díaz, and it reflects his willingness to work as a team.

17. See above.

18. San Martín, a Chilean who has served with the Publishing House since 1984 and is now working in domestic sales, has a very interesting story about the Miniature Bible (Casa publication #48816). He says it was evidently being distributed among some who worked at New York's World Trade Center and that its presence on one of the few bodies rescued after the 9/11 terrorist attacks helped identify the body.

19. David Fajardo came to specifically replace Dr. Antonio Rengifo who had accepted

student ministry responsibilities in Oklahoma. Jorge Rousselin came with a specific assignment in the Art Department to help in the graphic design of all these new pieces. Vilma Fajardo has served continually as an Assistant Editor or an Editor; she recalls with special gratitude the way the Tuckers helped them get settled in El Paso. She says: "They even gave us some vacation time at a cabin in the beautiful mountains of southern New Mexico!"

20. Jorge laments that the collection never covered the whole Bible, but he notes that measures were taken to complete the series on the New Testament.

21. First to study at Southwestern Seminary in Fort Worth, then to return to her home country, Venezuela.

22. Peggy and her husband Dr. Bob E. Compton had come to the Publishing House in 1986 from Costa Rica; see chapter 8.

23. The unifying theme became "Encuentro con Jesús" (Encounter with Jesus) and publication was completed in 1993. It is still in use.

24. Among the representatives were Dr. Roberto Gama and Dr. Javier Elizondo.

25. Since the Book by Book series only contemplated materials for young people and adults, a new three-year program for children was published and has been used by some churches that opt for the Book by Book curriculum. This children's material goes under the title Descubre Tu Biblia (Discover Your Bible). It uses Bible personages to survey the whole content of Scripture. Marta Dergarabedián, from Argentina, was the original author; Vilma Fajardo was the CBP resident editor.

26. As explained in chapter 9, the Operations Division was created in mid-1993 and combined manufacturing (i.e., printing and binding), marketing, and maintenance.

27. The Maintenance Department was reassigned to the Division presided by Dr. Jesse Bryan.

28. See motion 3, Trustee Meeting, May 1994, p. 5; CBP Archives.

29. See chapter 10.

30. See chapter 9, where the retirement of Ananías and Nelly González in March 1997 is reported and the fact that Poe had purposely left that slot vacant so that the incoming General Director could name his choice.

31. Technically the division's name at this time was still the Product Design and Develop-

ment Division; but it was eventually renamed the Editorial Division and continues as such.

32. This couple hails from the South American country of Ecuador. Besides academic opportunities in their home country, both have studied at the Evangelical Seminary in Limón, Venezuela and at the International Baptist Seminary in Cali, Colombia, where Juan Carlos finished the doctoral studies. When the Casa employed them, they were already in the United States, having been brought here by Professor and Mrs. Alfred Tuggy, who, during their retirement years in South Carolina, were carrying on some very extensive editorial projects. Juan Carlos and María Luisa had emigrated to South Carolina to help in those projects.

33. Previously it had been customary to speak of "products," but "resources" became the term of choice in this period.

34. From a height of about 30 quarterlies (see chapter 4), circumstances had gradually brought elimination of all but these two.

35. In Baptist ecclesiology, the term refers to a fraternal organization of Baptist churches in a state.

36. Their departure left the Casa without talented and professionally trained missionary musicians, really since the Blairs arrived in 1957 and the Nelsons in 1970. Other "music missionaries" who had served at CBP included Ed and Kathy Steele, Shirley Ditmore, and Mary Stanton. Equally talented and professionally trained employees in this area had included Leslie Gomez and Salomón Mussiett.

As an example of how CBP musical publications link with church musicians in the Latin American countries, Vilma Fajardo has shared how much her brother, Ramiro Martínez, a church musician in Ecuador, has appreciated and used successfully Casa publications such as the youth musical Amar es esperar (True Love Waits). Vilma reports the church where her brother serves presented this youth cantata several times, that it was a real blessing, and that many young people gave their lives to Christ as a result.

37. See chapter 10.

38. See Trustee Minutes, Meeting, May 2001, Motions 12, 13, and 14, p. 8; CBP Archives.

39. This and all the quotes from Jorge Díaz in this chapter have been taken from a 25 page document prepared by Díaz and supplied to J. T. Poe as input for the last two chapters in this centennial book. Received March 10, 2004. At the end of that document, Díaz had words of thanks for the author of this project and special expressions to his family: "I want to express my gratitude to my wife Raquelita for her faithful support, her prayers, and her assistance throughout our life together." He had similar words for his two daughters, Miryam Raquel and Carol Elizabeth: "They have been understanding, cooperative, and the fountain of many ideas and suggestions for 'this old cat.' "

40. Ted and Mary's plans were to move to Little Rock, Arkansas the week following the Trustee meeting.

Chapter 12

Jorge Díaz Brings Experience and Vision
for a New Century
Part II

Arguably Jorge Díaz faces the most daunting task of any CBP General Director since Davis in 1916 or Patterson in 1943: The Casa must again be re-invented.[1]

The end of operational funding by the International Mission Board probably impacted more than had been anticipated or imagined. Furthermore, the downsizing of missionary staff and the announced plan of shortly withdrawing all missionary personnel, plus the dismantling of "the deposit system" of distribution—and all this in times of economic retrenchment for basically all of Latin America—has represented a most serious challenge to CBP.

But Díaz is not one to give up easily. He brings rich experience[2] and vision that bodes well for the future of this ministry. This final chapter presents the early years of Jorge Díaz's administration, takes a snapshot of CBP at age 100, emphasizes present projections toward the future, and ends with an appeal to all the "Friends of the Casa."

The Early Years of Jorge Díaz's Administration

The Trustee action naming Jorge Díaz as General Director of CBP gave a beginning date of November 14, 2001.[3] In effect his administration began the very day he was elected. What a transition! Perhaps his first official act was to recommend that Rubén Zorzoli be named Director of the Resource Design and Development Division, the position Jorge needed to vacate to give full time to the General Director's office. And in that same meeting of the Trustees, Rubén was so named.[4] Immediately following the Trustee week, Jorge asked the members of the Management Team to be much in prayer and requested that they reserve the week of December 3-5 for a work retreat together. Meanwhile he dedicated himself—day and night—to studying the Casa's general situation and the work of each division. He reviewed the Casa's history along with his own experiences there during his now more than twenty years, and developed a list of seven matters that required both immediate attention and long range consideration. He put these thoughts in writing, shared them with members of the Management Team, alerting them that this document would give a framework for their time together in the upcoming retreat. That experience gave opportunity to refine the document and to review and sharpen short range plans and budget projections for 2002. They adopted a slogan of "inversiones inteligentes" (intelligent investments), by which they meant that expenditures from the upcoming budget would need to meet stringent requirements: expenditures should advance the ministry of the Casa and there should be good reasons, defensible arguments, for every penny of outgo. A consensus was reached to make whatever adjustments necessary to preserve and continue the Casa's ministry. At this point the Management Team consisted of Díaz, the new General Director; Rubén Zorzoli, director of what was shortly renamed the Editorial Division; John Bayer, director of the Administration and Finance Division; Miryam Díaz (now Picott), Director of the Marketing Division; Velia Hodge, as an at-large representative of personnel; and Norma Armengol, as the group's secretary. To some degree, Jorge's first steps (and those of his Management Team) can be summarized as "planning for change(s)—immediate and future—and coping with unexpected changes."

As early as January 2002, those unexpected (and uninvited) changes began to present themselves. The first was when missionary John Bayer gave notice to Jorge that he and his wife Brenda had accepted another assignment from the International Mission Board that would send them to Europe. They would be leaving almost immediately. Added to this vacancy, Jackie Disselkoen, who had been serving the Casa in accounting for more than fifteen years but who had been battling cancer since the mid-1990s, had to completely cease her regular functions at the office because of continually deteriorating health. These two circumstances forced Jorge into another "adventure:" becoming interim director of the Administration and Finance Division. (He was doubly grateful for the presence of both Matthew Venhaus and Velia Hodge[5] who helped him keep things afloat!) Another undesired (though not quite as unexpected) change occurred when Russell and Annette Herrington advised that they would definitely be transferring to Mexico (for work at the Seminary in Lomas Verdes) rather than returning to the Publishing House after their six months leave of absence. Still another vacancy was produced when Mark Fricke advised that he had accepted the opportunity for him and his wife Debbie to return to Guatemala as resident missionaries there. Fricke had been director of International Sales, in the Marketing Division; and over half of the Casa's sales were still going outside the USA. He would be sorely missed. "In each of these cases," recounts Díaz, "we appealed to the Regional Offices [of IMB] asking for missionary replacements. In each case, we were treated courteously and told possibilities would be investigated. But we were warned that finding help would not be easy."

An unexpected positive development occurred within a few months when Jorge received a phone call from missionary Tim Shupp[6] who inquired if the spot Mark Fricke left was still available. Happily, all Mission Board clearances were obtained, and Tim and his wife Louise were transferred to the Publishing House, where he became Mark's successor in the International Sales Department.[7] Still another happy development was the appointment of emeritus missionary Ray Turner and his wife Betty[8] to come to the Publishing House on a two-year ISC assignment. They arrived in February 2003. Díaz's comments: "The contribution of Brother Turner has been very valuable and has come just at the right time. Firmly but with courtesy and great tact, he has signaled the need for our attention to certain financial matters and has helped us control expenses, improve productivity, and take advantage of opportunities."[9]

Probably the most difficult decision that came in these early years of Jorge Díaz's administration had to do with the print shop. Jorge reflected on the matter: "During all of 2002 we carefully studied every angle related to the Casa's print shop. We worked out three criteria to guide us in deciding where we would manufacture products; these were quality, timely delivery, and cost of production. We gradually came to the conclusion that our printing and binding equipment had rendered good service and had done so for a long time. Implied was a certain limitation to the quality we could expect from our aging equipment. A more subtle factor was that our production crew had, perhaps unconsciously, developed a culture of production rhythm whose result seemed to be slower output than was needed. This, in the midst of developments in the world-wide printing industry where new technologies and modern equipment resulted in costs of production that, even after adding transportation costs for delivery to El Paso, were better than those from our own shop! Every member of our Management Team had to confront the hard questions of: 'What is our main business—printing or publishing?' 'In what can we excel and really stand out?' 'What is absolutely inherent to our ministry?' "

Jorge continues his reflection on this complex matter: "After long hours of dialogue, prayer, and consideration of 'the cold numbers,' we arrived at the decision to close our print shop and manufacture on contract all our products with other providers. We set May 12, 2003, as officially 'the last day' for the print shop, though it took some days more to complete all the work in process. At that time we had eight people working in the Production Division. We offered them a benefit package[10] to assuage the situation and promised positive recommendations to assist in their search for new employment." No doubt it was a difficult decision for Jorge and his team. The Casa had basically been bifocal (a printery and a publications house) since its birth. Poe found an interesting parallel in the experience of the Levi Strauss Company. The *El Paso Times*, on

January 9, 2004, carried an article in its Business Section, which told that the Levi Strauss Company, "the California Gold Rush outfitter whose trademark blue jeans have been an American clothing staple for generations" has just announced the closing its last two plants in the United States. "This spring," the article said, "Levi Strauss... will complete the shift to contract production..." Company officials cited changing markets and worldwide competition as major factors, and almost apologetically declared: " 'We're still an American brand, but we're also a brand and a company whose products have been adopted by consumers around the world.' " The survival of the company was at stake and required tough decisions.[11] Jorge and his Management Team confronted similar factors and came to similar conclusions.[12] Their courage should be both recognized and appreciated.

In some contrast to the difficult decisions related to closing the print shop, the early years of Jorge's administration have brought a positive development concerning a renovated curriculum for Bible study in the Sunday Schools of local churches. The matter had been left pending, since the Management Team determined to put the project on hold a few years earlier.[13] But in fall of 2003, Rubén Zorzoli approached Jorge as the General Director and told him of his strong desire to dedicate his full time and all his energies to the task of providing a new program of study for use in Sunday School. After exploring the implications and praying together, they decided to take the matter to the Trustees in the Board's November meeting. There, after more prayer and considerations, Rubén's resignation as director of the Editorial Division was accepted, and he was named as Editor of the Sunday School Bible Study Program. With the help of Mario Martínez, Rubén immediately set to work on the job and reports good progress. Publication of the new program is expected to begin in 2006. (Prayer is requested for Rubén.) One of the implications of this arrangement was that Díaz would shoulder, in addition to the General Director's office, the interim directorship of the Editorial Division. The Trustees also gave approval to this aspect of the plan. But in June 2004, Jorge recommended and the Executive Committee of the Trustees approved naming Alicia Zorzoli as Interim Director of this division. She began to function in this post on June 14.

Among the new resources recently launched by CBP is one that plows new ground, in terms of its format, and may indeed be a harbinger of things to come. It is a new CD entitled "Hispanic World Electronic Library" (Biblioteca Electrónica Mundo Hispano). This valuable resource includes Bibles, commentaries, Bible study helps, and eighteen other books to assist in pastoral ministry, preaching and teaching, and worship. Its reception has been close to phenomenal, and a second volume is already being planned. With development support received from the CBP Foundation, this project provided an opportunity for innovation and partnership that bodes well for the future.

Still another happening considered very positively by the General Director deals with property and buildings which the Publishing House has occupied since 1938.[14] The matter had been on Jorge's heart since he became General Director in late 2001. Finally, he took it to the Board of Trustees in their meeting of November 2003 and encouraged the Board to request the leaders of IMB's Middle America Region (specifically, Phil Templin, Regional Leader, and his Administrative Associate H. Rhea Chafin) give consideration to deeding the property (land and buildings) to the Casa's corporate entity (a fully legal nonprofit Texas corporation). The Regional Offices requested some data from the Casa files which was supplied forthwith. Then, somewhat to Díaz's surprise, the month of February brought news from Brother Chafin that the International Mission Board had approved the request and that the Casa should proceed to get the title deeds prepared for signing by the appropriate IMB representative. This was done, using a major title company in El Paso, and on March 15, 2004 missionary Brent Dix, power of attorney for IMB in the Region, came to El Paso and signed the necessary documents for the title transfer. Like a family that finally "owns its own home," the Casa now "owns its house."

In May 2003 Jorge encouraged the Board of Trustees to consider whether the new situation at the Publishing House required some changes in the structure of the Board itself. The Board named a study group, which subsequently brought its report to the Board Meeting in November. After thorough consideration of this delicate matter, the Board resolved to reduce its total membership from twelve to seven. Of these seven, two "memberships" would be held permanently by representatives of the Baptist constituencies in the United States and Mexico. The International Mission Board, SBC, (specifically its Middle America Region, whose offices are currently in Guatemala) would also have permanent representation. One of the remaining four seats on the Board would rotate among the other three Regions of Latin America where IMB has Spanish-speaking missionaries.[15] With the restructuring of regions done July 1, 2004, apparently there will be two permanent members representing IMB. And on a rotating basis, Baptist constituencies in three countries will be invited to name members who would serve terms of three years. This will provide for the total of seven board members.

A Snapshot of CBP at Age 100

Birthdays and anniversaries frequently become times for picture taking. The technology may vary, from a Brownie Kodak® to the latest digital Canon®; but the purpose is the same: to preserve a moment in the life of an individual or a family, for later enjoyment, appreciation, and perhaps even inspiration. Albums of such photos can easily become an informal volume of history. And, as someone has said, "Our history should be revisited from time to time to help us gain strength for facing the present and inspiration for facing the future."

This book has reviewed the life and ministry of Casa Bautista de Publicaciones since its founding in 1905. This particular section of the final chapter is an attempt to transmit a snapshot of "this lady" at age 100. Since the publication of the book itself its designed to be part of the centennial celebration, it is technically impossible to wait till the "birthday" to take the picture. What follows is a presentation of the personnel serving at CBP at a given date[16] during her hundredth year—and how they are relating to each other to carry forward Casa's mission:

Personnel:[17]

Jorge Luis Aguilar	Keith Morris[19]
Norma Armengol	Mixy Morris
Rafael Manuel Abascal	Eleazar Peña
Allan Cardet	Gilbert Pérez
Juan Carlos Cevallos	Jorge Rede
María Luisa Cevallos	Delores Robleto-Sodosky
Miriam Del Palacio	Terry Sánchez
Jorge Enrique Díaz	Exequiel San Martín
David Fajardo	Carlos Santiesteban
Vilma Fajardo	Carlos Simmons
Nancy Hamilton	José H. Torres
José A. Hernández	Ray Turner
Velia Hodge	Betty Turner
Violeta Martínez	Margarita Valadez
Mario Martínez	Juan Varela
Carol Ann Martínez.	Matthew Venhaus
Aida Medrano	Gloria Williams-Méndez
Olpa Mendoza	Rubén Zorzoli
	Alicia Zorzoli

Organization:

General Director: Jorge E. Díaz
    Executive Secretary, Norma Armengol
        Related entities:
            Management Team
            Health and Safety Committee
            Publications Committee

Editorial Division
    Alicia Zorzoli, Interim Director
    Administrative Assistant, Nancy Hamilton
    Editorial Department
    Alicia Zorzoli, Interim Director

Editorial quality control: Margarita Valadez
Supervising editor for books: Juan Carlos Cevallos
Supervising editor of materials for women: Alicia Zorzoli
Supervising editor for Bible teaching: Rubén Zorzoli
Team of editors: María Luisa Cevallos, Vilma Fajardo, Mario Martínez
Graphic Design Department
Gloria Williams-Méndez, Director
Carlos Santiesteban, Jr., artist and designer

Marketing Division

Miryam Díaz-Picott, Director
Administrative Assistant: Aracelis Vázquez
Receptionist: Aida Medrano
Factory Store and Volunteers: Olpa Mendoza
Office of Promotion, Publicity and Field Services:
Coordinator, David Fajardo;
    Others: Rebeca Sánchez, Carol Martínez, Olpa Mendoza
Domestic Sales and Services Department, Eleazar Peña, Director
    Others: Alan Cardet (Miami), Miriam Del Palacio, Teresa Sánchez, Exequiel
        San Martín
International Sales and Services:
    Director: Manuel Abascal
    Delores Robleto-Sodosky

Administration and Finance Division

Ray Turner, Director
Administrative Assistant: Velia Hodge
Office of Contract Production: Violeta Martínez
Office of Computer Services: Gilbert Pérez
Accounting Department: Ray Turner
Assistant: Matthew Venhaus
Accounts payable: Velia Hodge
Credit and collections: Velia Hodge
Inventory and Shipping Department: Jorge Rede, Director
Assistants: Jorge Aguilar, Agustín Hernández, and Carlos Simons
Maintenance: José Torres, Juan Varela

Celebration: Birthdays and anniversaries call for celebrations. Plans are in place to have a good "fiesta" for the Casa's hundredth! Jorge has made available the following list of things being planned: (Who knows? Additional ways may also emerge.)

1. Publication by the Casa, in partnership with the Baptist Spanish Publishing House Foundation, of two books, with editions in both English and Spanish (a total of four volumes). One of those is the very book you are reading! The other is a shorter presentation with a different focus. Its title is "Casa: The Partner in Ministry You Need." If you have not received it, please request a copy, using the reply sheet at the end of this chapter. Both are appropriate for

the Centennial Anniversary and will hopefully result in enlarging the active circle of "Friends of the Casa." (Maybe you can help get these books into the widest possible circulation.)

Very probably a few new publications will be launched during the anniversary year with the designation "Centennial Edition." One of these might be a new economy edition of the RVA Bible. (Would you be willing to help finance "Jorge's Bible?" If so, write him.)

2. Efforts to coordinate with each national Baptist convention in the various countries of the Americas and Europe (perhaps even beyond), in scheduling some event during the year that will celebrate the ministry of the Casa Bautista de Publicaciones.

3. The ample use of a logo that has already been designed and chosen. A unique design presents the centennial slogan: "1905–2005: A Hundred Years of Faithful Service to God and His People" (Spanish: "1905–2005: Cien años de servicio fiel a Dios y a su pueblo"). You will find it on this book. Perhaps there will be ways you too can use it to help promote consciousness of the Casa's centennial.

4. Trustees of CBP will have their mid-year meeting in 2005 in Mexico, where the Casa was born, probably in conjunction with the annual meeting of the National Baptist Convention of Mexico. It will be a unique venue in which to celebrate the Casa's "hundredth birthday" close to its "birth place" and in relation to perhaps its single most important constituency: the Baptists of Mexico.

5. A joint meeting, in the month of November, between the Casa's Board of Trustees and the trustees of the Baptist Spanish Publishing House Foundation. It will be held in El Paso, in the Patterson Building, erected during Aldo Broda's administration.

6. A public event, probably to be held in one of the Baptist churches of El Paso, while the trustees of both the Governing Board and the Foundation Board are still together. This will give an opportunity for brethren, especially from the Hispanic churches of El Paso, Ciudad Juárez, and Las Cruces to join in public celebration of the Casa's century of service.

(If you are reading this prior to one or more of these events and if it is possible for you to be present in person, please consider this as a personal invitation to do so! CBP needs your support!)

Projections Toward the Future

Allusion has already been made to the document Jorge prepared in the early days of his administration and used with the Management Team to begin projecting toward the future. With the support of that group and with the modifications it made, the document subsequently won approval by the Board of

Trustees in its meeting of May 2002. Jorge acknowledges: "To speculate about the future is always risky, but unless we have the capacity to dream of how we want our Publishing House to be in the coming years, and unless we put our hands to the plow in real efforts to make those dreams come true, economic globalization and the tremendous social and political changes that our world brings can threaten to put an end to a beloved ministry that is approaching its hundredth anniversary." Thus this document represents the vision of the current General Director, his Management Team, and the Board of Trustees for building *The House of Our Dreams*.

1. Create and maintain a persistent sense of urgency. The Publishing House has regularly had an attitude toward our work that may have fostered calm but also a degree of complacency. To a certain point we have permitted, in the name of "ministry," that each person should do "what they could and when they could." Now we must capture—or recapture—and cultivate a spirit of "here and now." A new "lifestyle" in which plans are made to produce results in the short term as well as over the long haul. Our mission is urgent and needs to be fulfilled—the sooner the better! Thus:

1. We must be aware of and face squarely the different crises that are before us:
    a. The crisis of competent personnel in various areas (examples: administration, music, sales)
    b. The financial crisis (the almost daily crisis of adequate cash flow)
    c. The crisis of motivation and enthusiasm toward the work to be done.
2. We must eliminate "small luxuries" we have permitted ourselves (such as none-too-strict daily work schedules, short absences during work hours, compensation days).
3. We must establish benchmarks and goals for income, margins, productivity, and efficiency that are so high they simply can't be reached with "business as usual" work.
4. We must insist that each "team" or departmental unit be responsible for reaching the agreed-upon goals of productivity and efficiency.
5. We must provide to more employees more information concerning the situation of our enterprise and bring them equally in the know on what we are achieving. Sometimes we have been fearful to share this kind of information lest we create a climate of insecurity. But the lack of information leaves employees in the dark concerning the gravity of the situation and deprives them of the opportunity to do their work with the urgency our circumstances demand. If we communicate openly to the personnel concerning the problems of our Publishing House, we will be in a better position to ask for their sup-

port, their ideas, and their suggestions for finding solutions to our problems.

6. We must insist that all employees be available to talk to customers about our products and services and that they share with colleagues the results of such conversations.

7. We must be willing, as necessary, to call on the help of "consultants" and "technical advisors" in the search for solutions to the problems and barriers we encounter.

2. *Foster constantly our commitment to team work.* The old paradigm under which everything depends on the Casa's General Director or on the relations which individual employees may have with their division director must change. The format of relationships between division directors and the department directors must also change, as must the individual relation of a department director with employees within his department. At each one of these three levels there must be a conscious, intentional, and well cultivated effort to deal with the constantly changing circumstances our House faces. Talents of each person must be taken into account and channeled to form a synergistic total in which the whole is greater than the sum of the individual parts. Therefore:

1. No one person, however competent he or she may be, should be thought capable of developing by himself a vision, or communicating it to all personnel, or eliminating all the obstacles we face, or generating the necessary changes. Hence, we need teams made up of:
   a. The right people,
   b. With a high level of responsibility and trustworthiness,
   c. Who share the same vision.

2. Though the phraseology may sound a bit ridiculous, we must therefore eliminate (or reduce to a bare minimum) the presence of persons who merit the description as:
   a. "Peacocks," whose self-centeredness barely leaves room for anybody else, since they tend to feel "indispensable" and behave like "know-it-alls."
   b. "Snakes," who are always criticizing decisions and suggesting "rebellion."
   c. "Tortoises," who seem to be in agreement but who move with their customary sluggishness.
   d. "Woodpeckers," who are always chipping away at the bark causing expenses that do not produce enough to even pay for their food.

3. To be successful, we must create a climate of trust
   a. Through events, retreats, and meetings with the members of each one of our teams

    b. And by giving opportunity to freely interchange ideas and opinions.

4. We must also develop common goals that appeal to our reason, touch our hearts, and move us to action.

3. Develop and communicate our vision and our strategies. We fervently believe that within the enterprise we have persons with capabilities to create, communicate, and generate enthusiasm so that *The House of Our Dreams* becomes a reality. Without a doubt we have some very good managers and administrators (persons who know how to get things done, administer budgets, and work with details); nevertheless, we must continue seeking and praying that the Lord will help us discover those who really have the ability to imagine, create visions, and chart—like pioneers—new paths never before even imagined. For now:

1. The vision/mission, the passion, and the economic goals that were written and adopted by the CBP Management Team and subsequently approved by the Board of Trustees declare:

   Our vision/mission: That Editorial Mundo Hispano/Casa Bautista de Publicaciones become either number one or number two [among evangelical publishing houses] in the publication and distribution of Bible-based Christian resources[19] that are of the highest possible quality and usefulness to equip the Hispanic Christian community to fulfill the Great Commission.

   Our passion: To communicate through printed and electronic media the message of the Word of God.

   Our economic goal: To cover the cost of each product with a contribution of one percent toward the growth of the enterprise.

2. Implied characteristics in the vision/mission statement that warrant emphasis:

   (1) It is *imaginable.* It makes possible for people to "see" what the future can be.

   (2) It is *desirable.* It has appeal for CBP personnel, CBP customers, and others who share an interest in the ministry of the printed page.

   (3) It is *feasible.* It presents reachable goals within a reasonable time frame.

   (4) It is *flexible.* Within general limits, it permits participants to take initiative and make necessary changes in light of how the circumstances change.

   (5) It is *communicable.* It can be explained in a simple and orderly way to whoever needs to understand it.

4. Delegate responsibility to, and share corresponding authority with, all employees. We must remove obstacles to the work of those who stand in the "direct line of fire," that is, those who are in direct relationship with our customers, be they individuals, churches, bookstores or distributors of whatever size. Those that stand in this "direct line of fire" with customers need to have the power and authority to make certain decisions that they feel are prudent, always in accord with the Casa's overall vision and strategy. What is desired is that we align all our work to be in harmony with those in front line relationships with our customer base. Some employees may understand the vision and want to make it a reality, but they encounter obstacles or barriers that we, then, need to help them overcome. We therefore desire:

1. To give more attention and more service to the customer than to the products, the paperwork, or the protocol.
2. To establish levels of authority that permit giving more responsibility to the employee.
3. To lower costs and produce results, instead of emphasizing "policies and procedures," the maintenance of which often takes good blocks of time and may provoke friction.
4. To seek constant interaction between all our personnel so that there is an atmosphere of mutual support rather than turf protection between departments or divisions.
5. How will we do it?
    (1) Providing training: on how to do the job, on how to relate to each other, on defining the results expected, and on the criteria to be used in evaluating results.
    (2) Defining how appropriately to reward those who really contribute toward achievement of the vision/mission.
    (3) Confronting leaders/managers/administrators who fail to facilitate the process of change. An honest dialogue will be attempted; but, as necessary, removal procedures will be followed if leaders/administrators/management personnel are not comfortable with the new demands. It should be made clear that interests of the Casa and its vision will be put ahead of individual considerations and of interests that are merely personal.
    (4) Improving and using new tools and instruments to detect, address, and follow-up on the process of delegating responsibility and sharing authority with personnel.

5. Establish and celebrate the achievement of short term, intermediate, and long range goals. Well stated goals share the characteristics of being purposeful, measurable, and datable. Only goals with these characteristics can move us along toward achieving *The House of Our Dreams*. We therefore:

1. Recognize that the establishing of goals and the celebration of their achievement help create confidence and trust in the whole process of advance toward the vision. Reaching some goals will take more time than others; but we all need to know if what we are doing is producing desired results.

2. The Management Team has established what we have called "Super-sized[20] Goals" (Spanish: Mega-Metas; and for Spanish an acronym of "Megas" has been launched based on letters taken from the phrase 'Metas grandes y audaces.') They will be revised each year; the five adopted for 2004 are as follows:

   (1) We will perform whatever heroic acts are necessary to serve well each Casa customer.

   (2) We will make our best efforts to produce, present, and promote each one of the products of the Publishing House.

   (3) We will share Jesus Christ and His message through our daily conduct in relating to our extended CBP "family," meaning our fellow workers and our customers.

   (4) We will work toward making Editorial Mundo Hispano/Casa Bautista de Publicaciones either number one or number two [among evangelical editorial houses], in the publication and distribution of Bible-based resources, of the highest quality.

   (5) We will achieve an overall sales volume of $2,800,000 in 2004, yielding a monthly goal of $233,333.33; the goal projects that 36% of the volume will come from international sales and 64% from the national/domestic market.

Each division and department is expected to establish its own goals, strategies, and operations that will contribute to all our Super-sized[21] Goals.

3. Department and division directors must find appropriate ways of celebrating goal achievement, whether the goals be short range, intermediate, or long range. The nature of the celebration should be such that it recognizes what has been done but also motivates toward the next goal. Some goals should celebrate:

   (1) Significant reduction in costs (while maintaining expected quality of production) as well as the achievement of quality itself, in both products and services,

   (2) Tightening of total time required for executing projects, and

   (3) Any reorganization that has notably improved team morale.

4. What a celebration should include:

   (1) Evidence that sacrifices made were worthwhile and productive,

   (2) Inspiration and motivation to continue advancing,

   (3) Opportunity for making corrections to agreed upon/established strategies,

(4) Identification of obstacles that have been overcome and how the present situation is better than before,

(5) Applause for leaders/administrators/managerial personnel, so that their affirmation moves us along toward realizing our dreams,

(6) Creation of the ripe moment when employees (workers/colleagues) who have been either neutral to our alliances, or doubtful about our systems, or marginalized as spectators can "convert" to the new team effort.

5. Another word concerning the sense of urgency: Doubtless we will hear the comment: "We should not pressure people." However, without sufficient and sustained pressure concerning the urgency of our goals and the achievement of our plans, our achievements will be small. Let all remember that together with the pressure, there must be celebration, motivation, and inspiration to continue toward "the vision."

6. Division directors must establish goals, develop plans and budgets, organize personnel, implement and control forward progress giving guidance, motivation, and support—all the while delegating work to subordinate personnel: this is the reason for having division directors! And each must maintain a constant balance between being good leaders, efficient administrators/managers, and resource people.[22]

6. Consolidate advances made and be open to new and even bolder changes. We must find ways to hire, promote, and develop employees who have the will to join our efforts and who will contribute effectively toward achievement of our strategic vision.

We must imagine new ways to accomplish things, design and develop new products that address new issues in new formats and accomplish the ministry of the Casa in new molds. Our corporate climate must be open enough and fertile enough to take advantage of the creative possibilities of every employee!

7. Develop a corporate culture that strikes a happy balance of ministry and business. We must create ways of working that open new avenues of relating with customers, new avenues of relating staff involved in the product development process with the leadership of the enterprise, fully recognizing that such will not be an easy task. If changing the "culture" of an individual or a family is difficult (and it is), changing the "culture" of an enterprise will be more difficult. But if we do not attempt it, the Casa is apt to wane to the point that its very existence and/or the validity of its ministry will be seriously jeopardized.

Another important aspect in the development of our corporate culture has to do with developing means to assure continuity and succession in the leadership of the Casa. To some extent, leaders have sometimes seemed to look at their work as something which when finished should give them freedom to "change clothes" and leave for "greener pastures," and this without having given training or assisted in the formation of a new generation that could take their place and carry forward the Casa's vision and ministry. At every level we should maintain an attitude of training and encouragement to growth so that those who come after us can actually do the job better than we.

The document concluded with the new CEO making an appeal to all personnel of the Casa in these words: "As the present General Director, I have essentially used the first six months of my new task to analyze, research, and diagnose the present situation of our enterprise. I have taken time to think about and develop these and other ideas that fit into the process of achieving *The House of Our Dreams*. I have put these thoughts in writing to share them with personnel at all levels. And I am purposely laying on the division directors a call for radical sacrifice and dedication so that they take this vision and these strategies to their field of everyday and practical reality, to the end that all of us together write a noble history of service for the next hundred years in *The House of Our Dreams*."[23]

Concluding Note: An Appeal to All

Some "history books" merely end with an implied or specifically stated conclusion: "That's the way it was." Other "history books" make some effort to connect with possibilities for the future.[24] This book goes even further. It hereby concludes its efforts at a carefully documented historical presentation, and turns to a sincerely made personal appeal: The Casa and its staff need friends— many friends, all kinds of friends. With its hundred years of rich experience and its keen vision for the future, its present friends–and all who would become "friends of the Casa"— are hereby called upon to give her the multidimensional support she needs to initiate successfully the second century of life and work. The kind of support needed begins with prayer support. In real sense this is the least "friends of the Casa" can do; and in another sense, it is the most they (you!) can do. Practical moral support is another dimension of what is needed. How many times have you been lifted up, revived, re-motivated in the midst of difficult circumstances in your job or ministry by a well spoken, or well written, word of thanks or encouragement. The Casa's main telephone number is 915-566-9656. Jorge Díaz's extension number is 265. Why not call him, when you finish reading this book, and tell him you are praying for him and for the Casa's gospel ministry? Or write: The Casa's physical address is 7000 Alabama Street, El Paso, Texas 79904. Visitors are always welcome, and some mail is received there, although most of the correspondence comes addressed to P. O. Box 4255, El Paso, Texas 79914. CBP's web page is found at www.casabautista.org. (Also: www.editorialmh.org.) E-mail can be directed to jdiaz@casabautista.org. Why not communicate in some way and tell Jorge that he and his staff are in your prayers and thoughts? You might ask how you can be an active part of the centennial celebration. "There's a place for you!" Or use the response page that follows this chapter. Let Casa hear from you!

Now,

Bugs Bunny would end with his customary, "That's all, folks!"

A southern gentleman would wave good-by and say, "Ya'll come!"

Bob Hope would sing, "Thanks—for the memory."

A gospel quartet would intone, "If we never meet again this side of heaven, I will meet you on that beautiful shore."

The author of this volume simply says, "Thank you for reading these chapters. Please become an active 'Friend of the Casa.' And may God richly bless you in all your service for Jesus Christ our Lord."

And all the people said, "Amen!"

Endnotes

1. In Jorge's first planning document, submitted to the Management Team in a study retreat that began December 3, 2001, he issued the challenge: "Let us build today our future; let's work in the present but build for the future." And he closed the draft with a section titled, "Not one step backward." In it he wrote: "The creation of a 'new' Casa Bautista de Publicaciones that can respond to the demands of the Twenty-first Century will require the dedicated participation of many people and with different perspectives but all working together."

2. Surveyed in chapter 11, which see.

3. See Motion 4, Trustee Minutes, Meeting, November 2001; CBP Archives.

4. See Motion 20, Minutes, Trustee Meeting, November 2001; CBP Archives.

5. Velia, a Casa employee since 1978, says she remembers on various occasions how the hand of the Lord has provided for the needs of the Casa. She specifically mentions a time when she and Betty Burtis were handling receipts and payments (Velia, receipts; Betty, payments). She recalls the day Betty commented (before the incoming mail was opened), "Velia, we need $20,000 today." Velia asked Betty, "And how much is really indispensable that we pay today?" Betty replied: "The really urgent total is $12,500." Velia counted the

receipts, and they totalled $12,525. Velia says, "This happened time and again."

6. Then serving in Spanish-speaking Equatorial Guinea, Africa, following earlier service in Spain. During at least five of his years in Spain, his responsibilities had included those of directing the CBP deposit there.

7. The Shupps arrived in August, 2002. Louise Shupp gave valuable and efficient part time assistance in Tim's department.

8. Betty has rendered part-time but greatly needed help in the Wilson Ross Library at CBP.

9. The Turners' ISC appointment will apparently end early in 2005, the Casa's centennial year. Ray writes of his appreciation for the Casa and its ministry, also of Díaz as its present leader. "And," he says, "it has been a privilege to have served, even for such a short time, at the Casa, with a group of God's faithful and special servants."

10. The package included two months' salary and medical insurance for the rest of 2003.

11. See "Levi Strauss closes its last 2 factories in U.S.," El Paso Times, January 9, 2004, p. F-1.

12. Violeta Martínez was already directing the office of Contract Production; but her responsibilities now became much more important. Now as "Coordinator of Production" she is essentially shopping the world for Casa's production. The

Casa's centennial year will mark her 25th anniversary of work with CBP.

13. See chapter 11.

14. See chapter 2.

15. In May 2003, these were Eastern South America, Western South America, and the Caribbean Basin; as of July 1, 2004, four regions of the Western Hemisphere were combined into two: South America, and Middle America and the Caribbean.

16. May 1, 2004.

17. Listed in alphabetical order according to each's customary surname.

18. Keith and Mixy Morris were a part of CBP staff on April 1, 2004, but were scheduled to be reassigned to Mexico by the summer of 2004, perhaps with some ongoing relationship to CBP.

19. David Fajardo, coordinator of the Office of Promotion, Advertising, and Field Services, in the Marketing Division, says he has seen, time and again, the marvelous manifestation of God's power working through the Casa's "printed page." He cites the case of a couple he met in a conference in San Pedro Sula, Honduras. The couple shared with David how much the book Señor, te consagro mi vida (Lord, I consecrate my life to Thee) had meant to their lives. The incident particularly impressed David, for the title they mentioned had been the first book he had edited after coming to the Casa in 1986. The couple had linked their lives and consecrated themselves to the Lord Jesus as a result of reading the book. Their case was "living proof" of the value of the Casa's ministry!

20. A novel or attention-getting translation has been attempted; a more literal translation would have been "Big and Bold."

21. Ibid.

22. Although the Spanish of this paragraph was written as a personal appeal from the General Director to the Division Directors, for purposes of the centennial book, the English has been made slightly less personal.

23. This and all the quotes from Jorge Díaz in this chapter have been taken from a 25 page document prepared by Díaz and supplied to J. T. Poe as input for the last two chapters in this centennial book. Received March 10, 2004.

24. See the concluding page of Estep's sesquicentennial history of the Foreign Mission Board, Whole Gospel Whole World, p. 388; or the similar conclusion of Jesse C. Fletcher's sesquicentennial history of the Southern Baptist Convention, pp. 386-388; or Harry Leon McBeth's sesquicentennial history of the Baptist General Convention of Texas, pp. 463-464.

THIS IS YOUR REPLY SHEET

Please separate this page and mail it (or fax it) to the Casa signaling your willingness to become a "Friend of the Casa."

(   ) Yes, please enroll me as a "Friend of the Casa."

Here is my name and address:

Name: _____

Mailing address:

_____

_____

_____

(City, state, country, zip code)

(   ) Please send me the quarterly newsletter.

(   ) I will pray regularly for the Casa and its ministry.

(   ) Please send me a bi-lingual catalogue of the resources published by CBP/EMH.

(   ) Please send me a copy of *Casa: The Partner in Ministry You Need*.

HERE ARE MY QUESTIONS AND SUGGESTIONS:

Questions:

_____

_____

_____

_____

_____

And here are my suggestions and/or recommendations:

_____

_____

_____

_____

_____

_____

Please mail this sheet to:

Casa Bautista de Publicaciones
Editorial Mundo Hispano
P. O. Box 4255
El Paso, Texas 79904

Or FAX it to us at: 915-562-6502

Appendix A: IMB Missionaries Who Have Served with CBP

Casa Bautista de Publicaciones was founded by missionaries of the then Foreign Mission Board, SBC (now International). During its hundred years of service there have never been fewer than two missionaries assigned to this publications ministry and sometimes more than twenty. This appendix intends to offer a list of IMB missionaries who have served in this work, sometimes for as little as a year, sometimes for as much as "a lifetime." The names have been gleaned from a variety of sources, including the archives in Richmond. The years served with the Publishing House are also indicated, with the best data available. (Insofar as possible, the years correspond to actual service in El Paso.) Our thanks to personnel both in Richmond and in El Paso who have helped us with important details. Where surnames have changed subsequent to missionary service with the Publishing House, effort has been made to include in parenthesis the current surname being used (for a variety of reasons), but the alphabetization has been done using the surname in use at the time of service with the Publishing House. If inadvertently, some name has been omitted or the years of service incorrectly registered, pardon is implored and information is requested that the list might be updated for its use in the future.

Ron Adams, 1994-1999
Freida Adams (Mrs. Ron), 1994-1999
Brian Allen, 1996-1997
Tina Allen (Mrs. Brian), 1996-1997
James Bartley, 1996-1997
Peggy Bartley (Mrs. James), 1996-1997
John Bayer, 1999-2002
Brenda Bayer (Mrs. John), 1999-2002
J. H. Benson, 1927-1934
Daisy Maurice Benson (Mrs. J. H.), 1927-1934
Judson Blair, 1957-1989
Dorothy Rose Blair (Mrs. Judson), 1957-1989
C. D. Boone, 1921-1925
Jesse Bryan, 1977-2002
Beverly Bryan (Mrs. Jesse), 1977-2002
Kirk Bullington, 1998-2001
Karen Bullington (Mrs. Kirk), 1998-2001
Betty Burtis, 1982-1997
Charles Campbell, 1981-1987
Bernadine Campbell (Mrs. Charles), 1981-1987
Viola Campbell, 1961-1982
Dan Carroll, 1973-1990
Betty Alice Carroll (Mrs. Dan), 1973-1990
Walton Chambless, 1973-1977
Lorena Chambless (Mrs. Walton), 1973-1977
John S. Cheavens, 1919-1921

Katherine Herndon Cheavens (Mrs. John), 1919-1921
Debra Collins, 1985-1997
Bob E. Compton, 1986-1987
Peggy Compton (Jones) (Mrs. Bob. E.), 1986-1987
Karl David, 2000-2002
Billie David (Mrs. Karl), 2000-2002
J. Edgar Davis, 1905-1943
Mary Davis (Mrs. J. Edgar), 1905-1943
Steve Ditmore, 1981-1993
Shirley Ditmore (Mrs. Steve), 1981-1993
Millie Douglas, 1986-1999
Hiram F. Duffer, 1948-1952
Charlotte Duffer (Mrs. Hiram), 1948-1952
Darline Elliott, 1981-1982
Siegfried Enge, 1978-1997
Donna Enge (Mrs. Siegfried), 1978-1997
Hoyt Eudaly, 1952-1977
Marie Eudaly (Mrs. Hoyt), 1952-1977
Kenneth Evenson, 1967-1978
Mary Ann Evenson (Mrs. Kenneth), 1967-1978
Edna Mae Franks (Brantley), 1958-1960
Mark Fricke, 1999-2002
Debbie Fricke (Mrs. Mark), 1999-2002
Max Furr, 1989-1991
Joan Furr (Mrs. Max), 1989-1991

James Giles, 1992-1994
Mary Nell Giles (Mrs. James), 1992-1994
Carroll Gillis, 1948-1956
Laverne Gregory, 1979-2000
Betty Gregory (Mrs. Laverne), 1979-2000
William F. Hatchell, 1921
Jessie Ennie Hatchell (Mrs. William F.), 1921
John Hatton, 1993-1996
Monica Hatton (Mrs. John), 1993-1996
Russell Herrington, 1989-2002
Annette Horton Herrington (Mrs. Russell),
    1989-2002
Dorothy Hicks (Pettit), 1958-1968
Thomas W. Hill, 1964-1976
Cornice "Connie" Hill (Mrs. Thomas W.),
    1964-1976
Gayle Hogg, 1977-1985
Sylvia Hogg (Mrs. Gayle), 1977-1985
G. H. Lacy, 1916-1917
P. D. Lee , 1986-1996
Brenda Lee (Mrs. P. D.), 1986-1996
Lewis E. Lee, 1971-1974
Jo Lee (Mrs. Lewis), 1971-1974
Roy Lyon, 1979-1980
Alma Ruth Lyon (Mrs. Roy), 1979-1980
Steve Manuel, 1997-2002
Barbara Manuel (Mrs. Steve), 1997-2002
Frank Marrs, 1921
Greg Massey, 1998-2000
Karen Massey (Mrs. Greg), 1998-2000
Ernie McAninch, 1987-1994
Lee Ann McAninch (Mrs. Ernie), 1987-1994
Cecil McConnell, 1980-1989
Mary McConnell (Mrs. Cecil), 1980-1989
James W. McGavock, 1945-1953
Catherine McGavock (Mrs. James), 1945-1953
Margaret McGavock (Woodward), 1949-1950
Mary Jo McMurray (Wilburn), 1968-1988
Harry Keith Morris, 1998-2004
Mixy Morris (Mrs. Keith), 1998-2004
Steve Murdock, 1998-1999
Lissy Murdock (Mrs. Steve), 1998-1999
Edward W. Nelson, 1970-1990
Gladys Nelson (Mrs. Edward), 1970-1990
Frank W. Patterson, 1939-1972
Pauline G. "Polly" Patterson (Mrs. Frank),
    1939-1972

A. P. Pierson, 1962-1970
Coy Lee Pierson (Mrs. A. P.), 1962-1970
Mell Plunk, 1988-1989
Suzie Plunk (Mrs. Mell), 1988-1989
Joe T. Poe, 1961-1997
Eleanor Poe (Mrs. Joe T.), 1961-1997
J. Wilson Ross, 1953-1988
Jimmie R. Ross (Mrs. J. Wilson), 1953-1988
Roberta Ryan, 1961-1986
Matthew Sanderford, 1961-1987
Dora Jean Sanderford (Mrs. Matthew),
    1961-1987
Sam Shaw, 1987-1988
Ruthie Shaw (Mrs. Sam), 1987-1988
Arthur Tim Shupp, 2002-2004
Louise Shupp (Mrs. Tim), 2002-2004
William Stennett, 1995-1996
Libbie Stennett (Mrs. William), 1995-1996
Ted Stanton, 1998-2001
Mary Stanton (Mrs. Ted), 1998-2001
Ed Steele, 1992-1998
Kathy Steele (Mrs. Ed), 1992-1998
Mary Jo Stewart, 1972-1989
Peter Stillman, 1982-1989
Jennie Stillman (Mrs. Peter), 1982-1989
Tom Sutton, 1993-1996
Peggy Sutton (Mrs. Tom), 1993-1996
Ann M. Swenson, 1962-1980
Cecil Thompson, 1977-1991
Jean Thompson (Mrs. Cecil), 1977-1991
Hugo Torres-Gómez, 1990-1992
Fifi Torres-Gómez (Mrs. Hugo), 1990-1992
Robert Tucker, 1984-1988
Margaret "Meg" Tucker (Mrs. Robert),
    1984-1988
Ray Turner, 2003-2005
Betty Turner (Mrs. Ray), 2003-2005
Weldon Viertel, 1972-1982
Joyce Viertel (Mrs. Weldon), 1972-1982
Jim West, 1981-1992
Bobbie West (Mrs. Jim), 1981-1992
Eddy Williams, 1997-1998
Russell Wills, 1996-2001
Nadine Wills (Mrs. Russell), 1996-2001
Rubén O. Zorzoli, 1997-present
Alicia Zorzoli (Mrs. Rubén), 1997-present

Appendix B: CBP Administrative Personnel from 1980–2004

For at least thirty-five years, the term "Director" has been used at the Publishing House to designate administrative personnel. The CEO has been designated the "General Director". Those who have supervised mayor areas of work (clusters of "departments") have been called "division directors" and the department leaders have also been called "directors." The intent of this appendix is to recognize those who have had leadership roles at CBP since 1980, either at the "department" or "divisional" or "general" levels. Here it has not been feasible to give further identifications either in terms of posts held or years served. Nonetheless the list will serve to highlight the scope of services rendered by an impressive list of God's servants across these twenty-five years in CBP's ministry of the printed page. The listing is alphabetical by surname.

Ronnie Adams
José Amézaga
Rubén Angulo
Steve Baumgardner
John Bayer
Laura Beamer
W. Judson Blair
Miguel Angel Blanco
Roberto García-Bordoli
Aldo Broda
Jesse Bryan
Viola Campbell
Jesús Carreón
Debra Collins
Bob E. Compton
Jorge E. Díaz
Jackie Disselkoen
Steve Ditmore
Millie Douglas
Donna Enge
Siegfried G. Enge
David Fajardo
Manuela Flores
Marcos Fricke
Max Furr
Guillermo García
Hugo Torres-Gómez
Ananías González
José González
Nelly de González
Laverne Gregory

Ibelís Guédez
John Hatton
Velia Hodge
Gayle Hogg
Russell Herrington
Donald E. Ivie
Hilda Kaplan
A. D. Lagrone
P. D. Lee
M. B. Lee
Roy Lyon
Exequiel San Martín
Carol Martínez
José Luis Martínez
Greg Massey
Ernest McAninch
Mary Jo McMurray
José Morelos
Edward W. Nelson
Linda W. Nodjimbadem
Yolanda Oseguera
Eleazar Peña
Gilbert Pérez
Dorothy Pettit
Miryam R. Diaz-Picott
Mell Plunk
Joe T. Poe
Elbin Porflit
Wayne Quarrier
Ignacio Ramos
Jorge Rede

J. Antonio Rengifo
Adolfo Robleto
Daniel Rojas
Jimmie Ross
J. Wilson Ross
Jorge Rousselín
Roberta Ryan
Matthew A. Sanderford
Sam Shaw
Tim Shupp
Fred Smith
Josie Smith
Ricardo Solís
Ted O. Stanton
William Stennet
Mary Jo Stewart
Peter Stillman
Tom Sutton
Cecil Thompson
Margaret Tucker
H. Robert Tucker
Ray Turner
George Villafuerte
James R. West
Eddy Williams
Gloria Williams-Méndez
Alicia Zorzoli
Rubén Zorzoli

Appendix C: CBP Trustees
1975-2004

As explained in chapter 6, a Board of Trustees was created for the Casa Bautista de Publicaciones in 1975. All who have, in the intervening years, served as members of this Board, have done so voluntarily. All have done so willingly, with sincerity and diligence. The Publishing House owes to each and all a hearty expression of thanks. They are part of "the Casa story." Thus the following list of Board members is presented for the years 1975–2004. The list is alphabetical by surname. Some have served for one meeting; others have served several years. Indication is given of the country each represented; those who have represented certain "fields" or "regions" related to the International Mission Board are indicated with the letters IMB, in full recognition that for most of the years covered in this survey the Mission Board was known as the Foreign Mission Board rather than the International Mission Board. Using the best data at our disposal, the years served are indicated in parenthesis. Apologies are expressed in advance for any discrepancies or inaccuracies. The list is intended as a sincere THANK YOU TO ALL WHO HAVE SERVED.

Moisés Poveda Castillo, Costa Rica
(1988-1991)
Aarón Ramírez Sabag, Mexico (2004-present)
Carl M. Rees, IMB (1999)
Eduardo Ríos Hernández, Chile (1977-1978)
Robert V. Roberts, Panamá (1984)
Jorge Angel Rodríguez, México (1977-1979)
Julio Ruiz, Venezuela (1992-1997)
Alberto Salazar, Chile (1991-1996)
Epifanio Salazar, United States (1977-1980)
Gustavo Sánchez, Colombia (1984-1989)
Julio Sánchez, Honduras (1979)
Harolt Sante, Ecuador (1986-1991)
Manuel Sarrias, Spain (2003-present)
A. Clark Scanlon, IMB (1975-1980)

Jim Sexton, IMB (2000-present)
Efraín Silva, United States (1998-2000)
Mark Smith, IMB (1993-1997)
Daniel Sotelo, United States (1985-1990)
Ted Stanton, IMB (1990-1997)
Delbert Taylor, Colombia (1977-1979
Reinaldo O. Toppin, Panamá (1977-1978)
Roberto Torres, México (1986-1991
H. Robert Tucker, Jr., IMB (1976-1984)
Kenneth Watkins, Paraguay (1977)
Kenneth Watkins, IMB (1997-2001)
Ronald Wilson, IMB (1986-1991)
Leoncio Veguilla, Cuba (1996-2001)
Roberto Velert Ch., Spain (1991-1996)
Manuel Zamora Rivera, Nicaragua (2000-2004)

Appendix D: Publications

Wilson Ross included two appendices to his M.A. thesis for Texas Tech University in 1957: One was a list of books published by the Baptist Spanish Publishing House from 1907 (the year of its first book publication) through 1957. The list was organized by author and gave the book title, the name of the translator (where pertinent) and the years of printing, both original and subsequent (if any). This appendix occupied twenty type written pages and, as is generally the case for such lists, has been discovered to be slightly incomplete. The second appendix contained a list of the periodicals published by CBP along with the dates of their issue, generally in terms of months and years. Titles and dates gave this list a length of two pages.

When this centennial book was envisioned, it seemed appropriate to update these lists and include them as appendices to this volume. The work has been done and is available on loan from the Wilson Ross Library of CBP, either in "hard copy" or electronic data format. But it has been decided not to include these updated lists as appendices in the printed book. Even in small type in three columns, they likely would have needed fifty or more pages in the printed book.

Other reasons for not including them also exist. To list "books" requires that one define "What is a book?" While at one point the U.S. Post Office defined a book as a printed piece, permanently bound, containing at least twenty-two pages of copy, it seems this definition is now out of date. And even accepting it, a list of printed books would fail to include tracts, booklets, maps, teaching pictures, recordings, calendars, certificates, church supplies, and other items in non-book formats but which have had a legitimate place in the publication program of BSPH across the years. Perhaps the most blatant omission would be materials in an electronic format (like the Biblioteca Mundo Hispano–Hispanic World Library–which includes twenty-five books on one CD).

With this explanation, the offer is reiterated to make available to any researcher that needs them the lists mentioned above. But emphasis is given here to the variety of resources (printed, visual, audio, and electronic) that the Publishing House presently offers. This is hereby done by reproducing the list of categories of resources announced in the CBP catalog available at this writing. These categories of resources–in a variety of formats–are as follows:

> Apologetics
> Bible, Book by Book, The (Annuals)
> Bible References
> Bible Studies
> Bibles, New Testaments, and Bible Portions
> Bookmarks
> Children's Materials
> Christian Discipleship Development
> Christian Education
> Contemporary Issues
> Church Growth
> Church Resources
> Commentaries
> Creative and Biblical Activities

Curriculum
Dialogue and Action (Curriculum)
Discipleship
Dramas
Doctrine and Theology
Evangelism
Family
French (Books and Tracts)
Hebrew and Greek Grammar
History and Geography
Inspiration
Leadership
Men
Missionary Education
Multimedia Resources
Music
Novels
Pastoral Ministry
Preschoolers
Prayer and Devotionals
Special Days
Special Products
Sunday School (Curriculum)
Sunday School (Supplies)
Tracts
Vacation Bible School
Women
Worship
Youth

Remember that the Reply Sheet included at the close of chapter 12 offers you the possibility of securing a copy of the current CBP General Catalog as well as a copy of the short book *Casa: The Partner in Ministry You Need.* Take advantage of these opportunities. Enhance your ministry through partnership with CBP.

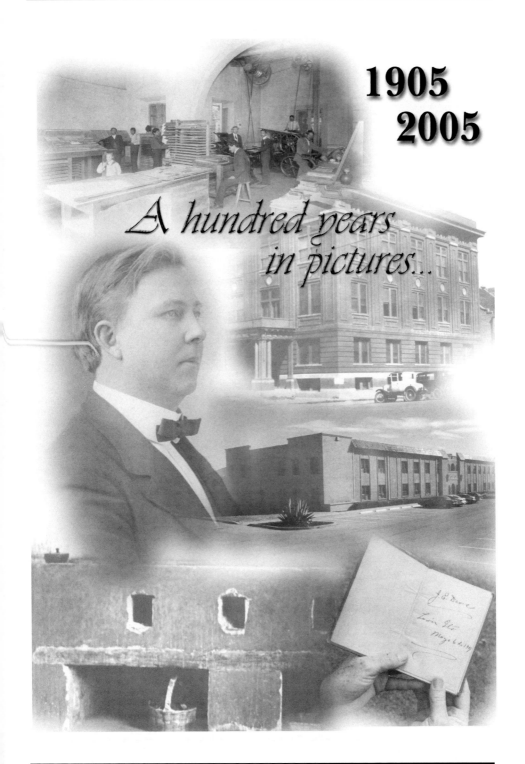

1905
2005

*A hundred years
in pictures...*

Casa's Print Shop in
León, Guanajuato,
México; see chapter 1.

Missionaries
J. E. & Mary Davis,
Founders of the
Baptist Spanish
Publishing House;
see chapters 1 & 2.

Publishing House office
in León, Guanajuato;
left to right: Josué
Valdés, Félix Baldain,
& J. E. Davis.

The Publishing House's first location in El Paso, on North Campbell Street

BSPH Print Shop at North Campbell Street location.

Personnel of the Publishing House, in front of the North Campbell Street location.

CBP's home from 1925 to 1938,
at 800 Myrtle Avenue.

CBP's new home,
beginning in 1938.

Ed Davis, son of founders,
Director of Print Shop.

Mrs. Mary Davis at the celebration
of her 80th birthday.

Dr. Frank Patterson (General Director 1943-1970)
& his wife Polly; see chapters 3 & 4.

Dr. Patterson with Clifford Smith,
Production Division Directo.r

Missionary Matthew Sanderford
& Dr. Patterson.

The Publishing House
staff in 1949.

Dr. and Mrs. J. W. McGavock;
see chapter 3.

Casa Bautista de Publicaciones.....
P. O. BOX 1648, EL PASO, TEXAS, E.U.A.

July 12, 1957

Dr. Frank K. Means
Box 5148
Richmond 20, Virginia

Dear Frank:

Enclosed herewith is a copy of the auditor's report
of the Publishing House for the year ending April
30, 1957.

I would like to explain that the decrease in sales, indicated in the comparative table, bottom of page 5, was
due to the fact that in 1956 we printed and bound 15,000
copies of a hymnal for the Methodists, in amount of
$13,000 plus, which was listed as book sales. That was
not a normal transaction. Discounting that, our sales were
actually up by almost $10,000.

No doubt there will be some items concerning which you
will wish to inquire.

We will appreciate you giving this copy to Mr. Deane after
you have studied it sufficiently. We are making some copies
on the Thermofax machine for use during the mission meeting,
so that another carbon copy like the one enclosed will be
available to you during and after the mission meeting.

Cordially yours,

Frank W. Patterson
Frank W. Patterson

1906 — Bodas de Oro — 1956

CBP Stationery commemorating
50th Anniversary in 1956.

A patio is enclosed and the Bindery Department
is enlarged; see chapter 4.

Viola Campbell, Olivia Lerín, F. W. Patterson
and Alfredo Lerín.

Lerín, Patterson, & Poe in a conference.

Dr. Poe, Polly Patterson & Olivia Lerín
discussing Sunday School materials.

Missionary N. H. Eudaly led toward
enlarged distribution.

Dr. Ann Swenson directed
ministry to students.

The El Paso Baptist Publications Mission,
about 1972; see chapter 4.

Laura Disselkoen takes care
of correspondence.

A new press was installed and dedicated in 1965.

"Floor men" Amézaga and Cienfuegos
preparing letterpress forms.

Dr. Patterson explains the marked
New Testament; see chapter 4.

A large interior patio was enclosed to house the Production Division.

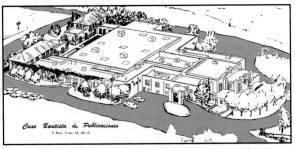

An artist's rendering of the CBP plant in the late '60s.

Frank Patterson, the writer.

Dr. & Mrs. Patterson posed for this picture with their three granddaughters after their retirement.

Mrs. Patterson and a display of the books she wrote

Alfredo Lerín teaches a Bible Study class in Ciudad Juárez, México.

Dr. T. W. Hill
(General Director 1970-1976)
& his wife Connie; see chapter 5.

Dr. Hill makes a presentation at an international gathering in El Paso; flags
symbolize the numerous countries where Publishing House materials are used.

Dr. Charles Bryan speaks at the installation
service for Dr. Hill; see chapter 5.

Dr. Hill and his library represent seminary and
church libraries wherever CBP books are used.

Hill unveils the portrait of F. W. Patterson to be hung
among those of CBP General Directors.

Adolfo Robleto reads one of
his poems.

Jack Disselkoen & Wilson Ross confer,
probably about Casa finances.

Elizabeth Angulo serves at
the reception for the Hills
just prior to their departure
for Richmond.

Norma Armengol presenting
a going-away gift to the Hills.

At Aldo Broda's installation service, Dr. T. W. Hill shares words of encouragement with his successor.

A map and picture display illustrates the Casa's outreach "for all nations".

N. Aldo Broda
(General Director, 1977-1986)
& his wife Dora; see chapter 6.

Josie Smith makes a presentation at an
international meeting.

The seal that represented
CBP's 75th Anniversary.

Dr. Jesse Bryan directed the
Marketing Division and later the
Finance Division.

Dr. William W. Graves, close friend and long
term trustee, along with Mr. Broda.

Aldo Broda (third from left) & others "break ground" for new the building.

258

Mr. Broda & missionary Judson Blair in front of the Casa's new addition.

Mr. Broda presents service pins to Cristóbal Mena & José Amézaga.

Broda & missionary Wilson Ross, who served as Interim General Director for about a year before the Brodas' arrival in El Paso.

Jackie Disselkoen

Artists Peter Stillman & Dorothy Pettit.

An aerial view of the Publishing House's plant after completion
of the addition built during Aldo Broda's years.

Velia Hodge

Ananías & Nelly González

Roberta Ryan, Mary Jo MacMurray, & Viola Campbell

Dr. H. Robert Tucker (General Director, 1986-1988)
& his wife Margaret; see chapter 7.

The invitation to the joint Recognition-Installation service
for Aldo Broda and Robert Tucker.

Dr. Tucker consults with
Josie Smith.

Books published by CBP are sold by Christian
bookstores in many places.

Miguel Angel Blanco & Maria Luisa
Porflit consult a grammatical point; for
many years both helped assure
quality Spanish —acceptable "for all
the nations"— in CBP materials.

Vicente Soto's life was changed
by a CBP book.

Artist Dorothy Pettit helped make materials
attractive "for all the nations".

Volunteers—like Darlene Elliot & Nola Granberry— are always needed and welcome!

The General Director's Staff, during Tucker's years of service: Dr. Roberto García-Bordoli, Norma Armengol, Dr. & Mrs Tucker, Dr. Daniel Carroll, Dr. Norberto Herrera & Rev. Judson Blair.

The International Board of Trustees, with Dr. & Mrs. Tucker and Dr. & Mrs García-Bordoli; taken around 1988.

A special seal adorned El Expositor Bíblico in 1990, its centennial year.

Dr. Roberto García-Bordoli (General Director, 1989-1992) and his wife Noemí; see chapter 8.

A women's Bible class in México using El Expositor Bíblico, as did similar classes in many nations.

Mrs. García-Bordoli gives special recognition to Bertha Valle.

Linda Wilson & Gayle Hogg supervise
publications in French and in English.

Missionary James West & Ibelís Guédez working
on a project related to Christian Education.

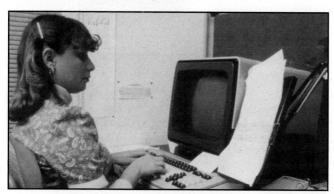

Nora Ávalos uses computerized
equipment in the typesetting
process.

H. C. McConnell, J. T. Poe, José Borrás, & Moises Chávez, one of the core editorial teams,
working on the translation of one of the Old Testament books for the RVA Bible.

CBP hosted a meeting of
the International Mission
Board that included a gala
banquet in the central patio.

Part of the CBP delegation
at a Christian Bookseller's
Convention; pictured: Hugo
Torres-Gómez, Steve
Ditmore, Shirley Ditmore,
Bertha Valle, Dr. García-
Bordoli, & Donna Enge

More CBP faces at a Christian
Booksellers Association event: José
Morelos, Betty & Laverne Gregory.

Dr. Joe T. Poe
(General Director, 1993-1997)
& his wife Eleanor;
see chapter 9.

Delores Robleto & Wayne
Quarrier sing a duet at Poe's
installation service.

Following his election as General Director in May of 1993, the Trustees lay
hands on Dr. & Mrs. Poe in the Publishing House chapel service.

In 1995, a visit by former General Directors created this "photo op" to catch the Hills,
the Poes & the Pattersons together; they represented more than a hundred years
of service in Christian publications "for all the nations."

This seal represented CBP's 90th Anniversary.

The year's first Anniversary cake.

Program for the climactic celebration of 90 years of ministry— "for all nations".

Trustee María Victoria Flores displays an Anniversary cake in Guatemala.

Nelly & Ananías González & Alicia Zorzoli, at a CBP celebration in Buenos Aires.

Mario Martínez, Alci & Carolina Rengifo in the Anniversary drama.

Various Anniversary plaques, flowers, gifts & other greetings.

268

Poe congratulates the editors responsible for Comentario Bíblico Mundo Hispano (CBMH).

CBMH volume on Psalms won a Gold Medallion Award.

The CBP choir, directed by Ed Steele, presents a Christmas cantata.

Organist and Music Editor Salomón Mussiett.

At the celebration of her 35 years of service with the CBP, Hilda Kaplan is greeted by Gladys Mussiett.

Rev. Ted Stanton
(General Director, 1998-2001)
& his wife Mary; see chapter 10.

Bro. Stanton presents service pin to Jorge Rede.

Millie Douglas

Miryam Díaz-Picott receives recognition
from the General Director.

Rev. Stanton with Rev. & Mrs. Roberto Velert
Chisbert, from Spain.

Aída & Raúl Medrano

Eduardo Escalante receives a recognition for distribution in Panamá from Eleazar Peña.

Agustín Hernández, Steve Strub,
Juan Varela, & Daniel Rojas.

Stanton awards service pin to artist Helen Reade-Curl.

See story of Mario, chapter 10.

Mary & Ted Stanton sing in chapel alongside Jorge Díaz; Dr. Juan Carlos Cevallos presides.

Jorge Díaz & David Fajardo share a moment at a book exhibit.

Dr. Russell Herrington & his wife Annette served several years at CBP, mainly in the area of Sacred Music.

CBP in México City; Hortensia Vásquez, manager.

Missionary Kirk Burllington leads a Music Workshop.

Rev. Jorge Enrique Díaz
(General Director, 2001-present)
& his wife Raquelita;
see chapters 11 & 12.

General Director Jorge Díaz
makes a presentation on
CBP publications.

Jorge Díaz, Gladys &
Salomón Mussiett share
a joyous moment.

The 2003 International Board of Trustees, with General Director; front row: H. Rhea Chafin, Eloy Coelho, Leandro González, Manuel Zamora, Alfredo Monje; back row: James Sexton, Rick Miller, Susana Martínez, Eduardo Henningham, and J. E. Díaz.

The Management Team for 2002; seated: Velia Hodge, Miryam Díaz-Picott, Norma Armengol; standing: Rubén Zorzoli, Exequiel San Martín, Jorge E. Díaz.

A children's Sunday School class in Panamá.

Missionary Mixy Morris and her daughter Génesis, at an International Christian Book Fair; children enjoy browsing at the Fair; the variety of books offered is indeed impressive! (Photos by missionary Keith Morris.)

Artist Carlos Santiesteban with editors Dr. & Mrs. Juan Carlos Cevallos; also Olpa Mendoza & Hermes Soto.

Missionary Alicia Zorzoli

Missionary Mark Fricke translates for Josh MacDowell at Expolit.

Editorial tasks are never done! Rubén Zorzoli, Vilma Fajardo & David Fajardo face fresh tasks in this ministry —"for all nations"— each day.